The Woman Suffrage Movement in America

This book departs from familiar accounts of high-profile woman suffrage activists whose main concern was a federal constitutional amendment. It tells the story of woman suffrage as one involving the diverse politics of women across the country as well as the incentives of the men with the primary political authority to grant new voting rights – those in state legislatures. Through a mix of qualitative and quantitative evidence, the book explains the success and failures of efforts for woman suffrage provisions in the American states and in the U.S. Congress as the result of successful and failed coalitional politics between the suffrage movement and important constituencies of existing male voters, including farmers' organizations, labor unions, and the Populist and Progressive parties.

Corrine M. McConnaughy is Assistant Professor of Political Science at The Ohio State University. She was Assistant Professor of Government and was affiliated with the Center for Women's and Gender Studies at the University of Texas at Austin from 2004 to 2007; she received her PhD in Political Science from the University of Michigan in 2004. McConnaughy's dissertation won a University-wide Honorable Mention as a Distinguished Dissertation at Michigan, as well as the Carrie Chapman Catt Award for research on women and politics from the Catt Center at Iowa State University. At Ohio State University, her work has been awarded a Coca-Cola Critical Difference for Women Research Grant from the Department of Women's Studies. She is the recipient of the Lucius Barker Award from the Midwest Political Science Association (2011), and she was recognized with the Distinguished Alumni Award from Pi Sigma Alpha at DePaul University in 2010. McConnaughy is on the Executive Council of the Women and Politics Research section of the American Political Science Association. Her work has appeared in the *American Journal of Political Science*, *Journal of Politics*, *Public Opinion Quarterly*, *Studies in American Political Development*, *Politics & Gender*, and *American Politics Research*.

Rather than focusing on the activities and perspectives of women's rights activists, McConnaughy asks what strategic considerations might be involved in convincing legislators to expand the suffrage when such an expansion affects the probability of their own reelection. This book is an important contribution to the areas of gender and politics, race and politics, and social movements, and to our understanding of how policy is created.

– Lee Ann Banaszak, Pennsylvania State University

McConnaughy is to be commended for addressing an important question, for rightly focusing attention on the state-level campaigns where so much of the suffrage fight was won and lost, and for articulating a nuanced and original theory to explain variation in suffrage success. McConnaughy's explanation resolves puzzles left unanswered by previous research and is simultaneously theoretically sophisticated and based in a deep understanding of 'real' politics on the ground.

– Christina Wolbrecht, University of Notre Dame

The Woman Suffrage Movement in America

A Reassessment

CORRINE M. McCONNAUGHY

The Ohio State University, Columbus

CAMBRIDGE
UNIVERSITY PRESS

CAMBRIDGE
UNIVERSITY PRESS

32 Avenue of the Americas, New York, NY 10013-2473, USA

Cambridge University Press is part of the University of Cambridge.

It furthers the University's mission by disseminating knowledge in the pursuit of education, learning, and research at the highest international levels of excellence.

www.cambridge.org
Information on this title: www.cambridge.org/9781107013667

First published 2013

Printed in the United States of America

A catalog record for this publication is available from the British Library.

Library of Congress Cataloging in Publication Data
McConnaughy, Corrine M.
The woman suffrage movement in America : a reassessment / Corrine M. McConnaughy, Ohio State University, Columbus.
  pages cm
Includes bibliographical references and index.
ISBN 978-1-107-01366-7 (hardback)
1. Women – Suffrage – United States. I. Title.
JK1896.M39 2013
324.6'230973–dc23   2013012175

ISBN 978-1-107-01366-7 Hardback

For Ismail, Khalil, and Meara

Contents

List of Abbreviations

AFL – American Federation of Labor
AWSA – American Woman Suffrage Association
CBA – Clara B. Arthur
CIO – Congress of Industrial Organizations
CSESA – Colorado State Equal Suffrage Association
CU – Congressional Union or National Woman's Party
CWSA – Colorado Woman Suffrage Association
HWS – *The History of Woman Suffrage*
IESA – Illinois Equal Suffrage Association
IWSA – Illinois Woman Suffrage Association
LSSA – Louisiana State Suffrage Association
MESA – Michigan Equal Suffrage Association
MSWSA – Michigan State Woman Suffrage Association
NAWSA – National American Woman Suffrage Association
NWSA – National Woman Suffrage Association
SSWSC – Southern States Woman Suffrage Conference
WCTU – Woman's Christian Temperance Union
WSPL – Woman Suffrage Party of Louisiana
WTUL – Women's Trade Union League

Acknowledgments

I first encountered the American woman suffrage movement as an undergraduate student in Beth Kelly's class on women and politics at DePaul University. Reading wonderful work by scholars like Eleanor Flexner, Nancy Cott, and Linda Kerber, I met a marvelous cast of protagonists in a daunting struggle. A movement that spanned more than seventy years, marked by personalities as large as those of Elizabeth Cady Stanton, Carrie Chapman Catt, and Alice Paul, and seemingly entangled in controversies of political corruption involving booze interests and machine bosses, was riveting course material. And yet I left that class still wondering if I understood the politics of it all. Why had the movement won and lost when and how it did? Why had politicians come to such different conclusions about the issue of women's voting rights at different moments and in different places throughout the country over those seventy-plus years? The puzzle was not just that women had been granted the right to vote in some states well before the Nineteenth Amendment, but that in some of those states the victory seemed quite surprising – that the issue had been turned down or ignored repeatedly, but somehow suddenly won.

That answers to the questions I had about the woman suffrage movement might be found by starting from the vantage point of the incentives of those who had primary control over and interest in the definition of the electorate – state legislators and their respective political parties – first occurred to me as I sat in a deeply engaging course on political parties taught by Pradeep Chhibber and Ken Kollman while in the political science PhD program at the University of Michigan. Still, I put the idea and interest aside for some time, working instead in the realm of the contemporary politics of race, ethnicity, and gender, and on the historic nature of city-state relations. For help seeing not only that I could take on my long-held interest in the woman suffrage movement, but that my other work had given me even greater tools to do so, I am deeply indebted to my incredibly supportive dissertation committee: Nancy Burns, Richard Hall,

Donald Kinder, and Terrence McDonald. To Nancy and Don, especially, I owe deep gratitude for the core of my training in doing the work of scholarship and for their patience and encouragement as I learned the essential lessons they each had to teach. Each gave me more time, constructive feedback, and opportunities for intellectual growth than a young scholar could ever expect. I thank both for their mentorship and continued support. To Rick, I am most thankful for encouraging me from my first day of graduate school to always be guided by – and never afraid of – interesting and important questions about the cultivation and deployment of social and political power. I am also thankful for his important insights into the incentives inside the legislative process, and the critiques he offered on my own, which helped refine my understanding of the treatment of woman suffrage legislation. Finally, I am grateful that Terry made time for me in his incredibly busy schedule as dean, to the great betterment of the historical method of the work.

I incurred many other intellectual and personal debts during the time I began working on this project while at Michigan. Hanes Walton, Jr., sought me out to share his own work on the history of blacks in the Republican Party, and his expertise on political parties in general, which informed my thinking about the intersection of race and partisan interests in my own argument. Jake Bowers, Vincent Hutchings, Arthur "Skip" Lupia, Rob Mickey, Nicholas Valentino, and all the participants in the National Election Studies workshop series asked constructive questions and made helpful suggestions at several stages of the project. Incredible, regular feedback and support came from my dissertation group: Matthew Beckmann, Sean Ehrlich, Laura Evans, Michael Hanmer, JungHwa Lee, Won-ho Park, Clint Peinhardt, and Ismail White. My work also benefited from a summer spent engaging it with the interdisciplinary group of Community of Scholars Fellows at Michigan's Institute for Research on Women and Gender. Finally, Janet Box-Steffensmeier reached out to me to provide productive comments on my use of event history analysis, and even shared her then-unpublished work on techniques useful to my final analysis of the forty-eight states' treatment of state suffrage issues.

While this project began as my dissertation, it grew in deeply important ways in the years that followed. For time and funds to collect and analyze more data as I began my career as an assistant professor, I am grateful to the Department of Government at the University of Texas at Austin. My time at Texas also provided opportunities for feedback and support from a new set of colleagues. Andrew Karch, Gretchen Ritter, Bartholomew "Bat" Sparrow, and Sean Theriault all read and offered advice on parts of the new book manuscript. Additional thanks are due to the junior faculty group at Texas, including Jason Brownlee, Jason Casellas, George Gavrilis, Ken Greene, Eric McDaniel, Patrick McDonald, Tasha Philpot, John Sides, and Ismail White, not only for their advice on portions of the project presented to our working group, but also for the supportive and friendly environment they provided for a new assistant professor.

As I grew a dissertation into a real book, I was incredibly fortunate to receive advice and support from scholars from other places whose work I greatly admired, and which has importantly shaped my own. Kira Sanbonmatsu was the first of these. She approached me with her first words of advice and support after my very first conference presentation of the project and has continued that support to the finish line of the book. Lee Ann Banazsak shared not only expertise on the suffrage movement, but her data as well. Frank Baumgartner gave me some of the most insightful critiques about the book's frame and contribution – and kindly did so over ice cream at the Berkey Creamery at Penn State. Holly McKammon also generously shared her coding of third-party presence in state legislatures and state constitution amendment procedures.

This book entailed a massive data collection effort, which included trips to archives scattered across the country. For the funding that made this possible, I thank the National Science Foundation (SES-0212419), the Carrie Chapman Catt Award for research on women and politics from Iowa State University, the Department of Government at the University of Texas, and a number of sources at the University of Michigan, including the Gerald R. Ford Fund, the political science department, Rackham School of Graduate Studies, the Institute for Research on Women and Gender, and the Innovation in Social Science Research Fellowship at the Institute for Social Research. The last fellowship was generously established by Dorwin "Doc" and Barbara Cartwright, who wrote me with kind words of confidence at an early stage in the research.

Several research assistants worked on this project at various times. In the data collection and coding stages, Nikki Beem, Megan McMillan, and Jason Tower merit special thanks for both the amount and the quality of the work they did. For heroic efforts to help me meet final deadlines for the book, I thank Nyron Crawford and Julian Wamble.

Like every researcher who uses archival data, I am incredibly appreciative for assistance from talented, dedicated research librarians and archivists at a number of institutions, particularly: The Arizona Historical Society Library, The Arizona State Archives and History, The University of Arizona Special Collections, The Hayden Library – Department of Archives and Manuscripts at Arizona State University, and The Phoenix Public Library; The Colorado Historical Society, The Colorado State Archives, and The Archives at the University of Colorado at Boulder Libraries; The Chicago Historical Society, The Illinois State Archives, and The Illinois Public Library; The Louisiana State Archives, The Louisiana State Museum, Special Collections – Hill Memorial Library at Louisiana State University, and The New Orleans Public Library; The Burton Historical Collection at the Detroit Public Library and The Bentley Historical Library at the University of Michigan; and The New Mexico State Library, The New Mexico State Records Center and Archives, and The Southwestern Collection at the University of New Mexico.

I undertook the final stages of data analysis and writing of the book after moving to the department of political science at The Ohio State University. For generous support of this final effort in his role as department chair, I am deeply grateful to Herb Weisberg. For his help in navigating the book process as a first-time author, I thank Larry Baum. Now my colleague, Janet Box-Steffensmeier proved to be an enduring source of encouragement. For making the details of the last financial costs of the book none of my concern, I thank our talented fiscal officer, Diana Camella.

I am extremely grateful to everyone at Cambridge University Press for their support of this book. I thank my editor Lew Bateman for his interest and encouragement – and Paul Kellstedt for making our introduction. The two anonymous reviewers provided richly constructive comments that greatly improved the quality of the manuscript. Mark Fox at Cambridge and Adrian Pereira at Aptara were both helpful and accommodating in the production stage of the project.

Of course, the biggest debts incurred in the course of researching and writing a book are most often personal. Such is certainly the case with this one. In writing this book, a voice from deep within often reminded me that girls like me weren't supposed to grow up to write books. That is, where I started is so far away from the world of academia I have entered. So I begin with thanks to the early encouragers of my pursuit of academia. Richard Zawack, my high school teacher of Philosophy and Government, not only nurtured my interest in politics, but also made sure that I survived my high school years and found my way to college. DePaul University offered an incredibly supportive environment for a first-generation college student. The entire political science department invested in me while I was there, but I owe special thanks to Patrick Callahan, Elizabeth Kelly, Wayne Steger, and J. Harry Wray. And I owe one more note of thanks to Nancy Burns for recruiting me to join the graduate program in political science at Michigan after my time at DePaul.

My family has been ever supportive of my intellectual curiosity and the demands it has often made on my time and on them. My parents, Kathryn McConnaughy and James McConnaughy, made untold sacrifices over the years to ensure that I could reach my potential. This book, I know, is the most tangible evidence I can offer that those sacrifices were well spent. My biggest regret, therefore, is that my father did not live to see it in print. My biggest hope is that both are, somehow, proud. I thank my sister, Jen Walts, for being my very first "teacher" on our little home chalkboard. To my brother, Jesse McConnaughy, I owe gratitude for the deep personal sacrifices he made as I set off for college and graduate school. My extended family has offered a network of support and love over the years, especially my late grandmothers Anne McConnaughy and Antoinette Zeitz, and my role-model grandfather Edward Zeitz. I acquired more supportive family members – the White family of Plaisance, Louisiana – through marriage. My thanks to all of you for your faith and presence.

Finally, there is the family that was created at the same time that this book was being written. Ismail White became my partner in everything at the moment this project was first beginning. He stood by me, supported me, cheered me on, and cajoled me when necessary through the ten years it took to see this project through. Not a page would have been possible without him. Our children, Khalil and Meara White, became my final and most joyful inspirations. For the love, devotion, sacrifice, and promise of this "new" family, I dedicate this book to all three of them.

Introduction

On States and Suffrage

"I don't know the exact number of States we shall have to have, but I do know that there will come a day when that number will automatically and resistlessly act on the Congress of the United States to compel the submission of a federal suffrage amendment."

– Susan B. Anthony

As their Women's Rights Convention assembled in Seneca Falls, New York, in the summer of 1848, organizers Elizabeth Cady Stanton and Lucretia Mott dissented on the prudence of one agenda item. Stanton had revised their Declaration of Sentiments – a document regarding women's rights modeled after the Declaration of Independence – to include a resolution in favor of women's voting rights. Mott balked. She worried the woman suffrage proposal was too far before its time; such extremity could threaten the viability of their broader women's rights agenda. Having her ideas about woman's place labeled as "too radical" even among fellow women's rights activists was hardly an uncommon experience for Stanton. She would, in fact, later become alienated from the organized woman suffrage movement over taking another radical position: her indictment of organized religion as an oppressor of women, the core of which she set down in a treatise entitled *The Woman's Bible*. This time, however, Stanton found an ally in convention delegate and eminent abolitionist Frederick Douglass. With Douglass introducing the suffrage appeal to the convention, Stanton managed to retain its inclusion. The Declaration, with Stanton's call for women to actively pursue the right to vote, was ultimately signed by a third of the convention attendees. Sixty-eight women and thirty-two men had put their names to the document that scholars have labeled the beginning of the struggle for women's enfranchisement in the United States.[1]

[1] The chapter's opening quotation of Susan B. Anthony appears in Catt, Carrie Chapman and Nettie Rogers Shuler, *Woman Suffrage and Politics: The Inner Story of the Suffrage Movement*

The end of the woman suffrage struggle came, of course, with the ratification of the Nineteenth Amendment to the U.S. Constitution in 1920, which barred discrimination based on sex in voter qualifications. That the struggle to realize the goal of woman suffrage spanned more than seventy years seems, perhaps, to validate Mott's worry that the idea of women's voting rights was still too radical for her time. Indeed, a proposal for a constitutional amendment did not appear in Congress until 1878, would not be voted upon until 1887, and seemed to stand no chance of passing until the second decade of the twentieth century. Yet, beneath the surface of the long wait for a federal woman suffrage amendment was a much more dynamic story of the politics of women's voting rights in the states. Woman suffrage measures were considered and adopted by states through legislative enactment, constitutional conventions, and popularly initiated referendums; the earliest of these extensions came in 1837, the latest during the push for ratification of the federal amendment in 1920. Some of these state-level measures provided for purely local electoral rights, enabling women to vote on local tax issues, school matters, or for municipal officers. Other measures provided women with limited suffrage rights in statewide elections, such as allowing them to vote only in presidential elections. And some states endowed women with truly full voting rights – as early as 1890.

Leaders of the national woman suffrage movement certainly noticed the story of the states, at least to the extent that they engaged the question of whether state-level adoption of woman suffrage would enhance the viability of their goal of a federal amendment. Although notable suffrage activists disagreed on the answer to that question, the state strategy – aiming to win the woman suffrage battle at the federal level by first accumulating a sufficient number of state-level victories such that Congress, the President, and the national party organizations would find support of a national amendment the only politically expedient option – ultimately became the dominant approach of the major national organization, the National American Woman Suffrage Association (NAWSA). When the U.S. Constitution was finally amended, more than half of the states already had adopted measures giving women voting rights in at least some statewide elections, and fully three-fourths of the states had instituted some form of voting rights for women. In turn, the argument that gains at the state level were key to effecting change at the federal level infused suffrage activists' accounts of their final victory. Carrie Chapman Catt, who lobbied Congress in her role as president of NAWSA, referred to the adoption of the state level suffrage measures as no less than "the most persuasive of

(New York, C. Scribner's Sons, 1926), 227. For a general outline of the history of the national movement, including the Stanton and Mott exchange, see Flexner, Eleanor, *Century of Struggle: The Woman's Rights Movement in the United States* (Cambridge, MA: Belknap Press, 1959). See also suffragists' own accounts in Stanton, Elizabeth Cady, Susan B. Anthony, Matilda Joslyn Gage, and Ida Husted Harper, ed. *History of Woman Suffrage* (Salem, 1985 (reprint)).

all arguments for extending full suffrage to women" at her disposal.[2] I will ultimately agree with Catt's conclusion, but demonstrate that progress at the state level mattered for political reasons well beyond any sense of accountability to women in the electorate.

Changes in women's voting rights in the states may have been essential to the achievement of a national commitment to sex equity in electoral qualifications, but the state and local politics of woman suffrage were also something more than mere stepping-stones to a federal amendment, even if nationally prominent suffrage activists viewed and treated them as if they were not. The states were filled with women who desired voting rights for their own sets of reasons, and who had their own ideas about how to attain those rights. Each state, moreover, presented a different political and social environment to be negotiated. These realities often led to clashes between "local" and "national" suffragists over state-level activism. There were disagreements about whose support should be sought, what type of suffrage legislation should be proposed, and when it was the right time for a public campaign. And the national suffrage organizations were quite regularly in the wrong. As women in Colorado, for example, mounted a campaign for a woman suffrage amendment to their state constitution in the summer of 1893, they found themselves defending their choice to act to the NAWSA leadership. Wrote one Colorado suffragist to Chapman Catt, then the NAWSA organizer appointed to her state: "You say you have talked with 'no one who feels the slightest hope of success in Colorado,' are you sure you have talked with anyone who understands the situation here?"[3] Colorado women were enfranchised in November of that year.

It is also true that the pursuit of women's voting rights was at times carried out in the states (and territories) without any intervention or assistance from the national organizations. Indeed, state lawmakers were considering the idea of woman suffrage before there was any national organization of which to speak. In states that were moving, in the score of years before the Fifteenth Amendment materialized, to dispose of clauses in their constitutions that defined voters in terms of race, removal of the sex barrier was not an uncommon digression in the debate. Michigan state legislators first contemplated female suffrage in this way in 1849 – just one year after Stanton met resistance to her women's voting rights proposal at a women's rights convention.[4] And yet a national organization dedicated to the goal of woman suffrage would not emerge until 1869.

---

[2] Catt and Shuler, *Woman Suffrage*, 340. I am attributing a passage of the text to Catt, which seems justified by Catt's role in the lobbying practices of the NAWSA, and Shuler's absence therefrom.

[3] Letter from Ellis Stansbury (Meredith) to Carrie Chapman Catt, June 30, 1893 (Ellis Meredith Collection, Colorado Historical Society).

[4] *Documents Accompanying the Journal of the Senate of the State of Michigan at the Annual Session of 1849* (Lansing: Munger & Pattison), 32–69.

Fixating on the story of the Nineteenth Amendment, then, or even taking a broader view by chronicling the woman suffrage issue from the vantage point of those in the national suffrage organizations, eschews important pieces of the history of woman suffrage in the United States. That prominent suffrage activists were convinced state-level developments were key to winning the federal amendment is certainly one reason to seek an explanation of state action – and inaction – on women's voting rights. That the states varied so widely, across time and geography, in their treatment of the issue is another. Simply put, it begs the question of why. Why did woman suffrage become a political reality in some states and not others? Why were women enfranchised at particular moments in their states' histories?

To offer an explanation of the states' treatment of the issue of women's voting rights will involve addressing the fundamental question about democratic development at the heart of the woman suffrage story: why would politicians *ever* decide to expand the electorate to which they are accountable? The aim of this book is to develop a general framework for understanding why politicians act to widen the democratic circle, and to use that framework to explain the politics of woman suffrage. Building this account of electoral expansion entails drawing on insights about the decision-making process of the legislators who control the supply of new voting rights, including how and when political parties structure the environments in which legislators make their decisions.[5] Centering the focus on partisan politics does not imply that suffrage activism is unimportant in the process of electoral expansion. Indeed, I argue that activism powerfully shapes the incentives of the supply-side actors in the enfranchisement equation. Yet previous accounts of voting rights extension that have focused almost exclusively on the demand-side actors have had difficulty explaining *how* activism influenced policy outcomes. By accounting for partisan politicians' motivations to expand the electorate, I gain new leverage on that question.

Why Woman Suffrage – What We Know So Far

Explanations for the extension of voting rights to women were first offered by suffrage activists themselves. NAWSA, the largest and longest-standing national suffrage organization, which emerged in 1890 as the reunification of the feuding National Woman Suffrage Association and American Woman Suffrage Association, published its own six-volume account of the movement – from start to finish and across state and federal levels. This *History of Woman Suffrage* allowed leaders from each state to write their own reports of state action; what was done by suffrage organizers, what legislation was introduced and

---

[5] In the category "legislators" I am including delegates to constitutional conventions, as well as members of regular state and territorial legislatures. Delegates do not have reelection goals per se, but are usually interested in legislative or other political careers after the convention. I deal with consequences of exceptions to this rule in later chapters.

how it was treated, and the characterization of "public opinion" in the state were all chronicled. NAWSA also kept copious records, for at least part of its existence, which were later deposited for public study. The Congressional Union/National Woman's Party (CU), which splintered off from NAWSA in 1914, also left behind a lengthy paper trail. And in both 1926 and 1940, NAWSA leaders authored book-length treatments on how woman suffrage was won.[6]

Despite the abundance of evidence left behind by suffragists, scholars were slow to come to the task of documenting and explaining the American experience with woman suffrage politics. Eleanor Flexner's *Century of Struggle*, considered the groundbreaking history of the American movement for women's rights by many contemporary scholars, did not appear until 1959. Flexner, and the scholarly literature on woman suffrage that followed, while cognizant of suffragists' lack of objectivity in documenting their efforts, nevertheless unapologetically concentrated on telling the woman's rights story from women's perspectives. Women as political actors had been missing from historical scholarship, and the line of research that emerged endeavored to redress that omission. As a result, what we know so far about woman suffrage is mostly about the suffragists themselves: the arguments they invoked, the ways they organized, and how they presented their cause. The cost for this tendency in research on woman suffrage, however, has been a relative paucity of work meant to address directly the question of outcomes.

To the extent that there are accounts about what determined woman suffrage successes or failures, they are developed from the vantage point of the movement. Indeed, most existing explanations of women's voting rights outcomes are found inside narratives meant to address other questions about the development of the suffrage movement. The consequence is a list of possible influences on the decisions made on the question of woman suffrage, but not clear answers to questions about how, when, and why each translated into the political behavior that produced voting rights policy outcomes.

Some scholars have identified changing ideologies as the primary mover of suffrage laws. In essence, the argument is that women were granted voting rights when and where the idea of their enfranchisement was no longer a radical one. Changing ideas about gender roles and the capacity of women, in particular, are often highlighted as the most important ideological shifts for facilitating woman suffrage success. The pattern of suffrage successes is thus fitted with two distinct societal developments that enabled women to establish legitimate claims to participation in electoral politics. First, early success in

---

[6] The Library of Congress (Washington, DC) and The Schlesinger Library (Radcliffe College, Cambridge, Massachusetts) each house extensive collections of papers from the national suffrage associations. Books by NAWSA leaders: Catt, Carrie Chapman and Nettie Rogers Shuler, *Woman Suffrage and Politics: The Inner Story of the Suffrage Movement* (New York, C. Scribner's Sons, 1926); The National American Woman Suffrage Association, *Victory: How Women Won It* (New York: The H. W. Wilson Company).

the American West is attributed to the changes in gender roles demanded by the frontier experience. Second, changes in women's levels of education and increases in their participation in both the workplace and the public sphere – what some have termed the "rise of the new woman" – are used to explain the increased success of demands for women's voting rights in the later years of the movement.[7]

Others have looked to variations in the organizational capacity of the suffrage movement to explain the pattern of its successes and failures. In these narratives, leveraging positive outcomes for the movement depends most on the development of sufficient resources or appropriate tactics. Developments of this sort deemed influential are generally those that map onto moments of increasing suffrage success. Inside this category are scholars who argue that success came when suffragists dropped principled arguments for extending voting rights to women – that is, appeals to issues of republican ideals and legal justice – and instead turned to arguments defined by political expediency. The key to success, then, was to find an argument for suffrage rights that fit into ongoing political debates, promising that enfranchised women might contribute to the victory of one side over another. Development of more sophisticated lobbying strategies over the course of the movement, particularly in the later years, has also been forwarded as an explanation for suffragists' patterns of success. A number of scholars explicitly credit the execution of Carrie Chapman Catt's "winning plan" strategy, which funneled NAWSA resources to a combination of key state campaigns and Congressional lobbying activities, as the determining factor in the increased generation of successes for the movement in the final decade before the federal amendment was ratified. With equal conviction, however, others have pointed to the explanatory power of the introduction of more militant tactics, such as confrontational White House pickets, employed by the CU in the same time period.[8]

---

[7] Baker, Paula, "The Domestication of Politics: Women and American Political Society, 1780–1920." *The American Historical Review* 89 (1984): 620–47; Beeton, Beverly, *Women Vote in the West: The Woman Suffrage Movement, 1869–1896* (New York: Garland Publishing, Inc., 1986); Grimes, Alan P., *The Puritan Ethic and Woman Suffrage* (New York: Oxford University Press, 1967); Mead, Rebecca J., *How the Vote Was Won: Woman Suffrage in the United States, 1868–1914* (New York: New York University Press, 2004); McCammon, Holly J., Karen E. Campbell, Ellen M. Granberg, and Christine Mowery, "How Movements Win: Gendered Opportunity Structures and U.S. Women's Suffrage Movements, 1866 to 1919." *American Sociological Review* 66 (Feb., 2001): 49–70.

[8] On the idea of the importance of politically expedient arguments for suffrage, see Marilley, Suzanne M., *Woman Suffrage and the Origins of Liberal Feminism in the United States, 1820–1920* (Cambridge, MA: Harvard University Press, 1996). For arguments about the influence of tactics, see Buechler, Steven, *The Transformation of the Woman Suffrage Movement: The Case of Illinois, 1850–1920* (New Brunswick, NJ: Rutgers University Press, 1986); Ford, Linda, "Alice Paul and the Triumph of Militancy" in *One Woman, One Vote: Rediscovering the Woman Suffrage Movement*, ed. Marjorie Spruill Wheeler, 277–94 (Troutdale, OR: New Sage Press, 1995).

Yet another set of accounts of woman suffrage outcomes is focused on factors that might explain delay or failure, implying that voting rights gains were achieved by somehow disabling opponents. Indeed, suffragists themselves were inclined to single out malicious opponents, such as liquor industry interests, "ignorant" immigrant men, and well-heeled women organized as anti-suffragists, as the key impediments to the adoption of women's voting rights. A fear of pro-prohibition voting by women was said to have driven the liquor lobby to campaign actively, and perhaps deviously, against woman suffrage. Vehement protection of traditional gender roles was the supposed motivation of immigrant men and the organized anti-suffragists. In this same vein, Southern resistance, tied to interests in keeping the "Negro question" closed by avoiding all discussions of voting rights, also has been implicated in the political stalling of woman suffrage.[9]

Finally, some scholars have looked to the political conditions under which women became eligible voters to explain suffrage success. Researchers have noticed that woman suffrage was often welcome on the platforms of minor political parties, including those of the Populists, Socialists, and Progressives. That woman suffrage was adopted in a number of states at moments when these third parties were actually having some electoral success is seen as evidence of their influence on the issue. In addition, scholars studying the Western suffrage successes have ascribed importance to the "unsettled" nature of partisan politics there, seeing in it a tendency toward political experimentation from which woman suffrage benefited. These are ultimately explanations about political opportunities – cracks in the system of politics as usual that might make space for the admission of new voters.[10]

Yet even as stories of partisan politics and political opportunities enter accounts of woman suffrage, lawmakers remain on the periphery, and their

[9] Green, Elna C., *Southern Strategies: Southern Women and the Woman Suffrage Question* (Chapel Hill: The University of North Carolina Press, 1997); Wheeler, Marjorie Spruill, *New Women of the New South: The Leaders of the Woman Suffrage Movement in the Southern States* (New York: Oxford University Press, 1993), esp. 100–32; Gilmore, Glenda Elizabeth, *Gender and Jim Crow: Women and the Politics of White Supremacy in North Carolina, 1896–1920* (Chapel Hill: The University of North Carolina Press, 1996), esp. 203–24; Kraditor, Aileen S. "Tactical Problems of the Woman-Suffrage Movement in the South" in *History of Women in the United States: Historical Articles on Women's Lives and Activities*, v. 19, ed. Nancy F. Cott (Munich: KG Saur, 1992), 272–90; Marshall, Susan E., *Splintered Sisterhood: Gender and Class in the Campaign against Woman Suffrage* (Madison: University of Wisconsin Press, 1997).

[10] Banaszak, Lee Ann, *Why Movements Succeed or Fail: Opportunity, Culture, and the Struggle for Woman Suffrage* (Princeton, NJ: Princeton University Press, 1996); McCammon, Holly J. and Karen Campbell, "Winning the Vote in the West: The Political Successes of the Women's Suffrage Movements, 1866–1919." *Gender and Society* 15 (2001): 55–82. For an exceptional work that considers legislators' incentives, see McDonagh, Eileen, "Constituency Influence on House Roll-Call Votes in the Progressive Era, 1913–1915." *Legislative Studies Quarterly* 18 (1993): 185–210.

incentives for making decisions on women's enfranchisement largely unexamined. Historian Aileen Kraditor observed in the preface of the 1981 edition of her book on the national movement that the effect of suffragist activity on Congressmen's votes was conspicuously missing from her own work, and that, "If someone tabulated the votes of all those Members of Congress who voted both when the amendment lost and later when it passed, and then searched the papers of those who changed their votes, we might know why they did so."[11] Systematic examinations of legislators' votes need not take on the form that Kraditor suggested – indeed, there are many other ways to get leverage on the reasons for legislative outcomes – but it is true that we won't understand why woman suffrage became law where it did and when it did without rigorous investigations of lawmakers' decisions on the issue.

Putting partisan politics and legislative decision making at the center of the woman suffrage story does not imply dismissal of the importance of the organized movement. Rather, it is the only approach that enables us to determine when and how suffrage activism – or any other factor – influenced state decisions on women's voting rights. As I show in later chapters, building legislative and partisan politics into the narrative of woman suffrage helps resolve empirical and theoretical difficulties in existing accounts of women's voting rights. For instance, while it is not incredible that opposition played a role in shaping political action on women's voting rights, the question remains of why the opposition would have been victorious initially and yet eventually overcome. Similarly, if ideological shifts pegged to changes in women's place drove suffrage outcomes, how can we explain why some frontier states held out longer than others, and why so many states in the Northeast, the region where the "new woman" was most common, never adopted woman suffrage? It is also unclear just how third parties could have delivered woman suffrage if they never controlled even a single state legislature. What is missing from all these accounts of woman suffrage, still concentrated on telling the woman's rights story from women's perspectives, is the mechanism by which each influence changed the minds of some lawmakers – and not others.

Suffrage through a Partisan Politics Lens: The Argument in Brief

Understanding what motivates politicians to work toward changing the makeup of the electorates to which they are accountable involves attending to their location in legislative institutions and partisan electoral environments. Legislators must be central to an account of electoral expansion because of their institutional power to grant or rescind voting rights. Changing voter qualifications, in fact, involves significant legislative work and institutional capacity: changes must be ushered past multiple legislative hurdles, usually

---

[11] Kraditor, Aileen S., *The Ideas of the Woman Suffrage Movement* (New York: W. W. Norton & Company, 1981), vii.

involving supermajority floor vote requirements, often in two successive sessions of the legislature. In many states, changes to voter qualifications made by the legislature must also be ratified by the existing electorate through a referendum. Such a long and complex path from proposal to policy implies that legislation for new voting rights is particularly vulnerable to defeat by neglect, delay, or procedural technicality. Ensuring success for the idea of new voting rights thus depends critically on whether the policy becomes not only an acceptable idea to a sufficient number of lawmakers, but an important one as well – one that legislators will expend their time and resources to advance.

Parties enter the account of voting rights extension not only as the political institutions centrally concerned with organizing and controlling electoral outcomes – and thus, with obvious interest in the definition of the electorate – but also as organizers of legislative bodies. Partisan interest in the extension of voting rights may thus provide the issue importance essential to ensuring its success inside legislative institutions. Given their central concern with electoral outcomes, a political party convinced that there is an electoral benefit for them in the enfranchisement of the new group would prefer to change electoral qualifications, and the more they need those new votes to win control of the government, the more important such a change should be. Conversely, if a political party sees more cost than gain in the enfranchisement of new voters, it should work to stymie the proposed change.

In defining the potential for success of a proposal for suffrage extension, then, the first question to answer is what the addition of new voters will mean for party politicians. How do they expect the group that might be enfranchised will behave as voters? From where do they draw those expectations? I argue that political identities – shaped by the influences of political comprehensions of race, class, and gender – are key to shaping partisans' expectations of likely voter behavior. It is possible that partisans might understand a disenfranchised group as likely to be supportive of a particular political party; common understandings of the political homogeneity of groups defined by their social location may credibly signal probable partisan benefit. In this case, the party expecting to reap the electoral rewards of enfranchising these new voters should be the only party interested in extending suffrage rights to the group. This simple partisan story of suffrage extension is what I term *strategic enfranchisement*. Importance of the suffrage issue, in this case, derives from a combination of a party's level of need for more support in the electorate and the would-be voters' (perceived) political tendencies. In other words, this is a story of parties seeking new sources of electoral support, finding in a disfranchised group the promise of a new voting bloc, and hence pushing suffrage changes through the legislative (and perhaps referendum) process.

It is also possible, however, that the future voting behavior of a disenfranchised group may be quite difficult to predict. Or the expectation may be that the group would be unlikely to exhibit any singular partisan pattern. That is, a proposed change in voter qualifications may not neatly map onto a politically cohesive group. What then? The change in the qualifications of voters must derive its political meaning and importance from some factor other than the promise of a new partisan voting bloc. In this case – when new voters are enfranchised not for the sake of the votes they themselves offer – new voting rights must somehow be distinguished as a real constituent demand, one for which unresponsiveness on the part of elected politicians and political parties would likely translate into real electoral consequences. Suffrage extension in an accommodation of the interests of existing voters in these new voting rights is what I term *programmatic enfranchisement*. The programmatic enfranchisement account takes on a level of complexity in how politicians come to perceive the importance of action on the suffrage issue; there are several political conditions that help suggest such importance, which I discuss in more detail in the following chapter. Essential to programmatic enfranchisement, however, is a credible pro-suffrage coalition to which elected politicians are already accountable.

Key Insights and Predictions for the Case of Woman Suffrage

My main argument about outcomes for the woman suffrage movement is that the *successful* path to enfranchisement for women was programmatic. This argument rests on the understanding that although gendered arguments for woman suffrage were common, real *political* essentialism of the category "women" was not. That is, politicians saw as much political diversity in "women" as they saw in "men," thus making women poor candidates for strategic enfranchisement. This argument does not imply that attempts at a strategic enfranchisement strategy never emerged. Rather, it asserts that the fundamental incentive structure of the strategic enfranchisement model was not realized; that where and when voting rights for women were actually delivered, it was through the coalitional politics of the programmatic enfranchisement model. To argue that woman suffrage was delivered through programmatic enfranchisement adds far clearer definitions of the relevant political opportunities, political barriers, movement resources, and activism strategies than previous accounts of the movement have managed to offer. In so doing, it also clarifies and even changes our understanding of how several of the oft-cited influences on the woman suffrage cause shaped the movement's potential, most notably race, third parties, political machines, and suffrage opponents like the liquor industry.

In arguing that women were not likely candidates for strategic enfranchisement, I am not arguing that expectations of women voting to support a particular cause or party were absent from the politics of woman suffrage. The groups that ultimately partnered with the suffrage cause likely wanted women sympathetic to their cause to add to the organization's electoral leverage once they became voters. It is easy to conflate the idea, however, that suffrage supporters expected that *certain groups* of women would be electorally supportive of their cause – such as those women that were locally active in the organized suffrage movement or those that were active within their issue organizations – with the idea that supporters believed "women" *in general* or *more than men* would support them. That distinction, however, is an important one, and one that helps explain why woman suffrage was not the result of strategic enfranchisement. And certainly some individuals or groups at some moments might have thought that they would get "women" on their side by working for suffrage. My argument, however, is that the dominant information defining the meaning of woman suffrage made such a calculation uncommon and unfounded – and, hence, prevented it from being the general incentive for supporting the suffrage cause. This information derived first from notions of gender and later from the policy feedback from the early adopters of woman suffrage provisions.

Perhaps ironically, both dominant contemporary notions of gender and woman suffrage activists' own feminist arguments about women's place in electoral politics worked against the possibility of strategic enfranchisement for women. Common notions of male leadership in the household and women's subservience made male politicians – party leaders, lawmakers, and interest group leaders alike – likely to expect women to "double the existing vote." This expectation that women would, generally speaking, vote the same way as the men to which they were related did is ubiquitous in the historical record and often called the "family vote" argument in the woman suffrage literature. For an entirely different gendered reason, suffrage movement leaders went to great lengths to emphasize that women would make electoral choices based on criteria other than their status as "women." Suffrage leaders were emphasizing the feminist notion that women were just as capable of "doing politics" in exactly the same way men did. If such feminist arguments were at all successful, however, their implication for the expectation of the partisan outcome of women's voting behavior was essentially the same: women promised no new voting bloc on account of their sex.

Not only did logics of gender push against the possibility of women becoming targets of a strategic enfranchisement approach, but so too did the information feedback from the early adopting states. When women were enfranchised, they did not turn partisan tides. This fact, as I highlight in Chapter 2, was one that politicians were quick to observe and underscore. Neither did suffrage states display a pattern of policy outcomes consistent with women electorally forcing a significant change in policy areas that were – at least rhetorically – linked to "female interests." Notably, suffrage states did not, as a rule, become dry states.

If women were unlikely candidates for strategic enfranchisement, then the fate of the woman suffrage movement rested on successful navigation of the politics of the programmatic enfranchisement model. Applying the programmatic enfranchisement model to woman suffrage specifies a key set of conditions that define what "political opportunity" was for the woman suffrage movement. It implies that women's voting rights should have been more likely when and where elections were competitive, politicians were electorally beholden to

organized constituent groups, and those groups could be engaged in the suffrage cause. Importantly, the programmatic model highlights that the suffrage
movement's ability to engage politically important coalitional partners was
key to its success. Thus, resources that would help attract political partners,
such as politically skilled movement workers, were the important ones for the
movement to accumulate. Also helpful in executing a successful coalitional
strategy were overlapping interests and social networks that defined a common
interest between women working for suffrage and interest groups wielding electoral leverage. In essence, it was particularly useful to have suffragists working
from within other organizations to push for support for the suffrage cause.
Farmers' interest groups, for example, the organizational roots of which were
often fraternal organizations whose ranks were populated by women as well
as men, could thus be engaged meaningfully through the demands of their
own memberships. On the other hand, some factors pushed against suffragists' willingness and capacity to build the necessary coalitions, particularly the
constraints of race and class. The organized movement was in many places
dominated by middle-class, white, urban women who had difficulty seeing and
establishing the necessary political common ground for successful coalitional
politics. Opportunities for promising partnerships with, for example, organized
labor were often missed or even, as I demonstrate with evidence from the case
of Illinois in Chapter 3, actively undone.

Adopting the programmatic enfranchisement model not only offers a general
explanation for the outcomes of the woman suffrage movement in the United
States, but also explains the influence of a number of the factors that repeatedly
enter the literature on the movement as ones relevant to the movement's failures
or successes. First among these is the role that third parties played in delivering
successes for the suffrage movement. It is the confluence of conditions that
define a political opportunity under the programmatic enfranchisement model,
I argue, that meant third parties stood as particularly promising coalitional
partners. When a third party took notable vote shares, it not only increased
political competition, but offered an unmatched level of certainty about the
electoral costs of failing to meet the demands of its constituent supporters.
Moreover, the leverage of third-party support could be heightened when their
vote shares represented the bolting of constituent groups that had been key to
previous winning coalitions and resulted in the overturn of previous partisan
control of the government.

Just as important as explaining political opportunities is explaining the conditions that frustrated the suffrage movement. Simply put, the key barriers were
those that constrained politics in a way that prevented the relevant political
opportunities from opening. Arguably, the strongest of these was race. Contrary to most existing accounts of woman suffrage, however, my argument is
not that the key barrier built by race was the resistance of black belt Southerners
to the idea of reopening the "Negro question" by considering the extension of
voting rights. Instead, I argue that the most important impediment to woman

suffrage forged by race was that race politics built political institutions that made movement for change difficult: ballot access laws, registration laws, and constitutional amendment procedures all had consequences for suffrage politics. The dominant story of race and woman suffrage was that a constrained one-party system built on ideals of white supremacy – which described most of the South – offered none of the electoral competition necessary for incentivizing partisan politicians to consider extending the franchise and few, if any, electorally consequential organizations with whom to partner. And even laws meant to protect the voting rights of racial minorities had implications for suffragists' ability to build sufficient political support for their desired change in state voter qualifications. Notably, unbendable electoral laws meant for the protection of racial minorities' rights could make the coalition required to win a change in women's voting rights an effectively impossible threshold. Of course, suffragists' own racial identities could also be part of the barriers built by race, ruling out some partnerships that were successful in states where racial interests were less central.

Political machines were another feature of the partisan politics environment that had consequences for the woman suffrage movement, often standing as a steadfast and powerful barrier to women's voting rights. Machines are in many ways the simplest of party organizations, functioning off of the notion of building a winning coalition through patronage and other tangible rewards for supporters. Suffrage extension, then, threatens a particular burden on machines: doing politics is literally expected to be more expensive with more voters to entice in this way. Machines would also be threatened by any movement tied to interests in increasing government transparency, increasing its efficiency, its reliance on expertise, and the like. All of these are threats to the machine's ability to use the apparatus of the state to entice its supporters. Any call for new voting rights packaged with calls for government accountability and reform, as woman suffrage typically was, would therefore meet with machine resistance. And because machines are particularly cohesive political structures, machine leaders stood well positioned to mobilize opposition to suffrage – both within government and in the electorate. This incentive and capacity for machine resistance, coupled the historical tendency for America's urban machines to count among their bases of support significant immigrant populations, helps explain the common refrain from suffragists that their efforts were stymied by "ignorant immigrant male voters." While suffrage measures that went to the polls undoubtedly encountered resistance that could be linked to immigrant voters, the suffragists' rhetoric missed the key role that machine politics played in ensuring such outcomes.

Finally, in a more general way, adopting the programmatic enfranchisement model as the framework for understanding the politics of woman suffrage helps explain the actions and leverage of alleged opponents, such as the liquor industry. An important part of the difficulty in understanding the role of suffrage opponents is explaining why opponents could have been so effective in staving off suffrage for so long, and yet could also be overridden in rather short order. Here, both the details of the programmatic model and the underlying observations about the institutional hurdles through which suffrage measures needed to pass are relevant. Given that the political institutions that must be cleared to change suffrage laws are designed to make change hard, there is an inherent inequality in the costs and benefits for opposition and support of new suffrage laws. Real efforts to change suffrage qualifications are always costly, and thus require strong electoral incentives to take on. In contrast, in a cost-benefit analysis, sometimes opposition is worth mounting based on even slight notions that the new voters might not be friendly. Effective opposition to woman suffrage, for example, might only require influencing a few lawmakers on the relevant legislative committee to keep a measure from being introduced into the legislative chamber. And because effective opposition can be relatively cheap, it might be mounted by interests like the liquor industry even if they only perceived small risks to their interests if women were enfranchised – in other words, they need not realistically fear imminent prohibition. When electoral incentives vest a partisan interest in effectively delivering a change in suffrage laws, however, opposition becomes much more expensive, because suffrage opponents would need to mount a campaign against the party organization. And because electoral tides can and did turn quite quickly, the relative advantage of opponents could quickly disappear.

Evaluating the Theory: A Mixed-Methods Approach

This book is motivated by two goals: evaluating the general theoretical argument I offer about suffrage politics and explaining the outcomes of the woman suffrage movement, in particular. Both of these aims are served by a research design that engages enough historical detail and captures enough variance in political circumstances to parse out the effects of demand-side and supply-side factors on the political fate of the issue of new voting rights. The design I offer, then, is one that begins with detailed investigations in five case study states, then tests the conclusions from the case study states with relevant data from all forty-eight states, and then finally turns to analysis of the politics of woman suffrage at the federal level. I rely on both qualitative historical work and quantitative statistical analyses in what some call a mixed-methods approach, where qualitative and quantitative data are employed in tandem. The underlying logic of this approach is that a deep familiarity with the on-the-ground details derived from the rich qualitative data enables the appropriate use of quantitative models to test my argument and its implications. The qualitative work is used to help determine the specification of what belongs in the quantitative models, how to interpret their results, and how to think about and defend quantitative models where, by necessity of the historical record, proxies rather than ideal measures must be employed. In sum, neither the qualitative nor the quantitative evidence is meant to stand on its own; both are to be taken up and interpreted together.[12]

To begin, I selected a sample of five states for which I track the development of the issue of woman suffrage over time, from its earliest mention in the public sphere in that state until the adoption of woman suffrage in that state – either through its own policy change or the ratification of the federal amendment. Colorado, Illinois, Louisiana, Michigan, and New Mexico are the central cases. These states were chosen as a set in order to capture not only significant variation on the key explanatory factor – the character and competitiveness of the partisan politics environment – but with attention to variation that would allow for investigation into the roles of state political institutional and demographic differences in this partisan process. The set, then, includes party environments marked by one-party dominance, two-party competitiveness, and significant third-party successes. Also represented is a range of racial and ethnic demographics; the set purposely includes states to account for differences in party politics and political institutions where populations of blacks, Spanish Americans, and/or new immigrants were significant. These demographic differences were deemed important not only because race and ethnicity are oft-cited factors in existing accounts of woman suffrage outcomes, but moreover because my argument about their role in defining the chances is quite different from those existing accounts. Thus, having empirical leverage on these factors is particularly important. Additionally, with an assortment of industrial and agricultural bases to the economies of these states, and with North, South, and West represented in the case set, the issue of woman suffrage can be traced across a range of distinct backdrops of interest arrangements in state politics.[13]

The primary goal of the qualitative historical work in the book is to map out what organizations and political figures were involved in the politics of woman suffrage over time in each state, the positions they took, and the actions they undertook. This work enables me to shed light on the building of the programmatic enfranchisement strategy by suffrage activists where it did emerge, illuminating when and how pro-suffrage coalitions developed. This mapping,

---

[12] For more information and arguments about the unique empirical leverage and validity of this sort of approach, see Brady, Henry E. and David Collier, eds., *Rethinking Social Inquiry: Diverse Tools, Shared Standards* (Lanham, MD: Rowan & Littlefield Publishers, Inc., 2004.).

[13] It may be noted that there is no Northeastern state in the set. This choice was deliberately made in part because so much of the existing literature focuses on Northeastern states, particularly New York and Massachusetts. This fact is likely attributable in part to the ease of availability of the historical record as well as the fact that the Northeast was home to some of the most famous of the national activists. As such, it is possible to turn to other secondary sources for some comparison of the Northeastern state politics to the politics of the Southern, Western, and Midwestern states included here. Doing so suggests that suffrage activists in the Northeast were likely frustrated in their efforts by the Republican Party dominance in that section of the country, a point I highlight in the cross-state analyses in Chapter 6.

in turn, enables appropriate statistical analysis of the decisions taken by state lawmakers on the issue of woman suffrage. I track every legislative consideration of woman suffrage in each state and test, where some sort of vote makes doing so possible, the effectiveness of the particular suffrage coalition that existed in that state at that moment on the outcome. The assessment of state legislators' decisions on the issue includes not only decisions on final roll call votes once woman suffrage measures reached the floor of the legislature, but also decisions on whether to push these measures through the legislative process at all. Paying attention to the entire legislative process is particularly important in revealing the interests and leverage of the party organizations on the issue. To piece together the histories in each state, I combed through national, state, and local suffrage organization documents; personal correspondences of suffrage activists; documents of coalitional partners; state legislative records; and papers of state political parties and individual state politicians. The state-specific data on which I rely to specify the statistical analyses come from the records of state legislatures, suffrage organizations, political parties, state election returns, and the U.S. Census. These sources allow me to account for the roles of suffrage activists, interest groups, political parties, and even the average voter in the politics of women's voting rights, and to show how and when each influenced state action or inaction on the issue.

Delving into local histories in five states across some of the major geopolitical divides of the United States enables the illustration of important nuances to the general explanation of suffrage politics. Each of the state case studies offers some unique insight, and the case studies are presented separately across chapters that highlight what piece of the politics that each case is particularly useful in unpacking. Commonalities across the case studies, however, demonstrate that indeed one framework can help us understand the suffrage story in markedly different sociopolitical environments. Put another way, the comparison is evidence that there is, indeed, a general story of woman suffrage to tell. This generality is also more rigorously tested in the penultimate chapter of the book, where statistical analysis on the timing of woman suffrage adoption across all forty-eight relevant states is presented. It is the work of the case studies that enables specification of the appropriate model across all the states. And it is the cumulation of the lessons from the state-level politics that provides the framework for understanding the national story of woman suffrage, including the analysis of the actions of the national political party organizations and the U.S. Congress, which is also presented in the penultimate chapter of the book.

What Is to Come

In the next chapter, I place the story of woman suffrage inside my general account of suffrage extension. Doing so involves first a brief review of the decisions that have been made over the course of American history about the qualifications of electors. The chapter then turns to developing, in greater detail, the general theoretical framework for explaining decisions to expand the electorate. Strategic enfranchisement and programmatic enfranchisement incentive structures are elaborated, including the crucial role of political identity in defining which type of enfranchisement is possible for previously excluded groups. Finally, I engage the question of whether woman suffrage should be considered an exceptional case of suffrage extension. I contend that it should not by highlighting the general lessons the case of the politics of woman suffrage offers about the interplay of political identities and partisan incentives in shaping electoral qualifications.

Chapter 2 engages the argument that the *successful* path to enfranchisement for women was programmatic. Using the case of Colorado, the first state in which male voters ratified a legislative decision to grant women the right to vote and a common example in other states' discussions of woman suffrage, I show how this early success for woman suffrage congealed the partisan understanding of woman suffrage in a way that defined out strategic enfranchisement. I also show that suffragists began to learn how it was that electoral partisan incentives could nonetheless secure women's voting rights – to learn the basics of programmatic enfranchisement politics.

The next two chapters illuminate both the difficulties of negotiating the coalitional politics of programmatic enfranchisement and how it was that those coalitions paid dividends. In Chapter 3 I take up the case of Michigan to explain how suffragists made and capitalized on connections to influential interest groups, and how they floundered in legislative politics without them. In Chapter 4 I explain how and when woman suffrage was linked to third-party movements, and, using the case of Illinois, demonstrate the particular leverage such connections brought the issue in state politics.

Finally, Chapter 5 investigates the significant barriers to woman suffrage constructed by issues of racial – and class – interests in state politics. The evidence for this chapter comes from Louisiana and New Mexico. Louisiana demonstrates suffragists' difficulty finding political leverage in a constrained, one-party environment. Tensions between protection of Spanish-American men's rights and an Anglo-run woman suffrage movement are explored with the case of New Mexico.

Although I argue that understanding the state and local politics that delivered state woman suffrage victories is central to explaining the historic change of women's place in American politics resulting from the woman suffrage movement, answering the question of the national outcome is still an underlying goal. Thus, in Chapter 6 I return to the national story of woman suffrage, and approach explanation in two ways. First, to ensure that the state-by-state account I build in Chapters 2 through 5 is not particular to the small set of states I study in detail, I offer a test of the general explanatory framework's applicability to woman suffrage across all forty-eight states between the start of the woman suffrage movement in 1848 and the adoption of the Nineteenth Amendment in 1920. Statistical analysis of data on all the states across these years is marshaled as evidence for the role of partisan incentives in decisions about the expansion of the electorate. Second, I revisit the decisions of members of the U.S. Congress on the Nineteenth Amendment to show how the framework can help us understand the long wait for federal action, as well as the final relenting.

As I draw conclusions about the particular case of woman suffrage in the final chapter of the book, I also revisit the question of what contribution this work makes to our general understanding of American politics. Most obvious is a set of lessons that change our understanding of how and why voting rights have changed and continue to develop; a discussion of new thinking about black voting rights provides an example. There are connections to other realms of political inquiry, too. Retelling the woman suffrage story in this partisan way holds insights for our thinking about gender in politics, particularly for the growing literature on the place of "women" and "women's issues" in the political parties. The accounts of states' experiences with woman suffrage also speak to just how significant third parties have been in the development of American politics, even if they show up only intermittently and primarily at the state level. In the end, I also hope the reader will find that these state stories of the struggle for women's voting rights underscore the reality that much more than the effort of the few famous suffragists that Americans now remember was necessary to enfranchise "one half the people."[14]

---

[14] "One half the people" is the terminology of Anne Firor Scott.

I

Bringing Politics Back In

Suffrage Supply and Demand

In the chapters that follow, I turn to state politics to explain how and why American women won the right to vote. Women, however, were not the only group for whom the enfranchisement story began at the state level. In fact, most of the voting rights protections that have become canonized in the U.S. Constitution followed behind state action. Defining the American electorate is thus a deceivingly difficult task; at no point in the history of the nation has there been a single answer to the question of who can vote. Despite a founding based on the republican principle of the "consent of the governed," neither the Articles of Confederation nor the subsequent U. S. Constitution offered protection of the people's right of consent – their right to choose the officers of their government. Protection and definition of that right was left to the states, to do with as they might. Therefore, there have always been at least as many answers to the question of who may vote as there have been states.

It is true that the national government has at some points adopted measures through both constitutional amendments and legislative acts to constrain the states' ability to delineate the eligibility of citizens for the elective franchise. Yet all of these actions – the bans on discrimination by race, sex, ability to pay a poll tax, or age – followed in the footsteps of similar policies already adopted by a significant number of states. Furthermore, beyond these specific categories of discrimination, states have made and continue to make distinctions between categories of their residents who may vote and who may not, and who the process of voting is designed to include and exclude. What, then, have state governments done with their power to define the American electorate? How have they chosen whom to include and exclude? What has prompted states to change the composition of their electorates over time? What has stalled that change?

This chapter develops a general framework for answering these fundamental questions about the development of voting rights in the United States, which will be applied in the remaining chapters to women's voting rights in particular. My account of suffrage extension is informed by two literatures that have been oddly disconnected in their approaches to issues of voting rights. Previous scholarship has tended to focus either on the role of political elites or on the role of social movements in bringing about changes in electoral qualifications. One might label these two lines of investigation "supply-side" and "demand-side" accounts of the politics of voting rights. Yet it is obvious that we need to understand the interaction of supply and demand politics to account for suffrage outcomes. Social movements demanding changes in voting rights have numerous strategies and resources they could pursue; seeing when each is likely to facilitate the desired policy change (if ever), and under what conditions we would expect failure in spite of resources and political savvy, involves detailing politicians' motivations for response. In so doing, we need to understand these supply-side actors as both partisans and lawmakers, elucidating the incentives and constraints engendered by electoral considerations *and* political institutions.

To give an overview of the landscape of changes, I begin in this chapter with a very brief history of suffrage qualifications in the United States. Next, I offer a concise review of the approaches of others to explain what has brought about changes in the legal composition of the American electorate, highlighting what pieces are missing from the politics in these accounts. Delving into the incentives for suffrage extension that are produced and constrained by politicians' locations in political parties and legislative bodies, I then detail my general framework for understanding decisions to expand voting rights. Finally, I explain the utility of using woman suffrage as a case to test the theoretical expectations implied by that framework.

The Journey from Propertied White Males – A Brief Overview of U.S. Suffrage History

The U.S. Constitution as drafted in 1787 offered only two comments on the subject of voting rights: one direct statement about voters in the first article and one indirect remark in the second. In Article I, Section 2, the Constitution proscribed that members of the House of Representatives would be "chosen every second year by the people of the several states, and the electors in each state shall have the qualifications requisite for electors of the most numerous branch of the state legislature." This clause meant that states were entrusted with the exclusive power of defining the electorate not only for the purposes of state elections, but also, by extension of that same process, for elections of the people's representatives in the national lawmaking body. It was a truly federalist institutional design, both reserving power to the state governments and tying decisions about state politics to the fundamental workings of the national government. Election of Senators was the jurisdiction of state legislatures (until the ratification of Amendment XVII in 1913). Article II,

Section 1 offered the process by which the President should be chosen, allowing each state "to appoint, in such manner as the legislature thereof may direct, a number of electors," which would cast the state's votes for the national executive. Although there is no explicit mention of a public vote, the power of the state legislatures to control the appointment of presidential Electors allowed state legislatures to define the qualifications of voters for the offices of President and Vice President.

At the time when the colonies became states, most states decided to tie voting rights to property rights, in much the same way the colonies had under British rule. Ten of the original thirteen states required voters to be freeholders of some set amount of property and/or of a set level of personal wealth. Pennsylvania and Georgia required voters to be taxpayers; Georgia also required certain personal worth or that the voter be a mechanic by trade. New Hampshire required only the payment of a poll tax. Voting was restricted to men in all the states save New Jersey, where widows of sufficient property were for a short time qualified to vote. Property qualifications waned in the early nineteenth century as new states entered the Union without such requirements for their electorates and existing states wrote them out. Tax-paying requirements, however, remained commonplace.[1]

Questions of race and the non-citizen vote were the next contentions in the history of American voting rights. Whereas only three of the thirteen states had constitutional bans on voting for persons of color in 1790, by 1840, twenty of twenty-six state constitutions included such clauses. In the 1840s and 1850s, state constitutions began to address the question of the vote for resident aliens. Three states – Wisconsin, Michigan, and Indiana – adopted provisions for suffrage rights for immigrants who declared an intention to become citizens in this time. More Midwestern, Southern, and Western states would follow suit in the 1860s and 1870s. Northeastern states, however, typically adopted citizen-only clauses. The political welcoming of alien voters where it existed was short-lived; by the 1920s, the "alien declarant" provisions were largely repealed. Exclusion of non-whites from electorates in the North, South, and West, persisted until the ratification of Amendment XV to the U.S. Constitution in 1870.[2] Redemption of the South in the last decades of the nineteenth century pushed black men back out of the electorate through various means, both constitutional and extra-legal. To pull out black voters without direct appeals to race, Southern state constitutions gained literacy and competency tests for the franchise, alongside grandfather clauses exempting those whose immediate ancestors were previously qualified to vote.

[1] Keyssar, Alexander, *The Right to Vote: The Contested History of Democracy in the United States* (New York: Basic Books, 2000), Appendix; Williamson, Chilton, *American Suffrage from Property to Democracy, 1760–1860* (Princeton, NJ: Princeton University Press, 1960).
[2] Keyssar, *The Right to Vote*, Appendix, Tables A.5, A.12; Kleppner, Paul, *Continuity and Change in Electoral Politics, 1893–1928* (New York: Greenwood Press, 1987), 165–66.

Between the end of the Civil War and 1920, there were several other major adjustments made to electoral composition across the states. Voter registration and complex residency requirements began to emerge immediately following the war. Literacy and competency tests – those common elements of Redemption constitutions in the Southern states – made their way into Northern and Western states by the early twentieth century. These non-Southern versions focused on required competence in the English language, holding new immigrant influxes out of the electorate. Women's voting rights first appeared in limited form in the mid-nineteenth century as states east and west of the Mississippi, and north and south of the Mason-Dixon Line, adopted provisions for women's participation in school or municipal elections. Full voting rights for women first took hold in the 1890s in the states of Wyoming, Colorado, Idaho, and Utah. By the time of ratification of Amendment XIX in 1920, which prohibited the denial of voting rights on the basis of sex, thirty states had granted women significant access to the polls. In this time period, disfranchisement of convicted criminals of various sorts also began to appear in state constitutions.[3]

The mid-twentieth century witnessed two major adjustments to voting rights. Although the practice of "military suffrage" had given a number of eighteen- to twenty-year-old males the right to vote in at least some elections since colonial times, extension of full voting rights to this age cohort did not occur until after World War II. Georgia became the first state to amend its constitution to include suffrage rights for this group in 1943. Before passage and ratification of Amendment XXVI to the U.S. Constitution in 1971, which provided for the right of eighteen- to twenty-year-olds to vote in all elections, seven other states acted to lower the legal voting age. In the same period, black Americans were re-enfranchised in states that had employed various legal and quasi-legal provisions to subvert their voting rights since the turn of the twentieth century through the ratification of Amendment XXIV in 1963, which outlawed poll taxes, and passage by Congress of the 1965 Voting Rights Act.[4]

There remains, of course, additional room for expansion of voting rights in the United States. Voting rights for non-citizens, now a reality in only a handful of local jurisdictions, have emerged on the political agenda in recent years in a number of states, including New York, California, and Massachusetts. Felon disenfranchisement provisions continue to be adjusted by the states. Debates

---

[3] Kleppner, *Continuity and Change*; Keyssar, *The Right to Vote*, Appendix, Table A.13; Scott, Anne Firor and Andrew MacKay Scott, *One Half the People: the Fight for Woman Suffrage* (Urbana: University of Illinois Press, 1982).

[4] Cultice, Wendell W., *Youth's Battle for the Ballot: A History of Voting Age in America* (New York: Greenwood Press, 1992). The Voting Rights Act has, of course, been renewed multiple times to preserve the federal oversight of voting and registration rights practices in places with conspicuously low registration and turnout. All of this federal legislation produced a long history of court challenges to state voting rights practices; the politics of such decisions, although certainly meriting their own systematic examination, are beyond the scope of this discussion, which seeks to explain initial state action to extend voting rights.

also endure about the voting rights of U.S. citizens residing in its territories; only residents of the District of Columbia cast votes for the offices of President and Vice President, and no territory claims a voting representative in the U.S. Congress. Recent decades have also borne renewed interest in regulation of voter registration and other procedural technicalities of the voting process that might be seen as effectively shaping the size and scope of the electorate. The U.S. Supreme Court's June 2013 ruling in *Shelby v. Holder* undid the federal government's legal formula under the Voting Rights Act for subjecting states and local jurisdictions to preclearance of any changes of their electoral laws and procedures. This decision reopens questions of the protection of racial and ethnic minorities' voting rights, and has already prompted new legislative proposals in a number of the previously covered states. And so the process of defining the American electorate is ongoing.

Suffrage Supply and Demand – Existing Accounts of Suffrage Changes

Even a cursory glance at the history of the franchise in the United States suggests that those with institutionalized political power – political elites – routinely make decisions that enable a broader electorate. It also illustrates, however, important patterns of diversity: that many states never relented on specific forms of electoral expansion, that no state or region can claim a consistent pattern of suffrage qualification liberalization, and that each change has come at different moments for different states. Such diversity would seem to challenge narratives of a steady march toward universal suffrage, including that offered by perhaps the most famous observer of American democracy, Alexis de Tocqueville. Writing in the 1830s, the French thinker believed he saw confirmation of the inevitability of consistent suffrage extension:

There is no more invariable rule in the history of society: the further electoral rights are extended, the greater is the need of extending them; for after each concession the strength of the democracy increases, and its demands increase with its strength. The ambition of those who are below the appointed rate is irritated in exact proportion to the great number of those who are above it. The exception at last becomes the rule, concession follows concession, and no stop can be made short of universal suffrage.[5]

Despite evidence of retrenchment and resistance in the history of voting rights in the United States, as well as other nations, de Tocqueville is not alone in his belief in the surety of universal suffrage. A number of scholars confronting the question of suffrage extension since de Tocqueville, however, have underscored the idea that political elites should not be willing to extend suffrage rights. Those with power should have an interest in maintaining it for the benefits that accrue to them; control of government institutions, of course, yields

---

[5] Vol. I, Ch. IV.

control over social and economic policy, as well as government coffers. Expanding access to the elective franchise to new groups would seem to threaten the benefits political elites reap by increasing the constituent demands that they must meet to maintain their control of the government. Indeed, elite interest in maintaining suffrage exclusion is emphasized by work in political economy that demonstrates a – perhaps unsurprising – pattern of increased public expenditures following suffrage extensions, generally attributed to greater demand for redistributive policies among the new electorate. As economists Humberto Llavador and Robert Oxoby have stated the question, "If greater democracy (extension of the franchise) implies a poorer median voter, and hence higher levels of redistribution, why would elites choose to extend voting rights?"[6]

Social scientists thus have searched for explanations of what might provoke elites to act against their seemingly simple self interest in maintaining the status quo in electoral qualifications. The answers they have provided can be grouped into two main veins: suffrage extension is seen either as a consequence of the politics of competing or divided elites, or as the acquiescence to pressure from the disenfranchised.

Accounts that center on elite division, quite simply, paint suffrage extension as a strategy by one set of elites to increase their leverage over another. A number of versions of this story have been offered. Economists have tended to focus on elite division over economic policies, and the idea that the franchise might be extended to create increased demand for some elites' preferences. Llavador and Oxoby, for example, point to asymmetrical economic sector benefits for government policies ranging from reduction in tariffs to increased spending on education and health care infrastructure, and see extension of the franchise as an attempt by particular elites to increase electoral support for the policies that produce increased returns in their own economic domains. Other economists have seen the ways in which certain elites might benefit from greater provision of public goods or a stronger national government as incentives for some to look to the disenfranchised for new electoral support. Political scientists have used the same divided elite logic, but indicted partisan politics more broadly, arguing that competition between political parties can push political elites to look for new bases of support among the disenfranchised. In the words of V. O. Key, the logic is that "if competition for power prevails,

---

[6] Llavador, Humberto and Robert Oxoby, "Partisan Competition, Growth, and the Franchise." *The Quarterly Journal of Economics*, 120 (2005): 1158. On the trend of increased public spending following enfranchisement see, for example, Cnudde, Charles F. and Donald J. McCrone, "Party Competition and Welfare Policies in the American States." *The American Political Science Review* 63 (1969): 858–66; Fry, Brian R. and Richard F. Winters, "The Politics of Redistribution." *The American Political Science Review* 64 (1970): 508–22; Abrams, Burton A. and Russell F. Settle, "Women's Suffrage and the Growth of the Welfare State." *Public Choice* 100(1999): 289–300; "Why Did the Elites Extend the Suffrage? Democracy and the Scope of Government with an Application to Britain's Age of Reform." *Quarterly Journal of Economics*, 119 (2004): 707–65.

invariably some of those within the privileged circle will hope for allies by the admission of their friends from without."[7]

Building partisan politics into theories of suffrage extension is certainly an important move toward placing elite decisions within the institutional arrangements that shape their incentives and capacity for effecting the policy changes they might desire. Although political parties are not political institutions established through either constitutional or statutory law in the United States, they are fundamental organizations in the American political process. Parties structure the electoral choices of citizens, mobilize citizens for participation, and generally facilitate the process of distilling public policy from the preferences of the electorate.[8] What parties do, and how they do it, follows from the political party's main objective: an organized endeavor to control the government through running candidates for elective office.[9] Thus, the most basic interest of the political party is to establish and maintain a winning coalition, one that puts their candidates in the offices of government. The composition of the electorate, and the needs and preferences found therein, must therefore figure centrally into the strategy of the political party – meaning that an account of suffrage extension needs to contend with partisan interests.

Political parties, however, are not the only political institutions that wield significant influence over elite action in the process of enfranchisement. Changes in suffrage qualifications are changes in law – meaning, quite obviously, that they must pass through legislative institutions. Yet, the legislative process is absent from existing accounts of suffrage extension offered across the social sciences. This omission has masked important pieces of the politics of voting rights, notably the significant constraints legislative institutions place on elites' ability to enact their desired suffrage policy. It has also limited our understanding of how demand from the disenfranchised influences elites' preferences and decisions, a point to which I return momentarily.

---

[7] Key, V. O., *Politics, Parties, and Pressure Groups* (New York: Thomas Y. Crowell Company, 1958), 671. On elite competition and suffrage extension see also Collier, Ruth Berins, *Paths Toward Democracy: The Working Class and Elites in Western Europe and South America* (Cambridge: Cambridge University Press, 1999); Lizzeri, Alessandro and Nicola Persico, "Why Did the Elites Extend the Suffrage? Democracy and the Scope of Government with an Application to Britain's Age of Reform." *Quarterly Journal of Economics* 119 (2004): 707–65; Llavador and Oxoby, "Partisan Competition"; Conley, John P. and Akram Temimi, "Endogenous Enfranchisement When Groups' Preferences Conflict." *The Journal of Political Economy* 109 (2001): 79–102; Rokkan, Stein, *Citizen, Elections and Parties: Approaches to the Comparative Study of the Processes of Development* (New York: David McKay Company, Inc., 1970); and Schattschneider, E. E., *Party Government* (New York: Farrar and Rinehart, Inc., 1942).

[8] Rosenstone, Steven J. and John Mark Hansen, *Mobilization, Participation, and Democracy in America* (New York: Macmillan Publishing Company, 1993); Key, V. O., *Politics, Parties, and Pressure Groups* (New York: Thomas Y. Crowell Company, 1958).

[9] Ranney, Austin and Willmore Kendall, *Democracy and the American Party System* (New York: Harcourt, Brace & World, Inc 1956), 126; Schattschneider, *Party Government*, ix.

A number of scholars have argued that suffrage extension is, at least at times, less an elite-initiated political strategy, and more an elite response to demand "from below." Much of this work focuses quite specifically on enfranchisement as acquiescence to the use or threat of violent coercion on the part of the disenfranchised. Daron Acemoglu and James Robinson, for instance, have argued that expansion of the franchise across many Western nations in the nineteenth century should be understood as attempts by elites to avoid escalation of civil unrest into outright revolution. Ruth Berins Collier, who treats expansion of the franchise within an investigation of patterns of democratization, argues that elites are often motivated to expand the democratic circle when faced with "the emergence of dissident allies within the army, coup rumors or attempts, and successful coups and citizen rebellions." Effective demand in these accounts, then, comes in the form of insurgency, a common function of social movements. And insurgency is deemed effective because it imposes certain costs on political elites for continuing to exclude particular disenfranchised groups: resources must be marshaled to deal with insurgents, and the attention of politics diverted from other policy matters. Voting rights are extended to invest insurgents in the existing government, to thereby quell costly rebellious behavior and perhaps avoid a greater loss of power through revolution.[10]

Scholars of social movements, however, might caution that successful movements for voting rights are not necessarily violent, nor particularly rebellious. Certainly the American experience of franchise expansion has not been regularly marked by violent insurgence, nor the threat thereof. Social movement-centered treatments of the extension of voting rights, therefore, point to such insurgency as only one of a number of versions of demand that might leverage success. These accounts of voting rights movement success borrow from frameworks originally developed to explain the rise of social movement activity, notably the ideas of resource mobilization and political opportunities. Resource mobilization accounts focus on the organizational capacity and tactical effectiveness of the group demanding new voting rights as explanations for successfully leveraging acquiescence from the state. Political opportunity explanations for successful demands for suffrage extension, in contrast, point to changes in the political environment (such as the constellation of elite alignments and the openness of political institutions) that facilitate the effectiveness of demand. Indeed, several scholars have used these concepts of resource mobilization and political opportunity structures – at times in tandem – to think about conditions that might generally make the adoption of woman suffrage more likely. Lee Anne Banaszak argues, for example, that in both the United States and Switzerland, woman suffragists' chances for success were shaped by the resources they could mobilize, their abilities to perfect political lobbying tactics,

---

[10] Acemoglu, Daron and James Robinson, " Why Did the West Extend the Franchise? Democracy, Inequality, and Growth in Historical Perspective ." Quarterly Journal of Economics (November 2000): 1167–99; Collier, *Paths toward Democracy*.

and the coalitions of political actors drawn into the cause. Holly McCammon and her coauthors, in contrast, argue that success for American suffragists was facilitated by instability or conflict in partisan politics, which made the political system more vulnerable to their demands, as well as the changing economic and political standing of women, which made the idea of women voters less controversial.[11]

Whereas social movement-centered accounts of voting rights extension have thus raised the idea of interplay between activists demanding inclusion and the political actors that must act to supply changes in suffrage laws, just as in the elite-centered accounts of suffrage extension, the incentives for those supply-side actors are not fully developed. The result is that these existing accounts still do not explain *how* activism influences voting rights policy outcomes. Importantly, there are no clear theoretical expectations about which activist tactics or resources should be most influential on those in the institutional positions to change voter qualifications, nor which changes in the political context should offer real political opportunities. This problem is not unfamiliar in the social movement literature, where, in the words of William Gamson and David Meyer, the term political opportunity "threatens to become an all-encompassing fudge factor for all conditions and circumstances that form the context for collective action."[12] By beginning with partisan politicians' motivations to expand the electorate and adding in the institutional constraints on their actions, I specify what should constitute a political opportunity for voting rights movements, and also what demand resources and tactics can be used effectively to take advantage of those opportunities. Starting with supply-side incentives, in other words, actually offers new leverage on the question of how both the supply and demand sides of the enfranchisement equation shape the development of voting rights.

The Supply-Side Politics of Extending the Franchise – Incentives and Constraints

Again, to develop a coherent model of suffrage extension, I allow supply and demand actors to interact, but begin by specifying the incentives and constraints of the supply side. Simply put, I consider the cost and benefit calculations of the political elites involved in supplying new voting rights provisions, including the limits placed on those elites' actions on the issue of suffrage by the arrangement of political institutions. Unlike previous elite-centered accounts, I specify two

[11] Banaszak, Lee Ann, *Why Movements succeed or Fail: Opportunity, Culture, and the Struggle for Woman Suffrage* (Princeton: Princeton University Press, 1996); McCammon, Holly J., Karen E. Campbell, Ellen M. Granberg, and Christine Mowery, "How Movements Win: Gendered Opportunity Structures and U.S. Women's Suffrage Movements, 1866 to 1919." *American Sociological Review* 66 (February 2001): 49–70.

[12] Gamson, William A. and David S. Meyer, "Framing Political Opportunity" in *Comparative Perspectives on Social Movements*, ed. Doug McAdam, John D. McCarthy, and Mayer N. Zald (New York: Cambridge University Press, 1996), 275.

sets of interrelated actors as the relevant elites in the enfranchisement equation –
both political parties and legislators. I offer here first an outline of the incentives
and constraints of these elites. In the next section, I detail the two models of
suffrage extension these considerations imply, and then turn in the following
section to more detail about how those interests play out in suffrage politics,
where they interact with demand-side actors.

By invoking political parties as supply-side elites, I am referencing what are
termed in the American context *major parties*. Rosenstone, Behr, and Lazarus
offer a clear definition of a major party as a political organization which "runs
candidates for local, state, and federal offices in a majority of the states" and
which "prior to the contest . . . holds one of the two largest blocs of seats in the
House of Representatives."[13] The major-party status, therefore, is conferred
only on those political parties that can maintain electoral success for more than
one election and who do so at all levels of American government. All other
organizations offering candidates in American elections are bearers of the title
third or *minor* party.[14] I ultimately offer an argument about the important
and unique role that third parties can play in leveraging the major parties
to deliver new voting rights provisions. The major parties, however, *must* be
central actors in the political story of suffrage rights extensions because of both
their vested stake in the composition of the electorate and their unique degree
of influence over the institutional hurdles that suffrage changes must cross –
legislatures and, often, elections.

The parties' central purpose of influencing the outcomes delivered by the
electorate necessarily implies a partisan interest in the constellation of that electorate. Because the distribution of preferences in the electorate is, of course,
key to the process of assembling a winning coalition, considering the possibility that parties may see groups of potential new voters as likely benefits
or likely costs to their electoral endeavors is important. Yet parties are also
beholden to existing voters' preferences – although certainly, and importantly,
under some conditions more than others – and thus it is also important to
note that party organizations may also make calculations about extending the
franchise that derive from the demands of their current electorates. This consideration of pressure from existing voters has been scarce in existing work
on suffrage extension, despite being easily recognized as generally important
to party position-taking, the policy process, and legislative outcomes. And it

[13] Rosenstone, Steven J., Roy L. Behr, and Edward H. Lazarus, *Third Parties in America: Citizen
Response to Major Party Failure* (Princeton: Princeton University Press, 1996), 9.
[14] Note that this definition deviates from those that would allow the titles of major and minor
parties to differ at various levels of government. For instance, Ranney and Kendall, *Democracy
and the American Party System*, 422–23, confer the title of "third party" on "any party which
seldom finishes better than third [in a two party system]." They regard parties' status in national,
state, and local party systems as separable, stating that although the Democrats and Republicans
have clearly been the major parties in the national party system since 1868, in some state and
local party systems Democrats have been relegated to third party status by Socialists and
Progressives.

is my argument that suffrage extension in acquiescence to existing voters is a far more likely model of enfranchisement than the broadening of the electorate simply for the sake of the new voters' future electoral support.

Pushing for new voters either for their own sake or in acquiescence to existing voters, I argue, is a strategy that parties pursue only under some duress. That is, I agree with Key's assertion that partisan competition should be the common driving force behind suffrage extension, although it is not a sufficient condition. Competitiveness signals vulnerability for the party in power; only in response to the threat of losing an election does a party need to change its strategy.[15] Close margins of victory in the last election signal little certainty about winning in the next round. In such circumstances, a new bloc of support from a previously disfranchised group could resolve a party's electoral difficulties. At these moments, also, demands from current voters threaten to be particularly costly to ignore. But competition is particularly important as a necessary incentive for the provision of new voting rights because parties *always* face additional costs with the addition of new voters. A larger electorate means more work to congeal and mobilize winning coalitions – whether that cost is the additional payoffs to partisan supporters in the time of political machines or more dollars for media buys and advertising in modern campaigns. This inherent disincentive for extending the franchise helps explain why parties do not pursue suffrage extensions often. It also implies that the potential voter-preference-based payoffs need to be perceptible; the certain costs of suffrage extension must be outweighed by a real possibility of benefits.

The political tools wielded by parties give them ample opportunity to influence the outcome of any consideration of new voting rights in the direction they desire. Partisan leadership and organizational structures in legislatures can impede or facilitate the flow of suffrage-extending legislation. Previous research suggests that on issues that carry partisan implications – as I have argued suffrage extension inherently does – parties play a unique role in structuring legislative outcomes. In particular, several studies have shown an increased influence of party discipline on voting – an induced similarity in voting behavior by members of the same party, above and beyond the preference similarities shared by members of the same party – the more the party as an organization has at stake.[16] Of course, parties also have the means to influence the electoral

---

[15] This argument is similar to one on party position taking made by Edward Carmines and James Stimson in *Issue Evolution: Race and the Transformation of American Politics* (Princeton, NJ: Princeton University Press, 1989). See also Wolbrecht, Christina, *The Politics of Women's Rights: Parties, Positions, and Change* (Princeton, NJ: Princeton University Press, 2000).

[16] Ansolabehere, Stephen, James M. Snyder, Jr., and Charles Stewart III "The Effects of Party and Preferences on Congressional Roll-Call Voting." *Legislative Studies Quarterly* 26 (November 2001), 533–72. Aldrich, John H. and James S. Coleman Battista, "Conditional Party Government in the States." *American Journal of Political Science* 46(2002): 164–72. Bianco, William and Itai Sened, "Uncovering Evidence of Conditional Party Government: Reassessing Majority Party Influence in Congress and State Legislatures." *The American Political Science Review* 99 (2005): 361–71.

process. Their specific tools of influence have certainly changed over time – in the time of woman suffrage politics, for example, the major political parties directly controlled decisions such as ballot wording and distribution and the location of polling places. Although some of their previous specific powers have been transferred to the state, to this day no other political organizations stand ready to mobilize electorates in favor or against a cause as readily as parties. This electoral influence is of particular importance because voting rights changes at the state level so often require a constitutional amendment that must be ratified by the existing electorate. The costs of educating and mobilizing the public to actually vote in support of the proposed change are formidable, and difficult for the disfranchised to bear. In contrast, the party apparatus, designed to influence elections, could be a most effective ally or formidable obstacle in achieving the necessary public vote.

No matter the influence of parties, however, it is still through legislatures that suffrage provisions must generally pass. What is most important to note about the legislative process, itself, is how difficult it makes the provision of new voting rights. In other words, placing suffrage politics inside legislative institutions imposes some important constraints. In the United States, at both the state and federal levels, legislative institutions in general make status quo protection easier than change, but particularly so in the case of voting rights. Because voter qualifications are generally defined by states' constitutions, changes most often require the clearing of extra policy-making hurdles, including legislative super-majorities, passage in multiple consecutive legislative sessions, and final approval through public referenda. Thus, the process involves many opportunities to stall a new voting rights proposal, institutional rules that empower opponents to be effective veto players, even if they are in the minority, and significantly higher costs for lawmakers in terms of the time and effort that must be spent to push the issue to fruition than the average piece of legislation.

In order to even reach a vote in the legislature, of course, a change in voting rights must have had initial endorsement from a legislator who found it worth introducing and must be delivered to the floor by its assigned committee. Bill introduction is rather simple. Any member of the legislature may introduce a bill, and doing so can be an entirely symbolic gesture. Overcoming the introduction hurdle, therefore, may not be a particularly difficult task for advocates of new voting rights. Committee work, however, is more complicated, and it offers the first significant legislative hurdle. Lawmakers facing heavy legislative workloads turn to the committee system to deal with the formidable task of evaluating every proposal brought to the body. The committee may choose not to report a legislative proposal to the rest of the legislature for consideration, to report a version it knows will be difficult to pass, or to report a version designed to have a good chance at success on the floor of the legislature. Not only can committees thus block or diminish the chances of the passage of legislation, but they can provide ample opportunity for defeat even by an opponent who is in the minority.

The challenge of the committee stage of the legislative process begins with initial bill referral. Whether the assignment of committee membership is purely at the will of the partisan legislative leadership or tempered by norms such as seniority, committee assignments are not random; and, thus, committees can be quite different from the body in important ways. This means, of course, that there is the possibility that legislation for voting rights changes could be stymied by an unfriendly committee, even if it might pass on the chamber's floor. Moreover, when partisan legislative leadership is charged with bill referral, it can exercise that choice in a way intended to shape the legislation's fate.

What happens inside the committee, however, is not simply a function of the positions each member holds on the issue. As Richard Hall has detailed, those with particularly keen interests in the outcome for a proposed piece of legislation, whether they desire any form of the proposed new policy or not, have at this stage in the legislative process ample opportunity to exert influence on both whether a measure will be reported and in what form. The key is the deliberative work in committee that shapes what appears to the body of legislature for approval, the work that can facilitate or forestall the deliverance of an agreeable proposal. Hall and others have argued that how strongly legislators feel about the issue – the intensity of their preferences for or against the proposed policy – shapes their willingness to expend their time and effort on drafting and promoting proposed legislation. Thus, even if nominally agreeable to most members of the legislature, proposals without interested advocates in committee are likely to slip off the agenda. Or proposals that draw little attention from most members can be shaped for failure or success by just the interested few. In sum, even if some version of a voting rights extension indeed exists that would pass the floor, if those with intense preferences are against it and on the appropriate committee, or if no member of the committee has an intense interest in the policy one way or the other, the agreeable version of the enabling bill may never materialize.[17]

Once past the committee stage, legislation faces the further hurdle of actually gaining consideration on the floor. Legislative processes require multiple readings of bills before a vote on the floor of the chamber can occur, and the scheduling of all of this floor activity is typically controlled by the chamber's partisan leadership. These details leave ample room for defeat either by simple neglect – when no member advocates for the legislation to appear on the calendar – or through purposive delay by the party leadership in scheduling. From committee to calendar, then, legislation needs advocates to move forward and is vulnerable to the exercise of partisan control. With political parties inherently

---

[17] Hall, Richard L., *Participation in Congress* (New Haven: Yale University Press, 1996). On committees see also Shepsle, Kenneth A., *The Giant Jigsaw Puzzle: Democratic Committee Assignments in the Modern House* (Chicago: University of Chicago Press, 1978); Hall, Richard L. and Bernard Grofman, "The Committee Assignment Process and the Conditional Nature of Committee Bias." *The American Political Science Review* 84 (1990): 1149–66.

interested in the definition of the electorate, the most promising trip through the legislative process before the vote would seem to be when the party in control of the legislature sees partisan benefit in the proposed change in electoral qualifications.

If finally brought to a vote in the legislature, a change in voter qualifications obviously must satisfy the constitutionally required number of legislators. In many instances of voting rights changes, that number is a two-thirds supermajority of each chamber; many alterations to suffrage qualifications can only be made through amendment to the state constitution, and many amendment processes place the threshold of support higher than for statutory changes. One set of models of the legislative decision making (and perhaps common understanding) would propose that the outcome should at this point be a rather straightforward aggregation of legislators' individual preferences on the issue, with the voting rights change being adopted as long as it satisfies the preferences of the requisite majority. Some nuance, however, is necessary in understanding the origins of legislators' preferred positions and the role such preferences may play in the determining legislative votes on the voting rights issue.

As elected partisan politicians, legislators' voting behavior needs to satisfy their constituencies – either because they desire reelection or at least because their party seeks to retain that seat in the government. The resultant connection between the policy positions of legislators and their constituencies' has been explained by John Kingdon with the concept of the "explainable vote." In Kingdon's telling, legislators take account of salient issue preferences in their districts, weighing the likelihood that they can justify their votes to those who care enough to notice (or have group-elites to notice for them) their behavior on each specific issue. Legislators' positions, then, are a balancing of the opinions or preferences of salient members of their constituencies and their own preferences; the election process induces a fair level of agreement between the two, calculations about the ability to explain the vote to those who care accounts for the choice when preferences diverge. And studies of interest group influence would suggest that it is interest groups that effectively communicate the salience of constituents' preferences to lawmakers; "lobbying friends," or appealing to legislators who can be convinced that the interest group's goal is consistent with representation of their constituencies' preferences, is common practice.[18] The implication for voting rights politics of this model is simple – as long as legislators sense little interest in the issue among their voting constituents in extension of the franchise, they should be free to rely on their own preferences on the issue – either personal or partisan. The inherent interest of parties in voting rights legislation and their likely influence on members has already been stated. Personal preferences on voting rights could be driven by

---

[18] Kingdon, John, *Agendas, Alternatives, and Public Policies* (Second ed. NY: Addison-Wesley, 2003). Hansen, John Mark, *Gaining Access: Congress and the Farm Lobby, 1919–1981* (Chicago: The University of Chicago Press, 1991). Kollman, Ken, *Outside Lobbying: Public Opinion and Interest Group Strategies* (Princeton, NJ: Princeton University Press, 1998).

any number of attitudinal factors, although likely culprits would seem to be their attitudes about the group seeking voting rights or their general disposition on the idea of republican government.

There are other implications of the legislative process for voting rights policy changes. Not only is change difficult, the appearance of supporting change can be rather easy. The legislative process can enable legislators to undertake actions that seem to signal support for a change in suffrage policy, such as sponsoring a bill, voting it out of committee, and even voting in favor of the bill on the chamber's floor, yet remain confident that the new suffrage provisions will not actually become law. Moreover, because the inherent electoral costs of implementing a new suffrage policy are necessarily broadly shared, suffrage changes need true widespread support – new voting rights are not an issue that a small but committed minority can pass without arousing the interest of others. And, of course, at the end of the day, the path of electoral accountability from the policy beneficiary – would-be voters – to deciding legislators is indirect at best. Would-be voters need a way to create electoral consequence for their inclusion or exclusion. In sum, changing voter qualifications is particularly costly legislative work, the support needed is broad, and the most direct tool of influence on the outcome is missing.

Finally, there is often the additional layer of constraint on voting rights policy of the need to pass the policy change at the polls through a referendum that endorses a suffrage extension approved by legislators. Although it is not uncommon to conceive of a public vote on a policy as an expression of the public's preferences, elite influences on electoral outcomes are difficult to understate – particularly when those elites are partisan actors who control the timing of the election, the wording of the policy choices that appear on the ballot, and the partisan apparatus regularly used to persuade and mobilize voters. Certainly, this does not mean that partisan elites can push policies through at the polls despite widespread and deep-seated opposition among voters. Thus, the referendum process is, in fact, a constraint on the elite politics of suffrage extension. Yet, when the parties have a vested interest in the outcome of a ballot measure, as they inherently do in voting rights measures, they have unmatched means of influencing the outcome. Therefore, what may be far more important to understand about the referendum requirement for voting rights changes is the constraint it enables partisan elites to exert on the supply of new suffrage provisions.

The constraints partisan elites could and, as I show in later chapters, have introduced to the referendum process on voting rights issues include a variety of important strategic choices about the appearance of the suffrage issue on the ballot. Those wanting the suffrage issue to fail, for example, could push for the placement of the issue in a low-turnout special election or in a fast-approaching election that would leave little time for mobilization work. They could choose to place it on the ballot next to another issue, such as a prohibition measure, they know to be especially likely to turnout voters with less sympathetic views on the suffrage measure. Partisan actors also control ballot language – whether directly in the days preceding the Australian ballot or through the legislative process in contemporary times – and thus could also ensure that the ballot wording was sufficiently confusing to cloud voters' comprehension of their choices. Thus, although pro-suffrage activists and other political actors face the same task in a referendum – getting enough voters on their side on Election Day, party leaders in particular have far more tools at hand to accomplish that task. Not only do partisan influences over the referendum process grant them unique leverage on the outcome of a public vote, but politicians can use the referendum process in particular as a way to vote in favor of new voting rights and yet remain confident that the electorate will remain constrained. The referendum process, in other words, is an excellent opportunity for partisan politicians to have their voting rights cake and eat it, too.

Models of Suffrage Extension – Strategic and Programmatic Enfranchisement

Summing up the incentives and constraints of supply-side actors, I argue, leads to two possible models of enfranchisement. Both models are differentiated from other models of policy outcomes by the particular features of voting rights politics: that the institutional path to change is particularly difficult, that the costs of implementing the new policy are necessarily broadly shared, and that the most direct tool of the policy beneficiaries' influence on the outcome is missing. Across both models, I delineate three necessary political conditions for suffrage extension: information, incentive, and capacity. What varies across the models are the specific ways in which the three conditions can be satisfied. The sharpest distinction across the models is in the information condition, in how the political meaning that incentivizes the supply-side actors to act – the information about potential payoffs – is established. Differences in the particular incentive structures of the two models, however, also lead to important differences in the activism strategies that are likely to increase suffrage proponents' chances of success. I lay out the general framework and basic implications of both models here and delve into more detailed implications of demand-side politics in the section that follows.

Strategic Enfranchisement
The first model, which I label *strategic enfranchisement*, is essentially the dominant framework of existing elite-centered accounts of suffrage expansion. This is where a single party acts to enfranchise a new group of voters expecting to reap electoral rewards from that group. Paying careful attention to the incentives and constraints of supply-side elites, I argue, implies three necessary political conditions for suffrage extension under this model: information, incentive, and capacity. What I point out about the strategic model is just how difficult it is to jointly satisfy these three conditions, and thus the questionable utility of the model as our dominant framework for understanding the

development of voting rights in the United States, where the suffrage has, in fact, been regularly extended.

The information condition of the strategic enfranchisement model is that a political party needs to have information that a group indeed exists that would, if enfranchised, actually deliver its votes reliably to that party. That is, given the assumption that a political party's primary objective is winning elections in the interest of controlling government, and given the costs of legislative and electoral time and effort involved in and resulting from expanding the electorate, strategic enfranchisement should only be undertaken when a party has reason to believe the inclusion of the new group would surely shift the balance of power further in its favor. This is what I term the *expectation of a voting bloc*. By voting bloc, I mean a well-defined political group that is understood to be fairly coherent in its political priorities and allegiances. There is, of course, inherent uncertainty involved in predicting the voting behavior of the disfranchised (I discuss how both identity politics and specific demand-side actions can help provide relevant signals in the next section). Potential blocs, however, are likely to share a common socioeconomic status, which signals shared interests in the resource allocations made by government, and to have an identifiable set of leaders that help interpret politics for the group, who are thus likely to be able to keep the group loyal to a particular political party. Irish Catholics in the United States in the nineteenth century might be a prime example of such a group; the new immigrants lacked voting rights, but were tied together and to recently naturalized Irish Catholics not only by socioeconomic status and cultural ties, but also institutionally through the Catholic Church.[19]

Even in the presence of a potential voting bloc, however, a party lacks incentive to seek new voters – to pay the costs of changing the law and then the costs of influencing the voting behavior of a larger electorate – in the absence of competition. The partisan environment must be sufficiently competitive such that the party has an electoral interest in working to create new voters, rather than simply attending to its current electorate. Electoral vulnerability may come in several forms, from narrow victories for many offices to the overturn of a key office, such as the chief executive. Dominant parties, those that have already established a strategy that keeps their members in control of the state apparatus, however, clearly lack incentive to pay the costs associated with broadening the electorate; the potential gain in support is not worth the risk to a winning status quo.

Most overlooked in existing accounts of elite incentives for suffrage extension, including other versions of the strategic enfranchisement model, is the issue of institutional capacity. Simply put, satisfaction of the first two

---

[19] Scholars have made similar arguments about African Americans. See, for example, Michael Dawson's argument about the reasons for expecting a large degree of African-American political unity even in the face of increasing socioeconomic diversity of the group in *Behind the Mule: Race and Class in African-American Politics* (Princeton, NJ: Princeton University Press, 1995).

conditions is irrelevant if the relevant party does not already hold sufficient legislative seats to pass the necessary legislation. If the change in suffrage laws is meant to increase the strength of one party over another, as is assumed in the strategic enfranchisement model, such action surely should not receive support from the partisan opposition. In the American context, again, this often means the party seeking suffrage extension must hold a supermajority of the seats in two separate legislative houses – perhaps, at the state level, across two successive sessions of the legislature – or be able to call and control a constitutional convention.

The enfranchisement of blacks by Northern Republicans in the wake of the Civil War would seem to provide a prime example of this strategic enfranchisement model. The Republicans were still a new party, having just swept into national ascendancy in the previous decade, and continued to face tough competition at the polls – in Northern and Southern states – in the wake of the war. Grant, war hero and Republican candidate for president in 1868, polled popular margins of victory of less than 3 percent in California, Connecticut, and Indiana, and lost the popular vote in New Jersey, New York, and Oregon. Despite the tough competition, Republicans held three-fourths of the seats in the House of Representatives and nearly four-fifths of the seats in the Senate. Republicans had already become associated with rights for blacks through the Civil Rights Act of 1866 and the Reconstruction Acts of 1867 and had won endorsement from black organizations and leaders. Thus, Republicans had electoral incentive to seek new voters, promise from an out-group of loyal support, and the institutional capacity through their representation in Congress to pass the necessary constitutional amendment.

As well as the story about strategic elites responding to partisan competition may work for the case of the Fifteenth Amendment, the chronicle of the Fifteenth Amendment reveals the fortune of political circumstances necessary for the joint fulfillment of all three conditions – incentive, information, and capacity. Such coincidence is a rare experience in the American context; legislative supermajorities for electorally threatened political parties are infrequent, and their overlap with strong information about the electoral reliability of a legally definable group is especially scarce. Consideration of the enfranchisement of freed blacks does suggest, however, that where enfranchisers can be removed, as the Northern Republicans were, from real accountability to the new group of voters, the possible rewards of the strategy may be particularly appealing despite the risk inherent because of uncertainty about the groups' future electoral behavior. Enfranchising blacks served Northern Republicans because it spelled defeat for Southern Democrats through the votes of numerous newly enfranchised Southern blacks; population numbers of blacks in the North were too few to concern Northern states' politics. Looking to the states, similar conditions might be created by the geographic partition of partisans into urban and rural constituencies. If a party with a rural base, for example, saw new bloc potential in an immigrant group concentrated within city boundaries, the strategic enfranchisement model might be more viable.

Programmatic Enfranchisement

Although voting rights extensions are infrequent, they have been a far more regular part of the American political experience than the strategic enfranchisement model would predict. To resolve this discrepancy, I offer an alternative model of the politics of suffrage extension, which I term *programmatic enfranchisement*. In this model, suffrage extension occurs not as a consequence of a search for new supporters from the ranks of the disfranchised, but in accommodation to the demands of existing voters. That is, suffrage extension occurs as part of a program of policies known to appeal to existing necessary electoral coalition members. This difference in the source of the electoral incentive driving the enfranchisement politics implies differences in the information, incentive, and capacity conditions for the model. Unlike the strategic model, the programmatic enfranchisement model can explain suffrage extension in the face of unclear or diffuse expectations of the voting behavior of the would-be new voters. The information that is required is a clear and credible signal about organized demand for suffrage extension among existing voters. Although partisan competition also plays a role in this model, the key incentive is in the form of electoral vulnerability that is specifically linked to those making the demand. In other words, the disfranchised need coalitions with groups that carry real weight in electoral politics, and politicians need to see in those coalitions a real possibility of an exit option for their failure to respond to the articulated demand. Finally, because incentive derives from accommodation of constituent preferences that may cross party lines, the capacity condition within the programmatic enfranchisement model does not require a single political party to hold the necessary majorities to change suffrage laws.

Given the inherent disincentive on the part of partisan politicians to expand the electorate, the information required within the programmatic enfranchisement model is more than information about the direction of constituent sentiment on the issue of new voting rights. Legislators, and ultimately the major political parties, must perceive a real threat of possible electoral defection among existing voters for failure to deliver new voting rights.[20] Fulfilling this information condition requires the disfranchised to establish coalitions with groups able to convey demand with electoral consequence – groups that partisan politicians perceive as able to funnel constituent opinion into voting action. Two kinds of political organizations have this distinct capacity: interest groups and third, or minor, political parties. Interest groups are organizations that seek to influence the policy-making process on a particular set of issues on behalf of some constituency, in part by actively lobbying legislators to communicate the electoral benefit of adopting the group's issue positions. In the American context, third, or minor, parties are essentially defined as those political parties that fail to achieve the level of electoral success that would grant them the

---

[20] This argument draws on the logic of Albert Hirschamn in *Exit, Voice, and Loyalty: Responses to Decline in Firms, Organizations, and State* (Cambridge, MA: Harvard University Press, 1970).

status of major parties. That is, they are organizations that run candidates for office, but whose candidates do not win over multiple elections and/or across both state and federal levels of government. The real political purpose of the third party in American politics, however, is often said to be the championing of an issue or set of issues ignored by the major parties. Thus, third parties are also organizations that seek to influence policy on a particular set of issues, but ones that use organized electoral defection rather than lobbying tactics as their primary means of influence.

Although both interest groups and third parties have the potential capacity to convey that their interest in new voting rights provisions is organized, realizing that potential turns, in part, on the credibility of the coalitional partnership. Politicians, that is, need to know that the exit option is not only possible, but also has some real probability of being exercised over the issue of suffrage. Token endorsements, in other words, should carry little weight with partisans whose primary incentives are to retain or expand their voting bases. It is important to note, however, that coalition credibility – unlike a strategic partisan interest in new voters – does *not* require the group to be enfranchised to seem likely to coalesce politically with those demanding their inclusion. Although credibility surely entails the perception of some benefit for the advocating interest group(s) or third party, a number of structural differences between the major political parties and interest groups and third parties imply that the latter may reap meaningful benefits from demands for the extension of voting rights that are less important to the major political parties.

With a focus on forwarding sets of policy provisions, rather than a primary focus on control of the government, interest groups have the incentive to take actions that bolster their ability to advocate for their cause in both the public sphere and legislative chambers – that is, to engage in both outside and inside lobbying. As John Mark Hansen has argued, interest groups derive their political strength from the judgments of lawmakers about their representation of constituents. Such judgments derive not simply from lawmakers' assessments of the official memberships of interest group organizations, but also from their evaluations of how broad the constituency is that has similar interests as the group and is attending to and swayed by the interpretations of politics and political choices (including electoral ones) that the group offers. In other words, the potential reach of the electoral leverage of interest groups through persuasion and mobilization may be perceived as extending well beyond their membership rolls. Farmers' organizations might be seen, for example, as conduits for the general interests of farmers, not just those enrolled in the organizations. It is this leverage that gives interest groups power to influence policymaking.[21] This

---

[21] Hansen, John Mark. *Gaining Access: Congress and the Farm Lobby, 1919–1981* (Chicago: The University of Chicago Press, 1991.) Note that I am not referencing lobby groups that focus on inside strategies only, relying primarily on the provision of monetary subsidies and narrow expertise to influence policy outcomes. Again, I am taking the issue of suffrage as one that cannot be accommodated by a purely inside politics strategy because of the broad costs

leverage, however, can be bolstered by a stronger public presence and increased organizational capacity.

The determinants of interest groups' leverage imply a number of incentives for groups to partner with the cause of expanded voting rights. First, there may be real value in activities that simply serve to sharpen attention to the particular policy domains they champion. Interest group support for suffrage extension, therefore, may rest credibly on a rhetorical refrain of common principles, such as on a common theme of government reform or fairness and equality, that helps to increase popular attention to and support for their main causes. Similarly, a confluence of interests with even just part of the disfranchised group could allow interest groups to use the issue of enfranchisement as one that might help advance their primary cause by building or maintaining their organizational capacity. That is, enfranchisement may be endorsed as a benefit for the specific set of disfranchised persons who offer some institutional support for the interest group's main cause, even if the new suffrage law would encompass others. Such a confluence may, in fact, derive from the origins of the interest group organization; interest groups are often simply the political arms of organizations built on a variety of common interests and may thus be populated from the start by both voters and the disfranchised. Organized labor, for example, developed first as a means to negotiate better working terms and conditions with firms and industry, but eventually became enmeshed in advocacy for pro-worker policies from government. As such, labor organizations have perennially counted disfranchised workers in their ranks, and there is non-electoral value in keeping them loyal to the organization. Of course, pushing for new suffrage provisions could serve not only as a strategy to retain disfranchised members, but also to swell the electoral strength of the group. Again, unlike the major parties whose primary leverage over policy is dependent on winning sufficient seats in government, interest groups serve their primary purpose of increased leverage for their cause simply by increasing the size of the electorate they are perceived to represent.

Although third parties, like major parties, are seekers of control over elected offices, significant differences in their capacities and the unique reason for their existence may engender markedly different interests in endorsing and advocating for new voting rights. In the American context, third parties that take more than trivial vote shares tend to emerge in response to extreme voter discontent. That is, the appearance of third parties is instigated by a fundamental failure of either major party to address the salient policy interests of some constituent group. Thus, in contrast to major parties whose interests lie in maintenance of the status quo political process, third parties are necessarily seekers of drastic change. To effect such change, however, emerging third parties must face the

to partisan politicians that come with an expanded electorate. For discussion of the range of interest group types and strategies, see, for example, Walker, Jack L., Jr., *Mobilizing Interest Groups in America: Patrons, Professions, and Social Movements* (Ann Arbor: University of Michigan Press, 1991).

reality of their resource deficits in comparison to their major party rivals. Less money, fewer qualified and experienced candidates, and inferior organizational capacity for mobilization are all common characteristics of third parties. It is exactly in the third party's origins and deficits that would-be voters can find their political opportunity. These coalitions that would be parties need things that a well-organized suffrage movement can offer: funds, political skills, and members to carry out campaign tasks. Thus, resource sharing may be the benefit key to engaging third party support of new voting rights. Because third parties often emerge from issue-based movements, it is also possible that support for suffrage extension could be a way for third parties to draw disfranchised members of the social movement from which the party emerged into the efforts to build an explicitly partisan organization. Moreover, the deep ideological convictions that lead some citizens and candidates into third party politics could make coalitions bound in part by principles of change, reform, and justice less politically dubious. Indeed, seekers of fundamental change may find that a new voting rights plank fits well as an addition to their new party's platform as it diversifies in attempts to gain and maintain political momentum.

Incentive within the programmatic enfranchisement model, as in the strategic enfranchisement model, derives from electoral vulnerability of the major parties. In the programmatic enfranchisement model, however, such vulnerability derives from the specific threat of electoral consequence for failure to respond to existing voters' demands for new voting rights policies. The threat of electoral consequence necessarily depends on the demanding groups' abilities to mobilize or stifle voters' support of particular candidates or political parties. Track records of mobilizing voters are certainly powerful signals about the groups' capacities. Also informative are the groups' current political resources – organizational membership numbers, financial coffers, and leadership capacity are all indicators to partisan politicians about the influence these groups may wield in future elections. Also important, however, is the degree to which candidates and parties are dependent on voters from those groups for their particular electoral fortunes. That is, political competition is also integral to encouraging the expansion of the electorate in the programmatic model, but that competition needs to be linked to the group of existing voters making the suffrage demand.

Again, the incentive for responsiveness to demand is the understanding that electoral fortunes are tied to responsiveness to the constituency demanding new voting rights – the importance of satisfying that constituency to electoral outcomes. The relative size of the constituent group, its previous partisan commitments, and the competitiveness of electoral politics all help shape this understanding. The size and partisan leanings of the constituent group help convey which politicians – individual lawmakers and political parties – are reliant on the group to construct a winning coalition. For example, legislators with significant numbers of union members in their home districts would generally stand more vulnerable to the demands of organized labor, as would a

political party that organized labor had actively supported. Electoral competitiveness, however, helps convey to those in office a particular need to expend
some effort to maintain their winning coalitions. Such competition may be
localized to only some lawmakers who represent uniquely contested districts.
Or it may be broader, as in moments generally marked by close elections. Localized competition in the face of an organized constituency demanding suffrage
extension serves to make individual lawmakers more responsive on the issue.
Moments of broader competitiveness, however, are times when partisan politicians need to be most responsive to the demands of the electorate, when the
loss of support of any members of partisan politicians' electoral coalitions can
readily turn over both individual legislative seats and partisan control of government. In these moments, when support of the groups demanding suffrage
extension is fundamental to a political party's success, the party organization
itself ought to become involved in pushing for, or at least enabling, enfranchisement, despite the costs for the inclusion of those new voters in future elections.
These, then, are the greatest political opportunities within the programmatic
enfranchisement model.

The electoral costs and payoffs, and thus the incentives for politicians to
respond, can be made especially clear in the attachment of constituent demand
for electoral expansion to third parties. What third parties uniquely offer is an
unmatched degree of certainty about their electoral influence reflected in the
vote shares they accumulate. The unique influence of third parties, however,
derives not simply from the number of voters they attract in any one election,
but also from the extremity of voter discontent reflected in the attraction of
any significant number of voters from the major parties to a new or minor
one. To (re)capture the votes given to third parties, the major parties must
address the discontent. Where third parties seize considerable portions of the
popular vote, would-be majority party coalitions must be rebuilt. Thus, the
common political outcome for successful third parties is to have their issue(s)
included, ultimately, in the design of one – or both – of the major parties, thus
doing away with their original purpose of existence. As political scientist Fred
Haynes, writing in 1916 in the wake of the Progressive Party's ascendancy into
American politics, aptly stated:

Looked at from the social point of view the chief function of third parties has been to
bring new issues before the people: they force new policies upon the older parties, and
after accomplishing their work they pass away.[22]

Third parties, if successful, change the political debate. And perhaps, by so
doing, they rearrange the coalitions that previously formed the basis of the

---

[22] Haynes, Fred E., *Third Party Movements since the Civil War* (Iowa City: The State Historical
Society of Iowa, 1916), 3.

two major parties.[23] Given these strong electoral incentives for major parties to respond, third parties can be tremendous allies for would-be voters.[24]

Lastly, the capacity condition for the programmatic enfranchisement model is importantly different from that of the strategic enfranchisement model. Given that incentive may derive from constituent demand that crosses party lines, the programmatic enfranchisement model does not require single party control of government. Instead, the issue of capacity is simply of there being a sufficient number of lawmakers electorally vulnerable to the demands of the pro-suffrage coalition. Of course, if the suffrage coalition is one that strongly favors a particular party, then only members of that party may, indeed, be vulnerable to the demand for new voting rights. This point is important, as it indicates that a single-party push for suffrage extension does not necessarily distinguish strategic from programmatic enfranchisement.

There is also a rather unique way in which the capacity condition may be fulfilled in the presence of a successful third party. Of course, although third party electoral success is not an American experience, third parties can face better odds at the state level and thus could also deliver suffrage rights as a fulfillment of their own platforms once in government. Yet, third parties need not actually take majority control of government to leverage suffrage extension. Even just a few third party legislators could exert significant pressure on state lawmaking bodies to pass voting rights measures when those bodies are otherwise evenly split between the major parties. That is, in legislative institutions set up with majority voting rules and partisan organizational and leadership structures, the third party politicians can become uniquely pivotal voters.[25] A chamber's business may be completely forestalled, for example,

---

[23] Burnham, W. Dean, *Critical Elections and the Mainsprings of American Politics* (New York: Norton, 1970); Rosenstone, Behr and Lazarus, *Third Parties in America*.

[24] Although scholars typically argue that major parties are induced to co-opt the issues of third parties to address the discontent of voters who have bolted, major parties do have another alternative, which is to adopt and promote an entirely separate issue that they believe will divide the issue base of the third party. One such issue may well be the expansion of the electorate to include new voters they believe can be herded into their electoral bases – a strategic enfranchisement response. It could also be the strategic *dis*enfranchisement of some element of the third party coalition. Scholars including J. Morgan Kousser, John Hope Franklin, and Doug McAdam have characterized the Southern Democratic response to the Populist movement in the South in this way. White supremacy was promoted to split the budding coalition of white and black farmers that threatened the Democratic planter class's control of the postwar South; in the name of white supremacy blacks were disenfranchised and white farmers herded back into the Democratic Party, without any significant acquiescence to their Populist demands. Kousser, J. Morgan, *The Shaping of Southern Politics: Suffrage Restriction and the Establishment of the One-Party South, 1880–1910* (New Haven, CT: Yale University Press, 1974). McAdam, Doug, *Political Process and the Development of Black Insurgency 1930–1970*(Chicago: The University of Chicago Press, 1982); Franklin, John Hope *From Slavery to Freedom: A History of Negro Americans* 5th ed.(New York: Knopf, 1980).

[25] That is, where the third party politicians are pivotal voters in the legislature. Both majority and supermajority pivots can wield significant influence, especially under some state legislative rules that required quite a lot of business to be carried out by two-thirds of the members.

if third party members refuse to agree to one of the major party's choices for state house speaker or, in the days before the Seventeenth Amendment to the U.S. Constitution, U.S. Senator. This ability to thwart the progress of policymaking of any sort can be a powerful tool for leveraging concessions from the major parties. Thus the capacity condition may actually be fulfilled through vulnerability of lawmakers to the leverage of third party members in government. I detail politics of exactly this sort on the issue of woman suffrage in Illinois in Chapter 4.

Seeing the Role of Demand Inside the Partisan Story – Identities and Activism

Although the central imperative for those demanding new voting rights is attaching a clear electoral consequence to politicians' actions on their enfranchisement, each of the two partisan paths to enfranchisement I have detailed implies a different key role for demand-side actors. The politics of strategic enfranchisement turn on expectations of solid electoral support from the new voters, meaning that demand activities that convey the political cohesion of the group should be most effective. Programmatic enfranchisement, in contrast, requires a coalitional strategy from demand-side actors, rather than one that maximizes the internal cohesion of the group. Demand-side implications of both models are elaborated in the following sections. Yet, before discussing the development of effective demand strategies for the disfranchised within each of these enfranchisement models, a crucial variable that shapes the possible path to enfranchisement for previously excluded groups, one over which they may not have tremendous control, must be introduced: political identity.

Political Identities as Information and Constraints

By political identity, I mean comprehensions of group differences and belonging that are brought to bear in politics. We commonly refer to race, class, and gender as markers of such identities. Political identities are defined by both in-group attitudes that ascribe importance of that identity to those who belong in the group category, and out-group attitudes that link traits and behaviors to the category. Nominal members of some group category may feel more or less of a sense of common interest with others in the same grouping; they may perceive that they share experiences that should commonly define their political behavior, or they may not. Likewise, a group may be defined by nonmembers with stereotypes that assign notions of common political behavior, or they may not. These identities, then, can play key roles in the politics of voting rights by shaping the incentives of both supply- and demand-side actors, shaping the possibilities for strategic or programmatic enfranchisement.

Introducing political identity into our explanations of voting rights politics illuminates an initial role of the demand side of the equation, one that, in part, precedes any political action. In the absence of revealed information about groups' behavior as voters, common understandings of these identity categorizations, I argue, shape partisans' expectations of likely voter behavior, thereby defining groups' potential for strategic enfranchisement. This important role of political identity is one that is driven by out-group attitudes – those in power are obviously of a group somehow distinct from the disfranchised – wherein stereotypes about the attitudes and behavior of disfranchised groups are infused with likely political consequence. Partisans, for example, may see political homogeneity in groups defined by their socioeconomic location, expecting the demands that the group will bring to electoral politics will be shaped by their common economic needs. Certainly, this is the implied assumption that a number of previous models of suffrage extension have made. Yet, the categorizations used to define new groups of voters do not necessarily map neatly onto a politically cohesive group identity. Removing sex, age, or citizenship criteria from voter qualifications, for example, are changes that would seem more likely to bring groups perceived as politically diverse into the electorate. The group "women," after all, would not only include people of different classes, but also of significantly differing levels of integration into the labor market. Only groups perceived as politically cohesive, through the lenses of those holding political power, should be targets for strategic enfranchisement.

Although notions of political identity can convey likely electoral cohesion, they also can provide strong predispositions against a disfranchised group's potential as a well-defined or politically promising "group" in electoral politics. That is, the repertoires of attitudes about and common understandings of some groups may contain information that works decidedly against the possibility of a group being considered for strategic enfranchisement. Notions of gender, for example, have historically included ideas about women's subservience to and dependence on men and their attachment to the home instead of the public sphere. As Aileen Kraditor has observed, these ideas about women were used in the time of the woman suffrage movement to undergird a gendered belief in women's representation via the "family vote" of her husband or father. Not only did such ideas form a strong argument against women's need for the franchise, as Kraditor and others have argued, but they also implied that there was no expectation of a women's voting bloc. These ideas actually suggested that women were politically heterogeneous – just as their husbands, fathers, and brothers were – and yet also unlikely to be mobilized reliably as voters. That is, they were expected to toe the party line dictated by the men in their households – but only in the unlikely event that they were permitted and motivated to engage in the masculine realm of electoral politics.[26]

Finally, as I discuss in more detail later in this chapter, political identities can constrain the politics of demand actors in important ways. In making this argument, it is important to note that "demand" is necessarily articulated within the public sphere by a subset of the disfranchised – and perhaps other

---

[26] Kraditor, Aileen S., *The Ideas of the Woman Suffrage Movement* (New York: W. W. Norton & Company, 1981).

strong sympathizers. This set of actors – those who are publicly engaged in forwarding suffrage as their primary political cause – are what I term suffrage *activists*. Activists are not necessarily a representative subset of the disfranchised group in question, and thus their own ideas about themselves and their fellow members of the disfranchised group can powerfully shape which strategies they choose to pursue and their effectiveness in executing those strategies. These politics of identity can cut both ways for activists. Cross-cutting political identities within the disfranchised group may cause activists to miss opportunities to mobilize members of the disfranchised group that are unlike themselves. Political identities may also hinder activists' ability to see or capitalize on possible coalitional partnerships; to see and advocate for the political common ground they may have with other groups that could wield electoral leverage on their behalf. Strong sentiments of shared identity and linked fortunes, however, can be particularly effective tools for mobilization and can encourage and facilitate coalitional partnerships.

Strategic Enfranchisement – Signaling Voting Bloc Potential

Given that extension of the franchise in the strategic enfranchisement model depends on perceptions of a likely voting bloc from the ranks of the previously disfranchised, conveying political cohesion of the disfranchised group through activism is key for those seeking new voting rights. Political mobilization, of course, may serve to alter perceptions of disfranchised groups as politically cohesive. In particular, extensive mass mobilization can be a powerful signal that conveys not only episodic unity of the group but also reveals the mechanisms for perpetuating and channeling the group's political engagement. Successful mass mobilizations, of course, demonstrate that members of the group are motivated to participate and make political demands on account of their identification with that group, perhaps despite interests deriving from some other group membership. They also offer opportunities to observe relevant political capacities of the group's internal structure – its institutions of interconnection, such as churches or civic associations – and its leadership. Because a promising voting bloc is one that will reliably turn out in favor of the party, the group's own key mobilization resources are of central interest to potential enfranchisers.

Cohesion, however, is not sufficient information for the disfranchised group to be attractive candidates for strategic enfranchisement. Partisans, again, are looking for signals that the group will not only cohere, but also reliably deliver their votes to a particular party. Political identity may certainly do some of this work for the disfranchised; party politicians' predispositions, or existing attitudes, about the group may make a partisan advantage seem readily apparent. Such was the case, it seems, with black Americans in the wake of the Civil War. Notions of race combined with the association of Republicans with the emancipation of slaves conjured powerful sentiments about blacks' likely partisan loyalties. If notions of political identity, however, do not suggest a clear partisan advantage, activism will also need to be overtly partisan to encourage strategic enfranchisement.

Programmatic Enfranchisement – Recognizing, Attracting, Maintaining, and Leveraging Coalitional Partnerships

Shared primary political identities are not required for groups to attain voting rights under the programmatic enfranchisement model, which requires instead of those seeking voting rights an effective strategy to establish coalitions with groups able and willing to exercise electoral influence on their behalf. As discussed in the previous section, the effectiveness of such coalitions depends in part on their credibility, which in turn involves some benefit for the coalitional partners. One of the chief mechanisms for disfranchised demand actors to increase their potential for success under the programmatic enfranchisement model is therefore the amassing and mobilization of resources to make themselves attractive coalition partners. Smaller but well-resourced and organized movements, therefore, can actually be highly effective. Sufficiently large coffers and politically skilled memberships may be ample incentive for partnering interest groups. Activism on the part of the disfranchised, then, need not be mass grassroots mobilization, nor include sufficient representation of the group to be enfranchised to demonstrate any sort of promised political cohesion. What is required of those demanding voting rights in this model is a willingness to expend their resources for causes other than their own enfranchisement.

As discussed previously, not all coalitions are equal under the programmatic enfranchisement model; some partnerships offer more electoral influence than others. Thus, activists demanding new voting rights must learn not only to forge coalitions, but to foster coalitional relationships that engender political clout. This can be a daunting task for the electorally excluded, and may also be conditioned by identity politics. Activists' own perceptions of group differences may preclude some potentially beneficial partnerships, even when some objective interests are shared. Moreover, how activists choose to organize themselves can shape their coalitional strategy possibilities. On one hand, a narrower base for the active movement membership – the more it is drawn from a limited set of social networks within the disfranchised group – is likely to engender fewer possible overlapping interests. Yet, such a narrow base may also make for stronger coalitional politics if the appropriate partner can be found, as the willingness to resource exchange and the external credibility of the coalition should be strengthened by a greater degree of interest similarities among activists.

Lingering Alternative Accounts

I have outlined two models of voting rights extension, drawing together theories of the incentives of political elites and of the effects of social movement activism. Still, I have not touched on some ideas about why voting rights are expanded. Notably, I have endeavored to offer a theoretical framework for understanding expanding definitions of the electorate absent the threat of violent rebellion, for elaboration of the democratic project within the confines of existing political institutions. As mentioned earlier, so much of the American experience calls for a model that does not invoke the threat of insurrection as the main incentive for a broadening electorate. Explanation of the role of insurgency that threatens existing political institutions, therefore, has intentionally been left to others.

Also largely absent from this discussion of both the strategic and programmatic paths to enfranchisement has been the demand tactic of direct appeal to legislators' personal preferences for a policy. Certainly, we would expect that some legislators would have their own salient preferences about the inclusion of a new group into the electorate. In particular, strong egalitarian or liberal convictions, we might presume, would make the issue of salient personal interest, as might strong personal sentiments against the group in question, such as racist or sexist beliefs. Personal connections to the causes of the disfranchised may even include kinship ties to active members of the group, as was the case with a number of politicians and woman suffragists. Appealing to both these personal beliefs and associations surely could win the support of a legislator, even without the support of his voting constituency, if the legislator felt he could offer a workable "explanation." This approach may indeed be part of getting the issue on the agenda, perhaps attracting bill sponsors, for instance. Yet, for establishing winning coalitions in favor of new voters, this approach is far less than expedient.

The greatest complication of the direct, personal appeal for the enfranchisement of new voters derives from the fact that the policy in question by definition carries consequences for parties and legislators, and its corollary that voting rights changes cannot be forwarded by a small, intense minority without arousing the interests of others. The resultant complication is that a successful direct appeal strategy would have to indoctrinate, one by one, a majority (likely supermajority) of legislators with a personal preference for new voting rights, and would have to engage any salient personal preferences against voting rights to stave off opposition. Winning wars based on principles, when those principles have political costs and consequences, is tough work. Additionally, building a winning coalition based on personal preferences is extremely sensitive to legislative turnover; if convinced members leave office, there is no mechanism to increase the chance that their replacements will be friendly to the cause as well. In contrast, garnering support within key constituencies provides incentives for politicians to act independent of their personal preferences, meaning that activists' work is not necessarily undone by a change in the legislature's membership. This distinction is particularly crucial for state-level voting rights struggles given that state legislatures are typically populated by members who serve only a term or two.[27] Hence, direct appeal to legislators'

---

[27] Burns, Nancy, Laura Evans, Gerald Gamm, and Corrine McConnaughy. "Pockets of Expertise: Careers and Professionalism in 20th-Century State Legislatures." *Studies in American Political Development* 22 (September 2008): 229–48.

personal preference may work as *part* of either the strategic or program-matic enfranchisement process, but partisan electoral incentives offer far more promise.

Finally, I have also laid aside accounts of voting rights extension that imply, in one way or another, that voting rights are extended simply because they are an idea whose time has come. This would include accounts that paint changing attitudes about the disfranchised as the primary impetus for changes in suffrage qualifications, as well as those that ascribe legal changes in voting qualifications to moments of heightened attention to democratic governance – the most cited of the latter being times of war. I have done so not because ideas play no role in voting rights politics, but because, given the incentives of political elites, attitude changes are insufficient as an explanation unto themselves. As I have outlined, and illustrate in later chapters, attitudinal shifts may help form new ideas about what groups could be promising targets of strategic enfranchisement, or to influence the coalitional possibilities available to the disfranchised, thus affecting their chances for inclusion under the programmatic enfranchisement model. Without partisan political incentives attached to them, however, ideas lack the leverage to change policy.

Assessing the Theory – The Case of Woman Suffrage

To evaluate the theoretical framework for understanding the development of voting rights offered earlier, I turn to the struggle for adoption of woman suffrage in the American states. Although Amendment XIX of the U.S. Con-stitution, barring discrimination in state voter qualifications based on sex, was not ratified until 1920, woman suffrage measures were considered and adopted by states as early as 1838. Some of these measures provided for purely local electoral rights, enabling women to vote on local tax issues, school matters, and/or for municipal officers. Other measures provided women with limited suffrage rights in statewide elections, such as allowing them only presidential suffrage. And some states endowed women with truly full voting rights – as early as 1890. There were thirty years between the earliest and latest adoptions of state-level woman suffrage, and nearly eighty years between the earliest and latest adoptions of local-level woman suffrage (see Figure 1.1). This variation, itself, begs explanation, which the literature on the woman suffrage movement has yet to fully provide. Moreover, it is through investigation of this variance that we can empirically demonstrate the institutional and sociopolitical fac-tors that make attainment of the right of electoral participation more or less possible for previously excluded groups.

Some might argue that the politics of women's voting rights were unique and therefore not instructive as we seek to understand the expansion of the franchise generally. Yet there are a number of reasons why the case is partic-ularly informative. To begin, because the American story of woman suffrage unfolded across a span of nearly eighty years, it overlapped with a number of

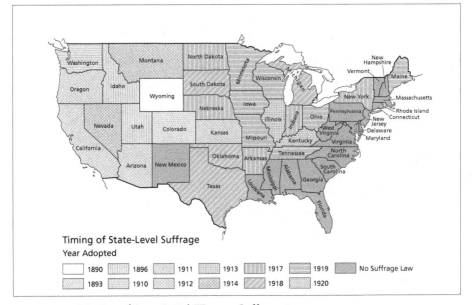

FIGURE I.I. Timing of State-Level Woman Suffrage.

other developments in voting rights. This fact enables direct and contemporaneous comparison of woman suffrage politics to consideration of the enfranchisement of other groups, notably black men, illuminating how differences in the groups being considered for enfranchisement engendered distinct reactions from partisan politicians. Moreover, although many treatments of voting rights politics in the United States have focused on the rights of African Americans, it would seem that politicians often lack the level of clarity about partisan expectations of new voters that characterized that case. Consider, for example, the layers of uncertainty involved in the question of enfranchising non-citizens. There are the questions of which immigrant groups are likely to support which party and which groups are likely to turnout to vote, and the issue is further complicated by ambiguity about what incoming immigrant streams will look like in both the short and long term. Turning to woman suffrage sheds light on this sort of politics of voting rights, where the promise of a new voting bloc does not seem likely to be the incentive for partisan politicians. In addition, following both failed and successful endeavors to enfranchise women across a variety of political contexts does unearth attempts at a strategic enfranchisement approach. The circumstances surrounding and results of these attempts further underscore the host of difficulties in satisfying the conditions of the strategic enfranchisement account, undermining its feasibility as the dominant model of voting rights politics.

2

Political Meaning for Woman Suffrage

> At every political convention all matters of right, of justice, of the eternal verities themselves, are swallowed up in the one all-important question, "Will it bring party success?" And to this a voteless constituency cannot contribute in the smallest degree, even though it represents the Ten Commandments, the Sermon on the Mount, the Golden Rule, the Magna Charta, and the Declaration of Independence.
>
> — National American Woman Suffrage Association[1]

Making headway with the partisan politicians that controlled state and federal governments was an incredibly difficult task for disfranchised women. It was, in fact, the nearly paradoxical reason for many suffragists' insistence on voting rights in the first place: frustrated in their endeavors to influence legislation on issues ranging from prohibition, to protection for women and children in the labor force, to provision of public parks and playgrounds, women with reform interests increasingly saw a need for electoral leverage.[2] Yet, if unable to influence reform legislation without the vote, how would women influence legislators to adopt legislation for new voting rights? The challenge, suffrage movement leaders realized, was to find a way to give woman suffrage political meaning that entailed consequences for party success.

Why was finding a foothold in partisan politics such a difficult challenge for woman suffrage advocates? Quite simply, the frustration was that attempts to take the simplest partisan path to enfranchisement of women – what I have termed strategic enfranchisement – were bound for failure. Although a credible

---

[1] Anthony, Susan B. and Ida Husted Harper, *The History of Woman Suffrage*, vol. IV (Indianapolis: The Hollenbeck Press, 1902), 444–45.

[2] Kraditor, Aileen S., *The Ideas of the Woman Suffrage Movement, 1890–1920* (New York: W. W. Norton & Company, 1981). Flexner, Eleanor, *Century of Struggle: The Woman's Rights Movement in the United States* (Cambridge, MA: Belknap Press, 1959).

claim that newly enfranchised women would become faithful voters for the political party that granted them voting rights could have been tempting to a major party with fleeting control over a state government, such claims were hard to come by. Women, most partisans discovered, were far too diverse a group to hold promise as a voting bloc. Despite gendered arguments for woman suffrage that claimed women would purify politics – not only through their more "civilized" conduct at the polls, but also their supposed support for reform policies and alcohol prohibition – politicians had ample evidence that women were, indeed, just as politically heterogeneous as their husbands, fathers, and brothers. Politicians knew, in short, that "women" were a much larger group than those who organized and lobbied for voting rights. Women were differentiated, just like men, by their race and ethnicity, social class, immigrant status, education, and even occupation. Indeed, it was a gendered belief in women's representation via the "family vote" of her husband or father that implied there was no expectation of a women's voting bloc. Politicians may have had gendered expectations of women's political dispositions, but they had no evidence to suggest political cohesion from the female sex.[3]

Even the relative class and racial homogeneity of the organized suffrage movement did not translate into political cohesion. National suffrage organization leaders clashed over the degree to which partisan strategies ought to factor into campaigns; although the National American Woman Suffrage Association (NAWSA) early adopted an official policy of "non-partisanship," dissention on this tenet eventually grew to become the central basis of the defection of some suffragists into the Woman's Party or Congressional Union. Regardless of whether they believed their partisan leanings ought to be invoked in their suffrage work, prominent suffrage advocates were identified with nearly every political party that entered national electoral politics during the seventy-plus years of the movement, through their commitments to other political causes, their kinship ties to prominent male politicians, or their own partisan activism outside of suffrage activities. Republican ties were easy to see from the start of woman suffrage organization, which drew a number of ardent abolitionists, including Lucretia Mott and Lucy Stone. NAWSA treasurer Harriett Upton Taylor was, in fact, brought into the early suffrage movement by her father, a Republican Congressman. Yet there were plenty of Democrats, even among the leadership, including many of the Southern women. Kate Gordon, a long-serving NAWSA officer, was perhaps the most vocal proponent of the decidedly anti-Republican cause of white women's voting rights in the place of black men's. NAWSA vice president Catherine Waugh McCulloch served as a Democratic presidential elector in 1916, whereas fellow Illinois resident and NAWSA vice president Jane Addams was a central actor in the Progressive Party, serving as a delegate at the 1912 national party convention. A number

---

[3] On the "family vote" logic of representation and anti-woman suffrage arguments that explicitly invoked the variation in "women," see Kraditor, *The Ideas of the Woman Suffrage Movement*, 14–42.

of the NAWSA leaders joined forces at some point with the Socialist Party, and yet others were connected to the Prohibition Party through their Women's Christian Temperance Union (WCTU) activities.[4]

At the state level, political heterogeneity of women was also the norm, although it took different forms based on population characteristics. In some states, politicians saw significant political divides between the laboring and middle classes; in others, the preoccupation was between the political tendencies of black or Spanish Americans and whites. And in still others, the divide was simply between whites of rivaling partisanship. There was sometimes more political cohesion among the state suffrage organizers. But such cohesion was typically the result of general partisan dominance in the state, rather than peculiar partisan expectations of women. Woman suffrage activists in the Deep South states after the Civil War were generally Democrats, just like their already enfranchised white male counterparts. In the South and, in fact, the Northeast, which was at times nearly as Republican-dominant as the South was Democratic, arguments for strategic enfranchisement indeed surfaced, but were unsuccessful. Those sorts of failures, resulting in part from a lack of need for a new voting bloc in one-party dominant states, and hence insufficient incentive for partisans to push for new voting rights, will be the subject of a later chapter. For now, I return to the question of what might bring sufficient partisan political meaning for woman suffrage.

Once suffrage activists recognized they were unable to promise the votes of women as a group, given their heterogeneous partisan leanings, it was not immediately clear to them how party politics would ever favor women's voting rights. Ultimately, they would discover that party politicians' need to respond to the already enfranchised groups with whom suffragists forged alliances would force acquiescence to demands for women's voting rights. Success, that is, came from a programmatic enfranchisement process in which woman suffrage became part of a program of policies enacted to satisfy organized demand from voting constituents. This chapter takes up the development of a programmatic enfranchisement understanding of the politics women's voting rights among both partisan politicians and suffrage activists with the key case of Colorado.

Learning from Success – Colorado and the Meaning of Woman Suffrage

In 1893, Colorado became the second state to grant women equal voting rights in all elections, and the first state to do so by a vote of its existing, male electors. The campaign that delivered Colorado's suffrage victory was

---

[4] Biographies of twenty-six national leaders in Kraditor, *The Ideas of the Woman Suffrage Movement*, 265–82. On Gordon, see B. H. Gilley "Kate Gordon and Louisiana Woman Suffrage," in Nancy F. Cott, ed. *History of Women in the United States*, vol. XIX (Munich: KG Saur, 1992), 254–71.

infused with partisan politics, which were churning around an insurgence of Populism in the state. It was also marked by initial disagreement between state suffrage activists and the National American Woman Suffrage Association (NAWSA) over the viability of the campaign, which gave way to tensions over the strategies that ought to be employed. As the campaign progressed, however, politicians and activists alike saw reason to expect that the result in Colorado would be used as an example for other states where the issue of women's voting rights might be raised.

Indeed, Colorado would become an example for other states on the issue of woman suffrage, much more so than Wyoming, despite its status as the first state to grant equal voting rights to women in 1890. Wyoming's experience was likely too unique, and thus hardly instructive for either politicians or activists. Wyoming had entered the Union with woman suffrage written into its first state constitution, providing little information about how woman suffrage could successfully endure the politics of legislative decision-making and public referenda that would be requisite for adding new voting rights to an existing state's laws or constitution. Moreover, Wyoming had experience with the practice of woman suffrage before its statehood, its territorial legislature having granted women full voting rights in 1869 – a time when the territory had fewer than 10,000 residents, only 20 percent of whom were female. Not only had that territorial decision on woman suffrage occurred in a unique political environment, but it had come without a protracted campaign on the issue, and thus offered few lessons for suffrage supporters hoping to take some action to increase the likelihood of new voting rights for women in other states.[5] In contrast, adoption of full voting rights for women in Colorado in 1893 – in a state of more than 400,000 residents, and a contentious partisan environment – provided an example rich with learning opportunities for policymakers and activists about the causes and consequences of woman suffrage. Thus Colorado became the state commonly invoked in both media accounts and political debates about the political meaning and implications of woman suffrage over the next score of years.

Seeing as many opportunities for learning about the politics of suffrage extension in the Colorado experience as did woman suffrage advocates and partisan politicians, the task at hand is explaining the determinants and meaning of success for woman suffrage in the state in 1893. That task entails first looking back over the failed attempts for woman suffrage in Colorado – in the territorial legislature of 1870, in the state Constitutional Convention of 1875–1876, at the hands of the male electorate in 1877, and again in the state legislature in both 1881 and 1891. Although the exact constellation of interests in the suffrage cause changed across the years, these failed attempts exhibit a common theme in the unsuccessful politics of woman suffrage:

---

[5] On Wyoming, see Beverly Beeton, *Women Vote in the West: the Woman Suffrage Movement 1869–1896* (New York: Garland Publishing, Inc., 1986).

politicians seemed unconvinced that their existing electorates were much interested in the cause. This lack of an electoral incentive for extending the franchise enabled two common patterns in the politics of woman suffrage. First, it kept the debate about women's voting rights in the realm of principles and attitudes, with the invocation of gender norms as common grounds for resistance to woman suffrage and republican principles of representation as the central reason to support the idea of women as voters. Second, it enabled politicians to essentially have the issue of woman suffrage both ways by choosing to send the issue to the polls. That is, knowing full well that woman suffrage was an issue for which it would require real work to mobilize sufficient support at the polls, legislators could feign acquiescence to suffrage supporters – or at least to the principles they invoked – by voting in favor of legislation for a suffrage referendum, but stave off actual democratization by simply withholding active party organization support of the issue in the referendum campaign.

Electoral tides, however, can turn quickly, and by implication of the programmatic enfranchisement model, so might the chances for new voting rights. This chapter demonstrates that such was the case in Colorado. Victory in 1893 came with the political endorsement of a suddenly powerful Populist Party, an endorsement that conveyed the necessary electoral consequences for engendering sufficient legislative and partisan interest in the enfranchisement of women. Yet, the electoral politics that followed the adoption of woman suffrage in Colorado clearly demonstrated for all those who would look to the state as political example that a partisan endorsement of the cause would not translate into a faithful women's voting bloc for that party. Suffragists offered reasons for the Populists – and other political parties – to work with them, but the promise of future electoral support from "women" was not one of those reasons. Colorado, that is, offered both a model of successful programmatic enfranchisement politics and important policy feedback about the implausibility of the voting bloc expectation necessary to the politics of strategic enfranchisement.

Principled and Personal Failures – Woman Suffrage Outside Party Politics

Public discussions of the idea of voting rights for women in Colorado began as the territory constituted itself in the wake of Reconstruction. Adoption of woman suffrage very quickly gained notable advocates, including several of its territorial governors and their wives. What developed first was a personal politics, where individual or small groups of politically influential suffrage supporters used their own clout to push for consideration and adoption of woman suffrage. In these early considerations, there was a search for a resonant broader political meaning for woman suffrage, which typically involved gendered arguments of opposition and arguments of democratic principles from supporters. Although personal political clout could deliver legislative consideration – particularly when that clout was attached to institutional powers such as the governor's office – without electoral leverage, woman suffrage ultimately failed. If suffrage supporters were strong enough, failure was simply delivered through a public referendum.

Personal Politics, Issue Definition, and Expanding the Scope of Conflict

Colorado's first legislative consideration of woman suffrage came at the request of its territorial governor, who signaled interest in the issue in an address to the legislature at the start of its 1870 session. Governor McCook and his wife were both known advocates for the suffrage cause. McCook's entreaty, however, reflected only the principled terms of his convictions: women were rightly considered equals to men, and their enfranchisement was an "inevitable result" of "progressive civilization."[6] The governor's charge was followed by active debate in the 1870 legislative session, a debate that not only engaged the normative terms that the governor set out, but also contemplated the political implications of women's enfranchisement.

Gender clearly played an important part in defining the suffrage issue at this stage, as arguments about the roles women should and could play in society were a central part of the legislators' disagreements. Opponents raised objections to granting voting privileges to citizens who they deemed incapable of carrying out the associated duties of suffrage, namely military service. As one legislator claimed, "the highest and dearest privileges of a freeman and voter are bought with a price that may be cheerfully and gratefully paid by those to whom God has given the resolute will, the firm muscle, and the daring heart which pertain to me, and ought to be inseparable from the estate of manhood." McCook's fellow woman suffrage advocates did not disagree with this fundamental assumption about women's capacity, but rather countered with arguments that women performed other duties as citizens that ought to earn them the ballot. There were also concerns among opponents about the ways in which women's involvement in electoral politics would conflict with their roles as caretakers and protectors of morality. In response came the contention that women's morality, rather than being destroyed by their involvement in politics, would contribute to the moral improvement of politics, itself. And in this last argument about gender roles and suffrage lay the first argument about the *political* meaning of women's enfranchisement: women as voters would elevate the moral content of politics.[7]

---

[6] *Council Journal of the Legislative Assembly of the Territory of Colorado* (Central City, CO: David C. Collier, 1870), 19.

[7] Quote on women's ability to carry out duties of voters from a speech made by Colorado Council member George A. Hinsdale in session on February 2, 1870, printed by the *Colorado Weekly Chieftain*, February 17, 1870. Morality concerns discussed in the speech of Representative

Suffrage proponents' argument about the expected change in politics was laid out explicitly in the minority report of the special committee on suffrage laws. The two suffrage-friendly members of the committee argued that women would attach themselves "to one or the other of the great political parties" and hence, with "women acting at elections as voters, each of the great parties will doubtless require of its representatives a higher and purer standard of morality." In short, they meant that women voters would not likely tolerate the "dirty" nature of politics; that those engaging in electoral corruption would be punished at the polls, and, perhaps, that women would require politicians generally to engage a greater range of social issues. Importantly, however, supporters saw no partisan advantage resulting from woman suffrage. To the contrary, the claim that, in partisan terms, "wives will vote with their husbands, mothers with their sons, and sisters with their brothers" was conceded. Women as voters would change how Democrats *and* Republicans were required to carry out electoral politics, not which of the parties would win at the polls.[8] Strategic enfranchisement for women was being defined out – by those who supported the extension of voting rights.

The other common argument about the political meaning of woman suffrage came from its opponents. This argument was quite simple: women's voting rights as of yet had no real political meaning. That is, opponents repeatedly alleged that there was "no real interest" among the public in changing the electoral status of women, and then contended that such a drastic change in policy needed real public interest before it was warranted. This argument was often invoked in tandem with concerns about the violation of gender norms that women's presence at the polls entailed, including an emphasis on the uncomfortable idea that women would be exercising power over men. Without an electoral impetus for change, such rhetoric seemed to signal, gender attitudes justified the prevention of women's enfranchisement. More important, opponents' comments spelled out their leverage in the politics at hand. A lack of widespread public interest gave them political protection against the push for woman suffrage by a small, but politically powerful, minority. Suffrage opponents could simply expand the scope of conflict, calling for the approval of the public for such a change. Those advocating expanded voting rights found it politically difficult to argue against the exercise of the franchise on the issue – to argue for further democratization but simultaneously against the idea that the popular will should prevail. Yet, all seemed to share the sense that a public vote was unlikely to deliver woman suffrage.

With endorsement from a few key political figures, woman suffrage had taken a place on the agenda of Colorado politicians, garnering attention and

---

C. L. Hall on February 4, 1870, excerpts printed by the *Rocky Mountain News*, February 5, 1870. Pro-suffrage positions outlined in detail in the Council's special committee on elective franchise minority report, *Council Journal*, 131–39.

[8] *Council Journal*, 134–35.

debate. With no sense of any partisan or public interest in women's voting rights evident in this early discourse on woman suffrage in Colorado, however – without the incentives that would drive either strategic or programmatic enfranchisement – the legislature defeated the proposed change, and did so in bipartisan fashion. The measure was first challenged in the upper chamber, where a resolutely opposed council member attempted to have the bill recommitted to committee three times and threatened a filibuster to prevent a final vote. He reportedly relented after being convinced of the inevitability of the outcome, allowing the council to vote to pass the measure, with seven in favor and six opposed. It is unclear, however, that the expected "inevitable" outcome for the measure was passage, as the bill faced stiff opposition and was defeated in the House just two days later. Four Democrats, seven Republicans, and four Independents joined to pass a motion to indefinitely table the House version of the suffrage measure. And even a number of those who supported the bill in the House were attempting, before the measure was tabled, to amend it such that a public referendum would be required before woman suffrage took effect. If legislators sensed that the public lacked interest in women's voting rights, as the earlier legislative debates implied, it would seem that even some of the nominal supporters of the woman suffrage bill were not interested in actually changing the status of women's voting rights.

Mistaken Opportunity – Failure in Convention
Despite the 1870 defeat, eastern suffrage organizers believed there was opportunity in the Colorado territory's transition to statehood just a few years later. Their logic was that inclusion in a new constitution meant woman suffrage would avoid the seemingly insurmountable hurdle of a stand-alone issue referendum. Colorado voters would be asked only to signal their support of the new state constitution as a whole. If Colorado men truly desired statehood, and convention delegates could be convinced to include woman suffrage, women's voting rights would be a constitutionally protected reality in the new state. The ensuing campaign would ultimately prove the eastern suffragists correct in their assessment of the issue's individual chances at the polls. But it would first reveal that they were decidedly unprepared for the politics of leveraging a place for woman suffrage on the draft of the new constitution. In short, the eastern organizers made attempts at a number of political strategies, but ultimately accomplished only a near replication of the 1870 personal politics. This time, however, the threat of a referendum was realized.

Even before the enabling legislation for Colorado's statehood passed Congress in early 1874, members of the American Woman Suffrage Association (AWSA), the east coast-based organization led by former abolitionists Lucy Stone and Henry Blackwell, were discussing a push to have woman suffrage included in the new state's constitution. The AWSA, however, had no real ties to the western territory, and no concrete plans for a campaign there. Ultimately, the organization sent just two organizers, Margaret and

J. B. Campbell. Moreover, the Campbells' campaign did not begin in earnest until mid-November of 1875, giving them just four weeks for organizing work before the Constitutional Convention began.

The Campbells' campaign strategy seemed to involve every activity that might influence convention delegates on the issue – perhaps because no tactic seemed particularly promising to the organizers. There was work to try to conjure and convey public interest in women's voting rights: canvassing as much of the territory as possible, holding public meetings on woman suffrage, and amassing signatures on a petition. And there were attempts at more backroom politicking through meetings with politically connected locals, including representatives to the Constitutional Convention, themselves, whenever possible. Traversing the territory proved tiresome and expensive, and seemed to bear little fruit other than occasional willingness of locals to sign their names to a petition. In reports to Stone and Blackwell, Margaret Campbell wrote consistently of the challenge to overcome disinterest. Public meetings proved mostly disappointing, with many suffering from utter lack of attendance, not to mention failing to generate any funds for the cause as such events often did in the east. Of this frustration, Campbell wrote to Blackwell: "[W]e were told in Central – one of the places where we could not get a hearing – that we must advertise *a dog fight*, then we could get a crowd." The resultant dwindling funds eventually forced J. B. Campbell, a lawyer by training, to leave the suffrage organizing entirely to his wife while he searched for work that would pay their living expenses.[9]

It seems that the eastern suffragists did attempt to cultivate some sort of coalitional strategy for the suffrage cause – the kind of strategy that might have engendered the politics of programmatic enfranchisement. The Campbells attempted to engage Albina and John Everitt Washburn, central figures in the newly founded Colorado Grange, in organizing for the suffrage cause. Margaret Campbell hoped the Washburns could leverage the agricultural fraternal organization, which was populated by both male and female members, to offer organizational support for the suffrage campaign. Politically promising as this strategy could have been, such a coalitional politics was not so easy to establish. Not only did the Grange refuse to become involved, deeming the issue too political, but with both Washburns elected to officer positions – John to the top position of Grange Master – the couple was distracted from suffrage work completely just as the delegates to the Constitutional Convention assembled in Denver in mid-December. On the first day of the convention, Campbell wrote

---

[9] The Campbells' work is documented in a series of letters from Margaret Campbell to Lucy Stone and Henry Blackwell collected in the papers of the National American Woman Suffrage Association. Quoted passage is from a letter from Campbell to Blackwell, December 15, 1875 (emphasis in original).

in despair to Stone and Blackwell of the Washburns: "[I]t is evident that even they put Grange business before suffrage."[10]

Notwithstanding disappointment and dwindling funds, Margaret Campbell continued her work attempting to convince the Constitutional Convention delegates to make Colorado the second state to grant women full voting rights. Her last effort was to work with a Denver physician, Dr. Alida Avery, to found an official Colorado suffrage organization in the capital city. At a January meeting, the Colorado Woman Suffrage Association (CWSA) was established, with Avery elected its president. Although the new organization was small in size – just thirty-six members signed on at the initial meeting – its inclusion of a number of politically connected individuals, including the Washburns, seemed to offer it some clout. Within days of the CWSA's founding, a delegation of its members was received by the Constitutional Convention's committee on suffrage and elections to discuss the prospect of including women's voting rights in the new state. The fledgling suffrage organization also held several open discussions of woman suffrage in Denver, and contracted with a newspaper to print a suffrage column.[11]

Ultimately, the small suffrage organization managed to gain access and some attention, but suffragists still found few friends for their cause. When the suffrage and elections committee delivered its draft of the suffrage qualifications clauses for the constitution, it included a provision stipulating that electors would be male. Although the provision was challenged by two suffrage-friendly members of the committee in a dissenting minority report, the resultant proposal to enfranchise the women in Colorado lost by a rising vote of eight in favor and twenty-four opposed.[12] Few delegates seemed to find any political imperative for woman suffrage in the minority's arguments. Indeed, woman suffrage was once again demanded largely on the basis of the republican principle of government by consent of the people and with the familiar refrain of no taxation without representation, although there was also an argument that women needed the vote to protect their own economic and physical welfares. Although this new argument introduced an additional consideration into the debate, it did so in a way that once again served as an argument from suffrage supporters against the strategic enfranchisement of women. The report raised the specter of exploitation of the growing body of women workers, but offered voting rights as the solution for these women to be "looked after by the politicians *of all classes.*" Women's political interests here bore no particular partisan implications.

[10] Letter from Campbell to Stone and Blackwell, December 20, 1875 (NAWSA papers).
[11] Colorado Woman Suffrage Association; Colorado State Equal Suffrage Association records, 1876–1881, Colorado Historical Society, Denver, Colorado
[12] *Proceedings of the Constitutional Convention held in Denver, December 20, 1875* (Denver: Smith-Brooks Press, State Printers, 1907).

Despite the largely dismissive treatment of woman suffrage at the Constitutional Convention, the delegates made two concessions to the suffrage advocates. Neither seemed meaningful or genuine. First, women's right to vote in school elections was included in the new constitution. This provision was tied to gendered arguments about women's interest in raising children; it was also completely ignored as a concession by the CWSA. The second accommodation was a clause in the new constitution that required the new state's legislature, in its first session, to submit the question of women's voting rights to the state's male electorate. Although this provision was of real interest to the suffragists, it was clearly not expected to bring woman suffrage to the new state – as suffrage advocates were well aware. John Washburn had warned the Campbells early on that such an outcome would spell defeat because of "the voters that cannot be reached and will not read the arguments."[13] The Campbells' difficulty in generating public interest in the suffrage issue before the Constitutional Convention attested to Washburn's concern. And the small, newly formed suffrage organization was clearly incapable of staging a major public campaign across the territory on its own.

Indeed, even the legislative treatment of the woman suffrage ballot measure in that first legislative session suggested suffrage opponents felt electorally insulated on the issue. Despite the constitutional mandate, passage of the ballot measure in the legislature was not uncontested. An alternative measure that attempted to increase the required simple majority among voters to a two-thirds threshold appeared in the House of Representatives. One House member, in expression of his own dismissive attitude toward women's voting rights, offered a motion to place the measure on the ballot in 1977. The 100-year delay, the *Denver Times* reported with amusement, was justified by the representative with the mocking desire "to wait until Susan B. [Anthony] should become of age." And when the constitutionally required election-enabling legislation finally came to a vote, some members of both chambers of the legislature still voted against it: four in the Senate and twelve in the House.[14] Without a sense of electoral importance for the issue of woman suffrage, politicians were free

---

[13] Washburn's concern about the viability of separate submission for woman suffrage was reported by Margaret Campbell in a letter to Stone and Blackwell dated November 20, 1875 (NAWSA papers). The school suffrage provision was introduced by delegate Byron Carr on January 22, 1876 with a speech justifying his proposal. The *Rocky Mountain News* summarized his statements, ascribing to him the position that "[u]pon the matter of education of our children, no class of citizens are more deeply interested than the mothers of those children." Carr's proposal was accepted by the convention's committee on rights of suffrage two days later. In a speech delivered after the Constitutional Convention adjourned, Margaret Campbell was reported to have referred to the school suffrage provision as "'the sop' offered to her sex" (*Rocky Mountain News*, February 13, 1876).

[14] Motion to delay election made by Representative W. D. Anthony of Denver (*Denver Daily Times*, January 25, 1877). House roll call vote reported in the *Denver Daily Tribune* (January 26, 1877).

to disregard even a constitutional mandate with only reference to their own gendered prejudices as justification.

The similarities in the treatment of the suffrage issue at the Constitutional Convention and the 1870 legislature's treatment are marked. Both times the efforts of friendly political entrepreneurs secured consideration for woman suffrage, but fell far short of delivering the desired policy change. Debate revolved around principled and gendered attitudinal reasons to support or oppose women's voting rights. And opponents seemed to take the lack of electoral incentives as insulation from a policy change. Given that consideration across both bodies was delivered in response the inside politics pressure of a small group of politically connected advocates, the similarities are also unsurprising.

The Referendum Campaign

As the politics that delivered the suffrage ballot measure suggested, suffragists were on their own in the referendum campaign. Their difficulty in meeting the demands of a public campaign were evident from the start. Not only was the CWSA small and resource poor, the support it received from the eastern-based "national" suffrage organizations in the form of eastern suffrage speakers was of questionable local political value. Given that the referendum occurred before the advent of the Australian ballot system, the suffragists also discovered that their mobilization efforts were made even more challenging by the complication of localized ballot wording decisions by the party organizations. Whether partisans purposely complicated the suffrage campaign or delivered complication through benign neglect, the ballot issue made clear that the suffrage issue lacked partisan organization support. The cost was the unsurprising failure of the referendum. Although it is clear that suffrage activists understood the failure to be connected to their lack of organizational capacity, their public response to failure was to conjure an explanation that blamed an "undesirable" element of the male electorate for the outcome. It was, perhaps, a strategy to assert a new political definition for woman suffrage – one that connected the issue with a particular set of voter interests.

The CWSA was clearly unprepared for a referendum campaign. Although the enabling legislation was enacted in January and the vote scheduled for October, CWSA work did not begin until the summer. Ultimately the plan was simply to attempt to sway voters directly by canvassing the state in the few months preceding the election. A lack of sufficient resources meant CWSA leaders needed to appeal for support to the AWSA and a number of eastern state suffrage associations. They asked, as stated in a request from Albina Washburn published in AWSA's newspaper, *The Woman's Journal*, for "money to promote the distribution of Woman Suffrage papers and tracts" as well as "speakers who will thoroughly canvass the State." The requested assistance arrived in September. Lucy Stone and Henry Blackwell, as well as Susan B. Anthony of the National Woman Suffrage Association (NWSA, then feuding with the AWSA), traveled the state making speaking appearances in the month before the public referendum. Their work would be the main effort to reach voters outside the areas where local suffrage activism was already being cultivated – beyond cities such as Denver, Boulder, and Greeley – although some friendly state politicians, such as former governor John Routt, whose wife was a declared suffragist, also made occasional appearances.

Accounts suggest the eastern suffragist speakers drew audiences throughout the state, but that speeches by activists from the east were not necessarily warmly received by, let alone conversion experiences for, the men of the western territory. Anthony, who traveled extensively through the southern, mining industry-dominated part of the state, wrote in her diary repeatedly of experiences marked by contempt or disregard. Incidents ranged from difficulties in securing a location to deliver her speeches in the mining towns to jeering from audience members. Local newspaper accounts of the speakers' tours reflected Anthony's sense of the underlying sentiments: some were resolutely antagonistic and worked to discredit the arguments in favor of women's voting rights, some were just dismissive, often referring to her and Stone as "shriekers," and still others simply expressed dubiousness that the time had come for the subject being addressed. Endorsements of the cause or optimistic speculations about its fate in the upcoming election did appear, notably in the pages of the *Rocky Mountain News*, the Denver paper that carried the CWSA column.[15]

Conducted before the advent of the standardized, state-issued Australian secret ballot, however, the suffrage election depended not only on the sentiments of Colorado voters, but also on navigation of the ballot choices presented to them by the party organizations. Although the legislature had mandated the exact phrases that needed to appear, once a vote was cast, for a ballot to be counted for or against woman suffrage, it had not mandated how the ballots should appear when voters received them. The importance of this fact became clear as Republican and Democratic Party committees in each of the counties revealed their individual decisions about the suffrage issue ballots. Although there were some distinct patterns to the ballots printed by each party, those patterns did not suggest a clear partisan interest in delivering support. Democrats tended to provide both of the legislatively mandated phrases "woman suffrage approved" and "woman suffrage not approved," meaning Democratic voters needed to determine which one to select and which to cross out. In some counties Republican voters needed to ask their election officials for the appropriate ballot to indicate their choice, as half were printed to signal approval and half

---

[15] Endorsement and/or optimism also appeared in the *Greeley Tribune, Colorado Springs Gazette,* and *Colorado Transcript* (Jefferson County). Antagonistic and dismissive coverage appeared regularly in the *Colorado Weekly Chieftain* (Pueblo County) and the *Denver Daily Times.* For summaries of relevant passages of Anthony's diary, see Ida Husted Harper, *The Life and Work of Susan B. Anthony* (Indianapolis: The Bowen-Merrill Company, 1899) and Marcia T. Goldstein, "Colorado Women and the Vote" *Denver Westerners Roundup,* July/August 1995.

to indicate rejection. Republican ballots in other counties might be read as tipping in suffragists' favor, as they provided only the phrase "woman suffrage approved," with a blank between the last two words to be left in order to signal a vote of approval, or filled with the word "not" to signal rejection. Regardless of whether these ballot wording choices were, as some newspaper editors indeed alleged, designed by party leaders to produce a particular outcome for the ballot measure, the variation underscored the scope of the challenge facing suffrage advocates. Indeed, Anthony would write years later that her experience was that the suffragists needed a "man or men – in every election district in the state – who will devote himself to helping men to rightly scratch their tickets."[16]

Given the adversity that generally characterized the campaign, Election Day delivered an unsurprising outcome. The suffrage measure failed, with only 6,612 votes in its favor, and 14,053 opposed. All but one county – Boulder – delivered a majority vote against it. Suffrage organizers were quick to offer an account of their failure that turned on some factor other than their own organizational or political shortcomings. Their account, which turned up in newspapers and in correspondence between suffrage advocates, prominently featured accusations of resistance among the Mexican-origin population in the state. One newspaper quoted Margaret Campbell as claiming woman suffrage's "enemies are the ignorant, degraded and superstitious Mexican of the south... and the uneducated and uncultivated negroes of the north." Yet, as historian William Faherty has observed, resistance among these groups, even if it was universal, cannot account for the loss. As Faherty noted, U.S. Census records do not report the number of Mexican Americans living in the state, but the number born in the Territory of New Mexico is likely a good proxy. Neither does the Census break down the New Mexican and black populations by age and sex. Still, even if every one of the 2,358 black Americans and 9,500 New Mexicans living in Colorado at the time were a qualified male elector who turned out and voted against the measure – an extremely unrealistic assumption – their votes would fall thousands short of the entirety of the negative votes cast. Although it is true that counties with larger New Mexican born populations registered greater percentages of negative votes than others, the most important feature of the returns was the general lack of approval across the state.[17] Hence, the result is more consistent with the difficulty in achieving a policy change with no real organization to forward its approval by voters

[16] Quote of Anthony is from a letter written to Colorado Equal Suffrage Association, July 16, 1893 (Ellis Meredith Papers, Colorado Historical Society, Denver, Colorado). Details on the ballots were reported in a number of newspapers, including the *Colorado Transcript* (October 3, 1877), the *Colorado Weekly Chieftain* (September 27, 1877), and the *Denver Daily Times* (September 26, 1877).

[17] Campbell quote appears in the *Colorado Weekly Chieftain* (October 25, 1877). Faherty, William B., "Regional Minorities and the Woman Suffrage Struggle." *The Colorado Magazine* (vol. 33, no. 3, July 1956): 212–17.

across the state, and with the idea that the political parties had no interest in an expanded electorate. Clearly a political party with an interest in delivering a woman suffrage victory could have enabled much greater support at the polls; ballot printing practices and mobilization efforts were within the purview of the parties, and neither was broadly employed in favor of women's voting rights.

Learning Coalitional Politics

In the face of the 1877 defeat, the CWSA dissolved. Interest in women's voting rights in the state did not disappear entirely, but was funneled through other organizations. Thus, the collapse of a formal suffrage organization actually provided a clearer opening for the beginning of a coalitional politics for woman suffrage in Colorado. Although coalitional politics would be key to delivering woman suffrage through the politics of programmatic enfranchisement, the programmatic model also makes it clear that not all coalitions provide the electoral leverage necessary to incentivize the requisite partisan interest in providing new voting rights. In particular, suffrage advocates would need to learn how to make connections to groups that wielded significant electoral leverage, as well as how to build those connections strongly enough that the partner would be willing to actually exert its leverage on the suffrage issue. These lessons were evident in legislative failures as suffragists negotiated a politically strong but unproductive relationship between suffrage and temperance organizations and a developing relationship with agricultural interests, including the Colorado Grange. Analysis of an 1881 vote suggests that the lack of broad political interest in temperance undercut the effectiveness of that partnership, and the lack of electoral leverage from farmers' organizations left legislators unconvinced of a need to appease constituents with the provision of woman suffrage.

Commitment of the state chapter of the Women's Christian Temperance Union (WCTU) to the suffrage issue came just after its 1880 founding. With suffragists, including Albina Washburn, at the center of the temperance organization, such a development is unsurprising. That is, an overlap of suffrage politics and temperance politics was reflective of an overlapping interest in the two issues among individual activists. It seems the same might be true of the connection between agricultural interests and suffrage, although the historical record here is a bit less clear. Washburn certainly appears to have continued her efforts to interest farmers' organizations in working for suffrage. Although the Colorado Grange withered organizationally in the 1880s, the Washburns remained active in the farmers' movement, with John Washburn even running for office several times as a Greenback candidate. The Greenback Party, which attempted to pull the support of farmers and laborers in Colorado, had little electoral success in the state, but did become the first political party to endorse full and equal voting rights for Colorado women.

A new state suffrage organization, the Colorado State Equal Suffrage Association (CSESA), finally emerged in 1881. Populated by many of the same figures active in the WCTU, the organization itself represented obvious overlap with temperance interests. Like the CWSA before it, the CSESA fell far short of its title of "state" organization, with the majority of its membership being drawn from Denver and Greeley. And despite the nascent connections between suffrage and other organized causes, when the CSESA quickly turned to the state legislature for a woman suffrage bill, it was clear once again that Colorado's suffrage activists were relying on the inside leverage of a few friendly politicians to advance their cause.[18]

Although the legislative strategy did not seem to involve attempts to leverage pressure from temperance or farmers' organizations on lawmakers, the temperance and agricultural roots of the suffrage organization were reflected in the legislator who took on the task of introducing and forwarding its measure in the state House. Jared Brush, a Republican state representative, was both a prominent Grange member and from the temperance movement stronghold of Greeley. Indeed, consistent with the suffragists' tactic of reliance on the support of a friendly political entrepreneur, throughout the legislature's consideration of the suffrage measure, the press referred to the bill as Brush's "pet scheme." Like earlier inside or personal politics attempts at securing suffrage legislation, the CSESA's approach was not wholly unsuccessful. The suffrage measure was pushed through committee consideration with a favorable report and brought up for a vote on the House floor. Resistance on the floor, however, was insurmountable. On their first vote, twenty-three of the forty-one representatives present voted in favor of the measure, but the bill failed for lack of the constitutionally required two-thirds supermajority. One of the dissenting legislators was convinced to call for a reconsideration of that vote, but when the House faced another vote on the suffrage bill, the opposition was more resolute. The suffrage measure narrowly escaped an attempt at indefinite postponement before failing again to pass the House, this time by a vote of twenty-two in favor versus twenty-three opposed.[19]

With state legislators casting roll call votes three times on the bill for women's voting rights – twice on the question of final passage, and once on the movement to indefinitely postpone its consideration in the House – it is possible to cast some light on the influences on legislative interest and opposition, to investigate whether the incentives of the strategic or programmatic enfranchisement models were at work. If the defeat of woman suffrage was a failed attempt at strategic enfranchisement, the votes should exhibit a clear partisan pattern; if there were expectations that women voters would turn electoral tides, the

[18] The CSESA founding and activity is documented in its own record book, which is actually the same book used by the CWSA (Colorado Woman Suffrage Association; Colorado State Equal Suffrage Association records, 1876–1881, Colorado Historical Society, Denver, Colorado).

[19] For newspaper accounts, see, for example, *Rocky Mountain News*, January 22, 23, and 27, 1881. Legislative activity and votes recorded in *House Journal of the General Assembly of the State of Colorado* (Denver: Tribune Publishing Company, 1881), 124, 160, 175–76, 203, 210, 242–43.

parties should have delivered party-line votes. Given that the primary advocate was a Republican, moreover, it would seem a strategic failure in this case would be driven by insufficient Republican votes to carry the measure. If the defeat of woman suffrage was a failed programmatic enfranchisement attempt, then the pro-suffrage coalition should have shaped legislators' support for the bill. In particular, comparisons of the district characteristics of supporters and opponents should suggest that legislators representing constituencies where the interests that overlapped with the organized suffrage movement were stronger were more likely to support the suffrage bill. If, however, woman suffrage failed because it had yet to attain the political meaning to drive either strategic or programmatic enfranchisement, then supporters and opponents could be delineated by factors other than partisan or coalitional influences, including their personal preferences.

Given the lack of discussion of the measure as one of any partisan interest, it seems unlikely that woman suffrage was seen in strategic enfranchisement terms. Consistent with the basic condition for strategic enfranchisement, Republicans held sufficient control of the state government to change the state's suffrage qualifications if they desired to do so, including thirty-six of the forty-nine seats in the state House of Representatives. Contrary to the strategic enfranchisement model expectation, however, Republicans were divided almost evenly on the question of whether the legislation should go forward across all the three roll-call votes in the House on the woman suffrage measure. Thirteen Republicans voted against the woman suffrage bill both times it came up for final passage, whereas fifteen Republicans cast their votes in favor on both of those roll calls. Neither did the party display a sense that allowing its suffrage-supportive members to forward their cause bore consequence for party fortunes; the vote on postponement saw Republicans line up in nearly identical groups, with only one Republican who voted no on the question of final passage being unwilling to support the motion to table the bill indefinitely. Democrats also lacked partisan unanimity; three of the thirteen House Democrats were consistent supporters of the suffrage bill, and another three were consistent opponents. The other members of both parties either spilt their votes or simply failed to show up to cast them. Neither party, in sum, behaved as if enfranchising women was expected to provide a clear benefit to one party over the other.

If Colorado politicians failed to see strict partisan incentives in enfranchising women, they may still have gleaned some sense of electoral consequence for their votes on the issue from their voting constituencies, providing the incentives for programmatic enfranchisement. The only perceptible connections between suffrage advocates and other interest groups lay in the notable overlap in the membership of the WCTU and the CSESA, and in the suffrage endorsements offered at various moments by Grange and farmers' movement leaders. If any electoral consequence was read in these coalitional politics, it should be reflected in legislators' willingness to support the woman suffrage measure.

TABLE 2.1. *Votes on Woman Suffrage Amendment by District Characteristics, Colorado House 1881*

	Temperance		Farmers	Constituent Vote
	WCTU	No WCTU	Mean Farms per 100 Population	Mean % in Favor in 1877
Consistent Supporters	8	9	2.5 (2.8)	36.2 (8.6)
Inconsistent Voters	2	17	3.4 (2.1)	27.4 (19.0)
Consistent Opponents	2	11	4.4 (4.0)	28.9 (12.6)

Note: Standard deviations of means in parentheses.
Sources: House Journal of the General Assembly of the State of Colorado, 1881; U. S. Census, 1880, Ninth Annual Report of the Convention of Colorado Woman's Christian Temperance Union, 1888.

At the time the legislature considered the suffrage bill, only a handful of localities registered any organized temperance interests; records of the Colorado WCTU show only Colorado Springs, Denver, Fort Collins, and Greeley had active branches by the start of 1881. Although the female membership of the WCTU itself could not hold legislators accountable for their votes on the suffrage measure, the WCTU's centrality to the temperance movement makes their organizational presence the best available proxy for systematic measurements of wider temperance interest influence in the legislators' districts. With no systematic measure of the strength of farmers' movements in each district, the best available proxy for gauging their influence on the woman suffrage measure is the relative presence of farmers, themselves, in each district, which can be derived from the U.S. Census counts of farms in each county. Given the recent referendum on woman suffrage, it is also possible to investigate whether the level of expressed district support correlated with legislators' voting behavior.[20]

Table 2.1 summarizes the analysis of the possibility of programmatic enfranchisement influences on Colorado legislators' votes on the 1881 woman suffrage measure. Legislators were first divided into three categories: consistent supporters, or those who voted in favor of the bill's progress on all three roll call votes; consistent opponents, or those who voted against the bill all three times; and inconsistent voters, a category that includes those who switched

[20] Dates of establishment of local Colorado WCTU affiliates are listed in the *Ninth Annual Report of the Convention of Colorado Women's Christian Temperance Union* (Denver: Challenge Publishing Co., 1888), 32. Legislators from Arapahoe, El Paso, Larimer, and Weld counties are coded as having a WCTU presence in their districts. Farming presence is calculated from the 1880 U.S. Census as the number of farms per 100 people in the counties that constitute the member's district.

their stance across the votes and those who failed to cast at least one of their votes. The rows of the table display the presence of each of the influences of interest across the three categories of legislators. These results suggest that consistent supporters were differentiated from both the other categories of legislators in terms of all three district characteristics, although not in the anticipated direction in each case. Consistent with the overlapping of activist involvement in favor of both the suffrage and temperance causes, supporters of the suffrage bill were more likely to come from districts with organized temperance interests, with fully eight of the twelve legislators from districts with local WCTU affiliates voting for the suffrage measure each time. Also consistent with the idea that greater constituent demand should increase legislators' willingness to endorse new voting rights, consistent supporters were indeed from districts that cast more favorable votes for woman suffrage in the 1877 referendum. The comparisons of supportive and oppositional legislators by the relative presence of farming interests in their districts, however, are inconsistent with the idea that the endorsements the woman suffrage movement had thus far received from farmers' organization figures had conveyed a sense of electorally meaningful demand from farming interests. In fact, consistent supporters were from districts with noticeably less farming interests than other legislators. Whether this negative connection between the relative district presence of farming interests and legislators' votes on woman suffrage was because of a failure of coalitional credibility or a lack of sufficient coalitional electoral strength, however, these data cannot parse.

After their failure, the CSESA folded. For the next decade, organized demand for women's voting rights would be lacking in Colorado. With a number of ardent suffragists still among its ranks, the state WCTU organized a division charged with forwarding the goal of woman suffrage. Seemingly aware of its political limitations, the organization did not actually invest much effort or resources. In her 1889 annual report, for example, the chair of the WCTU's franchise department concluded that petitioning the legislature for action on woman suffrage was "a waste of time and force." Because the political obstacle of getting the constitution amended seemed too insurmountable, her decision was to wait for the opportunity of a new Constitutional Convention. "Until then," she concluded, "our energies must be given to educating and arousing the public sentiment." Even that plan, however, was not extensive. And the assertion about the uselessness of petitioning the legislature was validated two years later. The WCTU presented a petition to the state legislature in 1891, asking for a new suffrage bill. That request was quickly denied by the legislature; the committee charged with considering the petition simply refused to draft or introduce any legislation on the issue, and the chamber validated that choice by accepting the report of the committee's decision.[21]

---

[21] *Twelfth Annual Report of the Woman's Christian Temperance Union* (Colorado Springs: Republic Publishing Company, 1892).

The Meaning of Success – The Suffrage Campaign of 1893

In the span of just two years, the treatment of women's voting rights in the Colorado legislature would go from complete dismissal to passage with strong support. Indeed, the change in suffrage politics in the state of Colorado was so quick that it took national suffrage organizers quite by surprise. Convinced that the suffrage situation was at a standstill in Colorado in the early 1890s, NAWSA – the organization formed by the merger of the previously feuding AWSA and NWSA – was focusing its efforts on Kansas, and would have to be persuaded to join the campaign in Colorado. The rapid change in suffrage circumstances in the state was not produced by a new investment by activists in the state, nor a sudden sea-change in gender attitudes in the state, but rather by a sudden change in partisan politics. A suddenly successful Populist Party – a party built on a base of disaffected farmers and laborers – brought women's voting rights to fruition, not only ushering the policy change through the legislature, but also shaping the politics of the necessary referendum for public approval.

Suffrage activism was not entirely irrelevant to the 1893 success story. Its most important role, however, was an indirect one. Suffrage advocates shaped Populists' willingness to engage their cause, and they did so through their location in the organizations that the Populists hoped to bring along in the new party's efforts. Rising to challenge the two major parties was a task that required instant infrastructure and a political agenda that drew together a coalition wide enough to affect sufficiently the major parties' electoral dominance. Endorsing woman suffrage could be a way to pull in the infrastructure of the well-organized temperance movement, which rested on the base of the WCTU, and to do so without directly alienating the laboring men that might value their saloons. It could also be a way to enlist the full organizational support of the farmers' movement, which had been relying on the support of female membership for decades. Because woman suffrage had already become an important issue to activists in these two movements, and because a new party would be in particular need of new sources of organizational support in order to mount an electoral challenge, the Populist Party offered an unprecedented opportunity for the issue of women's voting rights in partisan politics.

Woman Suffrage on the Populist Agenda

Woman suffrage appeared on the Colorado Populists' agenda during the 1892 campaign, the election season in which the party made its debut in the state's politics. Colorado's Populist Party emerged in the midst of particular concern about demonetization of silver, which was heavily mined in the state. "The silver issue" was pitched as the common interest of the states' miners, farmers, and urban workers. As the chair of the state party was reported to have remarked during their 1892 convention, "[workers'] income had been affected by the depreciation of silver, and if the mines closed every farmer would find it difficult to pay his taxes, so if a man came from the mines, from the farms, or from the city, all would suffer alike if silver was crushed." In addition to their dominant refrain on "the silver issue," Colorado's Populists took up other "money issues" that were framed as pitting the common interests of ordinary Americans against the wealthy elite, such as the income tax, banking laws, and corporate monopolies. The new party was clearly looking to pull together a broad constituency to challenge to the established Republican and Democratic parties. Farmers and laborers – from the mines and the cities – offered Populists organized bases through which the new party could recruit and mobilize. And the established parties found themselves sufficiently threatened by the building Populist organization and sentiment throughout the state during the 1892 campaign season that they fractured, with many Democrats supporting a fusion with the new party and some of the Republican ranks desperate enough for votes that they aligned themselves with the Populist agenda in opposition to the official platforms of the regular party.[22]

A party built from labor unions and farmers' organizations – most notably the Farmers' Alliance – found itself immediately with women in its midst, including some of the state's most active suffragists. Although women were still few in labor organizations, they were noticeably present as active members in both the state's farming organizations and the ranks of the national leadership of those federated organizations. With their organizational skills and resources as leverage, these women pushed for a role in the new party, and for the party to address the issue of women's rights.

From the first organizing activities of Colorado's Populist Party, the push for women's inclusion and woman suffrage was evident. Emma Ghent Curtis, an active member of the Colorado Farmers' Alliance, reported to the national suffrage publication *The Woman's Journal* that she and her fellow Fremont County delegates to the May 1892 state Populist convention pushed for consideration of woman suffrage and for women delegates to attend the state party's nominating convention later that summer. When the party reconvened in July, at least a dozen female delegates were seated; among them were both Ghent and Albina Washburn. By all available accounts, the women were well received, and several of them served on committees during the convention. A woman suffrage plank for the state party's platform was drafted at this convention, although the convention failed to adopt it before adjournment. Woman suffrage did, however, appear among the endorsements of many county-level Populist conventions and in the campaign pronouncements of Populist candidates for state offices. One newspaper's announcement of a campaign event for

---

[22] Quoted passage is the remark of Populist Party state chairman Steven Pratt reported in the *Aspen Weekly Times* (July 30, 1892). On the Populist ascendance in Colorado, see Robert W. Larson, "Populism in the Mountain West: A Mainstream Movement." *The Western Historical Quarterly* (April, 1982) 143–64; James Edward Wright, *The Politics of Populism: Dissent in Colorado* (New Haven, Connecticut: Yale University Press, 1974).

two of the Populist candidates it endorsed for the state legislature, for example, included the line that "[t]he ladies are especially invited, as Captains Boyd and Benton are firm believers in the justice of woman suffrage."[23]

The campaign season brought with it further reinforcement of the ideas that women advocates were central to the push for a People's Party, and that endorsement of women's rights was part of ensuring their support. Women in the Alliance and Populist Party from other areas of the country were an important part of that reinforcement. Kansas-based reformer and populist writer and speaker Annie L. Diggs published an article in the Boston-based populist magazine *Arena* underscoring the contributions of women across the country to Farmers' Alliance and related Populist Party activity in July, 1892 – just as the Colorado convention concluded its activities. There is evidence that her arguments reached the western state, as several Colorado newspapers implored their readers to take note of her piece, entitled "The Women in the Alliance Movement," at times printing passages from it. As one newspaper remarked, the article informed readers about "the social conditions which made the present [farmers'] movement inevitable, and why women from the first played such an important part in the agitation." In similar fashion, the Populist lecturer chosen to accompany the party's presidential nominee James Weaver to the state around the time of the nominating convention underscored the importance of women and women's interests in the farmer-labor driven organization. The lecturer was reformist orator Mary Elizabeth Lease – perhaps chosen because of her known ability to draw large crowds. Not only did the sex of the chosen lecturer serve as an indicator of the importance of women in the new party, but Lease's public comments about the need to support the new party were at times accompanied by explicit remarks in the interest of greater rights for women.[24]

Translating Campaign Rhetoric into Legislative Outcomes
Given the positioning of women and women's rights advocates inside the Populist movement, Colorado suffragists, it seemed, had reason to be hopeful when the new state government was seated at the start of 1893. The state had elected

---

23 Ghent, Emma Curtis, "The Forces that Carried Colorado" *The Woman's Journal* (December 2, 1893). Washburn, Albina L. "Colorado Suffrage Items." *The Woman's Journal* (August 27, 1892). Account of the convention, including seating of the female delegates and the woman suffrage resolution in *The Aspen Weekly Times* (July 30, 1892). Campaign announcement in the *Greeley Tribune* (October 6, 1892).

24 Diggs, Annie L. "The Women in the Alliance Movement" *The Arena* (July 1892), 161–79. Papers that covered the Diggs *Arena* article included the *Greeley Tribune* (September 29, 1892) and the *Aspen Union Era* (June 30, 1892 and July 14, 1892). Quoted passage from the *Aspen Union Era*, June 30, 1892. On the involvement of women generally in the Alliance and Populist Party, as well as on Lease's speaking for the party, see Mary Jo Wagner, "Farms, Families, and Reform: Women in the Farmers' Alliance and Populist Party" (Ph.D. diss., University of Oregon, 1986).

a Populist governor, put twenty-seven Populists in its state House of Representatives and twelve in its Senate, and had witnessed the influence of Populist
ideas on the platforms and campaign promises of Democrats and Republicans.
Moreover, by the time the new legislature convened, the state organizations of
both the Farmers' Alliance and their Populist Party allies the Knights of Labor
had issued official endorsements of legislation to grant Colorado women equal
suffrage rights. The first act of a Populist in the state government, however,
was slightly disappointing. In his opening address to the state legislature, the
governor, Davis Waite, endorsed only the idea of voting rights in municipal
elections for Colorado's women, rather than full equal suffrage. Still, Populist
legislators went on to take the lead in forwarding legislation for full suffrage
rights for women during their 1893 session. Bills were introduced by Populist
members in both the House and Senate, although the Senate would ultimately
wait for the House to settle on its version of a full suffrage bill before taking
any real action on the issue.[25]

What would become the enabling legislation for a referendum on woman
suffrage was introduced in the House by a Populist, J. T. Heath. A fruit farmer
from the western part of the state, Heath – like the 1881 suffrage bill sponsor,
Brush – reflected the agricultural roots of the state's suffrage sentiment. Heath's
bill, introduced early in the legislative session, would face weeks of wrangling
in the House before its passage. But at each important juncture, this time the
suffrage measure drew enough support to overcome legislative obstacles. This
time, enough legislators seemed convinced of a need to be responsive to the
demands for woman suffrage in the state – demands which they had heard
clearly articulated not only from women organized in suffrage associations
and the WCTU, but also from already enfranchised men organized in a strong
Farmers' Alliance and labor unions.

Referral to the committee on elections and appointments presented the first
hurdle for the suffrage measure. After ten days of consideration, the committee
reported back with a split position on the measure: of the eight committee
members, only three supported its passage. The partisan division on the committee was marked, with the only two Populists on the committee lined up
in support of the measure, and four of the five Republicans signing on to
the adverse report (the lone Democrat sided with the Republican majority).
Despite the majority of opposition registered on the committee, a motion from
the House floor to accept the minority report of the committee and push the
bill forward through the legislative process was carried by a vote of thirty-nine

[25] Partisan composition of the state legislature in *Rules and Joint Rules of the Senate and House
of Representatives and Standing Committees of Both Houses of the Ninth General Assembly*
(Denver: The Smith Brooks Printing Company, 1893). Waite's remarks in *House Journal of
the General Assembly of the State of Colorado* (Denver: The Smith-Brooks Printing Company,
1893), 49–121. Knights of Labor endorsement reported in the *Leadville Daily and Evening
Chronicle* (January 10, 1893) and Farmers' Alliance endorsement in the *Greeley Tribune*
(January 5, 1893).

in favor and twenty-one opposed. Here, too, a partisan division was evident, but not as stark. Only three of the House's twenty-seven Populists failed to live up to their party's endorsement of woman suffrage and cast their votes against the minority report, but the Populist supporters were joined by a third of the thirty-five Republican representatives and three of the five House Democrats. At this point in the legislative process, then, the bill's treatment suggested that legislators did not see the enfranchisement of women as exclusively beneficial to the Populists, although certainly a Populist interest in the bill was registered. Support drawn from more than one party, that is, hints at a programmatic enfranchisement, rather than strategic enfranchisement, response to woman suffrage.

Indeed, the incentives for the programmatic enfranchisement of Colorado's women had been clearly spelled out in the 1892 campaign. Although Populist legislators should surely have been responsive to farmer and labor organizations' articulated demands because of their centrality to the new party organization, so too should have legislators from the major parties who faced strong farmer and/or labor constituencies within their districts. The sudden ascendancy of the Populist Party through the support of those farmer and labor constituencies ought to have communicated the electoral consequences of ignoring those constituents' demands. Failure of major party legislators from districts with significant farmer or labor interests to be responsive risked not only turning over their own seats in the next election, but also foreclosing the possibility of their party recouping seats from districts that had been taken by the Populists in the last election.

With a roll call vote taken on the motion to adopt the minority report in favor of the suffrage bill, it is possible to test this argument that the legislators' understanding of and incentives on the issue were driven by the vote-wielding coalitions that had endorsed women's enfranchisement: farmers' organizations and labor unions. Although direct measures of the presence of farm and labor organizations in each legislative district are not systematically available, the U.S. Census provides information on the relative presence of farms and manufacturing interests in each county, enabling sensible proxies for the presence of the key pro-suffrage coalitions in House members' districts. If the programmatic model explains the response of the Colorado House in 1893, then major party legislators willing to push the woman suffrage measure past its adverse majority committee report should be from districts with greater farming and/or labor interests than those who were not.

Table 2.2 summarizes the statistical assessment of the argument that Colorado legislators were responding to woman suffrage within the programmatic enfranchisement model. The top section of the table displays the average presence of farmer and labor interests in the districts of four groups of legislators: major party legislators voted for the minority report, major party legislators who voted against it, major party legislators that failed to vote, and all of the Populist legislators. Comparison of these means suggests that

TABLE 2.2. *Votes on Minority Committee Report on Woman Suffrage by District Characteristics, Colorado House 1893*

		Farmers	Labor
		Mean Farms Per 100 Population	Mean Per Capita Investment in Manufacturing (logged)
	For	6.2	3.6
	(n = 15)	(5.2)	(1.3)
Major party legislators	*Against*	4.9	3.1
	(n = 19)	(4.7)	(1.8)
	Not voting	2.7	3.3
	(n = 4)	(2.2)	(1.9)
All Populist legislators	(n = 27)	4.0	3.0
		(3.6)	(1.2)
Regression coefficients, major party legislators	(n = 34)	.09[**]	.28[**]

[**] p < .01, two-tailed t-test.
Note: Standard deviations of means in parentheses.
Sources: House Journal of the General Assembly of the State of Colorado, 1893; U.S. Census, 1890.

those major party House members who supported the motion to move the woman suffrage bill past its first legislative hurdle were from districts in which farmer and/or labor interests were more widespread, consistent with the programmatic enfranchisement model expectation. Major party supporters of the motion not only had greater farming and labor presences in their districts than all other major party legislators, but they also faced heavier farmer and labor concentrations than the average Populist. The fact that the nearly unanimously supportive Populist legislators faced, on average, less farmer-labor influence in their districts than major party supporters is consistent with the argument that Populists had not only district-level incentives, but also party organization level incentives for being responsive to demands for woman suffrage.

Finally, the bottom section of Table 2.2 presents the coefficients from a regression model that uses both the farmer and labor measures to predict major party legislators' support of the motion to adopt the minority committee report. Placing both measures into this single model even more directly assesses the original argument that those legislators' facing stronger concentrations of at least one of these two key constituencies should be more likely to support the advancement of the suffrage legislation, and that their propensity to support the bill should be greater the larger the presence of these interests were. The estimated positive and statistically significant coefficients are consistent with this argument, and Figure 2.1 illustrates the effects estimated through a comparison of the probabilities of support for the minority committee report predicted by the regression model. The first two columns highlight the differences between

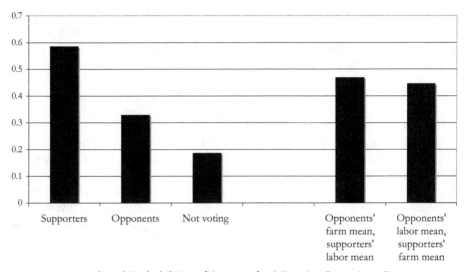

FIGURE 2.1. Predicted Probabilities of Support for Minority Committee Report.

supporters and opponents created by their district characteristics. Although a major party legislator from a district that had the same levels of farmer and labor interests as the average supporter's had a nearly 60 percent probability of being supportive of the minority report, his counterpart from a district that looked like the average opponent's had slightly more than a 30 percent probability of casting his vote in favor. The last two columns of the figure highlight how far in the direction of supportiveness a greater concentration of *either* farmer or labor interests could push legislators. For both a legislator from a district with the opponents' mean level of farming interest (4.9) but the supporters' mean level of labor interest (3.6), and a legislator with the opponents' level of labor interest (3.1) but the supporters' level of farming interest (6.2), the predicted probability of support for the minority report would reach near 50 percent. Particularly given the geographic spread of farms and laborers, suffragists clearly benefited from having both groups on their side during this legislative session.[26]

Once delivered to the House from the Elections Committee, the woman suffrage bill faced several more legislative challenges. As a bill proposing a constitutional amendment, the measure was subject to referral to the committee on revision and constitution, and faced another floor vote on whether it should be delivered out of committee for further consideration. Challenges also

[26] The regression model includes only the farming and labor variables and a constant term, and was run only on the thirty-four major party legislators who voted on the motion to adopt the minority report. The estimated constant term is −.98 with a standard error of .45, and the adjusted R-squared is .20.

arose when supportive legislators attempted to place the bill on the House's calendar for consideration by the committee of the whole. And at one point, one
particularly adversarial Republican from Denver motioned to disable the bill by
striking its enacting clause. NAWSA's *History of Woman Suffrage* reports that
two women suffragists – Minnie Reynolds and Louise Tyler, both members of
the state's WCTU and the reconvened state suffrage association – were lobbying the legislators throughout to encourage the bill's progress. Although no
other record of their effort has been located to detail or substantiate Reynolds
and Tyler's activities, it is clear that the bill benefited at each point in its jour-
ney through the legislature from the same basic coalition of House members.
Thus, if the lobbying activity had any effect, it seems it was simply to keep
legislators reminded of the constituency pressures that put woman suffrage on
the agenda in the first place. In this effort, the woman suffrage lobbyists were
aided by Farmers' Alliance and labor union organizations. One petition to the
legislature spelled the electoral pressure out particularly clearly, announcing
that "[t]he Trades Assembly of the City of Aspen, Colorado, composed of
duly elected delegates from nine different trades union organizations and one
Farmers' Alliance, *embracing a large voting population within their numbers*,
hereby petition your honorable body to pass the bill submitting the question
of female suffrage to the voters of Colorado."[27]

By the time the woman suffrage bill reached a vote on its final passage in the
House, little had changed in the coalitions in support of and opposition to the
measure. The bill passed by a margin similar to that which carried the minority
report: thirty-four House members voted for the bill and twenty-seven against
it. Indeed, only six members who had voted for the minority report defected
to vote against the bill on its final passage. One of those six explained his vote
away by claiming that he had only voted against the measure because he feared
it would not pass, and he wanted to be able to motion for a reconsideration
of the vote. Reconsideration could only be called for by a legislator on the
prevailing side of vote. Two legislators switched from opposition to support
across the two votes, and a few only registered a vote on one or the other.
With so little movement, it is difficult to offer any systematic account of why
any legislator might have changed his mind, but it is clear that the original
coalitional lines were fairly well held.

As it had in the House, woman suffrage legislation in the Senate faced
difficulties throughout the legislative process. Although two different woman
suffrage bills had been introduced in the Senate – one for municipal suffrage
and one for full equal suffrage – by Populists, that body chose to take no real
action until the outcome on the House had been decided. Both Senate bills were
referred to the committee on privileges and elections. Despite being constituted

---

[27] *History of Woman Suffrage*, vol. IV, p. 511. Petition and challenges to suffrage bill in *House
Journal of the General Assembly of the State of Colorado* (Denver: The Smith-Brooks Printing
Company, 1893), 708–09, 712, 757–58, 795. Emphasis added in quoted passage.

by just one supportive Populist and four major party legislators who would remain opponents of woman suffrage through the Senate's final vote on the issue, the committee forwarded a qualified adverse report on both measures. Although the committee's report announced that it was opposed to either suffrage measure, it stated that it chose to report the full suffrage bill "so that the whole subject of women suffrage many be considered by the Senate." Still, the report went on to recommend that the Senate's bill be tabled nonetheless, because the House already had a full suffrage bill under consideration, which "if favorably acted upon by the House will be before the Senate; and if the House refuses to pass the same bill it is useless for the Senate to discuss the measure." This report was accepted by the body without a roll call vote. And so the Senate waited for the House bill.

On its arrival in the Senate, the adopted House measure was referred to the same committee that had considered the Senate measures. Despite its earlier nominal endorsement of reporting out a suffrage measure for the sake of its discussion by the Senate body, this time the committee attempted to stall such deliberation by recommending referral to a special committee on constitutional amendments. The committee's recommendation, however, was challenged by one of the Senate's vocal Populist suffrage supporters, and the House bill was instead referred from the elections committee to the committee of the whole. Suffrage supporters also faced challenges in placing discussion of the suffrage bill on the legislative calendar. When the bill was finally called up for a vote on final passage, however, the Senate delivered a sufficient majority to carry the measure: twenty in favor and just ten opposed. Although the small number of voting members in the Senate makes statistical analysis of the vote equivocal, it is clear that Populist support was key. Eleven of the twenty supportive senators were members of the Populist Party.[28]

Delivering Votes for Women at the Polls

Success in the legislature did not guarantee that Colorado would become an equal suffrage state. The issue still faced a statewide popular referendum, a challenge the state's suffragists knew from previous experience was especially daunting. And as the state's suffrage organization was small in both numbers and assets, support from outside the state suffrage association would clearly be necessary to mount a successful campaign. Securing that support was at

---

[28] The Senate also did not conduct roll call votes on any of the procedural motions regarding the woman suffrage legislation. Senate consideration in *Senate Journal of the General Assembly of the State of Colorado* (Denver: The Smith-Brooks Printing Company, 1893), 226–27, 401, 445, 679, 694–96, 842, 887–88, 909, 1062, 1513, 1585–87. A challenge to discussion of the bill in the Senate was also reported in the *Aspen Weekly Times* (March 25, 1893). The house also needed to vote on the measure an additional time, as the Senate had made slight amendments. That vote was carried thirty-five to twenty-one by the same basic coalition of members who had passed it originally (*House Journal*, 2140).

times both a delicate and difficult task for Colorado's suffragists, as they navigated the incentives for and consequences of assistance from the national
suffrage leadership, the WCTU, and the state's political parties. Yet, although
the particular campaign efforts of the state and national suffrage organizations
were surely of consequence, ultimately, the results of the referendum would
depend critically on the actions of suffrage coalition partners whose organizations were equipped and practiced in delivering electoral results. This crucial
political point was one that seemed acknowledged in only fits and starts by
suffragists throughout the state campaign, but crystallized in its aftermath.

Although the enabling legislation for the suffrage referendum had been
signed into law by Governor Waite in April, it would be several months until a
campaign for its passage would be underway. The state's suffrage association
first reconstituted itself under new leadership. A woman with no known ties
to any other reform organization, Martha Pease, was elected president, and
Ellis Meredith, daughter of the editor of the Denver paper the *Rocky Mountain News*, was chosen as the vice president. Other offices of the organization
were filled by women with more obvious ties to the WCTU and/or the Populist
Party, including the legislative lobbyists Tyler and Reynolds. Rather than to the
WCTU or the Populist Party, however, the state association turned for its primary support to NAWSA. Meredith apparently took the lead in this effort, as
her collected papers contain regular letters to and from the national leadership
beginning in June.

NAWSA leaders were dubious of the chances for suffrage success in Colorado, and Meredith faced a significant challenge to convince them otherwise.
Correspondence between Lucy Stone and Henry Blackwell reveals that Stone
was particularly doubtful from the start. Stone articulated the concerns that
Colorado suffragists had "no money and only one small society," which led
her to the conclusion that "Colorado seems to me a hopeless case, but we are
to confer once more with the Colorado woman [Meredith]." Blackwell was
far more optimistic, suggesting that Colorado could be carried if the suffragists
could enlist the aid of "1. The Republican machine of Colorado 2. The Labor
Organizations & 3. The Newspapers" to "get a committee of men at each voting precinct of Colorado" to promote the ballot measure. Although it actually
foreshadowed the eventual strategy of the suffrage association in Colorado,
Blackwell's assessment did not seem to carry much weight with Stone or other
NAWSA leaders at this point.

The promised conference between Meredith and Stone took place weeks
after Stone and Blackwell's exchange, while both women were in attendance at
the Chicago's World Fair. Stone's follow-up letter to Meredith suggests that,
although she still had little confidence in the possibility of woman suffrage
passing in Colorado, Stone was willing to have NAWSA start to investigate the
matter in greater earnest. Thus, even though Stone still expressed to Meredith
that she felt "the whole case is at a disadvantage from the fact that there was
no preparation in advance in Colorado," she went on to concede that NAWSA

"must see what can be done." Carrie Chapman Catt, the prominent NAWSA organizer who would take over as its president after Susan B. Anthony, followed Stone's letter with one of her own, however, in which she laid out much more forcefully NAWSA's stand on the Colorado matter. "[T]he general sentiment," Catt informed Meredith, "is that something ought to be done to help Colo[rado], but there is no money in [the] National American [Woman Suffrage Association] treasury and all effort is being pushed to get financial aid from all [local] ESA Clubs for Kansas." The reason for this stance was that the eastern organizers had concluded Kansas was "the one place where there was a reasonable hope of carrying such an amendment." Colorado would receive some help from NAWSA, Catt intimated, but only as an instrumental aid for the Kansas woman suffrage referendum campaign on which the organization was focusing. "I have talked with no one who feels there is the slightest hope of success in Colorado, yet everyone feels that a small vote there will have a disadvantageous effect on Kansas and a larger vote would help."[29]

Pushback from NAWSA's leadership in part reflected a lack of knowledge of Colorado's circumstances. Catt seemed unfamiliar with the support that had already been proffered by the Populists, Farmers' Alliance, and labor organizations. She wrote off Democratic support, claiming that "as a party they have been against us," despite the fact that Colorado had just witnessed a fusion of Democrats and Populists that included an agreement on woman suffrage. And she seemed to know nothing about the electoral laws that would govern the referendum, which included both a newly adopted Australian secret ballot and a provision that the ballot measure would carry with just a simple majority of the votes cast on the issue. The former fact meant that partisan considerations in ballot printing were a moot concern; the latter gave Colorado a lower threshold for passing its suffrage amendment than nearly every other state in the Union. Of these ignorances and others on Catt's part, Meredith quickly wrote back to the NAWSA leader. "[W]e feel we have twice as much show as Kansas to get suffrage," Meredith wrote, and then proceeded to offer a litany of reasons for her claim. She informed Catt of the electoral law considerations, of the support already given and promised by Populists and labor organizations, and of the fact that the Colorado suffragists had observed "not a single particle of organized opposition in the state." Meredith also challenged the NAWSA plan for campaigning that Catt had conveyed, pointing out why some of the suggested speakers would not be advisable and who among Colorado politicians could and should be approached for advice or support. And she argued that while she agreed with NAWSA's plan that suffragists should remain non-partisan in

[29] Letters from Stone to Blackwell May 21, 1893 and from Blackwell to Stone May 19, 1893 are quoted in Leslie Wheeler, *Loving Warriors: A Revealing Portrait of an Unprecedented Marriage* (New York: Dial, 1981), 350–51. Letters from Stone to Meredith, June 12, 1893 and Catt to Meredith, June 23, 1893 (Ellis Meredith Papers, Colorado Historical Society, Denver, Colorado).

their campaign in order to draw as broad a base of support as possible, they perhaps should look to connect to the silver issue, which was still dominating public discussion.[30]

Meredith's thorough review of the situation in Colorado apparently won Catt and other NAWSA leaders over. Catt wrote back that she had been convinced that "there is as good and fair a chance for carrying Colorado as Kansas" and that "you [Colorado suffragists] are not being treated quite fairly." She conveyed that Blackwell, Stone, and Anthony agreed on the new assessment and that the organization was working to conjure resources accordingly. Ultimately they would raise the funds to send Catt to canvass the state in the fall and to support some other speakers. Catt stressed that her initial work should be small meetings and, especially, speaking engagements during meetings of "any Chatauqua Assemblies... Populist or Knights of Labor picnics... Republican or Democratic clubs or anything of that sort." As Anthony justified this strategy, the NAWSA leaders felt that "for all possible assemblies of men to pass such [suffrage-endorsing] resolutions will help create sentiment on our side much faster than anything we can do." In their efforts to build as broad a base of support for the suffrage measure as possible, Catt and Anthony not only insisted that the campaign remain "quiet" in this way until just a few weeks before the vote, when larger public meetings could be added, but also that a strict nonpartisan, single-issue stance be taken by the Colorado suffragists. "[K]now nothing – push nothing – but suffrage," Anthony implored Meredith.[31]

For the most part, it seems, the approach advocated by NAWSA was followed. CESA undertook most of its organizational work in Denver, where its leadership was based, holding meetings and canvassing door to door on the issue. Work to reach the rest of the state was a combination of Catt's in-person canvassing efforts and a correspondence campaign by CESA that included a newspaper column printed in various newspapers throughout the state and contacts with county party conventions asking them to adopt pro-suffrage platforms. Catt's work was intended to establish local associations of suffragists throughout the state that would carry out their own canvassing and meeting campaigns once she left. Although systematic evidence on the effectiveness of these efforts in unavailable, newspaper accounts suggest that the local associations left behind varied from a mere handful of women who expressed some interest to a real organization that indeed undertook its own canvassing efforts. CESA's correspondence efforts aimed to paint the suffrage issue as a widely supported nonpartisan issue throughout the state. Thus, their column offered quotes of supportive statements from a variety of public

---

[30] Letter from Meredith to Catt, June 30, 1893 (Ellis Meredith Papers, Colorado Historical Society, Denver, Colorado).

[31] Letters from Catt to Meredith, July 5, 1893 and July 16, 1893; and from Anthony to Meredith, July 18, 1893 (Ellis Meredith Papers, Colorado Historical Society, Denver, Colorado).

figures and from newspapers of various partisan sympathies. For similar reasons, CESA distanced itself from the WCTU. Although the suffrage-supporting state WCTU was better resourced than the suffrage association, CESA and NAWSA leaders worried about voters linking suffrage with a push for prohibition.

There was one notable departure in the Colorado campaign from the original NAWSA advocated plan. Despite the directive to push for suffrage as a stand-alone issue, both Catt and the CESA ultimately attempted to link suffrage with free silver – a tactic that had been advocated by Meredith from the start simply because she perceived the silver issue to be so widely popular. The overtures to a connection between suffrage and silver, however, lacked much substantiation. The CESA column, for example, simply heralded that "[a] vote for equal suffrage is a vote for free silver. The man who goes to the polls . . . and votes to exclude the ballots of half of the citizens of Colorado from the ballot box on account of sex is a traitor to the white metal and to the best interests of the state." No reasoning for equating the two issues was given. Similarly, Catt at times chose to open her suffrage addresses with her personal endorsement of the free coinage of silver, but apparently stopped short of claiming that the suffrage association was similarly supportive, or that woman suffrage would bring more votes for free silver.

Although their efforts were certainly greater than those mounted by organized suffragists in the 1877 campaign, just how much of a role the CESA and NAWSA – or the independently campaigning WCTU – played in shaping the broader pro-suffrage campaign in the state is unclear. Farmer and labor organizations as well as the Populist Party, of course, had supported the issue before the CESA had organized itself. Those organizational endorsements continued through the referendum campaign season, and public pronouncement thereof regularly appeared in newspapers across the state. And although the organized suffragists had hoped to keep the issue nonpartisan, the state's Populists appeared to be attempting to claim the issue as their own, to fully link woman suffrage with its partisan interests. Public pronouncements, such as one made by Lafayette Pence, one of Colorado's two Populist representatives in the U.S. Congress, tried to assert such issue ownership by pointing to the Populists' early endorsement of voting rights for women. In Pence's words, "[t]he Populists declared for woman suffrage years ago and now everybody else is beginning to think it is a good idea." Moreover, the Populists were actively courting the suffrage association. Meredith wrote to Anthony in the late summer that "the Populists have been trying to get us to come out for them." Although Meredith claimed that the CESA would "not hear of it" she went on to admit that "individually many of us are with them, but the association is and will remain strictly non-partisan."

What is clear about the referendum campaign is that it ultimately had the full backing of the state Populist Party organization. Partisan pronouncements were common in Populist-friendly newspapers, such as one in the *Aspen Weekly*

Times that instructed its readers to "[r]emember that the populist party of Pitkin county is pledged to the proposition of giving to women the right to suffrage. In making the canvass of the county in behalf of the people's party ticket this question should not be ignored. Advocate this reform movement." Positive editorials that linked woman suffrage with democratic ideals and reform, with the cause of free silver, and with thus with Populist politics were not uncommon. Nearer to Election Day, some papers offered explicit instructions on casting ballots in favor of the suffrage issue. At times these were statements of principled support, such as the directive to "let every man who loves his mother, his sister, his wife or his sweetheart or who respects the female sex and is a friend of justice, get out and vote for the amendment to the state constitution for woman suffrage this fall." But there were quite often explicitly Populist partisan mandates, like the *Fort Collins Courier*'s reminder that "the populist convention endorsed the equal suffrage law as passed last winter. Now let us approve it and don't fail to put your X opposite 'Equal Suffrage Approved.'" Although it is true that the suffrage ballot measure also garnered at least a nominal endorsement from the state Republican Party and a number of county Democratic organizations, evidence of those parties' efforts to actively promote the cause was far less pervasive than the Populists' push.

With so many political players in the state publicly backing the ballot measure, suffragists and newspapers alike speculated in the weeks before the vote that woman suffrage would, in fact, carry at the polls. Those speculations were confirmed on Election Day, when Colorado delivered the first successful statewide referendum on the issue of woman suffrage conducted in the United States by a vote of 35,798 in favor and 29,451 opposed. Although a number of the actors in the referendum campaign were quick to claim credit for the suffrage victory – notably the organized suffragists, the WCTU, and the Populist Party – the question remains of what influences actually shaped the votes of Colorado's men. Without individual-level data to bring to bear, answers to that question are imprecise. Yet with county-level vote returns it is possible to answer related questions about whether greater presences of the various political forces active during the suffrage campaign were predictors of greater support for woman suffrage in those counties. The county-level support for woman suffrage is simply modeled as a function of county-level indicators of each of those forces: Populists, farmers' organizations, labor organizations, the WCTU, and suffrage organization.

Developing measures for some of the pro-suffrage forces at the county level is more difficult than it is for others. Populist strength can be captured rather straightforwardly through the county-level returns for governor in the previous election. The same proxies for farmer and labor organization presence employed in the earlier analyses of legislative behavior, drawn from U.S. census county-level data on farms and manufacturing capital, can be employed here. Records of the Colorado WCTU provide counts of the number of active WCTU members in each county as a direct measure of their organizational presence.

TABLE 2.3. *Predictors of County-level Support for Woman Suffrage Referendum, Colorado 1893*

	Regression Coefficient	Statewide Mean
Percent gubernatorial vote for Populist candidate	.71**	46.5
Farms per 100 population	.97*	7.7
Per capita investment in manufacturing (logged)	.01	24.1
Members of local WCTU per 1,000 population	.72	2.1
Percent gubernatorial vote for Republican candidate	.26	42.9

* p < .05, **p < .01 two-tailed t-test.
Note: Regression n = 48.
Sources: U.S. Census, 1890; *Fourteenth Annual Report of the Convention of Colorado Woman's Christian Temperance Union, 1893; House Journal of the General Assembly of the State of Colorado, 1893.*

Accounting for the work of organized suffragists – the CESA and Catt – is more difficult, as no systematic record of that work remains. Yet, because a main focus of the CESA effort was to build broad support through contact with existing organizations of men like labor unions and farmers' organizations, their main influence would be expected to channel through those forces. Although most of these organizations were already active on the suffrage issue before the campaign, there is no record of any actors other than the CESA attempting to press the Republican Party organization into garnering support for the suffrage measure. Thus, organized suffragist influence might be gauged best indirectly through assessing whether there was any influence of Republican Party strength on the county vote returns.

The results of the model predicting county-level support are found in Table 2.3. To aid in the assessment of the model's estimated effects, Table 2.3 also provides the statewide mean of each variable in the model, and Figures 2.2 and 2.3 illustrate the influences of the key predictors. In short, the model offers strong support of the Populists' claim to influence on support for woman suffrage, and little support for idea that women organized in the WCTU or CESA delivered support for the ballot measure through the referendum campaign. It also suggests that the endorsements of farmers' organizations mattered beyond the Populist realm, whereas labor union support did not. As Table 2.3 highlights, the only forces found to be statistically significant predictors of county-level support for the woman suffrage measure are Populist strength and farming interests.

Just how much Populist Party strength and support for woman suffrage were intertwined is made clear in Figure 2.2, which displays the predicted support for the woman suffrage measure at the polls at the county level at various levels of Populist voting in the previous election. In order to give a sense of how Populism shaped the woman suffrage outcome in the typical Colorado county,

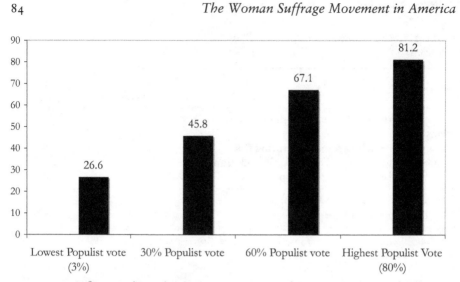

FIGURE 2.2. Influence of Populist Support on Percent of County's Vote Cast for Woman Suffrage Referendum, Colorado 1893. *Note:* Values are predicted from the regression model displayed in Table 2.3. All variables other than Populist support are set at the statewide mean.

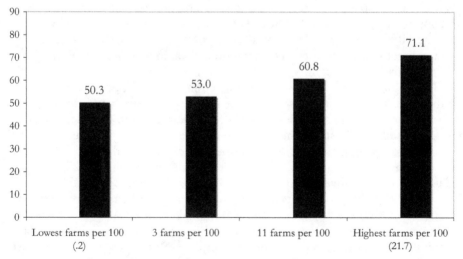

FIGURE 2.3. Influence of Farming Interests on Percent of County's Vote Cast for Woman Suffrage Referendum, Colorado, 1893. *Note:* Values are predicted from the regression model displayed in Table 2.3. All variables other than farming interests are set at the statewide mean.

independent of any other factors that might have shaped suffrage support, the predicted suffrage support values were generated from the regression model in Table 2.3, with the values for all variables other than the Populist vote set at their statewide means. Four levels of Populist voting were selected based on the range of actual observed values in the 1892 election: the lowest observed value of 3 percent, the highest observed value of 80 percent, and two values around which a number of counties clustered in the 1892 election, 30 percent and 60 percent. The increase from the minimal level of Populist sentiment to a strong, but still minority, electoral presence for the Populists of 30 percent, the figure illustrates, nearly doubled the amount of support registered for the woman suffrage referendum – even though woman suffrage would still have been a losing proposition in those counties. In counties in which Populists dominated the partisan environment, the last two columns of the figure illustrate, woman suffrage support also decisively dominated at the polls. Where the Populists reached at least 60 percent in the 1892 returns, woman suffrage was likely to gain super-majorities of two-thirds or greater of the votes cast in the 1893 referendum.

Figure 2.3 illustrates the independent effect of farming interests on woman suffrage support, which although not insignificant, was much smaller than the Populist Party influence. This figure was generated in the same manner as Figure 2.2, this time with all variables except farming interests set at their statewide means and four levels of farming interests chosen for their representation of the actual range of farming interests present across Colorado's counties. Consistent with the idea of farms per 100 population as a measure of the electoral presence of organized farming interests in the counties, the figure reflects that significant farming interests in a county were needed to deliver a real bump for the suffrage measure. Little difference in registered support for woman suffrage is reflected between a county with the absolute minimal farming presence of .2 farms per 100 population and one with 3 farms per 100 population. Where farmers were a dominant portion of the electorate, however – in counties where there was one farm for every five residents – support for woman suffrage was more than twenty percentage points higher. The agricultural roots of suffrage sentiment and organizational pressure, then, seemed important to the referendum's positive outcome, above and beyond the purely partisan Populist push. Although their independent contribution to the referendum's outcome does not look as great as that delivered by the partisan organization, as a coalitional partner, farmers' organizations, it seems, delivered their own pressure in favor of the pro-suffrage ballot. This fact offers some support of the outcome as a more programmatic – rather than strategic – enfranchisement result. That coalitions of voters that stretched beyond the bounds of simple partisan divisions shaped the deliverance of the voting rights policy change diminishes the likelihood that a purely partisan strategy of enfranchising women in the simple interest of capturing the "women's vote" was a politically sensible impetus.

Spreading Understanding of Woman Suffrage – Feedback to Partisans in Other States

With the Populist Party playing such a key role in the story of the adoption of woman suffrage in Colorado, it might seem that the effort was one of strategic enfranchisement; that Populists worked to enfranchise women expecting them to deliver their votes to the party in appreciation. As politicians had little information about the partisan behavior of women voters, assuming women would reward the party that enfranchised them might not seem entirely unreasonable. The information that Colorado women offered to partisan politicians after their enfranchisement, however, undermined the feasibility of a successful strategic enfranchisement strategy. Women did not become a voting bloc for the new party. As prominent Colorado Populists were quick to underscore, in both private correspondence and public statements, the conduct and results of the 1894 election suggested that women voted in much the same way their male counterparts did, and that they certainly did not cohere politically just because of their sex, nor because of some gendered political interest.

The 1894 campaign season made it clear that partisans saw electoral benefit in being seen as responsible for the provision of woman suffrage, as political parties attempted to credit claim in their campaigns. Populists and Republicans debated each other about which party had *truly* supported the suffrage extension. Populists highlighted their party's superior voting record on the issue in the state legislature, underscoring how many more Republican than Populist members had voted against the enabling legislation. The support of the Populist masses was also touted, as the party pointed out the strong correlation between the level of support for its ticket and the level of support for woman suffrage at the polls. Republicans attempted to substantiate their own claims to the suffrage mantle by questioning the Populist commitment to the woman suffrage cause, implying their party was the home of more true believers in voting rights for women. A story questioning Governor Waite's true position on the issue, for example, made the rounds of several papers. The account offered was one of "a gentleman well acquainted with Governor Waite" who insisted that the governor had voiced objection to the issue before the Populist convention. Of course, although the governors' reported position of "I'll work and vote against such a plank in the platform, and if it carries against my objection I'll quit the convention," was unsubstantiated, neither had the governor come into office with a position in favor of women's full enfranchisement.[32] Rather than as an appeal to "women," however, it would seem more sensible that such credit claiming for woman suffrage would have been an appeal to the underlying constituent coalitions – farmer and laborer groups – that had demonstrated an interest in the measure.

---

[32] Quoted passage from *Fairplay Flume* (October 25, 1894), which cites its source for the story as the *Creede Sentinel*. See also *Aspen Weekly Times* (September 15, 1894; November 3, 1894).

Indeed, despite the parties' appeals, the results of the 1894 election offered little evidence that Colorado's women made their ballot choices based on the parties' suffrage records. Populist support dropped off in the 1894 election, and Waite was badly routed in his attempt at reelection to the governor's office. In turn, the former governor played a key role in disseminating the information that women as voters were unresponsive to the argument that they should be loyal to the party that spearheaded their enfranchisement. Waite delivered his message through both public and private venues, making statements to the press as well as writing to reformist politicians in other states giving his interpretation of the election results, including what they implied for the promise of woman suffrage as a strategy for Populist electoral success. And when *The New York Times* reported on the end of Populist rule in Colorado in 1894, the paper noted its concurrence with the comments of "Gov. Waite, in explaining his defeat, [who] admits that the women voters did it."[33]

Not only had women failed to become a voting base for their enfranchisers, but even suffrage activists – those women who had expressed a keen interest in their voting rights – were not loyal to the party. This point was publicly, and emphatically, aired by Governor Waite's wife, Celia Crane Waite. Celia Waite had been active in encouraging the Populists to deliver the voting rights change, and was critical of other suffrage advocates' abandonment of the party. Her comments on the matter were carried in newspapers around the country. In November of 1894, for example, the *New York World* published Mrs. Waite's accounting of woman suffrage in Colorado, which was particularly disapproving of Capitol Hill women – the society ladies that had come to populate suffrage organizations in Denver – for allegedly voting for the Republican ticket:

It was due entirely to the efforts of the Populist party that women were given the ballot at all. They have simply gone and cut the throat of the party which gave them the right to vote and have disgraced their womanhood.... I know lots of them who sold their votes as the men did and were not ashamed of it, either. There were numbers of them who sold out for a package of chewing gum and a carriage ride.... The women of Denver and Capitol Hill especially have voted for the return of the saloon element to power and this is what they have pretended to be so much against.[34]

In addition to the immediate messages fed to other places and politicians about the political meaning of women's voting rights in Colorado, the state also became a perennial touchstone for such information over the course of the suffrage movement. In the years following the enfranchisement of women in Colorado, media outlets regularly turned to the state for information about the political consequences of women's enfranchisement. The regularity with which

---

[33] "Women Saved Colorado," *New York Times*, November 17, 1894.
[34] Quoted in the *New York World*, November 14, 1894.

Colorado was consulted as the source for information about how woman suffrage worked was, in fact, noted by the author of a 1906 piece in the news journal *The Outlook* on "How Woman's Suffrage Works in Colorado." Noting that women had been fully enfranchised for some time in three other states (Wyoming, Utah, and Idaho), the author observed that nonetheless "most people regard women's suffrage in Colorado as *the* type." They turned, the author noted, to the state for two kinds of information: information on whether the nature of electoral politics was changed by a female presence in the electorate and information on what type of women voted.

The political meaning information delivered by the media over the years regularly reinforced the initial messages of Waite and his ousted Populist Party. Using observations of the general conduct of elections in the state, for example, the *Outlook* piece drove home the claim that women did not change the conduct of electoral politics, that they "had no effect upon the kind of order and decorum maintained at polling places" and that their presence did nothing to change the fact that "[b]allot boxes are stuffed and stolen." The author then used registration and turnout data gathered from what he deemed "representative" districts in Pueblo county to demonstrate the registration and turnout patterns of different "types" of women – those of the "best residences;" those married to skilled, native-born laborers; those married to unskilled, immigrant laborers; those who resided in brothels or female rooming houses; those who lived in ranching communities; and those who resided in agricultural centers. Although the author did not offer explicit assertions on the electoral choices of each type of woman, his preoccupation with the relative involvement in electoral politics of each group clearly reflected a sentiment that the groups made different political choices. Indeed, the author pointed to his personal knowledge of a class of "good women, thank Heaven!... who vote because it is their duty... because they feel that they must help to overcome the votes of the vicious and depraved of their sex."[35] Similarly, the *Woman's Home Companion* ran an article in 1909 attributed to "a Denver politician" that engaged the questions of whether women voted, and to what effect, in Colorado's capital city. The politician reinforced the refrain that women surely voted, but failed to do so as any sort of political unit or voting bloc:

...the woman voter is a political power to be reckoned with. In the State of Colorado fifty-one percent of the registered voters are women and in many districts, such as certain wards in Denver, the women voters outnumber the men at the ratio three to two. The woman voter, then, if she were a social unit, could do pretty much what she pleased, and the popular conception is that she is a social unit. 'If women had the vote,' we often hear, 'the saloons would be closed' or 'child labor would be abolished,' or some other evil would be checked. If the women of Denver voted as one woman plenty of good

[35] Lewis, Lawrence, "How Woman's Suffrage Works in Colorado," *The Outlook* (January 27, 1906). Emphasis in quotation appears in the original.

things would be done. But does she? Bless you, of course not! There are just as many different kinds of women voters as there are men voters.[36]

Although the information about women's partisan loyalties fed back to other states was discouraging of a strategic enfranchisement approach, suffragists became well aware of the need to establish some political meaning for woman suffrage – some reason, other than principled rights arguments, that others should actually institute such a policy change. What resulted was a concerted propagation of feedback about suffragists' support for their coalitional partners, particularly organized labor. It is important to note that the claim was one of the *movement's* support for its coalitional partners, not of support of "women" for labor causes. What was underscored was the extent to which labor goals were accomplished through cooperative pressure politics, not broad electoral threat from enfranchised women. It was a story of political resource exchange of the concurrent movements, and it gave organized suffragists unique leverage in securing protection of women's voting rights despite their inability to promise or demonstrate political cohesion from women.

Conclusion

There were clear lessons in the case of Colorado. Not only did it help define out possibilities for the strategic enfranchisement of women, but it helped clarify how electoral partisan incentives could nonetheless secure women's voting rights. It is difficult to overstate the importance of information about the success of coalitional politics. Such information undermined the messages from suffrage leaders like Anthony about keeping the issue of suffrage extracted from all other political debates and justified the expenditure of suffragists' resources on causes other than narrow campaigns for women's voting rights. Before the Colorado success, coalitional politics had, indeed, hurt the suffrage cause. Suffrage leaders were wary of coalitional politics in part because of the failures they witnessed when the causes of the temperance and suffrage movements were intertwined. Such failure, indeed, seemed part of the earlier history of woman suffrage in Colorado. What the 1893 success taught, however, was that not all coalitional politics were detrimental. The fate of woman suffrage rested not simply on whether or not it was interwoven with other interests, but rather, as the programmatic enfranchisement model specifies, on whether it was connected to interests that wielded sufficient electoral leverage to invest partisan interests in the deliverance of women's voting rights.

The Colorado case also made clear just how quickly electoral incentives could be rearranged, and thus how quickly the possibilities for winning women's voting rights could change. In 1891, winning woman suffrage was

---

[36] "Votes for Women: What They Look Like from the Inside," *Woman's Home Companion*, November 1909.

impossible in Colorado; a request to consider the idea was simply rebuffed by state lawmakers. In 1893, Colorado women were fully enfranchised – and politicians were expending effort to claim credit for that outcome. This sharp turn in Colorado was particularly helpful in clarifying that success was tied to engaging partisan interests in the cause because the other factors that might commonly be used to explain suffrage outcomes had not changed so quickly – certainly not gender norms and roles nor the resources of the suffrage movement. Suffragists now had evidence that they ought to be evaluating their chances in terms of the dynamics of state politics, and in terms of where and how electoral pressure could invest partisan organizations in overcoming what had previously seemed insurmountable hurdles of legislative process and public referenda.

Of course, just because Colorado had such lessons to offer does not mean that they were easily or uniformly learned. And there were questions about the politics of suffrage coalitions that the case left unanswered. In the Colorado case, success came with the key addition of an extremely successful third party to state politics. Was such an unusual electoral landscape necessary to leverage partisan interest? Could third parties help the suffrage cause even if they didn't win so many votes? Could interest group partners be effective in the absence of third party pressure? How would they do so? Colorado also did not answer a range of questions about building and maintaining coalitional partnerships. Were overlapping networks, such as the overlap of suffragist and farming organization interests that seemed to characterize Colorado key? Could resource exchange indeed help solidify partnerships? What choices did suffragists need to make to retain their partnerships and what might undo them? And finally, what were the implications for suffragists when state politics were uncompetitive and citizen groups were not generally active in electoral politics? All of these questions imply there is more to know about suffrage politics than the case of Colorado can offer, and they motivate the chapters that follow.

3

Programmatic Enfranchisement

Coalitional Strategies for Voting Rights

> First: Farmers – we must keep their interest and vote . . .
>
> Second: Socialists – of which almost all are friends of ours . . .
>
> Third: Laborers – while we have many of them, many more are not yet converted, and we need them . . .
>
> Fourth: The women of all of these classes need [suffrage] education . . .
>
> – Ruth A. Gay, President of the Oklahoma Woman
> Suffrage Association, 1911[1]

In its later years, the woman suffrage movement was interwoven into the fabric of American politics through its ties to farmers' and labor movements, and, by extension, third parties including the Populists and Progressives. It was these connections to groups doing business inside partisan politics, suffragists discovered, that gave the extension of voting rights to women sufficient appeal not only to entice legislators to vote in its favor, but also to convince political parties to help push the issue past legislative hurdles and public referenda. This politics of woman suffrage is what I have termed programmatic enfranchisement – when politicians act to make themselves accountable to a new group of voters in response to pressure from their current electorate.

Although success for the American woman suffrage movement would eventually come through such coalitional politics, the challenges suffrage activists faced in coming to that end are difficult to understate. There was a steep learning curve involved. Suffrage activists needed to realize the political benefit in expending their scarce resources in cultivating coalitions. This learning process was complicated by the fact that not all coalitions could, in fact, leverage

---

[1] Letter from Ruth A. Gay to (NAWSA vice president) Catharine Waugh McCulloch, February 28, 1911. McCulloch Papers.

sufficient political might to help the suffragists advance their cause, and so failed coalitional politics could stand in the way of seeing the promise of stronger partnerships. Moreover, partnerships with the sorts of groups capable of exerting electoral pressure were not always particularly easy to cultivate or maintain. The dominance of the movement, at least in many places and at the national level, by white, middle-class activists meant that there were issues of political identity and diverging preferences that could pose real challenges to coalition building and maintenance. Nonetheless, coalitional politics emerged and were translated into successful legislative and public referenda outcomes.

This chapter turns to the case of Michigan to illustrate a number of lessons about how both politicians and activists came to understand the issue of woman suffrage as one made imperative through the pressure of coalitional partners who exerted electoral leverage. Michigan displayed a common pattern of early discourse on woman suffrage, wherein the issue was devoid of much political meaning and argued in principled terms – and made no notable progress toward enactment. Michigan suffragists also learned from early failures that personal politics – relying on the inside leverage of politically well-connected suffrage advocates – were unable to invest the partisan interest necessary to actually deliver women's voting rights. When inside politics leveraged some movement on the issue in legislative politics, ultimate failure was simply delivered by expanding the scope of conflict to a public vote. Failure of an early coalition with the WCTU was also instructive about how the issue of woman suffrage garnered political definition. Michigan suffragists also learned about partisan interests in woman suffrage through the failure of an attempt to deliver voting rights to only a particular subset of women through strategic enfranchisement politics. Finally, suffragists in Michigan began to develop more politically promising coalitional strategies. Somewhat ironically, these coalitional politics began as would-be suffragists turned their central attention from suffrage to other causes in response to frustration with their failures in the state. Some invested effort in protective labor legislation and found partnerships with organized labor. Others were active in farmers' organizations. Although the work of investing these interest groups in the suffrage cause was new and complicated, it is clear that suffrage advocates ultimately understood it as key to their success. As the evidence in this chapter shows, when women's voting rights were finally delivered in the state in 1918, legislators' acquiescence was tied to the sense that their existing constituents harbored real interest in woman suffrage, particularly those tied to the interests represented by farmers' and labor organizations. Moreover, coalitions between woman suffrage advocates and these organizations were key to mobilizing voters to sign off on constitutional amendments presented to them at the polls. Yet, evidence from repeated attempts at passing women's voting rights beginning in 1911 also shows that even effective coalitional partnerships faced important challenges, including the engendering of opposition. In the case of Michigan, an increasingly agrarian and reformist-backed coalition encountered resistance from urban interests, which would include political machines.

Again, my argument about the programmatic enfranchisement politics of woman suffrage is that success came when partisan politicians were vulnerable to the demands of the groups interested in women's voting rights. Without such vulnerability, party politicians had no incentive to make themselves accountable to new voters – to pay the costs necessarily inherent to a larger electorate. Clearly, interest group politics varied; so too did political vulnerability. Such vulnerability came both from partisan struggles to maintain control of the state government and from legislators' individual electoral welfares. Although Michigan was a predominantly Republican state from the 1850s through 1918, the party's grasp did not go unchallenged. At times, Democrats surged close to taking the governors' office and began putting members in the House and Senate. In some of these instances, Democrats were helped along by Prohibition Party spoilers who siphoned voters from the Republican base, and in one instance – when Democrats actually took the executive office – the culprit was a decidedly successful Progressive Party. These were the times when the Republican Party needed to be most responsive, when it was most vulnerable to constituent demands. And of course legislators who wanted to keep their seats – and even in early statehood, some of them did – but who were hardly in safe territory, were vulnerable to demands as well. That is, electoral dynamics – not just coalitional partnerships – were important in defining the chances for woman suffrage.

To say that women interested in their own voting rights could not carry the day for woman suffrage without partnerships with organizations comprised of existing, male voters is not to say, however, that the work of Michigan's woman suffrage organizations was not essential. Building organizational capacity made suffrage groups attractive partners for political allies with other primary goals, such as prohibition, labor rights, and government reform. Fundraising, carrying out massive petition campaigns, monitoring elections – demonstrating effectiveness at all of these tasks increased the attractiveness of coalitions between suffrage advocates and other interest groups. For Michigan suffragists, it won them partnerships with Prohibitionists, labor unions, farmers' organizations, and, most effectively, the Grange and the Progressive Party. Ultimately, Grange and Progressive Party influences, which overlapped significantly in Michigan, would help Michigan suffragists carry the day in the legislature and at the polls. All along the way, the interest of other groups in women's voting rights gave meaning and consequence to the issue, for politicians and for the public.

Considering Political Meaning – Early Discussions of Woman Suffrage

That the programmatic – rather than strategic – enfranchisement model would be the key to success in Michigan seemed evident from its earliest contemplations. Discussions of woman suffrage among state lawmakers began to appear in the 1840s, even before organized demand for woman suffrage was viable. These early legislative considerations of woman suffrage emerged, as did the organized woman suffrage movement, in the wake of debate over the concept of universal male suffrage. Michigan legislators early on expressed doubts that admitting women to the electorate would greatly change its political makeup; it was argued that women currently bore influence on their husbands' votes, that granting them voting rights would only change vote totals, and perhaps the manner in which voters conducted themselves on Election Day. Indeed, notions of gender roles and women's subservience – political as well as social – to the men inside their kinship circles seemed part of the reason that politicians generally failed to perceive in women the promise a new, distinct voting bloc that would turn electoral tides. And these notions were starkly contrasted against the discussions of suffrage for non-white males, where expectation of a partisan advantage was quite commonly invoked.

The early impetus for discussing woman suffrage certainly seemed linked to the incongruence between arguing for "universal suffrage" and continuing to exclude women from the polls. When woman suffrage was first mentioned in Michigan legislative politics in 1849, for example, it was in a special committee report on revision of the state's constitution that made an unequivocal case for inclusion of universal suffrage "which reaches every resident citizen of the body politic, arrived at the age of majority" in a new state constitution. Although the committee seemed certain that the impetus of universal suffrage entailed male suffrage without regard to race, it also advocated that "the policy that excludes females is worthy of rigid and mature examination."[2] It is perhaps striking that just one year after the Seneca Falls declaration made the first known public demand for women's voting rights in the United States and before any woman suffrage organizations had been assembled, Michigan politicians had begun to deal directly and even somewhat sympathetically with the question of women's voting rights. The issue, however, died quickly in committee, with no further mention in the following discussions of constitutional revision. Principles gave little political impetus for action.

Through the 1850s and 1860s, the state legislature was routinely petitioned for universal suffrage, with some of those petitions explicitly referencing female suffrage as part of that universe, and was also increasingly petitioned solely for female voting rights.[3] These petitions were referred to committee, and the resultant committee reports delved into debates on the essence of republican government, representation, and the meaning and rights of citizenship.[4]

---

[2] Note that the first state constitution had already outlawed slavery. Report in *Documents Accompanying the Journal of the Senate of the State of Michigan at the Annual Session of 1849* (Lansing: Munger & Pattison), 32–69. Quoted passage on pages 37–38.

[3] Petition activity summarized in Virginia Ann Paganelli Caruso, *A History of Woman Suffrage in Michigan* (Ph.D. diss., Michigan State University, 1986).

[4] Portions relevant to female suffrage from a number of the reports are collected in *Legislative Action of the State of Michigan Relating to Universal Suffrage; or, Woman Suffrage* (Compiled by Executive Committee, State Woman Suffrage Association, 1874).

Sometimes the conclusion was that republican principles necessitated extension of voting rights to women, as well as to men of color. An 1857 report, for instance, surmised that "[w]oman, then, in possession of her citizenship, acknowledging her allegiance, and subjecting herself to the legislature of the land, clearly and undeniably acquires the right of participation in the structure of all legislative authority," and recommended a resolution for female voting rights.[5] At other times, lawmakers returned to the logic of female influence through their husbands, the idea of representation of the household, and to the conclusion that the greatest change effected by granting women voting rights would not be a change in the balance of political interests, but rather a disturbance in gender roles. This sort of argument was reflected in an 1859 report, which stated:

Your committee have also declined to submit an amendment in accordance with the prayer of numerous petitioners, to extend the elective franchise to women, from a full conviction that such an innovation upon the long-established customs of the country, while it would in no material degree add to the real influence of the women of our land, would, by bringing them into the exciting, and not unfrequently [sic], revolting arena of political strife, so destroy and overthrow the high regard for female character, which is now such a world-wide characteristic of Americans, as to really defeat the objects which the friends of this measure seem to have in view, viz.: – the enlargement of the sphere of female influence.[6]

Although the committee reports issued in these early considerations of woman suffrage in Michigan reflected some disagreement over the propriety of female voting rights, the response of the legislature to every report was arguably identical, for there was never a response to any committee recommendation. With no suffrage organizations in the state, and no constituent interest expressed beside petitions from small groups of "concerned citizens," and hence no clear sign of political consequence, legislators had little reason to spend any significant time or effort on the issue. Thus, whether the committees' reports were positive or negative, resolutions for women's voting rights never left the purview of their assigned committees to reach consideration on the floor of the legislature.

That politicians were at least as much interested in electoral consequences as they were in principled arguments of representation was especially evident in the debates of Michigan's 1867 Constitutional Convention. Delegates discussed the possibility of two major innovations in suffrage qualifications: non-white male voting rights and women's voting rights.[7] The two possibilities were often discussed in tandem, with various delegates pointing to the relative merits of tribal, "savage" American Indian voters and "ignorant" African descent

---

[5] *Documents Accompanying the Journal of the Senate of the State of Michigan, at the Biennial Session of 1857* (Lansing: Hosmer & Fitch), Document No. 27. Quoted passage on page 3.

[6] *Documents Accompanying the Journal of the Senate of the State of Michigan, at the Biennial Session of 1859* (Lansing: Hosmer & Kerr), Document No. 12, 2.

[7] There was also some discussion of both the residency and the age requirements.

voters versus intelligent, civilized, white female electors. Characterizing American Indians, black Americans,[8] and white females in this way was not simply a discussion of the qualifications of responsible citizens. Instead, it reflected beliefs about the voting propensities of each group, and their consequences for party politics. Women's voting rights were discussed *explicitly* as *white* women's voting rights, and white women as a group were differentiated from black Americans and American Indians primarily in the extent to which delegates expressed concerns about each group voting as a political bloc.

Delegates discussed instances of the political use of both "the Indian vote" and "the African vote," pointing out the ways in which each could affect party politics. Of American Indians, one delegate warned, "[t]hese identical ignorant Indians which you have today, you will have tomorrow; and the party in power will control the Indian vote."[9] Another, in the same vein, argued, "[t]hey always go with the side that furnishes the most whisky, whether it be Republican or Democratic."[10] Others acknowledged the unease about an American Indian voting bloc, but argued their presence in the state too small to be of consequence: "If I thought the white people of this State were to be overpowered by the Indians – the gentleman from Washtenaw (Mr. Norris) seems to think there is some danger of that – I would go for limiting them, for keeping them in close quarters. But we all know that seven or eight thousand Indians can do no harm."[11]

Black men's voting rights, in their turn, were discussed as a strict partisan issue. One delegate termed the discussion "a question of paramount importance to the Republicans as a party," referring to the Republican nature of the push for the inclusion of black male suffrage in the new state constitution.[12] On account of the partisan politics of the war effort that had ended the enslavement of people of African descent, Republicans in Michigan, as elsewhere, were expecting to reap those votes; the push for black men's voting rights was clearly a *strategic* one. Apprehension about the admission of "ignorant Africans" to the electorate was heightened by the suspicion of Democrats that they would be an unbreakable bloc.

Discussions of white women's voting rights, in contrast to those of American Indian and black suffrage, contained none of the concerns of party politics. No delegate suggested that white women would constitute a voting bloc of any

---

[8] The terms used most often by the delegates to refer to any person of African descent were "African" "colored" and "Negro." I use "black American" throughout as a less pejorative but still historically appropriate term. "American Indian" was occasionally used by the delegates, although more commonly they simply used the term "Indian."

[9] *The Debates and Proceedings of the Constitutional Convention of the State of Michigan* (Lansing: John A. Kerr & Co., 1867), 272.

[10] *Debates*, 1867, 263.

[11] *Debates*, 1867, 268.

[12] *Debates*, 1867, 718.

sort, whereas some returned to the question of whether their inclusion would only replicate the patterns of current politics set by their husbands, fathers, and brothers. On that issue, one asserted, "I say that the [white] females are now represented at the polls.... The vote deposited by men is but a representative of the principle."[13] Another elaborated on that assertion with the reasoning that "women now have an indirect political power by their influence on men." Delegates argued over whether women really wanted the right to vote. They also debated whether the principles of republican government meant women ought to have voting rights, whether suffrage rights were natural or political. Although several members advocated an amendment to the voting qualifications that would eliminate the word "male," that amendment not only failed to be adopted, but also failed to garner serious consideration from a number of the delegates. Indeed, discussions of the woman suffrage topic often trailed off into light-hearted remarks and laughter about the proposition.[14] Without a place in party politics, women's voting rights slipped easily off the convention's agenda, whereas a proposition to submit the question of suffrage rights for men of color to Michigan voters won not only serious consideration, but final approval from a majority of the delegates.[15]

Lessons to be Learned: Personal, Coalitional, and Strategic Failures

Although Michigan politicians considered the issue of women's voting rights as they contemplated other expansions of the franchise through the mid nineteenth century, there is no evidence of organization in favor of women's voting rights until the first state suffrage association constituted itself in 1870. This first organization would pursue its suffrage goals largely through personal politics. The result was similar to early personal politics pushes for suffrage consideration in Colorado: inside politics leverage could pressure legislators only into symbolic approval tied to the requirement of a public referendum that was bound for failure. Suffrage would then become connected, as it had in Colorado, to WCTU activities. The political disadvantage of temperance interests in Michigan rendered that connection ineffective. Finally, suffrage advocates in Michigan found themselves in the politics of strategic enfranchisement, when some Republican lawmakers suggested a measure that would tie women's voting rights to literacy requirements. Failure in this case was particularly informative. It further congealed the notion that lawmakers did not expect to reap particular partisan advantage from enfranchising "women," and yet also revealed that politicians were nervous about the feasibility of qualifiers that attempted to strategically carve out an advantageous bloc. Repeated failure was sufficiently frustrating that it dispersed suffragists from suffrage

---

[13] *Debates*, 1867, 273.
[14] E.g., *Debates*, 1867, 279, 717.
[15] *Debates*, 1867, 717. The new constitution, however, was ultimately not adopted.

organizing to other primary causes, ones that eventually bore coalitional fruit for the suffrage cause. Failure was thus politically informative and productive, although the lessons may have been difficult to learn.

Inside Victory, Outside Failure

The Michigan State Woman Suffrage Association (MSWSA) was established by a small group of both men and women, many with political connections, in 1870. With sights set on a constitutional amendment for full suffrage rights, MSWSA's small initial membership began organizing local suffrage clubs, collecting petitions, and lobbying the legislature. By 1873, the organization proudly counted a number of state legislators as members, as well as the governor's wife.[16] And in its first concerted push for a woman suffrage provision that year, MSWSA attempted to leverage these personal connections between the organization and state lawmakers into a constitutional provision of women's voting rights.

MSWSA's personal politics strategy surely helped them make some progress. The sponsor of the legislation was a representative who was listed as a member of the organization. When the committee charged to consider the bill tersely declared that "the time has not arrived for us to decide on so important a matter" and that they were "under the impression that there is no popular demand for change," and hence reported the resolution without recommendation, MSWSA's supporters managed to bypass the committee and push the legislation through to the floor of the state House of Representatives.[17] The bill's supporters also circumvented a last minute effort by one representative to have the resolution recommitted to a new committee, with instructions that it be amended to provide for a canvassing of Michigan women on the issue of their own voting rights. After the failure of the motion to recommit, the House then voted fifty in favor and twenty-four opposed to the woman suffrage amendment. Although the total failed to reach the two-thirds majority required to pass a constitutional amendment, the level of support was certainly not dismissive.[18] In the politics that followed this initial defeat, however, the inadequacy of personal politics' ability to deliver an expansion of the franchise would become clearer.

MSWSA counted the governor among its supporters, and he used his institutional powers to push for the constitutional amendment even after the failure of the House bill. He placed the issue of woman suffrage on the agenda of a commission he appointed that year to consider revisions to the state

---

[16] Executive committee and officers for 1870 in *The History of Woman Suffrage* (HWS) vol. III (page 516) for 1873–1874 in *Legislative Action of the State of Michigan Relating to Universal Suffrage; or, Woman Suffrage.*

[17] *Legislative Action of the State of Michigan Relating to Universal Suffrage; or, Woman Suffrage*, 9.

[18] *Journal of the House of Representatives of the State of Michigan* (Lansing: W. S. George & Co., 1873), 833, 2099–100.

constitution. The commission, however, rejected the issue altogether.[19] The governor pushed back, calling the legislature back into special session, charging them to consider recommending a new state constitution to Michigan voters, presumably including woman suffrage therein. Legislators produced a resolution for a constitutional amendment for woman suffrage in the special session. MSWSA, continuing to lobby in principled and personal terms for their cause, had a memorial presented on the House floor, wherein the suffrage advocates argued for voting rights due them by the merits of the republican principle of government by the consent of the governed and the Revolutionary era slogan of no taxation without representation.[20] Within days, the committees returned their joint report, recommending adoption of the resolution to submit the question of woman suffrage to Michigan voters at the next election, citing some agreement with the points made by MSWSA in their memorial. The report also insinuated, however, that the legislators' acquiescence did not necessarily reflect full support of the issue, but rather a willingness to let unrelenting pro-suffrage lobbyists try their luck at the polls – where, perhaps, failure seemed likely:

As the reasons given above are strongly urged by the advocates of woman suffrage, and as several petitions, numerously signed by citizens of the State, asking for some action on the part of the House in this matter, are in the hands of the committee, we have deemed it advisable, although not equally agreed as to the main question involved, to recommend the passage of the resolution by the House, in order that the people of the State may have an opportunity of expressing their will at the ballot-box as to the expediency of extending the right of suffrage to women.[21]

One week later, the measure passed both houses of the legislature. Suffragists' Republican friends, it seemed, pressured within the party for acquiescence to the demand for the referendum, but made no inroads with Democratic representatives. The entirely Republican state senate voted twenty-six in favor, with just four opposed. In the House, the majority was less overwhelming; sixty-six members, slightly more than the necessary two-thirds majority voted for the resolution, and twenty-seven against it. None of the five House Democrats was among the sixty-six representatives that voted for the measure.

Success delivered through inside lobbying pressure was short-lived for the woman suffrage advocates. Having lobbied the legislature into delivering a referendum on women's voting rights, public approval now had to be won, and MSWSA's political model was ill-equipped for that task. Although MSWSA commenced to planning a campaign during their spring convention in Lansing,

[19] The commission split seven in favor and seven opposed on the issue of separate submission, and four in favor and ten opposed on the inclusion of woman suffrage in their suggestions for a newly drafted constitution. *Journal of the Constitutional Commission of Michigan* (Lansing: W. S. George & Co., 1873), 26, 29–32, 71–72, 147, 163–67.
[20] Reproduced in HWS, vol. III, 517.
[21] Reproduced in HWS. vol. III, 517.

reaching voters across the state before the fall ballot would be an overwhelming task. Indeed, it was one at which the fledgling organization ultimately failed. With a limited infrastructure, few resources, and no organizational allies behind it, MSWSA's issue fared dismally at the polls. Woman suffrage collected 40,987 yes votes out of the 176,944 votes cast, or slightly more than 23 percent.[22] The decisive defeat caused the disbanding of MSWSA, and allowed legislators to put off consideration of a woman suffrage amendment for years to come. Lobbied only by a limited suffrage organization and its politically connected advocates, legislators had been suspicious that constituent interest in women's voting rights was lacking. They were right. It was now clear that interest in woman suffrage needed to be cultivated somehow. It was not enough to win principled approval of inside politics advocates. Women's voting rights needed to become an issue with *political* endorsements that could engender both legislative and public support.

Ineffective Alliance – Suffrage and Temperance

Although the 1874 loss unraveled MSWSA, it did not eliminate all interest in woman suffrage in Michigan. A new set of actors was taking interest in the cause, just as it was being written off by Michigan voters: prohibition advocates. The Prohibition Party had endorsed woman suffrage at its national convention in 1872, and Michigan Prohibitionists were beginning to warm to the idea as well. Michigan was at a crossroads on the idea of prohibition, moving in the direction of weaker prohibition laws, to be replaced by liquor licensing. Temperance organization was growing in response, including the Michigan WCTU, which was founded in 1875. Michigan's fledgling Prohibition Party endorsed woman suffrage during its 1874 campaign, claiming that women's votes would increase the chance of a definitive victory on the issue of prohibition versus licensing, and advocating female suffrage as one among several reform issues to give the party an agenda, and thus political appeal, larger than the temperance question.[23] Endorsement from the Michigan WCTU came in 1881, with hope that the right to vote would make their lobbying efforts on state liquor laws more effective.[24] The idea was growing that woman suffrage and prohibition were partnered causes.

With some prodding from NAWSA activists, including visits from Susan B. Anthony and Elizabeth Cady Stanton, suffrage organizations also began to reemerge. Some local suffrage clubs were formed after Stanton's or Anthony's speeches in cities, including Manistee, Lansing, and Detroit. Grand Rapids was host to a NAWSA convention in 1880, after which a local suffrage club

---

[22] *Manual for the Use of the Legislature of the State of Michigan, 1875–76.* (Lansing: W. S. George & Co.: 1875), 234–35.

[23] On the party's position and logic: Williams, Albert. *Prohibition and Woman Suffrage*, 1874. Williams was the Prohibition Party's candidate for Michigan Attorney General in 1874.

[24] Caruso, *A History of Woman Suffrage in Michigan.*

was formed there. In May of 1884, at a suffrage meeting in Flint, a new state suffrage organization was finally formed, the Michigan Equal Suffrage Association (MESA).[25] The new organization was clearly intended to be broader in its membership reach than its predecessor. MESA welcomed both individual memberships and affiliations of local suffrage clubs, and intended to organize statewide efforts for woman suffrage legislation. The state association met yearly, in Lansing during legislative session years and rotating through other cities in the off years. For the first several years, its program was largely informational, offering speeches by both prominent Michiganians who supported woman suffrage and nationally visible suffrage advocates, including Anna Howard Shaw, then of the WCTU, and Lucy Stone and Henry Blackwell.[26] During this time they also clarified women's right to vote at school board elections, a privilege that was established first on a technicality of the incidental omission of the word male in some legislation, then granted explicitly, without opposition, to mothers of school children.

With the small success of school suffrage behind them, MESA members and their WCTU partners grew more optimistic about the political viability of their issue. Adding to their confidence was a much-publicized pro-suffrage speech made by one of Michigan's U.S. Senators, Thomas Palmer, on that chamber's floor as that body considered (though quickly rejected) a woman suffrage amendment to the U.S. Constitution in 1885. That same year MESA and the Michigan WCTU made their first concerted push for suffrage legislation on a bill for voting rights for women in all school and municipal elections. The political task was carefully chosen: it was a feat that could be accomplished by the legislature by majority vote, and needed no referendum as a constitutional amendment would. A petition drive was carried out by both organizations, resulting in a deluge of petitions delivered to the state legislature throughout the session.[27]

A sponsor for the legislation was secured in the state Senate, and his commitment to the measure was strong enough to push for a vote on the floor, despite the fact that the committee to which it had been referred declined to support it. When the bill failed by a vote of fourteen in favor and fifteen opposed, there was some evidence that the coalition between suffrage and temperance activists was conveying political meaning for the issue of women's voting rights – that legislators were getting the message that woman suffrage might have consequence for the battle they were waging on prohibition. Unfortunately, the political meaning the coalition offered seemed to work to the detriment

[25] HWS, vol. III, 529–30.

[26] "Michigan Equal Suffrage Association, Second Annual Convention." Announcement. 1885. "Programme of the Third Annual Convention of the Mich. Equal Suffrage Association. Lansing, Jan. 13–14th, 1887."

[27] *Journal of the Senate of the State of Michigan* (Lansing: W. S. George & Co., 1885), 150, 172–73, 175, 278, 378, 424, 440, 448, 488, 538, 610–11, 618, 636, 652, 673, 706, 865, 1065, 1100, 1221, 1268–69, 1288, 1341.

of the suffrage cause. Those legislators attempting to defeat prohibition were also loath to vote for women's voting rights. Eleven senators voted against that year's prohibition measure; eight of those senators also voted against woman suffrage.[28]

Despite the resistance they experienced in the state legislature, suffrage activism continued in Michigan through a partnership between MESA and the WCTU. And the results of those efforts continued to exhibit the issue-based residue of that partnership. When MESA petitioned the state conventions of all four Michigan political parties in 1886 – Republican, Democrat, Prohibitionist, and Greenbacker – to adopt a woman suffrage plank in their state platforms, only the Prohibitionists and Greenbackers did so. Still, MESA and the WCTU secured the introduction of municipal suffrage legislation at every session of the legislature over the next several years, petitioning and lobbying for its passage. As legislators continued to struggle with partisan battles over liquor laws, however, suffrage bills continued to meet similar resistance. When brought up for votes in 1887, 1889, and 1891, the municipal suffrage bills drew more support from prohibition supporters than others, and thus also more support from Republicans than Democrats; but the bills still failed. Suffragists seemed to have given women's voting rights political meaning through the coalitional partnership with the temperance movement, but that meaning translated into too narrow a base of support. This was an important lesson about coalitional politics, but one that activists had some trouble internalizing.

Strategic Failure and Coalitional Beginnings
Although their repeated failures through the 1880s suggested a failed strategy, it was unclear to Michigan suffragists what other political options there might be. In 1893, some Republican politicians friendly to the budding movement made a suggestion: add a literacy clause. This was a decidedly strategic enfranchisement model tactic. Adding a clause that required would-be women voters to be able to read the Michigan constitution in English was meant to construct an enfranchised female population whose presumed voting propensities would appeal to Republican candidates: white, educated, native-born females, deemed more likely to vote Republican as did their male counterparts. MESA leadership resisted the idea for its departure from the equal rights principles they had been advocating, but its president admitted she would acquiesce if municipal suffrage first failed again to pass without the new clause.[29] Indeed, the bill without the clause failed, and the measure was recommitted to committee where it was amended to include the English literacy requirement. The amended bill passed the House in a manner consistent with its strategic enfranchisement model appeal, but met resistance in the Senate. Although the bill passed and was signed

---

[28] *Journal of the Senate of the State of Michigan* (Lansing: W. S. George & Co., 1885) 999, 369. The measure did not emerge in the house.
[29] Michigan Equal Suffrage Association, *Report*, 1893.

into law, it was overturned by the courts. Frustration with this failure finally led suffragists away from the cause – and into politics that unwittingly laid the groundwork for the more promising productive programmatic enfranchisement path to women's voting rights.

If the bill was, indeed, an attempt at the strategic enfranchisement of only the subset of women deemed likely to support the Republican Party, lawmakers should have lined up their votes accordingly. This was clearly the case in the House. First, the vote reflected a near party-line split: fifty-seven Republicans in favor, twenty-five members opposed, only six of whom were Republicans. Those who switched positions from opposition on the original bill to support of the version that included the literacy requirement were also all Republicans. Moreover, those who switched their votes across the two bills were exactly the members who were likely to reap more benefit from the English literacy requirement – those Republicans whose home districts had heavier concentrations of foreign-born populations, where enfranchised native born women would be most helpful in ensuring future electoral success. Although the typical representative who supported both versions of the bill came from a district where native-born men constituted more than 40 percent of the population, native-born men made up just more than 30 percent of the typical vote switcher's district.[30] In addition, all six Democrats who had supported the version without the English literacy requirement withdrew their support for the amended version.

Even to the amended form, however, senators were less receptive than House members to the measure. After its arrival in the state Senate, a number of attempts, three of which came to a floor vote, were made to prevent the measure from passing by adding amendments. After attempting to remove the literacy requirement in its entirety, the very same legislators attempted to add a clause that would criminally punish registrars who failed to administer the literacy test. Failing on both of these fronts, the bill's opponents attempted to remove only the section that referred to competency in English. Unsuccessful in derailing the House's version of the bill, one more attempt was made, and lost, to table the bill. With opponents out of options, the senators came to a final vote of eighteen in favor and eleven opposed. All of the opponents of final passage had been involved in the efforts to amend and table the bill.[31] Lacking the same marked partisan split on the final vote that the measure received in the House, it appears that the Senate did not trust the assumption that the English literacy requirement would engender a new Republican bloc in municipal elections. Senators, in other words, were not convinced that even this particular class of women made good candidates for strategic enfranchisement.

---

[30] For those who voted yes both times, median percent native-born (adult) men was 42.0%, mean 40.1%. For those who voted no, then yes, median was 33.0%, mean 35.0%. The mean difference is significant at p=.03.

[31] *Journal of the Senate of the State of Michigan* (Lansing: Robert Smith & Co., 1893), 1540–43.

As the amendment that proposed to punish registrars for failure to administer the literacy test underscored, at least some of the senators ascertained that the literacy requirement would only shape the female electorate in so far as it was actually executed by election officials. Partisan officials could easily bend the requirements to suit their districts.

As he had promised MESA, the Republican governor signed the municipal suffrage bill when it reached his desk and Michigan women had their first suffrage victory. But before most Michigan women had a chance to exercise their new voting rights, the Michigan Supreme Court overturned the measure. Ruling that fall on a case brought against the city of Detroit and its Board of Election Commissioners by two women refused registration, the court issued a decision that the qualifications of voters for offices that were created by or through provisions of the state constitution could only be changed by an amendment to the constitution's election qualifications clauses.[32] Not only did the court's decision take away arduously won new voting rights, but it also reduced woman suffrage advocates to a single avenue to extending voting rights – a constitutional amendment. Sensing the slim chances of capturing the necessary legislative super-majorities and approval at the polls, Michigan's suffrage movement stalled.[33]

Yet, in the Michigan suffrage movement's response to the overturn of municipal voting rights for women laid a political opportunity. When the court decision turned activists' attention away from lobbying for suffrage legislation, it helped open their political agendas. It was at this time that the suffrage activists aligned with MESA and its affiliated local suffrage clubs diverted their attention to a broader reform agenda. They began working for protective legislation for women and children, including in the workplace, and through those efforts began relationships with labor organizations. Labor unions, they found, were particularly receptive to working for equal pay for equal work, a reform that the suffragists desired for reasons of gender equity and labor unions desired, arguably, to keep employers from farming labor to women at lower rates that undercut union wage efforts.[34] Suffragists not only cooperated with labor unions, but populated the newly forming women's pro-labor organizations, such as the Women's Union Label League, which encouraged women to use their household buying power in the union effort by insisting on

---

[32] *Mary Stuart Coffin and Mary E. Burnett v. The Board of Election Commissioners of the City of Detroit*, and *Edward H. Kennedy and Henry S. Potter v. Hazen S. Pingree, Mayor, etc., et al.* 97 Mich. 188; 56 N.W. 567; 1893 Mich. LEXIS 867.

[33] Annual reports indicate they at times canvassed members to gauge interest in suffrage, but finding too few supporters did not pursue any legislation and decided to wait for a time when general revision of the constitution might be discussed. Michigan Equal Suffrage Association, Report, 1897, 1898, 1901.

[34] This confluence of interests discussed in exactly these terms by Mary Doe in her report as chair of MESA's Committee on Labor Organizations in 1900. *Report of the Sixteenth Annual Convention of the Michigan Equal Suffrage Association, Detroit May 15, 16, 17, 1900*, 4–5.

union labeled products. Suffragists also lobbied to have women appointed to government positions, starting with those that could be argued for on gendered terms – superintendent of the state reform school for girls, state physician at the women's sanatorium – and then those which fit with their reform agenda, especially the newly expanding factory inspector positions. Michigan suffragists were finally laying the groundwork for the sort of political coalitions that might leverage the depth and breadth of support needed to push for the extension of the franchise to women on equal terms with men.

Working Through Coalitional Challenges

Having begun the work of building political bridges between woman suffrage and organized interests that might influence lawmakers' decisions in their favor, Michigan's suffrage activists still had lessons to learn about how coalitional politics could be translated into success. Although work in this direction was already underway, suffragists would still struggle with enlisting the support of the rank and file of the groups to which they were making connections. This work was not to be taken lightly, either – politicians, the suffragists would discover, were less moved by nominal endorsements of group leaders than by stronger signals of true group-based support. Interest group leverage, that is, depended centrally on the credibility of a signal about constituent demand. Among the coalitional challenges that still lay ahead of suffragists were also the difficulties of knowing exactly who would be influenced by their coalitional partners and when those politicians would be most open to their demands. Particularly important would be how to use coalitional politics to intertwine the party organizations in their cause, not just individual politicians. The first score of years of the twentieth century offered opportunities in Michigan for learning these lessons and honing the programmatic enfranchisement approach.

Mistaken Opportunity – The Politics of Convention
State suffrage leaders had been anxiously awaiting a Constitutional Convention. Suffragists believed such a convention was a political opportunity, as it would afford the chance to change the election qualification clauses without clearing the high hurdles of support for the cause needed to simply add an amendment. They needed only a majority of convention delegates to agree to women's voting rights, as opposed to the two-thirds majorities needed in the legislature. There would be no single-issue public vote to won, either. A convention was finally called in 1907. Despite the progress that suffragists had made in developing new coalitional partnerships, however, the convention presented them with a political obstacle they had not anticipated. Delegates were divorced from electoral incentives – quite purposely – in a way that legislators were not. As such, they were less susceptible to electoral coalition pressure and more likely to invoke their personal interests in deciding the issue. Suffragists ultimately lost in convention not because they had failed to establish any new

politically relevant meaning for their cause, but because delegates used that meaning in a different way than legislators might.

The movement certainly had garnered enough political support that finding friends and sponsors was not a difficult task. MESA quickly secured the pledge of Republican delegate to introduce a proposal to strike the word "male" from the constitution's clause on voter qualifications. The organization also found itself with several delegates willing not only to endorse their cause, but to provide counsel to the organization as the convention considered the proposal.[35] Just days into the convention, MESA's memorial to the convention "to secure the elective franchise to citizens on the basis of needs and rights of a common interest and not on a sex restriction" was introduced.[36]

Suffragists had developed several new strategies since their last attempt at voting rights legislation. Early on, a plan of action for MESA was sent from NAWSA. The central piece of the NAWSA plan was to have women from each district hold personal and confidential interviews with their respective convention delegates on the issue of woman suffrage. This was to be the decidedly back-door element of the lobbying strategy; the importance of keeping the interviews private and certainly out of the newspapers was strongly underscored. More – and less clandestine – lobbying would occur throughout the convention in the form of petition and letter-writing campaigns and continued meetings with delegates. The newest strategies, however, were aimed at bolstering a coalition of support among friendly interest groups, enabling suffragists to signal to the convention political interest in women's voting rights that had not been conveyed when all the lobbying had been done by women from the suffrage organizations and WCTU.

The first step in the coalitional strategy was to establish an advisory board for the campaign, to consist of "women belonging to different organizations, such as the Maccabees, the Federation of Clubs, the Labor Associations, the Granges." MESA then sent petition forms to all these organizations that could be endorsed and then sent on to the Constitutional Convention delegates to convey the groups' interest in a woman suffrage provision.[37] General publicity work was also planned, to consist of distribution of standard NAWSA literature and a hearing in the convention on the issue of woman suffrage, featuring testimony from NAWSA president Reverend Ann Howard Shaw.[38] Ultimately,

---

[35] The agreement is discussed in a letter from MESA worker May S. Knaggs to MESA president Clara B. Arthur (hereafter CBA) dated November 1, 1907 (Clara B. Arthur Papers, Detroit Public Library – Burton Historical Collection). Barbour's presentation: *Journal of the Constitutional Convention of the State of Michigan* (Lansing: Wynkoop Hellenbeck Crawford Co., State Printers, 1908), 150–51.

[36] *Journal of the Constitutional Convention*, 212.

[37] This strategy discussed in an undated letter from May Knaggs to CBA. Knaggs stressed the need to get labor unions to sign on (Clara B. Arthur Papers, Detroit Public Library – Burton Historical Collection).

[38] NAWSA plan enclosed in letter from Kate Gordon to Arthur November 11, 1907 (Clara B. Arthur Papers, Detroit Public Library – Burton Historical Collection).

the suffragists were able to arrange a hearing in the hall where the convention delegates were meeting, although it was not an official part of the convention proceedings.[39] This would also become a key moment to demonstrate the breadth and depth of interest in woman suffrage. In addition to Shaw's remarks, the evening hearing held featured appearances by Illinois suffragist Catherine Waugh McCullough, MESA president Clara B. Arthur, and representatives from a number of organizations that endorsed woman suffrage, including the Michigan Grange and the Michigan Association of Farmers' Clubs, the Maccabees, the Michigan WCTU, the Michigan Federation of Labor, and the Detroit Garment Workers.[40] The event also featured the presentation of a large petition, signed by women requesting their voting rights.[41]

From the start, however, expectations of success at the convention were mixed. The delegate who introduced the woman suffrage provision assured MESA that he expected the proposal was quite likely to be adopted. Another delegate supporting the effort, however, warned "that while the Convention seems desirous of granting a measure of political liberty to women the prospect for a complete franchise is not favorable."[42] Certainly, the basic composition of the convention gave little reason to expect behavior markedly different from the state legislature: many delegates were former members of the legislature and most, just like most legislators, were Republican. Yet, there was one particularly notable difference, which could have implications for the fate of woman suffrage: diminished electoral incentives. Clearly *no* delegate would be running for reelection. More important, as the existing constitution barred current legislators from sitting in the convention, most of the delegates with political experience were either local politicians or former legislators past their prime. Under these circumstances, leveraging electoral demand from the home district to influence decision-making – the promise of the coalitional work suffragists had been doing – seemed a less promising strategy. Delegates were far more insulated from electoral pressure than legislators might be.

When the convention reached its consideration of the new constitution's suffrage provisions, MESA's friends were challenged in their attempts to have women's voting rights included. Although the committee, which included the MESA ally who had presented their memorial to the convention, put forward a

---

[39] *Journal of the Constitutional Convention,* 797–804.

[40] HWS vol. VI, 305. "Women Demand Suffrage," *The Detroit Free Press.* January 9, 1908, 10. "Women Flock Down on Con. Con." *The Detroit News.* January 9, 1908, p. 1.

[41] Quite a number of petitions were brought before the convention on the issue of woman suffrage, some containing well more than 1,000 signatures. There is no official record of how large the petition at the hearing was, and there are conflicting reports from the suffragists and the papers: HWS claims "225,000 names, 175,000 of individual women of voting age," but *The Detroit News* reported the petition bore 10,000 signatures. As the HWS number would represent nearly 10 percent of the entire state's population, gathered in two months' time, the *Detroit News* number seems more likely.

[42] Van Kleecks comments reported by Knaggs in her November 1, 1907 letter to Arthur. Tossey's comment from a letter he wrote to Arthur on November 11, 1907 (Clara B. Arthur Papers, Detroit Public Library – Burton Historical Collection).

set of voter qualifications that completely enfranchised women, the convention quickly overturned the committee's gender equity. On first consideration of the suffrage provisions in the Committee of the Whole, a motion for the insertion of the word "male" into the voting qualifications was carried by a rising vote of forty-seven in favor and thirty-four opposed. Debate on the suffrage clauses continued until another of MESA's political sponsors moved to strike again the word "male" and demanded the yeas and nays on that motion. This forced the convention into a roll call vote on whether to include voting rights for women in the revised constitution. Women's voting rights lost by a vote of thirty-eight in favor and fifty-four opposed.[43] MESA supporters pushed for and won, however, a measure of progress for women in the new constitution – the right of tax-paying women to vote on tax and bond issues. This right was adopted by the convention in a roll call vote, and passed easily by a vote of sixty-five yeas and five nays.

Suffrage activists had been hoping that their new coalitional strategy would spell new success for women's voting rights, that their cause would be tied to labor and farm interests that pulled weight in Michigan politics. Yet, they failed to consider the unique political challenge of influencing convention delegates that were largely divorced from electoral incentives. Moreover, woman suffrage had maintained its ties with the prohibition issue through the continued visibility of the WCTU in the suffrage campaign. With delegates struggling to resolve the prohibition issue, any connection between suffrage and that political hot button may have worked to the detriment of a positive outcome for women's voting rights. In the end, of course, the convention conceded only a small victory, and there was indeed evidence that the coalition effort had actually worked against the achievement of full voting privileges.

Systematic analysis of the incentives delegates invoked in their decisions on woman suffrage is possible by modeling the roll call votes they cast on woman suffrage – on the motion to strike the word "male" from the new constitution's electoral qualifications clause and on the inclusion of the provision for tax-paying women to vote on tax and bond issues. To capture the possible influence of suffragists' growing labor and farm-group coalitional partners, measures of the relative farming and labor presence in the delegate's district are drawn from the U.S. Census. The farm measure is the per capita number of farms in the district, and the labor measure is the per capita number of manufacturing workers. To gauge the possible connection between suffrage and prohibition decisions, the delegates' votes on the convention's decision on whether or not to include a liquor prohibition clause in the constitution are included in the model. Given the Republican leanings of the politicians most closely involved in pushing for suffrage to this point in Michigan, an indicator of whether the delegate identified as a Republican is also included. Finally, the possibility that the delegates' personal interests were uniquely relevant to

---

[43] *Journal of the Constitutional Convention*, 1033, 1115–21.

TABLE 3.1. *Predicting Support for Woman Suffrage,*
Michigan Constitutional Convention, 1907–1908

	Strike Male Requirement	Tax Suffrage
Republican	− 1.80*	.62
	(.99)	(.96)
Anti-Prohibition	− 2.79**	− 1.73
	(.69)	(1.13)
Farms	− 10.65	12.15
	(9.52)	(12.86)
Labor	3.94	12.63
	(8.87)	(12.60)
Corporate Interest	− 1.64*	− .06
	(.91)	(.96)
Constant	3.65	.71
	(1.86)	(2.42)
N	85	72
Log-likelihood	− 44.45	− 26.08

Results from logistic regressions. $*p < .10$, $**p < .05$, two-tailed t-test.
Sources: U.S. Census, 1900; *Journal of the Constitutional Convention of the State of Michigan,* 1908.

their decisions as lawmakers that faced little electoral pressure is gauged by including a measure that indicates whether or not the delegate had a significant personal economic interest in working against suffragists' most notable coalitional partner, labor. This measure identifies delegates who owned or headed manufacturing corporations, as reported in their official state biographies.

Results of the statistical analysis of the model predicting delegate support of the two suffrage measures are displayed in Table 3.1. Opposition to the full suffrage measure, the results show, came both from delegates opposed to prohibition and from delegates whose personal business interests as owners and executives of manufacturing firms put them squarely in the anti-labor camp, even when those delegates came from districts where labor interests were strong. Significant negative coefficients on both the anti-labor and anti-prohibition positions suggest that these sentiments were the source of opposition to the full suffrage measure, and the presence of farm and labor interests did little to structure the decision of the delegates on the issue. Because these delegates would not be running for reelection, there was even greater room than for the typical legislator to serve personal rather than district interests. Thus suffragists' hopes for success in the convention because of lower majority thresholds than the legislature were trumped by lesser needs for responsiveness to constituent group interests and greater presence of individuals with interests opposed to their coalition members' objectives.

Navigating Coalitions and Compromise

Having won limited suffrage rights with very little opposition, despite significant resistance to full voting rights for women, Michigan suffragists pushed
forward on their coalitional strategy. Suffragists were finding that partnerships
with the Grange and labor unions looked promising, but not uncomplicated.
In particular, suffragists found that although they had secured support from
the leadership of these organizations, the rank and file seemed less willing to
sign on to the suffrage cause. Nonetheless, the 1909 session of the Michigan
legislature delivered new municipal voting rights for women, to the extent that
they were allowed under the new constitution. Yet, full suffrage did not even
reach the floor in either house for a vote. Progress was being made, but how to
overcome obstacles in the coalitional strategy seemed unclear.

MESA, nudged along by encouragement from NAWSA leadership, was
working to both deepen and broaden the coalition of groups that had supported women's request for voting rights, actively seeking to explicitly ally with
Granges, Farmer's Clubs, Maccabees, and labor unions.[44] Support seemed to
be growing on most of these fronts from the leadership, but not necessarily the
constituent membership. Some prominent members of the Michigan Grange
had individually voiced support for women's voting rights, but active mobilization of their members around the issue was slow to develop. The issue of
official Grange support for woman suffrage legislation had been broached at
the 1907 Michigan State Grange convention by a member of the Michigan
House of Representatives and chair of the State Grange legislative committee,
but there still had been no follow through by 1909.[45] MESA president Clara B.
Arthur had also managed to ally with the advertising manager of *The Michigan
Patron*, a statewide Grange newspaper, who promised to aid the cause as best
she could through the paper, but also confirmed a lack of discussion of the
issue within the local Grange meetings.[46]

The relationship with labor unions was even more complicated. Although
MESA had been working with labor groups on labor issues for years and suc-
ceeded in getting an endorsement of their petition from several labor organizations in the state, suffrage workers still sensed resistance on the ground. MESA
organizer and Women's International Union Label League member Mary Doe
reported on the contention in her correspondence with MESA president Arthur:

I am not too much surprised that the Labor Unions are both to sign the woman suffrage
petitions.... It is not that they oppose equal rights for women *per se* but the brewers and
distillers recognize a danger to their interests in the votes of women. At the last Con. of

[44] *Report of the Twenty-Sixth Annual Convention of the Michigan Equal Suffrage Association*
(Kalamazoo: November 16–17, 1911).
[45] Trump, Fred. *The Grange in Michigan: An Agricultural History of Michigan over the Past 90
Years* (Grand Rapids: The Dean-Hicks Co., 1963), 82–84.
[46] Rose Helme to CBA, February 1, 1909 (Clara B. Arthur Papers, Detroit Public Library – Burton
Historical Collection).

Mich. F of L the brewing and allied interests made the fight of the Con. to secure an anti local option resolution, which they did.... After our ESA Con. I went to Mrs. Young our Representative's wife and asked her to go to our Com. on Lab. Org. Mr. Young is a machinist and Lab. Organizer who was present said 'If it stands for prohibition I won't stand for it.' I explained as best I could, but... she finally phoned her refusal, with an excuse and regrets of course but I felt that I knew the real reason.... Under ordinary circumstances, the Labor Unions would be more willing to sign our petition, but the local option agitation has arrayed many unions against us. Those employed by distillers and brewers... Bottlers, etc. etc. You see where it would be easy to get resolutions it is difficult to get individuals to sign.[47]

Suffrage activists' experiences like this one suggest that a liquor industry threatened by Michigan's ever-expanding list of dry counties, so created by recent local option elections that the pro-woman suffrage Michigan WCTU had been active in promoting, was working to spread its unease through its workforce. Whereas suffragists were experiencing increasing receptivity from labor union leaders, who found in the women's organizations allies for labor reform and protective legislation, they were less sure about the rank and file who might see in the end of an industry the end of gainful employment.

Of course, the rank and file were not deciding the issue of woman suffrage in Michigan – yet. Legislators were, and they acted to extend women's voting rights that year. Yet, they also refused to introduce legislation that would grant women full voting rights. In fact, the only bill on woman suffrage that appeared in the Michigan legislature during the 1909 session was one authored by a representative without any consultation with organized suffragists. The bill's author touted himself an advocate of democratic rights, having previously introduced Michigan's first legislation for direct primaries.[48] And he made the choice to pursue a strategy of pushing only for municipal voting rights as the result of his own political calculation. MESA leaders lamented the lack of coordination, but abided.[49] The result of the push for woman suffrage disconnected from the movement was a small and uncontroversial victory for women's voting rights. The municipal suffrage bill moved through both houses with ease, getting favorable committee reports, passing quickly on through third readings to the unanimous votes on final passage. In both houses, the votes were unanimously in favor of the municipal voting rights measure, but

---

[47] Mary L. Doe to CBA, March 21, 1909 (Clara B. Arthur Papers, Detroit Public Library – Burton Historical Collection).

[48] This is listed in his biography in the *Michigan Official Directory and Legislative Manual for the Years 1909–1910.*

[49] Mary Doe wrote to CBA about the situation on April 11, 1909 and judged the practice not uncommon from her days as MESA Legislative Committee chair: "I judge that Mr. Colby has not consulted you or the Legislative Co. nor asked our help in any way. There have been cases in our history when champions of our cause have said that they felt more confident of success if we remained in the background." (Clara B. Arthur Papers, Detroit Public Library – Burton Historical Collection).

TABLE 3.2. *Vote on Municipal Suffrage by District Characteristics, Michigan House of Representatives, 1909*

		Interests in Representatives' Districts			
		Labor		Farming	Liquor
		Percent Urban	Percent Employed in Manufacturing	Per Capita Farms	Per Capita Liquor Tax
	Median	.38	.05	.08	.79
voted	Mean	.41	.06	.09	1.04
n = 31	(Std. Error)	(.03)	(.01)	(.01)	(.10)
	Median	.50	.06	.06	.85
did not vote	Mean	.49	.07	.07	1.28
n = 68	(Std. Error)	(.06)	(.01)	(.01)	(.19)

Note: No statistically significant differences.
Sources: United States Census (1900 & 1910); *Journal of the House of Representatives of the State of Michigan, 1909.*

the House had a significant number of abstainers. On final passage, the entirely Republican Senate vote was twenty-eight in favor with just four members not voting, while the House returned sixty-eight in favor with thirty-two members not voting – including one of the two House Democrats.

Although no members voted against the municipal suffrage measure, it may be that opposition was registered by abstaining from the vote. And although it is difficult to determine whether abstention really indicated opposition or not, we can determine whether voters and non-voters in the House differed along any of the dimensions that might make them more susceptible to political pressures for or against the bill. As it turns out, there are no notable differences between those who cast votes in favor of the suffrage bill and those who did not. Supporters' and abstainers' districts were indistinguishable in terms of the presence of labor interests, farming interests, and liquor interests – the three groups that had begun to express a stake in the woman suffrage issue in the state. This is evident in Table 3.2, which shows that median and mean values of district characteristics capturing each of these interests for those House members who voted for municipal suffrage and those who did not vote on the measure were nearly equivalent.[50] It appears the independent suffrage entrepreneur crafted

[50] None of the small differences is statistically significant. Moreover, a logistic regression predicting likelihood of voting on municipal suffrage using all four district characteristics confirms no significant differences, even when the members are split into safe and marginal seat holders (assuming marginal holders may feel more need to be responsive to their home districts). For all members:

$$\beta_{urban} = -.43 \ s.e. = 1.7 \quad \beta_{manufacture} = .97 \ s.e. = 8.0$$
$$\beta_{farm} = 3.35 \ s.e. = 11.5 \quad \beta_{liquor} = -.09 \ s.e. = .46$$

a quiet compromise that pleased all sides within the legislature. Suffragists, however, were still left wanting more.

Finding the Key Constituency – Leveraging the Political Power of the Michigan Grange

If any year marked a turning point for the issue of women's voting rights in Michigan, it was 1911. The year was significant not because of new legislation passed; in fact no new voting rights were gained. Instead, 1911 proved consequential because the place of the issue of women's voting rights in state politics changed. Although the issue had been handled previously by women's groups – the suffrage organizations and the WCTU – with only nominal endorsement by other groups, women's voting rights were now being deliberated as part of other groups' active political agendas. Most important, 1911 was the year that the Grange in Michigan began to take up the issue of woman suffrage in earnest. During the annual session of the Michigan State Grange held in Kalamazoo in December 1911, the report on "women's work" included the statement that, "[t]he women of the Grange have been studying with quiet dignity the profound subject of equal suffrage." Certainly, MESA and NAWSA had made efforts to include Grange women in their lobbying activities previously, but the inclusion of this mention at the State Grange session signaled the beginning of a new, more active interest in working for woman suffrage from within the Grange organizations. Women in the Grange were using their own organizational capacity to leverage the interest group's commitment to the cause.

Additionally, 1911 was a politically ideal time for this interest to develop. Grangers sat in key places in the state government – in both the executive and legislative branches. Notably, both the governor and the Speaker of the House were active Grange members. In fact, the Speaker of the House sat on the executive committee of the State Grange. Twenty members of the Michigan House were also identified as active Grangers. Moreover, the Grange's potential as a lobbying power was reaching a crest: the organization was flourishing, reaching peak levels of membership in Michigan and prospering financially through its insurance offerings.[51] The Grange partnership would be key for suffragists. Credible interest in suffrage on the part of the Grange would translate not only into district-level pressure on individual lawmakers' votes, but also into incentive for Grange-affiliated politicians to do the active work of shepherding women's voting rights through the policymaking process. Indeed, the governor, who – along with his executive staff – had signed on to the NAWSA woman suffrage petition to Congress, would prove an unmatched political ally for

---

[51] On Grange activity, see Trump, *The Grange in Michigan*, 90–93. Quotation appears on page 92. On petition activity see *Report of the Twenty-Sixth Annual Convention of the Michigan Equal Suffrage Association*.

suffragists in the next two years, facilitating their first legislative success for full voting rights.

Despite the influx of support from the Grange, woman suffrage was not actually won in Michigan until 1918. Woman suffrage would fail in the legislature in 1911 and at the polls in both 1912 and 1913. In these failures there is evidence of resistance from the liquor industry and, later, as the explicitly reformist Progressive Party pushed for woman suffrage, from Michigan's urban center of machine politics, Detroit. Indeed, suffragists and their coalitional partners would question whether outright electoral fraud was responsible for one lost referendum. Yet the investment of the pro-suffrage coalition was so committed, that it persevered, regrouped, and ultimately delivered victory.

Muted Message – Initial Grange Support in 1911
Although the State Grange had signaled its interest in working for woman suffrage before the 1911 legislative session, the push for woman suffrage that year was still led by MESA. MESA vice president and legislative committee member Clara Russell and her husband, a notable figure in the state's Republican Party organization, hand-picked a member of the House to shepherd through a resolution for a constitutional amendment for woman suffrage.[52] Charles Flowers, a Republican Party activist from Detroit, was the key figure in the advancement of the measure through the legislative process. He secured referral of the measure to and delivered a favorable report from the committee he chaired, and then pressed it quickly through consideration in the Committee of the Whole. In floor consideration, Flowers successfully moved for a suspension of the rules to push the resolution to a vote on final passage. Although fifty-five representatives voted in favor, the resolution failed to garner the two-thirds majority required to pass.[53]

A vote, even a failing one, was far more progress than was seen on amendment resolution in the Senate. The same resolution had been introduced there, but languished in committee. Neither the resolution's sponsor, a member of the woman suffrage friendly Maccabees and the Michigan State Agricultural Society, nor the senator chosen as the MESA sponsor in the Senate was able to bring the resolution out of committee – even though MESA's ally was the committee's chair.[54] But Flowers was persevering in the House. The day after the resolution's first failure there, he moved for and won reconsideration of

---

[52] Caruso, *A History of Woman Suffrage in Michigan*, 170.

[53] *Journal of the House of Representatives of the State of Michigan*, 1911, 27, 173, 203, 253, 258–60. Immediately after the vote, a new woman suffrage resolution, which provided for a referendum by the women of Michigan on the issue of their voting rights, was introduced and referred to Flowers' Committee on Revision and Amendment of the Constitution, where it would remain for the duration of the session.

[54] *Journal of the Senate of the State of Michigan*, 1911, 54, index on p. 41; *Michigan Official Directory and Legislative Manual for the Years 1911–1912*, 764–69.

the vote. He then had the resolution tabled, giving suffrage supporters time to lobby for the cause before another vote was taken. Although MESA's legislative committee reported "arduous efforts of that committee working in Lansing for the bill for the submission of an Amendment to the State Constitution which should enfranchise women," they did not report of any assistance in their efforts.[55] When Flowers finally moved the suffrage resolution from the table near the end of the session for a second vote on final passage, it fared no better than it had the first time. Again, only fifty-five members voted for the resolution; woman suffrage would not pass in 1911.

Although the new signal of interest in woman suffrage from the Grange did not translate into active lobbying or produce a legislative victory, there was some evidence in legislators' behavior that Grange influences and the issue of woman suffrage were connecting. First, with just two exceptions, those representatives from the fifteen districts in which the Grange organization had grown particularly strong, with memberships numbering more than 1,000, voted to support the suffrage resolution. Legislators whose main occupation was farming – those personally tied to the interests of the Grange, if not the organization itself – were also more likely than others to support the suffrage amendment. Of the forty farmer-legislators in the House, twenty-five voted to pass the measure, and, by the second vote, only ten voted against it; just 25 percent of the farmers in the legislature opposed the measure, whereas half of the non-farmer members voted to defeat it. What is most notable is that although there had been no evidence in previous votes of such a connection, House members who voted in favor of women's voting rights in 1911 tended to be from districts where farming interests – the Grange's constituent base – were stronger than in opponents' districts. The average number of farms per 100 people living was more than a third larger in supporters' districts.[56] Grange interest, it seemed, was beginning to give the issue of woman suffrage new definition in state politics.

A Programmatic Push – Granger-Led Reconsideration in 1912

Within months of the 1911 failure, there would be another concerted push for a woman suffrage amendment to the Michigan constitution. This time, however, the charge would not be led single-handedly by MESA, but would instead be shouldered in part by the Grange organization, including its members in key positions of state power as well as its organized legislative lobby. Although resistance was marked, Grange influence ultimately helped deliver a legislative

---

[55] *Report of the Twenty-Sixth Annual Convention of the Michigan Equal Suffrage Association.*
[56] The average number of farms per 100 population was 8.97 in supporters' districts and 6.71 in supporters' districts. That difference is statistically significant: $t=2.15$, $p=.03$, two-tailed test with unequal variances assumed.

victory. Legislators were converted to the extent that they were vulnerable to the Grange's constituent base of farming interests. This was, in other words, a true push for woman suffrage within the programmatic enfranchisement framework.

The 1912 consideration of woman suffrage was made possible by Michigan's governor – a Granger, himself – who called the already-adjourned legislature into special session. Although the governor called the session explicitly for consideration of direct presidential primaries, he also issued several messages during the session charging the legislature to act on a number of other issues they had failed to resolve in 1911. The governor placed woman suffrage inside a decidedly reformist agenda; notable additions to the legislative docket were direct democracy provisions and regulation of brewery-owned saloons. This was a remarkable expression of political support for the suffrage cause; constitutionally the legislature could consider only those issues with which the governor charged them during special session, and woman suffrage was put on a very short list.[57]

Although legislators considered a woman suffrage resolution, as the governor requested, it failed to pass. Brought to a vote only in the Senate, the resolution drew a majority vote in favor, but not a large enough majority to pass, with eighteen in favor and eleven opposed.[58] In fact, the special session ended without accomplishing any of the major legislative goals laid out by the governor, legislators having spent most of their time on disagreements over the issue of presidential primaries. The governor countered by calling the legislature immediately back into another special session. Again, he placed woman suffrage inside his reformist agenda, demanding that legislators further regulate the liquor industry; provide for the initiative, referendum, and recall; amend the primary laws, including the establishment of the direct presidential primary; and adopt legislation that would send the question of a woman suffrage amendment to Michigan voters.[59] The governor told suffrage lobbyists that he had confidence that the legislature could be prodded into delivering successful votes for the constitutional amendment in both houses, but it would take strong political pressure.[60] That pressure would come from the Grange. And resistance would come from those motivated to

---

[57] *Journal of the House of Representatives of the State of Michigan, First Extra Session 1912*, 1–3, 81–85.

[58] *Journal of the Senate of the State of Michigan, First Extra Session 1912*, 118, 125, 128–29. A movement was passed to have the vote reconsidered and then to lay the resolution on the table, but the session would close without the Senate pulling the measure from the table for a second vote.

[59] *Journal of the House of Representatives of the State of Michigan, Second Extra Session 1912* (Lansing: Wynkoop Hallenbeck Crawford, Co., State Printers), 7.

[60] Reported by MESA legislative committee chair Jenny Law Hardy, *Yearbook of the Michigan Equal Suffrage Association and Report of the 27th Annual Convention* (Lansing, January 15–16, 1913).

work against the other elements of the governor's agenda, including liquor interests.

The Senate quickly passed a resolution providing for a woman suffrage amendment to be sent to the polls, by a vote of twenty-three to five. Politics in the House of Representatives were more complicated. There was at first an attempt to circumvent the governor's directive through a resolution that proposed to bring the issue to a vote by the women of Michigan. Introduced by a Republican representative who had voted against the woman suffrage amendment during the 1911 session, the measure required a majority of *all* adult women in the state, as counted in the last decennial census, to turnout and cast their ballots for their own suffrage rights. Given that the last constitutional amendment referendum held in 1910 turned out just less than 30 percent of voting age men, and presidential voting turnout hovered around 60 percent, the required threshold of turnout from women made the underhanded purpose of the resolution quite clear.[61] And despite legislative dealings with and activism on the issue dating back to the middle of the previous century, the resolution also suggested woman suffrage was a new and unconsidered proposition, stating:

Whereas, the question of equal suffrage in the state of Michigan has been but recently brought forcefully to the attention of the electorate of the state, and the representatives of the people are in doubt as to whether the majority of the women of the state are in favor of, or in sympathy with, an amendment to the organic law of the state extending such right; therefore be it resolved that . . . the question be submitted to the women of the state at the November, 1912, election for an expression of their desire as to whether the franchise shall be so enlarged . . . and that in case a majority of the women of the state above the age of twenty years, as shown by the census of 1910, shall vote in favor thereof at said primary election . . . the act extending such right shall be in full force and effect.[62]

Note that this was a new version of the previous maneuver of expanding the scope of conflict to a referendum to only nominally appease suffrage advocates – and one that suggested a new sense of the viability of that strategy. The replacement of a straightforward referendum of existing male voters with an overly complicated canvass of women suggests that opponents this time sensed that the regular partisan-controlled electoral process could not be counted on to deliver a suffrage defeat. Although the resolution was tabled before it could be brought to a vote on final passage, its appearance suggests that suffrage opponents understood the political meaning and electoral incentives of woman suffrage were changing.

---

[61] The 1910 Census put Michigan's male voting age population at 870,876; 541,830 voted in the 1908 presidential election and 259,876 voted in the 1910 constitutional referendum, according to the *Michigan Official Directory and Legislative Manual for the Years 1911–1912*.

[62] *Journal of the House of Representatives of the State of Michigan Second Extra Session 1912*, 65.

Having discarded the resolution calling for Michigan women to vote on their own voting rights, supporters in the House pressed to take up the Senate's measure. Although opponents tried several procedural measures to keep the suffrage resolution from reaching a final vote, the House ultimately voted to concur with the Senate resolution, passing the measure with seventy-five in favor and nineteen opposed. Not a single member who had supported the measure in 1911 chose to vote against it the second time around, but twenty-two representatives who had voted against woman suffrage in the last session were drawn into the yes column in the 1912 vote.

What changed between the 1911 and 1912 to push the Senate to consider and pass woman suffrage and to move twenty-two representatives from no to yes on the same resolution? The key was a concerted lobbying campaign, the central feature of which was a strongly committed the Michigan State Grange organization. In the time between the 1911 State Grange convention and the 1912 special legislative session, the Michigan Grange established an official Equal Suffrage Campaign Committee. The committee undertook lobbying efforts directed both at ordinary citizens and individual legislators. The organizational commitment was real. The State Grange even cut down its regular Lecturers' conferences to put the money and time into the campaign.[63] Whereas previous support from the Grange had been in the form of resolutions endorsing the issue of women's voting rights and individual efforts by some especially committed members, the work in 1912 had the full backing of the Grange as a political institution, and a leadership willing to work to convey as much to state legislators. Writing to MESA president Arthur just after the resolution was finally passed in the House, MESA's legislative committee, in Lansing for all the votes in 1912, credited the Grange with all the last minute conversions that put the House vote over the required two-thirds majority:

[I]f ever things looked desperate it was Wednesday morning: 12 liquor dealers and some bonding men arrived and a number of members told me our case was lost. In despair I had Rep. McNaughton phone up every Granger he could get hold of, and in half an hour he came back saying that the Grandmaster, Mr. Hull, Helme of Adrian, and Bartlett would be there as soon as possible. When Hull arrived, I pounced on him and gave him a list of men to convert, farmers especially. He worked all day and next morning I gave him some more backsliders, especially Haviland, and he promised me in front of Hull to vote, saying he would not have done so if Hull had not come. Mr. Flowers told me we never could get Fralick, it was no use trying, but Helme got him. After the vote Haviland, Fralick, and a couple of others said to me, pointing to Hull: 'There is the man that has done the trick, I never would have voted for you but for him.' I myself attribute our victory to the Grange. The Labour men and Mr. Shippen were called by Mrs. Russell and Mrs. Sellers, and did fine work, but the Grangers did

---

[63] Trump, *The Grange in Michigan*, 95.

TABLE 3.3. *Presence of Farming Interests in District by Votes on Suffrage, Michigan House of Representatives 1911 and 1912*

Per Capita Farms in District	Voted Yes in 1911 & 1912	Voted No in 1911 & Yes in 1912	Voted No in 1911 & 1912
Median	.09	.08	.01
Mean*	.09	.08	.04
(Std. Error)	(.05)	(.05)	(.05)
Number of Legislators	52	22	15

* Mean for those voting no both times statistically different from those who voted yes both times at p = .001 and from those who voted no in 1911, yes in 1912 at p = .01.

Sources: United State Census, 1910; *Journal of the House of Representatives of the State of Michigan, 1911, 1912.*

stand by us. I had no idea there were so many in the House, but the work I did some years ago among them helped me wonderfully.[64]

If the politics of the programmatic enfranchisement model hold, then it should be that the Grange's lobbying efforts moved those legislators electorally accountable to its constituent supporters. Of course, a strong presence of Grange organization in a district was ready evidence of such accountability. Legislators from districts known to have strong local Grange organizations were already lined up in favor of woman suffrage; only two House members from districts in which the Grange numbered more than 1,000 members voted against the 1911 measure. In the 1912 vote, both of those representatives had moved to the yes column. But twenty other representatives changed their votes on woman suffrage from no to yes between 1911 and 1912. Although Grange organization may have been an especially crisp signal about the electoral incentive to vote in favor of woman suffrage, interest groups do represent constituencies greater than their official memberships. In the case of the Grange, their influence in state politics came not simply from their official membership rolls, but from their position as the most visible and well-resourced group representing the increasingly politicized interests of farmers.[65] Evidence of Grange influence on these vote switchers, then, is in the similarity of the level of farming interests in their home districts to those in members' districts who supported woman suffrage in both sessions, and the difference of both from continued opponents' districts. These patterns are displayed in Table 3.3, which reports the mean and median number of farms per capita in the districts of consistent supporters, those who switched from opposition to support, and consistent opponents. The mean number of farms per capita for legislators that switched

[64] Letter from Jenny Law Hardy to CBA, March 30, 1912 (Clara B. Arthur Papers, Detroit Public Library – Burton Historical Collection).

[65] Trump, *The Grange in Michigan.*

sides in 1912 was twice the mean number of farms per capita for the opposing legislators' districts, and effectively indistinguishable from the mean number of farms per capita in the districts of consistent supporters of the woman suffrage resolution.

What about the effect of the opposition? Suffragists, Grange activists, and state legislators alike commonly referenced the "liquor lobby" as a now active anti-suffrage force in the state, although they did not necessarily agree on its ability to influence representatives' votes. Certainly the governor had placed the enfranchisement of women and the regulation of the liquor industry side-by-side in a very narrow agenda. One House member who had switched from opposition to support, Republican Augustus Gansser, referenced the tension in an explanation of his 1912 vote:

Then too, the opponents have been accused of representing the liquor interests of the state in blocking this proposition. This never entered into my problem. The liberal element knows that Colorado, which for sixteen years has had woman suffrage, Washington, Oregon, and California, which have since granted it, are not prohibition states.[66]

Gansser's statement suggests that perhaps those members persuaded by the Grange were not only from districts with greater farming interests, but also somehow less vulnerable to liquor interests. Such variation was a reality in Michigan. Increasing numbers of dry counties in the state since 1890, thanks to local option referenda, had begun to cut down the number of liquor manufacturers and vendors and the amount of (legal) liquor profits.[67] By 1912, thirty-four House members were from districts that were at least partially dry (thirty-one fully). And the presence of the liquor industry varied substantially among wet districts.

Indeed, matching the presence of liquor interests to representatives' votes on woman suffrage finds a pattern consistent with the argument that those legislators whom the Grange could move were not only sympathetic because of the farming interests in their districts, but also less likely to be facing a powerful local liquor lobby. Most of the members from dry districts voted in favor of woman suffrage both in 1911 and in 1912; just two members from dry districts voted against the measure in both sessions. Table 3.4 presents the average number of liquor dealers – which includes manufacturers, wholesalers, and retailers – across the districts of consistent supporters, vote switchers, and consistent opponents. The table shows that, in general, opponents came from districts where the liquor industry was stronger. The median number of liquor dealers in woman suffrage opponents' districts was 229, compared to

---

[66] *Journal of the House of Representatives of the State of Michigan, Second Special Session 1912*, 85.

[67] The number of liquor dealers and the amount of liquor tax paid had increased steadily from 1898 through 1907, after which the numbers declined into 1910, with a very small uptick in 1911. See Liquor Tax Summary, *Michigan Official Directory and Legislative Manual for the Years 1913–1914*, 298–99.

TABLE 3.4. *Presence of Liquor Interests in District by Votes on Suffrage, Michigan House of Representatives 1911 & 1912*

Number of Liquor Dealers in District[68]	Voted Yes in 1911 & 1912	Voted No in 1911 & Yes in 1912	Voted No in 1911 & 1912
Median	32	45	229
Mean	215	228	776[a]
(Std. Error)	(72)	(109)	(221)
Number of Legislators	52	22	15
		Wet Districts Only	
Median	63	81	1023
Mean	372	312	969[b]
(Std. Error)	(118)	(145)	(246)
Number of Legislators	30	16	12

[a] Statistically different from yes both times at p = .03 and from no in 1911/yes in 1912 at p=.04.

[b] Statistically different from yes both times at p = .04 and from no in 1911/yes in 1912 at p=.03.

Source: Michigan Official Directory and Legislative Manual for the Years 1913–1914.

just 45 in the vote switchers' districts; among legislators in wet districts the same comparison is 1,023 dealers to 81. If the liquor lobby had any effect, it appears, it was primarily in retaining opposition to woman suffrage in those districts where its industry was strong.

The richness of the historical record in Michigan at this moment enables an even more detailed analysis of this particular outcome. Table 3.5 presents the results of multinomial logistic regression. This model allows assessment of which characteristics distinguished both consistent supporters and vote switchers from those members who voted against the woman suffrage amendment in both 1911 and 1912. The model includes the previously used information on the presence of liquor dealers and farming interests in each district, but adds several other measures to test whether Grange and liquor interests really did differentiate representatives' votes more than other possibly relevant differences. Most notable, MESA records include for this time period the rare information of a measure of the size of the organized movement across the entire state.[69] MESA leaders coded each county's strength of suffrage organization in 1912 on a three-point scale. This county-level information can then be mapped onto state legislative districts to assess whether MESA's organizational work had its own, independent effect on legislators' votes. The

[68] The number of liquor dealers in the district and the amount of liquor tax paid are perfectly correlated; the more dealers in the district, the higher the tax paid. Mean differences for liquor tax are also statistically significant.

[69] In MESA County Reports 1910–1918 (Florence Belle Brotherton Collection, State Archives of Michigan).

TABLE 3.5. *Predicting Support for Woman Suffrage Amendment, Michigan House of Representatives 1911–1912*

	All Districts		Wet Districts	
	Yes 1911 & 1912	No 1911 & Yes 1912	Yes 1911 & 1912	No 1911 & Yes 1912
Farms	27.73**	23.40**	42.64**	36.98*
	(10.85)	(11.95)	(21.40)	(21.42)
Liquor Lobby	− 2.67	− 3.38*	− 4.15	− 3.86
	(1.83)	(1.98)	(3.15)	(3.26)
Labor	19.23	26.51	65.63*	53.10
	(20.10)	(20.93)	(36.87)	(35.88)
Republican	− 1.14	− 1.13	− 2.32	− 2.89
	(1.51)	(1.57)	(2.57)	(2.49)
Suffrage Organization	.50	−.08	−.002	−.33
	(.69)	(.73)	(1.00)	(1.03)
Urban	1.08	1.59	− 2.64	− 1.69
	(2.30)	(2.51)	(3.63)	(3.45)
Constant	− 1.34	− 1.84	− 1.41	−.28
	(1.75)	(1.96)	(2.51)	(2.34)
N	89		58	
Log-likelihood	− 74.06		− 47.28	
LR ratio χ^2	22.67**		24.02**	

Multinomial logistic regression results. Base category is legislators who voted no in both 1911 and 1912.

Standard errors in parentheses. *p < .10, **p < .05, two-tailed test.

Sources: United States Census, 1910; *Journal of the House of Representatives of the State of Michigan, 1911, 1912; Michigan Official Directory and Legislative Manual for the Years 1913–1914;* MESA County Reports, 1910–1918.

model also includes the legislators' partisanship – a measure indicating whether they belonged to the Republican Party, which had appeared more friendly to the suffrage cause to this point. Two other district-level differences that may have structured legislators' voting behavior are included. First, there is a measure of the presence of labor interests, as captured by the U.S. Census's measure of the number of manufacturing workers per capita in the district – because suffragists had earlier established a relationship at least with labor leaders. Second, a measure of the district's urbanicity, captured simply by the Census's reporting of what percentage of the district lived in urban areas, is included as a check on whether the farming variable does not simply capture an underlying urban/rural divide, including possible urban-based political machine resentment of the broader reformist agenda within which suffrage had been placed.

The results in Table 3.5 support the conclusion that, in fact, liquor interests and Grange interests had separate but related effects on legislators' positions. The positive and statistically significant coefficients on Farms in both columns indicate that stronger farming interests in the legislators' districts differentiated those who supported woman suffrage either consistently or in 1912 only from those who voted repeatedly against it. That this relationship holds despite the inclusion of the measure of urbanicity, and that the coefficients on the urbanicity measure are statistically indistinguishable from zero further supports the conclusion that what mattered was legislators' vulnerability to farming interests, rather than some other urban/rural divide. The negative coefficient on the Liquor Lobby, which attains statistical significance at conventional levels only in the vote switchers' column, indicates that the vote switchers and those who still could not be swayed from opposition to woman suffrage were also differentiated by their vulnerability to lobbying from liquor interests. That is, the Grange's stance on woman suffrage garnered some support for the issue among legislators from farming districts in 1911, their lobbying efforts maintained that support and brought more legislators from farming districts into the fold in 1912, but representatives from liquor industry strongholds continued to register opposition. There is also evidence that the suffragists' alliance with labor interests, however tentative, was beginning to pay off, especially in the state's wet districts. Positive coefficients on Labor that reach statistical significance in the Wet District columns of Table 3.5 show that strong labor constituencies also convinced legislators to support woman suffrage, despite whatever efforts the liquor lobby might have made.

Just as notable as the relationships between district-level forces and legislative votes upheld in Table 3.5 are two that are not: relationships between legislator support for the suffrage bills and the measures of suffrage organization and legislators' party affiliation. The suffrage organization result is just as the programmatic enfranchisement model would predict. Legislators are not expected to be directly influenced by demand from those who wish to be enfranchised, but rather only by the coalition of existing voters with whom the disfranchised have partnered. Clearly, suffrage organization can be essential to building effective partnerships, but that argument specifies an indirect relationship between organization and legislative outcomes – one that these data cannot readily assess. This is in direct contrast to the strategic enfranchisement model expectation, however, for which level of organization of the disfranchised should convey to partisan politicians important information about the group's likelihood of mobilization for the party. The lack of a remaining relationship between partisanship and support for woman suffrage once the influences of the suffrage coalition are accounted for is further evidence that what mattered most in defining the political meaning of women's voting rights were those coalitions, rather than other, simpler, partisan calculations.

Coalitions and the Public Vote

Legislative approval for the constitutional amendment referendum was, of course, only half the battle. There was still a public vote to be won. Although the politics of the 1912 session do not suggest that the referendum was considered a reliable means by which to prevent the actual adoption of women's voting rights, the organizational challenge of carrying a public vote was still a formidable obstacle. Michigan suffragists would do a fair share of organizing, although they struggled at first with funding and throughout with establishing effective strategies for influencing male voters, including how to incentivize coalitional partners other than the Grange to engage in voter persuasion and mobilization work. Grange support, however, was steady. But so, too, was suffragists' sense that opponents were also mobilizing, particularly the liquor industry. In the end, the referendum was lost in an extremely close vote – and amid allegations of electoral fraud. And there was evidence that the key interests on both sides shaped the pattern of votes across the state.

The welcome, yet not quite expected legislative victory meant that suffrage activists in Michigan had just months to rally voters to support them at the polls and almost no money to begin a campaign – MESA records show just $250 was available at the start.[70] Although MESA pleaded with NAWSA for help, the answer came back that "before the amendment was submitted in Michigan, we had pledged every dollar . . . to other States, so there is not any of this fund left in the treasury . . . [b]ut . . . I will pledge to Michigan now $200 worth of literature."[71] As for expertise, suffrage organizations had become proficient in convincing women to express an interest in voting rights, working to get endorsements, and collecting women's signatures on petitions meant to lobby state and federal legislators. Managing a mass campaign was different, as the MESA president wrote back to NAWSA, explaining that their first move had been to hire a campaign manager who "has successfully managed six reformatory campaigns – not political – and not a woman in Michigan has done this. We can PLAN but we feel we cannot execute as well as an experienced man or woman."[72]

Ultimately, then, suffrage activists became even more dependent on other organizations, particularly the Granges and labor unions, to reach voters. Both NAWSA and MESA leadership acknowledged that they needed to appeal to men through their own venues. Responding to MESA's plans to arrange for public statements by prominent men throughout the state, NAWSA president Shaw wrote: "Then I think it is a very wise thing to utilize as many of the men as possible, to get them to speak for you and, after they have once stood up for you they would be much more likely to help when the time really comes. If you have the Labor men strongly with you and the Grange, I am sure that victory

[70] In *Yearbook of the Michigan Equal Suffrage Association and Report of the 27th Annual Convention* (Lansing, 1913). The President's report in that document states that at the beginning of the actual campaign, only $250 remained.
[71] Letter from Anna Howard Shaw to CBA April 2, 1912 (Clara B. Arthur Papers, Detroit Public Library – Burton Historical Collection).
[72] Letter from CBA to Anna Howard Shaw May 30, 1912 (Clara B. Arthur Papers, Detroit Public Library – Burton Historical Collection).

cannot help but come to Michigan."[73] But by late May, nearly two months after the passage of the suffrage referendum resolution, MESA was still struggling to establish a coherent campaign strategy, causing Shaw to write anxiously again encouraging a strategy of mobilizing through existing networks:

To my mind the first thing is to get together as many representatives of as many different associations as possible, getting each of these associations to appoint a representative on a Central Campaign Committee and let that Central Campaign Committee devise a plan of campaign. This, of course, must include organizers and distribution of literature, holding public meetings and, during July and August, they should be street meetings and automobile tours, as people will not go inside halls, especially men, and *it is the men we have to reach*. All farmers' picnics, all Chatauquas, all gatherings of any sort, no matter what the form, should have a woman suffrage speaker. Every convention which meets should have a petition for a speaker to go before it, no matter what kind it is, Ministerial, Sunday-school, Day-school, Butchers, Candlestick Makers, anybody who meets in a convention should be asked to allow suffragists to come before them and speak.[74]

MESA president Arthur replied to Shaw that MESA was, indeed, working with a number of organizations in the state: the Maccabees, WCTU, the Grange and the Michigan Federation of Labor. But Arthur's correspondence also revealed troubles. There were repeated difficulties in coordination of MESA efforts across the state. More troubling, Arthur's correspondence through the summer with suffrage workers in Michigan conveyed less confidence in the success of mobilization through outside organizations, with the exception of the Grange, than she expressed to Shaw. A member of the MESA campaign finance committee reported difficulties between MESA and the WCTU over whether suffrage ought to be lauded as a temperance issue.[75] Another MESA organizer reported that although support was evident among the Grange, the Gleaners, the Farmer's Clubs, and the Federation of Labor, that support still needed organization to channel it to the polls.[76]

The exception to the general rule of organizational difficulties was the Grange. The MESA organizer's troubling report on work amongst other

---

73 Letter from Anna Howard Shaw to CBA April 2, 1912 (Clara B. Arthur Papers, Detroit Public Library – Burton Historical Collection).

74 Letter from Anna Howard Shaw to CBA May 27, 1912 (Clara B. Arthur Papers, Detroit Public Library – Burton Historical Collection). Emphasis added.

75 Letter from L. Verna Simons to CBA June 1912 (Clara B. Arthur Papers, Detroit Public Library – Burton Historical Collection). Arthur had anticipated this issue and warned Shaw of it early in the campaign. Shaw's response to Arthur on April 18, 1912 was: "I greatly regret that what you say about the WCTU wanting to carry the measure as a dry and wet one, because nothing could be more absurd than to mix temperance and woman suffrage in a campaign; each is good and each should stand on its own feet without compromising either." (Clara B. Arthur Papers, Detroit Public Library – Burton Historical Collection).

76 Letter from Jenny Law Hardy to CBA June 18, 1912 (Clara B. Arthur Papers, Detroit Public Library – Burton Historical Collection).

organizations singled out the exception of the Grange, relaying that they were "having suffrage meetings and speeches all around," carrying out their own campaign with their own finances.[77] Indeed, the State Grange's own Equal Suffrage Campaign committee was in regular contact with MESA's Arthur, arranging for suffrage speakers at their local meetings through the summer. Even in the face of other organizational difficulties, both Arthur and Shaw found the support from the Grange promising for the referendum's outcome, as they counted on rural voters to carry the referendum, and expected urban centers increasingly led by political machines to be the most difficult to win over.[78] At the start of the campaign, with few resources to offer, Shaw had hoped to reach the rural voters she viewed key to a victory at the polls by getting sympathetic members of the U.S. Congress to have reports of the suffrage hearings before that body franked to voters in rural districts. Reaching those voters directly seemed a prohibitive task for suffrage organizations whose memberships were concentrated in urban areas.[79] By the end of the campaign, Arthur reported that all the rural areas in the state had been systematically worked over by the State Grange campaign, which paid all its own expenses for the work.[80]

Despite the short, taxing campaign, suffragists were hopeful on Election Day. They had managed to raise more than $6,000 for the referendum effort, which they spent sponsoring mass meetings, door-to-door canvassing, and distribution of literature in multiple languages. They had garnered support from a growing list of reform-minded organizations, including a plank in the platform of the newly emerging Progressive Party. And the Grange had done massive campaigning in the rural areas they hoped would be most conducive to supporting their cause.[81] As results began to come in the day after the election, it appeared that women's voting rights had prevailed. MESA members began receiving letters of congratulations from suffrage workers across the country. But when the final count was posted, the measure was lost: 247,375 votes in favor of extending the elective franchise, and 248,135 votes against, a difference of just 760 votes.[82]

Almost immediately allegations of voting irregularities and fraud surfaced as explanations of the loss. MESA workers, posted at polling places to observe the elections reported incidences of election officials failing to provide the

[77] Jenny Law Hardy to CBA June 7, 1912 (Clara B. Arthur Papers, Detroit Public Library – Burton Historical Collection).
[78] Letters from Anna Howard Shaw to CBA April 2, April 18, June 5, 1912 (Clara B. Arthur Papers, Detroit Public Library – Burton Historical Collection).
[79] Letter from Anna Howard Shaw to CBA April 2, 1912 (Clara B. Arthur Papers, Detroit Public Library – Burton Historical Collection).
[80] *Yearbook of the Michigan Equal Suffrage Association and Report of the 27th Annual Convention*, 15.
[81] Ibid.
[82] *Michigan Official Directory and Legislative Manual for the Years 1913–1914*.

separate ballots on which the woman suffrage amendment was listed.[83] Suspicion of vote fraud, stuffing the ballot box against the suffrage measure, however, was mostly fed by the fact that the measure was winning in all the early ballot counts, then lost as sizable majorities against it were reported late in mostly urban areas. MESA and Grange campaigners speculated liquor industry interests had a hand in somehow creating the eleventh hour overturn, although they failed to uncover proof of any wrongdoing. Their misgivings were bolstered, however, by the involvement of liquor industry lawyers in the legal proceedings that followed the election.[84] MESA officers and Grange Equal Suffrage Campaign leaders considered challenging the vote count. MESA's campaign manager attempted to gather evidence of actual fraud and to assess whether throwing out questionable ballots would change the election results in their favor before proceeding with any formal challenge of the election. Challenges were ultimately filed in Wayne and Kent counties, only to bring two discouraging results. First, it was discovered that the amendment would still be lost by several hundred votes in both counties after throwing out the ballots in question. Second, the Wayne County Circuit Court handed down a decision that a recount was unconstitutional. MESA and Grange leaders agonized over whether to challenge the circuit court decision or to work for resubmission in the next legislature, but with uncertainty about whether a statewide recount would actually resolve in their favor, the leadership made the decision to ask for resubmission.[85]

Evidence of the reasons for the 1912 outcome in the poll results is limited because only county-level vote totals are available. Although it is not possible with these data to thoroughly investigate the reasons individual voters chose to vote for or against the suffrage amendment, the county totals do tell a story that is consistent with the suffragists' understanding of their supporters and their opposition. Consonant with the strong suffrage support from the Grange, stronger majorities in favor of woman suffrage turned up in rural areas. Counties with heavy concentrations of farming interests returned a total vote of 52.5 percent in favor of suffrage; the remaining counties gave suffrage just 48.3 percent of their votes. The pattern of support among wet and dry counties also conformed to expectations given the effort at anti-suffrage mobilization from liquor interests; seventeen of the forty-five (38 percent) wet counties returned

[83] Michigan Equal Suffrage Association, *Report*, 1913. 50.

[84] Letter from Ida Chittenden to CBA, November 12, 1912 (Clara B. Arthur Papers, Detroit Public Library – Burton Historical Collection).

[85] Discussion of the deliberations over challenging the circuit decision in a letter from MESA vice president Clara Russell to CBA, December 18, 1912. Sentiment within Grange leadership to push for the recount reported by Ida Chittenden in a letter to CBA, December 19, 1912. Final decision discussed in letter from Anna Howard Shaw to CBA, December 31, 1912 and January 3, 1913. (Clara B. Arthur Papers, Detroit Public Library – Burton Historical Collection).

majorities against the suffrage amendment, whereas only seven of thirty-eight (18 percent) dry counties did the same.[86]

The Politics of Referendum Resubmission – Partisan Pressures on Elite Support, Waning Public Interest

Not only had woman suffrage lost at the polls in November 1912, so, too, had the Republican Party. Michigan's steady Republican base had been fractured by the Progressive movement, with its unmet demands for stronger direct democracy provisions and other government reforms in Michigan. The result was a decidedly different political landscape for suffragists to navigate as they pushed for resubmission of the suffrage amendment in 1913. This new landscape had some advantage. The newly formed Progressive Party, which had peeled both elites and voters away from the Republican Party, had already made a commitment to the suffrage cause. Its electoral success, then, provided not only supportive Progressive lawmakers, but also incentive for other politicians to acquiesce to woman suffrage among other Progressive demands to win over the inordinate number of voters who had bolted to the new party. The partnering of woman suffrage and the Progressive push for reform, however, also increased the ire of already resistant political machines. Suffragists, as a result, found themselves up against concerted resistance from the politically powerful Detroit machine, and its legislative arm, the Wayne County delegation. Although suffragists won resubmission, this new arrangement of interests structured the legislative deliberation and bore a losing consequence in the referendum that followed.

Suffragists had secured an endorsement from the Progressive Party during the 1912 campaign, something they had never managed to secure from the Republican Party in Michigan, no matter how many of its members individually supported the cause. The rising tide of Progressive support in turn pressured similar concessions from others. The Republican Party offered their own pledge for resubmission of the amendment referendum, as did the Democratic candidate who went on to win the governor's office. When the election put Progressives inside the legislature – eleven in the House and six in the Senate – MESA leaders saw potential for new leverage. In fact, with continued organizational commitment from the Grange to lobby other members, and so many members' districts actually returning majorities in favor of the 1912 referendum, MESA leaders were hopeful that resubmission would be easily achieved.[87]

---

[86] Multivariate analysis is difficult here because of to the collinearity of "farm" and "dry" counties. Regressing farming interests, liquor interests, labor interests, and urbanicity on the percent of the vote in favor of woman suffrage produces a significant effect only for the liquor variable ($b = -.04$, s.e. $= .02$, $p = .04$; R-squared $= .16$ n $= 82$).

[87] MESA report 1913.

Suffrage advocates hoped for submission of the amendment at the April 1913 elections, reasoning that their supporting rural districts typically turned out at higher rates than urban districts in off-year elections. This meant the resolution needed to be moved expeditiously through the legislature. Within a month, suffrage supporters in the House secured a vote on final passage and passed it easily with seventy-four in favor and twenty-four opposed. True to their campaign promise, Progressives had lined up unanimously in favor of the amendment. Progressive support also seemed important to the calculations of other members. First, although the House was markedly supportive of the Progressive-endorsed measure, it received significant resistance from exactly those legislatures who represented the interests that the Progressive reform push was trying to eliminate from state politics: the legislative arm of the Detroit machine, the Republicans of the Wayne County delegation. All but two Wayne County Republicans opposed the measure, accounting for more than half of the Republican opponents of the measure. Among other legislators, however, the Progressive's electoral fortunes seemed to provide a general impetus to support the Progressive agenda, regardless of other considerations. There were no indications of any systematic leverage of pro- or anti-suffrage coalitions on members' votes. Notably, supporters and opponents were not differentiated by the relative presence of farming, labor, or liquor interests in their districts. The only discernible systematic difference is that legislators from outside Wayne County who held out support for the resolution were perhaps more insulated from any Republican and Democratic party pressures that may have been exerted to support the measure, taking on average nearly 52 percent of their districts' vote shares in the last election, whereas supporters of the resolution averaged slightly less than 42 percent of their districts' votes.[88]

The suffrage resolution also passed with ease in the Senate. The Senate first passed its own version of the resolution, which included the decidedly anti-machine provision of an additional provision that required the wives of immigrant men to wait five years before becoming eligible for voting rights, by a vote of twenty-six in favor and five opposed. After receiving the House version one week later, the Senate again passed woman suffrage, this time by a vote of twenty-five to four. As in the house, resistance came from Wayne County Republicans, accounting for half of the opposition. Electoral incentive – or perceived protection – for resistance also seemed tied to the previous referendum results, with all but one of the dissenters on either measure coming from districts that had returned majorities against the amendment in 1912.

---

[88] Mean percentages of district votes taken in November 1912 election are .516 and .415. Difference is statistically significant at p=.03. Because Progressives voted unanimously in favor of the measure, the test of coalitional influence was a logistic regression on only Democrat and Republican members' votes of party, vote share, district vote on the previous suffrage referendum, farms per 100 population, per capita investment in manufacturing, and liquor tax in the district on votes of major party representatives. No significant relationships were estimated.

There was little time before the April elections to campaign throughout the state for the suffrage referendum. There were also few resources, so much money and energy having been expended in both the 1912 campaign and the investigation and legal proceedings that followed. Although MESA believed their strongest support was in the rural areas, they did little campaigning outside the urban areas of Detroit, Grand Rapids, Saginaw, and Bay City where most of the leadership lived, concentrating their efforts on hopes of vote conversion there, instead of mobilizing their supporters to turnout for the off-year elections.[89] It was a strategy they would soon regret. Although the 1912 measure had lost by just several hundred votes, when the 1913 votes came in, the amendment had lost far more decisively. The final state tally was 168,738 in favor and 264,852 against woman suffrage.[90]

MESA leaders studied the county vote returns to explain the dismal showing for suffrage. Although they publicly blamed anti-suffrage mobilization and even poor weather that kept rural voters home for the loss, in their private correspondence there was admission that they had failed to work hard enough to mobilize their own support. Eventually their standard explanation for the outcome was one centered on turnout, as they reported to NAWSA:

The preceding year the liquor forces had not realized the need of active work. Never in any other State campaign did these forces make so open a fight as in this one. They paid for columns of space in the newspapers and circulated vast quantities of the literature prepared by the women's Anti-Suffrage Association. This was in piles on the bars of the saloons and, according to reports, in even more questionable places. The defeat was not due so much to a change in public opinion as it was to an absence of the favorable vote which had been called out in the previous year by reason of the presidential election.[91]

Indeed, the county vote totals are consistent with a story of lopsided voter turnout in favor of the anti-suffrage interests. As a percentage of the voting-qualified population, counties had returned on average 30.4 percent of their votes for the amendment in 1912, but only 22.2 percent in favor in 1913, an average decline of 8.2 percent. On the other side, counties had returned an average of 27.9 percent of their vote against the measure in 1912, and in 1913 average opposition turnout grew to 29.4 percent. And, the average relationship between county vote totals is, in fact, typical across counties. Correlations of .78 between the supporting vote percentages and .85 for the opposing indicate that there was a marked linear pattern to both support and opposition across the two years, indicating all the districts experienced similar depressed turnout for suffrage and steady opposition.[92]

Although we cannot gauge with certainty whether these strong county patterns indeed indicate decreased turnout of pro-suffrage voters and steady

---

[89] Michigan Equal Suffrage Association, *Report*, 1913.
[90] *Michigan Official Directory and Legislative Manual for the Years 1913–1914*, 778.
[91] HWS, vol. VI, 309.
[92] Plots of the relationships confirm linearity as well, with no notable outliers.

TABLE 3.6. *Predicted Voter Transition Rates, 1912 to 1913 Vote on Woman Suffrage Thomsen Voter Transition Model, Conditional Probit Predictions*

	Yes 1912	No 1912	Not Voting 1912
Yes 1913	.49	.16	.02
No 1913	.35	.61	.07
Not voting 1913	.16	.23	.91

turnout of anti-suffrage voters, rather than any marked vote-switching, ecological inference techniques that have been shown to be accurate in capturing split-ticket voting and party switching between elections can also be applied here. Using information about each county's marginals – the number of votes for and against suffrage and the number of qualified voters who did not vote in each election – Thomsen's voter transition model suggests there may have been more vote-switching than suffragists believed.[93] Thomsen's model produces predicted rates of retention and defection from 1912 to 1913 for individual voters, which are displayed in Table 3.6. First, the model suggests that suffragists had a harder time retaining their support than did the opposition Slightly less than 50 percent of those who voted in favor of the amendment in 1912 did so again in 1913, but more than 60 percent of those who voted against it in 1912 did the same in 1913. Second, despite a notable rate of abstention of 1912 supporters in the 1913 referendum (16 percent), those who voted yes in 1912 were twice as likely to vote no in 1913 than they were to abstain. These results perhaps lend more credence to suffragists' concerns about the mobilization of the opposition, particularly of liquor interests, whose anti-suffrage mobilization would have been more widespread across the state than the locally concentrated Detroit machine. The model, however, suggests

[93] All ecological inference techniques suffer from the difficulty of making a suitable and realistic identifying assumption. The Thomsen model is an ecological inference approach that solves the identification problem by assuming underlying individual utilities that map onto a typical probit binary choice model, then assuming that the ecological correlation between the transformed vote proportions is the same as the individual-level correlation between the transformed vote probabilities. For more discussion on why this may be the most sensible possible assumption when estimating voter transitions (vote changes across elections), see Christopher Achen and W. Philips Shively, *Cross Level Inference* (Chicago: University of Chicago Press, 1995). On the model's accuracy in identifying split-ticket voting, see Michael J. Hanmer and Michael W. Traugott, "The Impact of Voting by Mail on Voter Behavior" *American Politics Research* 32 (2004): 375–405. On voter transition, see Won-ho Park, "Estimation of Voter Transition Rates and Ecological Inference." Paper presented at the 2003 annual meetings of the Midwest Political Science Association. For details on the model's development, see Soren R. Thomsen, "Danish Elections 1920–79: A Logit Approach to Ecological Analysis and Inference." Aarhus, Denmark: Politica (1987). Thomsen, Soren R., "Issue Voting and Ecological Inference." Unpublished manuscript, Aarhus University, Aarhus Denmark (2000).

some success of the suffragists' campaign for conversion of opposition as well; 16 percent of voters seem to have switched their votes from no to yes. To overcome the conversions by opponents, it seems, suffragists needed broader efforts to both preserve *and* turnout their original base of support. What is certain is that although Michigan's suffrage movement had established coalitional partnerships, their coalitional politics had yet to produce sufficient leverage for partisan politicians to ensure the deliverance of woman suffrage at the polls.

Final Victory – Friends Retained, Enemies Eliminated

Convinced that they had lost their battles for a woman suffrage amendment only through voter fraud and ineffective mobilization, suffrage activists returned to planning for another attempt. In no rush to fail again, they did not push for immediate resubmission in the next legislative session. Instead, time was taken to build organizational capacity that might be more effective in the next referendum campaign. Receiving advice and eventually a paid organizer from NAWSA, now under the leadership of Carrie Chapman Catt, MESA set about establishing an organization that mirrored the political districts of the state. There would now be a MESA member charged with each county, and to the fullest extent possible a member for each voting precinct within the county. Suffragists had also worked to retain and grow their political partnerships, especially those with the Grange and organized labor.[94] By 1917, it seemed Michigan might be ready for another attempt, although MESA leaders actually expressed some reservations about whether their organization and its budget had grown enough to take on a campaign. What suffragists failed to appreciate was that Michigan's recent adoption of statewide prohibition through referendum signaled the end of their greatest challenge in the past decade – the effectiveness of oppositional pressure exerted by liquor interests. In the absence of liquor-related politics and indeed in the face of strong prohibitionist sentiment, suffrage was easily won in the legislature and at the polls.

Two suffrage measures were drafted and introduced in the legislature that year, both a bill that would immediately grant voting rights for women in presidential elections only, and a resolution calling for another referendum on a constitutional amendment for full woman suffrage. Both measures passed. The resolution was opposed by only four senators, all representatives of the Detroit machine. Presidential suffrage drew opposition from seven senators, including three from Detroit. House members were also slightly less supportive of the presidential suffrage measure than the amendment resolution. A number

---

[94] Details of the organizational work in various documents and clippings in the Florence Belle Brotherton Collection, State Archives of Michigan (Box 1, Folder 11). Details of the organizational work, including consideration of a partial suffrage bill, are in a MESA report to NAWSA, 1915 (Florence Belle Brotherton Collection, State Archives of Michigan, Box 1, Folder 2).

of those voting against the presidential suffrage bill reserved the right to explain their votes, registering objection to enfranchising women without voter approval. Although appeals to the need for a referendum in previous legislative considerations had been part of a strategy to provide support for suffrage in the legislature yet remain effectively certain that the policy would not come to pass, it was less clear that legislators had sufficient reason to expect failure this time. These particular dissentions may, in fact, have been representation of district preferences, as opponents' districts were, on average, less supportive of woman suffrage in the 1912 referendum, giving approximately 47 percent of their vote to suffrage, whereas supporters' districts returned an average of slightly more than 51 percent of their vote in favor of the amendment.

The influence of the pro-suffrage coalition on legislators' votes on the issue can be demonstrated using a logistic regression to predict House members' support of both suffrage measures. Grange influence is again captured with the farming presence in the district, measured by the per capita number of farms. Labor influence is gauged with a measure of the per capita number of manufacturing workers in the district. Also included is the sentiment that the district registered for suffrage in the last referendum, and for the previously linked issue of prohibition. The model also includes possible sources of anti-suffrage influence: urbanicity of the district and an indicator of whether the member was from the anti-suffrage stronghold of Wayne County. Although the coalitional influences stretched across party lines, partisanship of the legislators is included to test whether a significant party divide remained despite coalitional pressures. The results of the model, displayed in Table 3.7, reveal that district approval of the 1912 referendum added to the Grange and labor interests already pushing legislators to support the measure: all three of these factors increased representatives' likelihood of voting yes on both pieces of suffrage legislation. Additionally, if any doubt had remained about whether legislators' woman suffrage and prohibition positions ought to be connected, passage of a prohibition amendment to the state constitution the previous year clearly and decisively separated their votes on woman suffrage from concerns about wet and dry interests. No relationship remained even between the districts' votes on the prohibition measure and House members' votes on women's voting rights. Still, resistance from Wayne County politicians remained – suffrage coalitional politics were unpersuasive in the state's largest urban center, suggesting the urban machine-based politicians were resistant to the reformist coalition's pressures.

Although it passed in April of 1917, the constitutional amendment would not go to Michigan voters until the November 1918 elections. This left more than a year to work up public support for the amendment. It seems, however, that MESA leaders had been right to be apprehensive about their ability to carry out a referendum campaign. There was difficulty securing commitments of time and money for the cause, a state of affairs that was relayed to

TABLE 3.7. *Predicting Support for Woman Suffrage, Michigan House of Representatives 1917 Logistic Regression Results*

	Constitutional Amendment	Presidential Suffrage
Per capita farms	28.12**	11.44
	(12.89)	(9.37)
Per capita manufacturing laborers	26.20*	36.81**
	(14.08)	(14.76)
District support for prohibition	3.86	−.58
	(6.67)	(3.03)
District support for suffrage	16.07**	7.56*
	(6.50)	(4.53)
Republican	.30	.44
	(1.09)	(.89)
Percent district urban	1.47	−1.14
	(2.34)	(2.10)
Wayne County	−2.81*	−3.70**
	(1.50)	(1.42)
Constant	−12.83**	−5.20*
	(4.40)	(3.08)
N	92	94
LR	37.23**	21.86**
Log likelihood	−30.8	−47.9

* $p < .10$, **$p < .05$, two-tailed test.
Sources: United States Census, 1910, 1920; *Journal of the House of Representatives of the State of Michigan, 1917; Michigan Official Directory and Legislative Manual for the Years 1913–1914, 1917–1918.*

NAWSA president Catt.[95] Catt responded with an organizational commitment from NAWSA unlike Michigan had received at any other time. For the first time NAWSA sent paid organizers, with experience in successful referendum efforts in other states, to run the campaign. The workers were accompanied by a cash infusion of $1,400 and a pledge to finance the printing costs of publicity literature.[96] Cooperation was maintained with MESA's previous allies, including the Grange, Maccabees, WCTU, and several labor organizations. When the votes were counted, the NAWSA investment had paid off: the suffrage amendment carried by 229,790 votes in favor to 195,284 opposed. Support was less strong in counties with large urban populations, but just eleven of Michigan's eighty-three counties, including Wayne County, failed to return majorities in

[95] Caruso, *A History of Woman Suffrage in Michigan.*
[96] HWS, vol. VI, 314.

favor of the amendment.[97] Michigan women were finally fully enfranchised citizens.

Conclusion – Lessons Learned

Looking back across the seven decades that the issue of woman suffrage lingered in Michigan politics revealed the important role that group interests played in both legislators' and voters' decisions on woman suffrage. Although activism for women's voting rights in the state began in isolation from other political interests, campaigns for voting rights on principle sustained neither lawmakers' or the public's interest. It was not enough for suffrage advocates to win a war of ideas; they needed to give legislators and voters reasons to do the political work it would take to turn principle into state policy. Some groups might have been able to accomplish this through the promise of their votes alone – to effectively navigate the politics of strategic enfranchisement. That strategy, however, required enough group homogeneity for a party in power to see in it the potential for a new voting bloc. Michigan politicians never saw that sort of homogeneity in women. In fact, they were so aware of the political consequences of the heterogeneity of Michigan's female population that some attempts were made to draft suffrage qualifications that would enfranchise only a specific segment of the group, such as the English literacy clause attached by Republicans to the municipal suffrage bill of 1893. Ultimately, constraining the definition of the female electorate in such a way that politicians could confidently anticipate a new voting bloc was an elusive goal. Michigan women simply were not good candidates for this sort of strategic enfranchisement.

Failing to be good candidates for strategic enfranchisement did not leave Michigan suffrage advocates without possibilities. There was still hope for programmatic enfranchisement, for convincing legislators that important segments of their existing constituencies had salient interests in women's voting rights. This path to voting rights, however, required credible commitments from groups other than disfranchised women. Suffragists needed to build politically viable and credible coalitions with other interest groups. In Michigan, suffrage organizations eventually found common ground with four particularly important groups: prohibitionists, the Grange, labor unions, and the newly forming Progressive Party. Each of these groups perceived some real benefit in aligning with suffrage organizations, and the suffragists worked for each group's causes in exchange for their support of women's voting rights. These coalitions moved woman suffrage in Michigan from a principled debate to a viable political issue,

---

[97] Percent urban and percent foreign-born both significantly negatively correlated with percent support. Regressing both on percent support reduces only urban to statistical significance, although both are significant in a regression predicting county support for prohibition. Urban opposition, it seems, was not entirely about foreign-born opposition, as some suffrage activists and later scholars have claimed.

one on which politicians were willing to expend real political capital to push for a change in policy. Politicians' need to be responsive to woman suffrage's political allies waxed and waned with the tides of party politics, but in the end persuaded legislators to see the issue through to adoption.

Of course, passing suffrage legislation to accommodate existing constituents did not mean that politicians would work to help suffrage supporters to pass the issue by the voting public. And as Michigan women discovered, work *was* needed to accomplish that task, even if the work was simply to encourage turnout among voters that already supported the cause. On this front, real partnerships with other interest groups were also incredibly useful, for the existing networks of those organizations could be used as means for voter mobilization, and perhaps conversion as well. In Michigan, suffragists' most powerful ally in this respect was the Grange, which, through its own Equal Suffrage Campaign Committee, included suffrage mobilization in its regular meetings and activities. Only with this these sorts of effective partnerships did the cause of woman suffrage finally emerge victorious.

The case of Michigan also revealed that opposition has its place in suffrage politics – but that the motivations and effectiveness of opponents should also be understood within the programmatic enfranchisement model. Across all the considerations of women's voting rights in Michigan, the common theme among organized opposition was, in fact, opposition to the interests of the suffrage coalition. Woman suffrage began to draw opposition from anti-prohibition interests and the so-called liquor lobby when the suffrage movement partnered with temperance organizations. An ongoing connection between suffragists and the WCTU made breaking that resistance difficult. A later connection to other reformers who were pushing for at least greater regulation of the liquor industry further cemented this opposition. Similarly, as suffragists partnered with those pushing for reforms aimed at undermining the power of political machines, machine politicians were particularly likely to work against the suffrage cause. It is important to note that, although opponents forestalled woman suffrage even in the face of growing pro-suffrage coalitions, as coalition strength grew opponents won by narrow – and perhaps not always entirely legitimate – margins. And under the right political circumstances, pro-suffrage coalitions could, and did, overcome opposition and deliver new voting rights.

4

Strong Leverage

Third-Party Support

> ...make a comparison between the Suffrage Association and the Anti Saloon
> League. The latter organization at the time of the Labor Convention would not
> ask for endorsement, because they said if the Labor Party does not win, it would
> surely mean defeat in the Constitutional Convention. So they would have nothing
> to do with the Labor Party, and kept their campaign strictly non-partisan. When
> it came to a vote in the Constitutional Convention on the separate submission of
> both questions, the anti Saloon League got 15 votes, and we got 19. So that our
> alliance with the Labor Party probably helped us that much even in a Democratic
> Convention, for as I said, the Democrats are bidding for the Labor vote.
>
> – Laura Gregg, NAWSA organizer writing on the woman
> suffrage campaign in Arizona, 1910[1]

Alliances with minor (or third) political parties were an especially effective tool
for compelling major party politicians to respond to the woman suffrage cause
in the states. Although, as demonstrated in the previous chapters, support for
women's voting rights from any well-organized, populous constituent group
could foster pressure on politicians, third parties wielded particularly clear
information about the electoral costs for lack of major party attention to their
causes. Successful third parties, by definition, were organizations that took
votes away from major parties. Third parties that took significant vote shares,
even if they failed to win any office, could, and often did, change the balance
of power between the major parties. This left both major parties with incentive
to respond to the third party's agenda, to somehow capture the third party
voters: the former majority party needed to reclaim its dominance, and the
former minority had a new opportunity to gain majority status. A place on
the agenda of an electorally successful third party thus gave woman suffrage

---

[1] Letter from Laura Gregg to Caroline I. Reilly, December 26, 1910 (Women's Suffrage Collection,
Arizona Department of Library, Archives, and Public Records, History and Archives Division).

unique immediacy in state politics; the clear electoral incentive pushed the major party organizations for responsiveness. Third party support, that is, was extremely effective in communicating the constituent demand and electoral vulnerability thereto required for partisan support for suffrage extension within the programmatic enfranchisement model.

Arguing that third parties provided particularly strong pressure on major party politicians to enfranchise women opens the question of why woman suffrage advocates could convince third parties to forward their cause when major parties found it in their interests to elude or even reject the issue. Simply put, third parties faced an entirely different set of incentives. First, lacking the finances and organizational capacity of their competitors, these coalitions that would be parties needed things that a well-organized suffrage movement could offer: funds, political skills, and members to carry out campaign tasks. In return for support from third party politicians, woman suffrage organizations often added some of the third party's key policy objectives to their own agendas and sent their membership to work in the party's electoral campaigns. At other times, the membership overlap between woman suffrage organizations and other issue organizations meant consistent policy work was already being performed, and the draw for the third party was bringing the women of the issue organization along in the new party. In other words, supporting woman suffrage was a way for third parties to draw the women from the social movement from which the party emerged into the efforts to build a partisan organization. Woman suffrage was also often added to platforms of parties that started as single-issue alliances, as the party diversified in attempts to gain and maintain political momentum.

Consider, for example, the Prohibitionist Party, which was the first to endorse woman suffrage in its national platform in 1872, at the same time it also added planks relating to issues relating to both farming and labor interests.[2] The concurrent action speaks to an attempt to pull temperance society members along in the work that would be necessary to run the new party. In other words, although the temperance movement flourished with an abundance of active members, convincing those members to defect from the major parties both electorally and organizationally might take more than appealing to their support of prohibition – temperance advocates needed to see how their other interests fit into a seemingly single-minded agenda. Indeed, Prohibition Party candidates addressed this concern explicitly, speaking in their campaigns directly to the point. One such speech noted that " . . . it is objected, '[t]hat is a 'one idea' party, having no purpose but the suppression . . . of intoxicating liquors,' and [we] countered with the claim '[t]hat the platform of our party . . . possesses so many valuable, noble and vital principles . . . that it

---

[2] McKee, Thomas Hudson, *The National Conventions and Party Platforms of All Political Parties* (Baltimore: The Friedenwald Company, 1901), 157–58.

would... gain a great triumph in a comparison with that of either of the other parties."[3]

To be sure, there were also common arguments in Prohibitionist rhetoric about women's ability to "purify" politics if enfranchised, and particularly about the certainty of prohibition victory following woman suffrage. Such comments could, indeed, be read as genuine conviction that women voters would deliver a prohibition triumph. Yet, there is also room to see in this rhetoric an appeal to the women of the temperance movement, in particular, to join the party in its organizational efforts. As the candidate quoted earlier emphasized the spreading policy agenda of the Prohibition Party, for example, he also spoke of "the women 'crusaders,' who [had] done so much in purifying and upbuilding a healthy public sentiment... " – the women who had carried out a great deal of the practical efforts of the movement. By some estimates, in fact, these women accounted for one-third to one-half of the movement's grass-roots support.[4] If the fledgling party was to bring these organizers along, rather than lose them to the decidedly nonpartisan wing of the temperance agitation, which became the Anti-Saloon League, Prohibitionists needed to give women their own reasons for joining a political party. Adding women's voting rights to the party's agenda was a good way to create a place for women in an organization whose main purpose was electoral.

Appealing to the female membership of the social movement at the roots of the political party also undergirded the support offered to woman suffrage by several farmers' and labor parties, most notably the Farmers' Alliance, the People's party, the Greenbackers, the Union Labor party, the Socialists, and the Socialist-Labor party. Women were already active members of a number of organizations charged with advocating the interests of American farmers, including the fraternal society of the Grange from its founding in 1867, where women's roles grew along with the organization's political agenda. Eventually, women would serve as Grange Lecturers, paper editors, and even Grange Master, and a number of state and local Granges would establish their own woman suffrage committees – special political arms of the Grange organizations charged with public and legislative lobbying for women's voting rights.[5] Women were also playing an increasingly important role in workplace

---

[3] Williams, Albert, "Prohibition and Woman Suffrage: Speech of Hon. Albert Williams." Michigan State Prohibition Party. Charlotte, Michigan. October 9, 1874, 8–9.

[4] Williams, Albert, "Woman Suffrage and Prohibition," 26–27. Using the term "crusaders" most likely references the Women's Temperance Crusade, an independent women's temperance organization formed in 1873 and replaced the following year by the Woman's Christian Temperance Union. On the importance of women to the temperance movement, see Jack S. Blocker Jr., "Separate Paths: Suffragists and the Women's Temperance Crusade," *Signs* 10 (1985): 460–76.

[5] Marti, Donald B., *Women of the Grange: Mutuality and Sisterhood in Rural America, 1866–1920* (New York: Greenwood Press, 1991). Trump, Fred, *The Grange in Michigan: An Agricultural History of Michigan over the Past 90 Years* (Grand Rapids, Michigan: The Dean-Hicks Co., 1963).

politics in the mid- and late nineteenth century, expanding the labor parties'
incentives to draw on their organizational strength. The 1870 U.S. Census
counted 323,506 women employed in manufacturing, meaning women already
accounted for approximately 16.8 percent of the adult manufacturing labor
force, and their presence in that labor force would grow steadily into the twentieth century.[6] Independent women's trade unions formed at least as early as
the 1860s, and their incorporation into labor union organizations with men
had begun by the 1870s. The Knights of Labor admitted women to regular
membership by 1881; the American Federation of Labor seated its first fully
accredited female convention delegate in 1890.[7] By the 1890s, the same middle
class women populating suffrage associations were also taking a sincere interest in labor causes, particularly those involving women and children. These
women became involved in the efforts to organize women workers through
the Women's Trade Union League and used their household purchasing power
to further the union cause through Consumers' Leagues and the International
Union Label League.[8] It was also in the 1890s that the larger labor union organizations began offering not only their endorsement of woman suffrage, but,
in some instances, their active support in suffrage lobbying.[9]

Bringing along the base of the social movement(s) from which it emerged
was not the only reason for a third party to offer an endorsement of woman
suffrage, however. The campaign assistance that woman suffrage organizations, themselves, could offer was also appealing. In Arizona, for example, as
the state's suffrage organization and its NAWSA organizer worked to have voting rights for women written into the first state constitution, they approached
the newly forming Labor Party for support from any delegate the new party
might elect to the Constitutional Convention. An endorsement was agreed on,
as was the suffragists' assistance in the party's campaign work. The NAWSA

---

[6] University of Virginia Geospatial and Statistical Data Center. *United States Historical Census Data Browser*. 1998. University of Virginia. Available: http://fisher.lib.virginia.edu/census/

[7] The first admission of women to a national trade union with men appears to be the Cigar Makers' International Union in 1867. Henry, Alice, *Women and the Labor Movement* (New York: Arno & The New York Times, 1971), 37–56. Flexner, *Century of Struggle*, 126–35.

[8] Some suffragist leaders, including Elizabeth Cady Stanton and Susan B. Anthony, began pushing for a connection between the middle class movement and the growing numbers of working women, going so far as to establish a Working Women's Association in 1868. The Association and Stanton and Anthony's trade union support were both short-lived, however. Their commit-ment to the cause of workingwomen seemed a bit less than genuine; the leaders' interests were more in converting workingwomen to the suffrage cause, rather than lending their support to wage and working condition battles. An unwillingness to compromise "suffrage first" apparently generated some disdain, especially for Anthony, in union circles. See Philip S. Foner, *Women and the American Labor Movement: From Colonial Times to the Eve of World War I* (New York: The Free Press, 1979), 122–62; Flexner, *Century of Struggle*, 195–207.

[9] Foner, *Women and the American Labor Movement*. Dye, Nancy Schrom, "Feminism or Union-ism? The New York Women's Trade Union League and the Labor Movement" *Feminist Studies* 3.1/2 (1975): 111–25.

organizer reported of this agreement that "we helped the Labor ticket in those counties where the other parties would not do anything for us, and they saw that we intended to stand by the people who would stand by us."[10] Suffrage organizations were also quite active in the 1912 Progressive party campaigns. In Illinois, for instance, suffrage organization members were enlisted to help in a number of fundraising and publicity tasks, including the running of Progressive campaign "stores" – venues where campaign literature was passed out and donations were accepted – and the arrangement of public rallies.[11]

Using the case of Illinois, this chapter investigates the politics of connection between woman suffrage and third parties. Third party support of woman suffrage, I show, gave unique leverage to the cause on two occasions. In 1891, support from the Farmers' Alliance helped deliver the right of Illinois women to vote in school elections. And in 1913, Progressive Party pressure was instrumental in making Illinois the first state east of the Mississippi River to allow women to vote in statewide elections when legislators passed a measure that enabled women to vote in presidential (as well as municipal) elections. Embedding these victories in the full history of consideration of woman suffrage in the state provides important lessons on how the connections between third parties were formed and also how they were undermined. Most important, it shows how third party support rested on important suffrage coalitions, notably with farmer and labor interests, and how the choices of suffrage activists could both strengthen and undo those coalitional incentives. The history of the Illinois case also shows how the lack of issue importance that left woman suffrage off the legislative docket for years could be overcome by the partisan incentives that sprang from third party success, and also how that incentive disappeared with the demise of the third party.

Digging more specifically into the legislative details of the 1891 and 1913 successes, in turn, reveals two important lessons about the politics of woman suffrage and third party support. First, the Illinois case reveals important insight about third party leverage that went above the general electoral incentive for major party politicians to recapture bolting voters. Although such emergent parties were extremely unlikely to win sufficient control of the state government to deliver woman suffrage unilaterally, the Illinois case shows how even just a few third party legislators could exert significant pressure on state lawmaking bodies to pass woman suffrage measures when those bodies were otherwise evenly split between the major parties. When third party legislators

[10] Letter from Laura Gregg to Caroline I. Reilly, December 26, 1910 (Women's Suffrage Collection, Arizona Department of Library, Archives, and Public Records, History and Archives Division).

[11] Illinois suffragists' involvement in the Progressive Party is well documented in the papers of Margaret Dreier Robins collected in *Papers of the Women's Trade Union League and its Principal Leaders* (Woodbridge, CT: Research Publications, Inc., for the Schlesinger Library, 1981). Straetz, Ralph Arthur, "The Progressive Movement in Illinois, 1910–1916" (PhD Dissertation, University of Illinois, 1951), 341–44.

held seats that could decide the outcome on otherwise straight party-line votes, they had a uniquely favorable opportunity to obstruct the business of the state legislature to leverage their demands. That this leverage often came at contentious partisan moments, when party-line voting was even more likely than usual, added to its strength.[12] Moreover, they could hold out on the usually party-line procedural, organizational, and rules decisions before policy business could even get started.[13] They could – and did – for example, bring legislative business to a standstill by refusing to side with either major party's choice for the state Speaker of the House and block the selection of U.S. Senators, voting for their own party's candidate, rather than aligning with either major party on the choice. Thus, third party membership in the state legislature added the pressure tactics of legislative bargaining, increasing the party's capacity to leverage adoption of its favored policies, including woman suffrage. Thus, the case shows how third party pressure on major party politicians came not only from the disruption at the polls, but, at times, also from the consequent need for bargaining within the legislature.

The second lesson – made most clearly in the details of the 1913 consideration – is how such coalitions could engender significant resistance of political machines. Machines, operating on a model of building a winning coalition through patronage and other tangible rewards for supporters, are inherently inclined to resist suffrage extensions for the new burden they threaten: doing politics is literally expected to be more expensive with more voters to secure in this way. When such voting rights are, in turn, demanded by the same actors calling for reforms that would undermine the machine's ability to use the state apparatus to do its electoral work, machine resistance is indeed inevitable. Such was clearly the case in Illinois in 1913, as Progressives emerged with an explicitly anti-machine agenda. Given the strength and electoral scope of the Chicago machine, this presented not only resistance in the legislature to be navigated, but also a strategy for woman suffrage that spared it the requirement of needing to clear a referenda hurdle, where machine influence would almost surely spell defeat. In short, the particular opposition to woman suffrage created by the Progressive meaning attached to the cause implied that every ounce of the political leverage deriving from the pro-suffrage coalition was necessary to its success.

Familiar Refrains – Women's Voting Rights Outside Partisan Incentives

Although organization for woman suffrage began quite early in Illinois – the first known suffrage society was established in 1855 and a state organization,

---

[12] This is conditional party government.
[13] That is, third party politicians could become uniquely pivotal voters in the legislature. Both majority and supermajority pivots could wield significant influence, especially under some state legislative rules that required quite a lot of business to be carried out by two-thirds of the members.

the Illinois Woman Suffrage Association (IWSA), was in place by 1869 – early politics of woman suffrage in the state demonstrated patterns of voting rights politics lacking the electoral incentives of either the strategic or the programmatic enfranchisement model. When the IWSA lobbied the convention that met to draft a new state constitution in 1870, it relied on the leverage of a small petition campaign and the direct appeal of politically connected husbands of several IWSA members to delegates. Among the appeals made for woman suffrage was the suggestion that delegates might pass a measure providing for a separate referendum on the issue, an option that the delegates duly considered, but ultimately rejected. Despite a good deal of principled debate on the subject, woman suffrage failed to claim political vitality in the convention. Although the endorsement of suffrage for blacks would be fought along party lines and eventually carried, women's voting rights floundered as a political issue and ultimately failed.[14]

Sitting in convention during the final push for ratification of the Fifteenth Amendment to the U.S. Constitution, the Illinois delegates extensively debated the definition of the state's electorate, arguing primarily over the propriety of voting rights for blacks and women. Although the Illinois legislature had already voted to ratify the federal amendment, significant resistance to writing the word "white" out of the state's constitution did not relent until the national decision on the issue was conclusive. Division on this question was clearly partisan, as some delegates explicitly acknowledged. For instance, when a Democratic delegate presented a resolution meant to forestall Illinois' ability to ratify the federal amendment, should it require resubmission, a Republican objected that he was about to "throw a fire-brand into this Convention." The Democrat responded, "[i]f by 'fire-brand' the gentleman ... means an attempt to excite party feeling, I assure him that I shall do no more than the ... minority report on the question of suffrage." The issue of the minority report was the removal of the word "white" from the electoral qualifications.[15] Delegates, who were evenly divided between the Democratic and Republican parties, clearly read the enfranchisement of blacks as a Republican Party strategy, and each side pushed for the inclusion or exclusion of the racial qualification accordingly. Even after the delegates received word that the Fifteenth Amendment had been ratified, some Democrats continued to push for the retention of the Illinois constitutional requirement that voters be "white," although enough conceded that the national measure compelled them to agree to race-neutral suffrage qualifications to allow for their passage.

---

[14] Buechler, Steven M., *The Transformation of the Woman Suffrage Movement: The Case of Illinois, 1850–1920* (New Brunswick, New Jersey: Rutgers University Press, 1986), 103; HWS, vol. III, 570–71. The suggestion for woman suffrage was rather demure. Catherine Waite's letter, for example, made references to the convention making woman suffrage possible "should the majority of the voters desire it." *Debates and Proceedings of the Constitutional Convention of the State of Illinois* (Springfield: E. L. Merritt & Brother, Printers to the Convention, 1870), 129, 156, 451, 479, 487, 510, 560, 613, 679, 1077.

[15] *Debates and Proceedings*, 161–62.

Women's voting rights, in comparison, were not construed as a partisan debate. Although some delegates made attempts to link the ideas of black and female suffrage, at issue was not partisan politics but racial privilege. One Democrat, for example, offered a resolution that deplored the convention for proposing "an arbitrary and oppressive discrimination in their political privileges, including the right of suffrage against the white female citizens of this State, on account of the providential accident of their sex, and at the same time to obliterate from the Constitution all political discrimination against the black persons of this State." The resolution went on to state that granting rights to black men and not to white women would "assert the natural and political superiority of the [N]egro by reasons of his sex and color, over white women, of our own race and blood."[16] Most of the discussion of the subject of woman suffrage in the convention, however, was not even so sophisticated as to make any overtly political argument. Delegates arguing in favor of woman suffrage offered arguments in terms of adherence to principles of justice and democracy. Moreover, debate easily steered to other topics, ending on several occasions with joking remarks on the woman suffrage measure. One member stated a preference to delay debate on the subject "for a personal consideration therein – I have not seen my wife in two weeks. I wish to go home on Saturday and return on Monday, so that I may find how she stands upon the question before I vote upon it." His comment was followed by laughter in the convention and an end to the discussion.[17]

A roll call vote on the issue of women's voting rights was successfully called for by an outspoken proponent. The convention's lack of interest in women's voting rights was firmly established. Only twelve of the convention's eighty-five delegates voted in favor of removing the sex qualification from voting rights: three Democrats and nine Republicans. Forty-six delegates voted against enfranchising women, and twenty-seven delegates failed to even cast a vote.[18] Although delegates clashed over even symbolic action on the partisan-charged issue of black voting rights, without compelling political reasons to address

---

[16] *Debates and Proceedings*, 212. Note that these are also arguments attempting to use the lack of general support for the issue of woman suffrage to undo support for blacks' voting rights.

[17] *Debates and Proceedings*, 857. In similar fashion, when a Democratic woman suffrage supporter moved to strike the word "male" from the suffrage clause adopted by the convention, a fellow Democrat countered by motioning to replace the word "male" with the word "female." Hanna quipped that "[i]f the females are to vote at all, I want them to do all the voting and let the males retire from voting altogether." *Debates and Proceedings*, 1281.

[18] *Debates and Proceedings*, 1281–82. There is no partisan pattern in the decisions to vote no or to fail to cast a vote: twenty-four Democrats and twenty-two Republicans voted no, fifteen Democrats and twelve Republicans did not vote. Democratic and Republican party identifications were derived from *Debates and Proceedings*, including self-identification during debate and votes on convention leadership positions, and supplemented with information from Eric Monkkonen, *Law and Finance In Illinois, 1868–1874* [Computer file] (Los Angeles, CA: Eric Monkkonen, University of California [producer], 1990; Ann Arbor, MI: Inter-university Consortium for Political and Social Research [distributor], 1992); and biographies archived on The

women's voting rights, delegates showed little interest. Even those who voiced support on the floor did not necessarily possess intense enough preferences to be sure to cast their own votes on the issue, let alone persuade others to lend their approval. Women's voting the rights, pushed only by personal politics, failed to garner sufficient political meaning to leverage even serious consideration, whereas the strategic enfranchisement incentive of expected one-party gain had ensured that black voting rights were vigorously contested.

Leveraging Success – The Farmer's Alliance and School Suffrage

Frustrations after the Constitutional Convention failure appear to have set the stage for the first woman suffrage success in Illinois. Would-be suffrage activists ended up engaging in other causes, laying the groundwork for the coalitional politics of the programmatic enfranchisement path to woman suffrage in the state. Indeed, the IWSA leadership perceived in the years immediately following the convention that a single-issue focus in the suffrage association cost them active members to broader reform organizations. They were nonetheless apprehensive about the subversion of the suffrage goal to other reform objectives if a broader agenda were adopted. In 1885, they went so far as to explicitly narrow the suffrage organization's agenda to the singular goal of political enfranchisement, and adopted new name to signal the organizational change, becoming the Illinois Equal Suffrage Association (IESA). Although the IESA endured, it stalled organizationally. Women who might have engaged suffrage work were instead actively building reform societies, such as the Illinois Social Science Association and local Woman's Clubs, and growing temperance convictions into a statewide Illinois Woman's Christian Temperance Union (IWCTU). Yet, all of these women's groups would eventually come to appreciate the desirability of the ballot, at least in some limited form, as a means to achieve their other political goals.[19] Indeed, by 1890, the IWCTU was running a full-fledged campaign for woman suffrage, organizing a massive petition drive and publicity effort to lobby state legislators for local voting rights for women.[20]

Political Graveyard website (http://politicalgraveyard.com/index.html). Self-declared independents (four delegates) who nevertheless consistently voted with one party are categorized as members of that party.

[19] Buechler, *The Transformation of the Woman Suffrage Movement*, 105–47. Beldon, Gertrude May, "A History of the Woman Suffrage Movement in Illinois" (M.A. Thesis, Department of History, University of Chicago, 1913), 21–29.

[20] Many of the petitions are preserved in the Illinois State Archives (37th General Assembly. 1891. For Woman Suffrage. Voting for School Officers. Petitions.) On the back of one of the petition forms are instructions from the IWCTU Secretary to have the bill noticed by the local papers as a measure of the IWCTU, to write to one's Senator and Representatives in the General Assembly concerning the bill, and to check in regularly on the progress of the campaign. See also *History of Woman Suffrage* vol. IV, 600.

The first success for woman suffrage in Illinois, in fact, came in 1891 in the form of school suffrage. The reformist activities of those women's organizations calling for suffrage at this point seemed to provide a bridge between the issue of women's voting rights and the third party who pushed for the 1891 success, the Farmers' Alliance. The Alliance's presence in Illinois politics at the time was an outgrowth of farmer discontent over fairly common populist themes of concentration of wealth (in urban hands) and related charges of corruption. The Alliance thus took up woman suffrage within a generally reformist policy agenda, which included calls for increased regulation of industry, including railroads, and new tax policies that moved burdens more squarely onto the wealthy.[21] The Farmers' Alliance leverage – on suffrage as well as their broader agenda – derived from the outcome of their candidates' participation in the 1890 election. The Alliance had run candidates for a number of seats in the General Assembly, and their fortunes at the polls turned control of the usually Republican lower house over to the Democrats.[22] More important, three Farmers' Alliance candidates were actually elected to the House, and the number of Democratic victories placed the Alliance members at the center of the partisan balance of power in the House.[23] The Alliance members, that is, were the pivotal members for any vote that would split Democrats and Republicans along party lines.

The political leverage of the Farmers' Alliance members in the state legislature was revealed as the body struggled to elect a U.S. Senator. By voting for their own third party candidate, the Farmers' Alliance representatives were able to force 153 votes on the senatorial election before compromising, delaying the state's choice for nearly two months. After rounds of stalemates, the Republicans made an attempt to compromise by supporting the Farmers' Alliance candidate, but could not convince all of their members to agree. Alliance members reportedly grew dissatisfied with the Republican leadership, and transferred their support to a new candidate. Republicans promptly abandoned the attempted compromise as well and put forth a new candidate of their own. Having clearly established their partisan resolve through the holdout, two of the three Farmers' Alliance members chose to vote with the Democrats for their candidate on the 154th vote. This action finally allowed the House to move forward in earnest with its legislative agenda, with the third party's representatives' place as pivotal voters clearly impressed upon Republicans and Democrats alike.

---

[21] Scott, Roy Vernon, *The Agrarian Movement in Illinois, 1880–1896* (Urbana: University of Illinois Press, 1962).

[22] The *Blue Book of the State of Illinois. 1909.* (Danville, IL: Illinois Printing Company), pages 248–318 has lists of members of the General Assembly from 1818 to 1909, including partisanship from 1881.

[23] Destler, Chester, "Consummation of a Labor-Populist Alliance in Illinois, 1894" *The Mississippi Valley Historical Review* 27:4 (March 1941), 589–602 (esp. 593–94).

The decision to side with the Democrats' choice for Senator was especially significant given the perception of the Farmers' Alliance as spoilers of Republicans' electoral success, and the failed candidate negotiations between the two parties.[24] It impressed upon both major parties that the Alliance was clearly independent of the Republican Party organization; they would bargain with Republicans to achieve their desired influence on legislative business, but would also defect to the Democratic side if too much compromise was necessary.[25]

The first measure on the issue of woman suffrage, introduced by one of the Farmers' Alliance members, offered further information on the Alliance incentives and potential leverage. Introduced during the partisan wrangling over the senatorial election, it was a resolution calling for a "woman's day" hearing in the House. It specifically requested "Mrs. Helen M. Gouger and others" to address the House "in behalf of municipal suffrage for women."[26] Singling out Helen Gouger – rather than an IESA officer – underscores the origins of the Farmers' Alliance tie to the woman suffrage issue. Gouger was a temperance and suffrage advocate involved in national Farmers' Alliance politics and the gathering momentum for a Populist Party.[27] The signal was that the proposal, and Alliance interest in advocating woman suffrage, derived from the Alliance's commitment to their female members' goals, members who were hard at work for the fledgling party lecturing, fundraising, and campaigning. Although enough representatives voted to carry the resolution, it did meet some opposition, and that opposition was decidedly Democratic.[28] As bolters from the Republican fold, it seemed the Alliance had less leverage on Democratic lawmakers, even on symbolic matters such as this one.

Resistance of some lawmakers even to the symbolic action of a suffrage hearing was, in fact, a signal about the difficulty the Alliance members would have, despite their unique institutional leverage, in securing a policy concession on woman suffrage. The Alliance ultimately forwarded two bills for women's voting rights, one that would grant women the right to vote for and hold municipal government offices, and another that would grant voting rights in school elections only. Neither received timely legislative attention. Municipal suffrage was finally brought up for a vote, and promptly defeated by a vote of sixty-five in favor and fifty-one opposed. One of the Alliance members, however, must have anticipated not having enough votes to pass the measure, as he voted against the bill and then invoked his right as a member voting

---

[24] Haynes, Frederick E., *Third Party Movements since the Civil War* (Iowa City: The State Historical Society of Iowa), 231–53.

[25] *Journal of the Senate of the State of Illinois*, 1891, 64–69, 327–29, 551–53; Haynes, *Third Party Movements since the Civil War*, 250–51.

[26] *Journal of the House of Representatives of the State of Illinois*, 1891, 76–77.

[27] Wagner, "Farms Families and Reform," 227–32.

[28] Twenty-six of the thirty opposing members were Democrats, whereas the 100 supporting members broke down into 59 Republicans, 38 Democrats, and the 3 Farmers' Alliance members.

not to pass to move to reconsider the vote.[29] On reconsideration weeks later, however, the bill failed again, this time garnering sixty-eight votes in favor and forty-three opposed.

Although the municipal woman suffrage measure failed, legislators found a less consequential school suffrage measure more palatable. In fact, it was the only version of woman suffrage the Senate would allow to come to a vote, despite Republican efforts there for other measures.[30] Finally, the school suffrage bill was introduced by a Republican. It was referred to committee, the Republican chair of which delivered a favorable report. School suffrage passed the Senate by a vote of twenty-nine in favor and four opposed, with eighteen members not voting. Support was bipartisan, with two-thirds of the Republican senators and nearly half of the Democrats in the yes column. Resistance once again was Democratic, however. All four opposing members were Democrats. Passage of the school suffrage bill in the Senate gave the House one last opportunity to pass a measure for women's voting rights. In fact, both a House and Senate version were under consideration.[31] The House ultimately chose to table its own version, making way for passage of the Senate bill by a vote of eighty-three in support and forty-two opposed. Limited suffrage rights for women were delivered with strong Republican support and some Democratic assistance – a compromise reached on one of the Farmers' Alliance demands.

IESA officer Catharine Waugh McCulloch would later credit the Farmers' Alliance with delivering the requisite votes in the House to pass school suffrage, but how were legislators who voted down the Alliance original municipal

---

[29] *Journal of the House of Representatives of the State of Illinois,* 1891, 1077. In addition to rejecting the municipal suffrage bill, the House had also turned down a resolution proposing an amendment to the Illinois state constitution that had been introduced by a Democratic Representative, with the express backing of his local Grange. See petition to Curtiss from Towns-Grange #1163 (37th General Assembly. 1891. Petitions for Woman Suffrage by Constitutional Amendment. Illinois State Archives.). The letter to Curtiss states that the local membership "is unanimously in favor of said bill."

[30] The school suffrage measure had been drafted by the IWCTU, which had already begun running its petition and publicity campaign throughout the state, and also had been endorsed by the IESA. Senators first tabled a resolution for an amendment to the state constitution to grant women full voting rights, drafted by the IESA. See *History of Woman Suffrage* vol. IV, 600. A municipal suffrage bill lingered in committee for months before being reported to the floor with a recommendation that it not pass. The Senate concurred with the committee by a strongly partisan vote of twenty-seven to twenty-one and the bill was laid on the table. Nineteen Democrats and eight Republicans voted to accept the committee recommendation that the bill not pass; three Democrats and eighteen Republicans voted against. *Journal of the Senate,* 1891.

[31] Although a number of school suffrage bills were proposed by members of the House – both Democrats and Republicans – none came to a vote in the body. Three were referred to the Committee on Elections, which recommended against their passage, and two others were referred to the Committee on Education, which recommended in favor of passage for one measure, House Bill 632. *Journal of the House of Representatives,* 1100, 1394–95.

suffrage proposal convinced to reach the final compromise?[32] Analysis of the floor votes on each of the woman suffrage measures allows for evaluation of the roles of both district-induced preferences and party pressure across legislative decisions. Although data on the Farmers' Alliance vote returns within each district are not available, data on the presence of the Alliance's base (farmers) are, which can be used to gauge the degree to which legislators based each decision on preferences arising from this presence in their constituencies.[33] In fact, if the Alliance endorsement was indeed key information about the political meaning and electoral impetus for supporting (or opposing) the measures, then we would expect both party and constituency composition to structure the votes. Because it was understood that the Alliance drew its electoral support from traditional Republican base, Republicans ought to have had greater electoral incentive to acquiesce to the Alliance's proposal, and, moreover, to have been particularly vulnerable to the demand if their districts were home to larger bases of farming voters.

Table 4.1 presents a simple look at the question of the Farmers' Alliance influence on legislators from the two major parties on the two votes on the Alliance-sponsored municipal suffrage bill. Legislators are divided by party in the table, and then by voting patterns – those who consistently withheld support across the two votes, those who consistently voted in its favor, and those who changed their behavior across the two votes. The mean number of farms per 100 people living in each category's members' districts, drawn from the U.S. Census, is reported. Comparisons of means across the cells of the table then provide information about how the relative presence of farming constituencies may have shaped legislators' decisions.

Consistent with the expectation of the Farmers' Alliance influence, for Republicans, the difference between those who held out their support and those who voted for the measure at any stage is significant. Republicans who resisted supporting the municipal suffrage measure even after the negotiation for its reconsideration tended to represent constituencies with significantly lesser farming interests than those who voted for municipal voting rights for women. Put another way, it seems Republicans needed to be quite certain that their constituencies were not interested in the Farmers' Alliance agenda, which included women's voting rights, to holdout on the issue. There is little evidence of a correlation, however, between Democratic votes on the issue of municipal woman suffrage and district farming interests; the average presence of farming interests in the district does not distinguish even those Democrats

---

[32] McCulloch actually singled out a specific member, Representative Moore. The credit appears in a pamphlet written in 1913 by McCulloch entitled "Chronology of the Woman's Rights Movement in Illinois."

[33] Election returns from the Illinois Secretary of State office available from the Illinois State Archives, but establishing party identification of all candidates was not possible. Farming interest was measured by the number of farms per 100 population in the county or counties of the legislators' districts, derived from the U.S. Census, 1890.

TABLE 4.1. *Farming Influence on Votes for Municipal Suffrage, Illinois House of Representatives 1891*

	Democrats		Republicans	
	Mean Farms (s.d.)	Number of Members	Mean Farms (s.d.)	Number of Members
No or abstain both votes	7.3 (4.1)	46	5.5* (4.1)	27
Yes first vote, No or abstain on reconsideration	8.1 (2.7)	7	7.0 (6.1)	5
No or abstain first vote, Yes on reconsideration	4.3 (4.1)	5	8.0 (2.3)	11
Yes on both votes	7.1 (4.6)	19	(8.8) (3.4)	31
All Members	7.2 (4.1)	77	7.4 (4.0)	74

* *Significantly different from both Republican categories that voted yes on reconsideration and Democrats that voted no on or abstained from both votes.*

Sources: U.S. Census, 1890; *Journal of the House of Representatives of the State of Illinois*, 1891.

who consistently voted against the municipal suffrage measure from those who consistently supported the measure. This suggests a uniquely partisan pressure to acquiesce to the Farmers' Alliance issue, to which Republican members from more vulnerable districts deferred.

Turning to similar analyses on the vote of final compromise – the school suffrage measure – reveals that success was built on the coalition established in favor of municipal voting rights and additional members from both parties with stronger farming presences in their districts than those who continued to resist any form of women's voting rights. Table 4.2 presents the average level of farming interests in Democratic and Republican representatives' districts by the members' voting patterns on both the municipal and school woman suffrage measures. Farming interests were, indeed, stronger in supporters' districts than in the districts of legislators who opposed women's voting rights for school elections. The average farming presence in Democratic supporters' districts was more than 40 percent greater than that of Democratic opponents'; Republican supporters hailed from districts with two times the average farming presence of Republican opponents'.

Looking down the table also reveals that the path to support for school voting rights was noticeably different by party, as was the overall level of support. Republicans retained more supporters of municipal suffrage in the vote on school suffrage, losing a total of just six members who had previously voted for municipal suffrage, of whom three simply did not cast a vote on the school

TABLE 4.2. *Farming Influence on Votes for Municipal and School Suffrage, Illinois House 1891*

	Democrats		Republicans	
	Mean Farms (s.d.)	Number of Members	Mean Farms (s.d.)	Number of Members
For School Suffrage Only	9.2^{ad} (1.7)	10	6.2^{bd} (4.2)	10
For School & Municipal Suffrage (first vote only)	9.0 (3.0)	3	11.5^{abc} (0.8)	3
For School & Municipal Suffrage (second vote only)	5.1 (4.9)	3	8.0^{a} (2.3)	11
For School & Municipal Suffrage (both votes)	8.7 (3.5)	11	8.9^{a} (3.3)	26
All School Suffrage Supporters	8.5* (3.2)	27	8.3† (3.4)	50
No or Abstain School & Municipal Suffrage (both votes)	6.8^{c} (4.4)	36	5.0^{b} (4.4)	16
No or Abstain School Suffrage Only	3.6^{c} (5.1)	6	7.7 (4.9)	4
No or Abstain School & Municipal Suffrage (first vote only)	3.3 (4.1)	4	N/A	0
No or Abstain School & Municipal Suffrage (second vote only)	7.4 (2.8)	2	0.4^{abc} (0.0)	2
All School Suffrage Opponents	6.0* (3.9)	28	3.8† (4.3)	11
All School Suffrage Abstainers	6.7 (5.1)	20	6.4 (4.4)	11

[a] Statistically different from *Against School & Municipal* (within party)
[b] Statistically different from *For School & Municipal* (within party)
[c] Statistically different from *For School Only* (within party)
[d] Statistically different across parties
* Difference between means statistically significant $t = -2.63$, $p = .01$
† Difference between means statistically significant $t = -3.19$, $p = .01$

measure. Democrats showed less incentive to retain their support; twelve who had previously voted in favor of municipal suffrage failed to lend their votes to school voting rights for women. Seven of the lost Democrats were legislators who actually cast votes against school suffrage and the other five were abstainers. And although the major parties each produced an additional ten supporters of women's voting rights on the school measure, beyond those who had supported the municipal measure in either of its floor votes, the converted Democrats came from districts with far more farm influence – nearly 50 percent greater farm presence – than the Republicans who were swept into suffrage coalition on only the school issue. Convincing Democrats, it seems, depended more crucially on the interests of their districts. The ultimate implication was a winning coalition driven by a combination of district pressures and Republican Party influence on legislators to reach a compromise on the Farmers' Alliance issue of women's voting rights.

The Collapse of Coalitions and Partisan Incentives

Encouraged by the success of school suffrage in 1891, IESA decided on an incremental plan for voting rights legislation, to begin with a township suffrage bill at the next legislature. But new voting rights would not be won in 1893. It would be more than two decades, in fact, before Illinois women won any further inclusion in the electorate, although suffrage bills were introduced in every legislative session. Looking back over those years, one Illinois legislator offered the following account of the many failures:

There are so many ways of defeating bills in legislatures that voting against them is only a trivial means and a last resort. In all the years in which the suffrage bill had been before the House of Representatives no member had had to vote for it. It had gotten into the wrong committee and had died. It had been amended to death on second reading. It had gotten to third reading and had perished at the close of the session. It had perished twice on third reading despite the fact that petitions had been presented to the Speaker signed by eighty members and asking that it be brought to a vote. For at the same time more than eighty members had privately besought the same Speaker not to let the bill come to a vote – seventy-seven being a majority of the House.[34]

This short summary of the fate of legislation for women's voting rights between 1891 and 1913 is fairly accurate, and highlights the challenge for suffragists facing politicians who either saw little advantage in their enfranchisement or found the idea of women's voting rights distasteful. With no strong political incentives to push legislators to a compromise like the one delivered in 1891, even with principled supporters, woman suffrage as an issue lacked the initiative needed to pull it through the legislative process, and opponents found it easy to bury the measures. The unique partisan circumstances of 1891, with woman suffrage on the agenda of a demanding and pivotal third party, had given the issue clear political consequence to party politicians. The Republican Party had incentive then to see a compromise through as part of its attempts to diffuse the Farmers' Alliance movement that threatened Republican electoral dominance in the state, and legislators from both parties representing particularly farm-heavy districts had found compromise with the Alliance in their electoral interests as well.

   Yet, Illinois suffragists seemed to have little comprehension of the political circumstances that had cultivated the legislative coalition that delivered school

---

[34] Fitch, George, "The Noiseless Suffragette" *Collier's* August 9, 1913, 6, 29–31. Fitch was a Progressive party first-termer in 1913, the year woman suffrage actually passed.

voting rights for women. The organized suffrage effort carried on not only in an explicitly nonpartisan manner, but also with little energy focused on forging coalitions with other organized political interest groups that could wield influence in partisan politics.[35] Notably, during this time, active support from farmers' organizations was lost. Even if suffragists had realized the potential of a coalitional strategy, however, they still would have faced the obstacle of steady Republican dominance in state politics from the mid-1890s through the first decade of the twentieth century. With secure control over the legislature and governor's office, Republicans lacked the vulnerability as a party that had aided in the leverage of the 1891 compromise.[36]

Although suffrage activists failed to follow through on the possibilities of a coalition with farmers' organizations revealed by the Farmers' Alliance influence on the school suffrage victory, growing and maintaining relationships with other women's organizations would ultimately lead to another productive path. IESA made some attempts in the late 1890s to enlist the aid of labor organizations, a growing force in Illinois politics, with some success. In particular, IESA secured signatures from thousands of Chicago labor union members, which were delivered to the state legislature in 1899.[37] A political coalition with labor could give woman suffrage the legislative viability it lacked, but only if politicians believed labor's support for the issue was credible.

Indeed, the recession of the suffrage-farmer coalition did not go unnoticed by lawmakers, but the political credibility of a suffrage-labor alliance was not easily established. In 1899, after IESA presented the petition signed by Chicago labor union members, the Senate voted down both a proposed township suffrage bill and a bill that would have given women the right to vote in presidential and municipal elections. Although the Republican lean of support characteristic of the 1891 vote had been retained – only two of the yes votes were from Democrats – the link between farming interests and legislators' votes on suffrage was gone. As Table 4.3 shows, there was only a small and statistically insignificant difference between the average farming presence in the districts of supporters and opponents of the 1899 suffrage bills. In addition,

---

[35] On the organizational decision to proceed in a nonpartisan manner see Beldon, "A History of the Woman Suffrage Movement in Illinois," 34–39.

[36] Republicans consistently held a majority of the House and a two-thirds majority in the Senate (except 1901 when they held just 63% of the seats) in addition to the governor's office. The difference between the House and Senate numbers likely derives from a cumulative voting system for House elections: the top three vote-getters from each district were elected, usually resulting in a two to one split in each district between the Republicans and Democrats – the two going to whichever party was dominant in the district. *Blue Book of the State of Illinois, 1913* (Danville: Illinois Printing Company).

[37] The claim in *History of Woman Suffrage* (vol. IV, 602) and by McCulloch in "Chronology of the Woman's Rights Movement in Illinois" is that 25,000 signatures of Chicago labor union men were delivered to the state legislature in 1899. There is no record of such a vast number in the Senate or House *Journals* or the Illinois State Archives files on legislative petitions (despite many of the 1891 petitions being preserved there).

TABLE 4.3. *Votes on Woman Suffrage by Farming and Labor Interest in District, Illinois Senate 1899*

Township Suffrage	Farms Farms per 100 Population		Labor Manufacturing Workers per 100 Population		N
	Mean	(s.d.)	Mean	(s.d.)	
Yes	8.9	(3.3)	3.7*	(3.8)	15
No	7.4	(4.2)	6.7	(5.1)	16
Not Voting	6.2	(4.4)	7.2	(6.2)	20
Presidential Suffrage					
Yes	8.9	(3.9)	4.0	(4.6)	17
No	8.1	(3.3)	5.5	(4.2)	12
Not Voting	5.8	(4.3)	7.9†	(6.0)	22

* Difference from *No* and *Not Voting* statistically significant[38]
† Difference from *Yes* statistically significant[39]
Sources: U.S. Census, 1900.

without any real connection between suffrage organizations and labor unions, there was little evidence that the endorsement by petition signaled a salient concern for women's voting rights on the part of union organizations and their constituent voters. Most of the Senators from labor-heavy districts – notably, six of Chicago's ten – abstained from voting on the woman suffrage issue all together. And on the township suffrage bill, supporters were Senators *without* a significant labor presence in their districts. In short, there was no evidence that the labor petition had convinced legislators of a committed labor interest in women's voting rights.[40]

Building a New Coalition – Suffrage and Labor

IESA would eventually lend the necessary credibility to a political coalition of labor and the initially middle-class suffrage movement to give it leverage in suffrage politics by establishing far more solid alliances with working women's organizations. The cross-class relationship was developed first through the growing settlement house movement in Chicago. Middle class reformers – the majority of whom were women – established residences (settlement houses)

---

[38] Difference between *Yes* and *No*: t = 1.90, p = .06. Difference between *Yes* and *Not Voting*: t = 2.07, p = .05. Two-tailed test, unequal variances assumed.

[39] t = 2.25, p = .03. Two-tailed test, unequal variances assumed.

[40] Analysis of Senators' votes on liquor licensing does not suggest this effect, or the general pattern of votes on woman suffrage, is explained by positions on temperance issues. Senators from strong labor districts were more likely to support licensing in 1899; license supporters' districts averaged 4.4 more manufacturing workers per 100 population than opponents' (t = 2.31, p = .03). But license supporters were no more likely to oppose, support, or abstain from voting on woman suffrage than license opponents.

in laboring, immigrant communities from which they offered the neighbor-hoods' residents programs intended to address issues of poverty and worker exploitation, and to serve the general educational and social needs not met by government in these communities. Leaders of the Chicago movement also joined the woman suffrage cause, including Jane Addams, who, with her settle-ment Hull House, gained national prominence in political reform circles, and Florence Kelley, who had been appointed Illinois Chief Factory Inspector by the governor in 1894. Women like Addams and Kelley became the first real bridge between the women of the organized suffrage effort and labor women. That bridge grew steadier through the Women's Trade Union League (WTUL), an organization dedicated to advocating for working women's rights primar-ily through unionizing efforts, but also by lobbying for protective legislation. Addams had been present at the national founding meeting in 1903 and months later held a meeting at Hull House to organize an Illinois branch. The overlap between the reform interested middle-class women who pursued labor rights in partnerships with working women and those who organized for women's vot-ing rights led to an increasingly strong link between woman suffrage and labor protection. By 1909 IESA was calling for legislation on work-hour limitations and "a law as to providing seats for women employees" and the WTUL was beginning to provide support for suffrage campaigns.[41]

As suffrage activists became more involved in working for labor interests by advocating for protective legislation and partnering with the WTUL, the cred-ibility of a suffrage-labor coalition would grow. Establishing that credibility, however, was a slow and somewhat complicated process. Building and main-taining cross-class cooperation between women whose primary electoral goals were the immediate protection of their health, safety, and financial well-being in grinding industrial workplaces, and women who sought voting rights as a tool for broad social reform and their inclusion into elite politics and profes-sional careers was difficult. The Illinois WTUL spent its first several years in pursuit of legislation to limit women's work hours, a goal they achieved in 1909 with the passage of a "ten hour bill."[42] WTUL success did not translate into improved chances for women's voting rights that year, but it did begin to open greater space in the WTUL agenda for woman suffrage.[43] Endorsed at first only by its more middle-class leaders, regard within the WTUL for woman suffrage as a tool for achieving working women's goals became more common by 1910, and culminated in the establishment of a wage earners' suffrage league in 1913.[44]

---

[41] Buechler, *The Transformation of the Woman Suffrage Movement*, 157–62; McCulloch, "Chronology of the Woman's Rights Movement in Illinois."

[42] *Journal of the Senate*, 1909, 1210, summary of bills.

[43] In fact, the two measures were considered in immediate succession in the Senate, with woman suffrage receiving just twenty-five yes votes, and the ten hour law garnering forty-one yes votes, with no Senator voting against the measure. The House continued its pattern of refusing to consider suffrage bills.

[44] Buechler, *The Transformation of the Woman Suffrage Movement*, 161–62.

Legislators' awareness of the slowly building relationship between suffrage and labor interests seemed evident in their general treatment of the suffrage issue. Although woman suffrage legislation had slipped off the Illinois General Assembly docket entirely in the early 1900s, being repeatedly buried in committee or stalled on second reading in both houses, it reemerged in as women's organizing for labor interests grew in strength. The state Senate finally considered a measure in 1907 for presidential and municipal voting rights; the measure garnered twenty votes in its favor and yet no special resistance or support from labor or farm districts.[45] For its part, the House ignored several presidential and municipal suffrage bills after they received unfavorable committee reports, but engaged the subject of women's voting rights symbolically through a resolution that called on the governor to participate in the summit on women's rights IESA was planning for its fortieth anniversary in February of 1909. Although the action appeared little more than a publicity ruse – the House and Senate passed independent versions of the resolution and then each laid the other chamber's on the table – it suggested that House members for the first time since 1891 felt compelled to address the woman suffrage issue in some way.[46]

Still, the suffrage issue lacked sufficient political incentive to leverage results from the legislature, although women's labor rights did not. The next legislative session brought two suffrage bills to a vote in the Senate: a statewide municipal suffrage measure and a bill providing municipal voting rights for Chicago women only. Both bills failed on final passage, after the statewide measure barely endured an attempt on the floor to strike its enacting clause. In the House, both measures were proposed but died in committee. Although legislators lacked the incentive to pull women's voting rights through, they produced a real gain for labor women in the form of the ten-hour law. Offered as a compromise to a General Assembly that had resisted several broader provisions for the protection of labor, the ten-hour bill received unanimous support in the Senate and nearly so in the House, where just nine members voted against it.[47] Both Republicans and Democrats from labor-heavy districts were sure to show their support; those legislators who voted against or abstained hailed from districts

---

[45] *Journal of the Senate, 1907–1908,* 944. Mean farms per 100 population (s.d.): yes = 5.4 (4.5); no = 5.7 (5.0). Mean manufacturing workers per 100 population (s.d.): yes = 8.6 (5.7); no = 7.6 (6.2).

[46] *Journal of the House, 1907–1908,* 1595–96, 1681–82; *Journal of the Senate, 1907–1908,* 1510, 1571.

[47] Measures not passed included a union label act, factory safety regulations, and a provision to require weekly payment of wages by employers. A resolution from the WTUL presented on the floor of the Senate before the final vote on the ten-hour law read in part: "Whereas, the eight-hour bill cannot pass the Legislature at this session, now therefore, be it resolved that the Women's Trade Union League of Chicago does hereby endorse and recommend for enactment into law of the substitute bill introduced by Senator Jones ... we urge upon all friends of labor and social welfare an united support of this substitute bill." *Journal of the Senate,* 1909, 1210, 1602; *Journal of the House,* 1909, 1263, 1411.

with comparatively little labor presence.[48] The ten-hour law, although only applicable to women, was perceptibly a labor issue, and one that received its due support from legislators accountable to districts populated with industrial interests. A more solid connection between women's labor rights and women's voting rights seemed a promising strategy for suffragists. The fact that labor organizations were still struggling to have most of their agenda items carried out, however, suggested that lawmakers were not as vulnerable to the groups' demands as might be necessary to pull women's voting rights through both chambers, even with a credible commitment of union support. What Illinois suffragists needed was not only a strong coalition, but also a disruption in the state's stable Republican control. Such an opportunity was about to present itself in the form of electoral success for a newly forming political party – the Progressives.

A Progressive Feat – Victory East of the Mississippi

Of the status of woman suffrage in Illinois in 1911 – just two years before the adoption of legislation that granted women voting rights in presidential, municipal, and some state elections – suffrage activist Grace Wilbur Trout complained, "I was indignant at the way the suffrage committee was treated [by the state legislature]. Some men who had always believed in suffrage were exceedingly kind, but *no one regarded the matter as a serious legislative question* which had the slightest possibility of becoming law."[49] Trout and her fellow activists were up against the biggest challenge for the disfranchised: how to garner not just agreement with, but issue importance for their cause.

The change across those two short years was an alliance with the suddenly important Progressive Party. The Progressives would offer Illinois suffragists an even stronger version of the political leverage they had achieved through the Farmers' Alliance endorsement of women's voting rights in 1891. As the Farmers' Alliance members had in 1891, Progressive party representatives in the Illinois legislature in 1913 held the balance of power; neither Democrats nor Republicans secured enough seats to constitute a majority in a party-line vote. The electoral success of the Progressive Party in 1912 not only put twenty-six of its members in the state House and two in the Senate, but also turned over the governor's office from the Republicans to the Democrats for the first time since the 1892 elections. Moreover, the issue agenda of the new party placed them between the traditional Republican and Democratic electorates; although first formed from bolting Republican reformers, Progressives also made appeals to

---

[48] Measure of labor presence is the U.S. Census report of the number of manufacturing workers per 100 population, 1910. House supporters averaged 8.2 manufacturing workers per 100 population, opponents just 4.9 (t = 1.83, p = .07 in a two-tailed test, unequal variances assumed).

[49] Trout, Grace Wilbur, "Side Lights on Illinois Suffrage History." *Transactions of the Illinois State Historical Society* (1920), 96. Emphasis added.

labor voters from the Democratic base. The result was a loss of thirty previously held House seats for Republicans and seven lost for Democrats – although Democrats did manage to pick up enough seats where Progressives had split the traditionally Republican vote to produce a net gain of four seats. Poised, then, as pivotal voters on the typically party-line procedural and leadership votes, including that for U.S. Senator, and representing voters and legislative seats lost for both major parties, Progressive Party legislators stood capable of leveraging at least consideration of, if not success for, their policy program. And thanks to a durable partnership between the new party and suffrage activists, forged from Progressives' need for the workers and coalitional appeal offered by the organized suffrage movement, women's voting rights would be part of the Progressive legislative program.

Progressive support was not without its own challenges. In particular, the explicitly anti-machine agenda of the Progressive Party meant that resistance from Chicago's notorious and powerful political machine was inevitable. There were two implications. First, because the machine's presence in the legislature was not undone by Progressive electoral fortunes, Progressives would have a solid bloc of resistance around which they would have to maneuver to secure their policy agenda, including woman suffrage. Second, given the sizable proportion of the Illinois electorate over which the Chicago machine held sway, expansion of the scope of conflict to a referendum on women's voting rights would likely result in the issue's demise. It is for this reason, it seems, that Illinois was the first state in which a carefully crafted measure to enfranchise women to vote for presidential electors and other offices not created by the state's constitution was passed. Illinois women, that is, became statewide voters of consequence without the need to pass the referendum hurdle.

The Origins of Progressive Support

The Progressive reliance on the organized suffrage movement in Illinois grew in part from its rather sudden emergence. Although related to the general trend of reform movements that emerged in the early twentieth century, the party did not grow out of a social movement in the way the Populist parties of the last century had. In Illinois in particular, the Progressive Party was founded by experienced politicians formerly of the Republican Party who bolted after first failing to forward their reform agenda within the major party organization.[50] The bolters were advocates of direct democracy provisions, the "short ballot" and increased government efficiency, and an end to the party's reliance on machine-based politics, which became particularly salient in Illinois following the expulsion of their Republican Senator William Lorimer from Congress in 1912 on charges that he bought his seat through bribes of state legislators. Ultimately unable,

---

[50] Among the Republican bolters were Charles Merriam, University of Chicago political science professor who served as a Chicago Alderman, and a score of legislative incumbents including Frank Funk, who would become the Progressive candidate for governor that year.

however, to convince the Republican Party organization to endorse the call for direct democracy, to agree on a slate of machine-independent candidates, and to come to terms on the question of the Roosevelt candidacy for President, the would-be Progressives split from the Republicans in the summer of 1912, in the midst of disagreement at the party nominating conventions.

To take on the party machine from which they split in elections that were just months away was a formidable task for the new Progressive Party. Progressive leaders began immediately to attempt to broaden their electoral appeal. To defeat Republican regulars would entail a new coalition, and so a broad policy agenda emerged in the new party's convention. In the convention's keynote address, temporary party chairman Charles Merriam articulated the new Progressive program, one designed to reach out to the traditionally Democratic labor voters by linking the government reforms at the base of the party's founding to economic and social reforms to benefit the working class. In particular, Merriam attributed the failure of a more extensive program of protective labor legislation to the corruption of political machines, and promised greater workplace reform under the Progressive banner:

This is not alone a battle to secure political machinery. Great questions of economic and social justice loom large before us and demand attention and solution. Tariff, currency, regulation of corporations and the working and living conditions of men must not be forgotten. The greatest loss inflicted on the community by the grafters is the prevention of a vigorous and aggressive policy of legislation for social and economic betterment. They have obstructed and prevented adoption of laws long since applied in other countries and have left the working man and woman in many instances the victims of exploitation and greed.... We must stand for a minimum wage for women, limitation of hours of labor in continuous occupations, appointment of an industrial commission to investigate working conditions and to codify and strengthen our labor laws and recommend other legislative dealing with this human situation.[51]

Appealing to labor voters was part of the Progressive Party's strategy for success in the 1912 elections, and commitments to protective labor legislation appeared accordingly. Beyond the labor appeals, however, the convention found another way to broaden its base through policy endorsement: it included a plank for women's voting rights in the party platform. Justifications for the inclusion of woman suffrage included both principled arguments of representation and the expediency argument that it would assist women in their efforts for protective legislation.[52] The utility of endorsing women's voting rights was actually two-fold for the Progressives. First, it was consistent with attempts to recruit organized labor into the party fold. Although it had taken years to grow, by this point the alliance between the WTUL and the organized suffrage movement was real, and woman suffrage was being advocated not only as a middle

---

[51] Straetz, Ralph A., "The Progressive Movement in Illinois," 190–330. Quote appears on page 323.

[52] Straetz, 328.

class reform issue, but also as a tool to protect working women's rights. Thus, the suffrage movement reflected exactly the cross-class reform-worker alliance Progressive Party leaders were attempting to build – and the WTUL's affili-ation with the Chicago Federation of Labor was one more inroad to voters through organized labor. The second appeal of the suffrage policy was the tac-tical assistance that the suffrage movement's workers, themselves, could offer. IESA, the WTUL, and local suffrage groups including the Chicago Political Equality League offered workers experienced in fundraising and public cam-paign orchestration, which the new party desperately needed. Jane Addams, who had been selected as one of the Illinois delegates to the national Pro-gressive Party convention, was given charge of the women's work within the party. This "women's division" reportedly pulled hundreds of women, many from the suffrage movement, into the party's work, setting up storefront oper-ations through the city where the women distributed campaign literature and collected donations. These women also arranged the party's first public rally in September, an event in Chicago that featured speeches by Progressive can-didates, including gubernatorial nominee Frank Funk, and well-known social reform, labor, and immigrant advocate Grace Abbott of Hull House.[53]

Progressive Leverage

Progressive success in the fall elections brought a new political landscape for the suffrage issue, especially in the House, with its twenty-six new Progres-sive members. Just as it had in 1891, the start of the 1913 legislative session quickly devolved into partisan deadlock on the election of a House Speaker and two U.S. Senators, one for the expired term, and another to replace the ousted William Lorimer. For three weeks, all other business halted, includ-ing the confirmation of the election of the new governor, while Republicans, Progressives, and several Democratic factions cycled through possible candi-dates and coalitions for the House speakership. After repeated attempts at a Democratic-Progressive alliance failed, with a machine-dominated faction of the Democrats refusing the compromise, a Democratic first-term representa-tive from Chicago was elected by a Democratic-Republican coalition on the seventy-sixth ballot. Taking only fifteen ballots, the decision on U.S. Senators was comparatively short. Republican Lawrence Sherman had won the advisory public primary, but with only his party's support in the legislature, he received only a third of the combined House and Senate votes on the first ballot for the open full-term position. Ultimately a coalition very similar to the one that

---

[53] Straetz, 343–44; *Chicago Tribune* September 24, 1912, 1. On Abbott, see Wallace Kirkland, *The Many Faces of the Hull House* (Chicago: University of Illinois Press, 1989). The Progressive Party supportive activities of suffrage workers are well documented in the Papers of the Women' Trade Union League and Its Principal Leaders (collected on microfilm), particularly in the Margaret Dreier Robins Papers (Department of Rare Books and Manuscripts, University of Florida Libraries, Gainesville, Florida).

elected the speaker would select a Democrat for the open seat, while giving the balance of Lorimer's unexpired term to Republican Sherman.[54]

Through the rounds of balloting, the Progressives had established two things: their willingness to coalesce if given a reformist option and their willingness to hold out when not presented with such an option. If Republicans hoped to recapture their bolters, rather than risk turning state politics over to Democrats, they would need to find some way to compromise. But they were unwilling to deliver that compromise on the most central Progressive issue of direct democracy, which was ultimately defeated. Republicans insisted on an amendment to the initiative and referendum provisions that would make popular referenda nearly impossible and refused even a largely symbolic resolution concerning the direct election of Senators. On both these scores they prevailed with the assistance of machine-supportive Democrats. This left the more peripheral Progressive measures, those that had been picked up as the new party attempted to broaden its appeal and strengthen its organization, including woman suffrage, on which to compromise. Women's voting rights therefore benefited not only from the committed support of Progressive legislators, but from a Republican Party interest in seeing the policy through as well. Also joining the cause was the progressive wing of the Democratic Party, as that faction also attempted to separate itself from machine politics and court the votes of organized labor through endorsement of protective labor legislation and the initiative and referendum.

Constrained by an Illinois constitutional provision that allowed only one constitutional amendment proposal to be referred to voters from each legislative session, and hoping that proposal would be for initiative and referendum provisions, Progressives had planned to introduce a woman suffrage measure in the 1913 session that, through simple legislative enactment, would grant voting rights to women for all offices not explicitly created by or through the state constitution. Essentially, such a measure would qualify women to vote in all municipal and presidential elections, and for a very limited set of state offices. This measure also had the desirable property of granting a broad swath of voting rights to women without needing to find a strategy to overcome almost-certain Chicago machine-mobilized resistance at the polls. Some confusion between Progressives and IESA developed, however, and two versions of the bill were drafted and presented in each chamber – one by Progressives in both houses, and one drafted by IESA and presented by a Republican in the Senate and a Democrat in the House.[55] In both houses, both measures were sent

54 *Journal of the House 1913*, p. 4–105, 222–419. On the general partisan politics of the session, including identification of machine and progressive Democrats, see also Richard Allen Morton *Justice and Humanity: Edward F. Dunne, Illinois Progressive* (Carbondale and Edwardsville: Southern Illinois University Press, 1997), p. 67–82.

55 New IESA president Grace Wilbur Trout claimed in several of her writings that this was the fault of veteran IESA legislative lobbyist (and attorney) Catherine Waugh McCulloch. Trout claimed that an agreement had been worked out with the Progressives for the Democratic and

to the same committee, allowing the confusion to be settled before reaching the floor. With the assistance of Progressive Representative Medill McCormick, husband of one of IESA's four legislative lobbyists, the Progressive versions were stalled, and the IESA version moved first through the Senate.

Throughout the legislative process, from the referral of the IESA-preferred version to committee in the Senate, to the final push in the House, there was evidence of particularly deliberate handling of the suffrage issue to propel it through a legislative process in which it had been locked and stalled for two decades. The referral in the Senate was to the Committee on Constitutional Amendments – rather than the more jurisdictionally appropriate Committee on Elections – from which it received a favorable report. As it had for the last several sessions, the bill traveled rather easily through the Senate, moving without opposition from committee report through second reading. On third reading, it encountered a motion by a Chicago Democrat to recall it to second reading so that it might be amended, but that motion was rejected by a simple voice vote and the bill moved straight onto a vote on final passage. With the support of both Progressive senators, most Republicans, and nearly half the chamber's Democrats, woman suffrage carried once again in the Senate by a vote of twenty-nine in favor, fifteen opposed, and seven members not voting.

Success in the Senate was perhaps not entirely attributable to the leverage of Progressives. After all, senators had also passed a suffrage bill in the last two sessions. There is evidence, however, that district support for Progressivism did make a difference in senators' 1913 votes. First, as shown in Table 4.4, the share of the votes given to the Progressives in the last legislative election significantly divided senators who voted for the bill not only from those who voted against it, but also from those who failed to cast their votes. The average percentage of the district vote that went to the Progressive candidate among those senators who voted yes on the 1913 suffrage measure was nearly twice that of senators who voted no or abstained. This would suggest that Progressive sentiment in the district provided not only a preference for the woman suffrage measure,

Republican legislators that Trout had secured as sponsors to introduce the Progressives' measure to "have it introduced as an absolutely non-partisan measure." McCulloch, Trout claimed, was not satisfied with the wording of the Progressive measure, and essentially strong-armed Trout and the three other IESA lobbyists to have her version introduced by the sponsors. Then, in response to the deviation from the agreed plan of action, the Progressives introduced their version in the House and Senate anyway and had to be convinced to withdraw the measures. See, especially, Grace Wilbur Trout, "Side Lights on Illinois Suffrage History" (*Transactions of the Illinois State Historical Society for the Year 1920*, 93–116). All of this is possible, but given the amount of personal acrimony evident between Trout and McCulloch, equally plausible is a version of the story in which Trout was to blame for the confusion, because she was apparently the one who desired that the Progressives not introduce the measure, and that McCulloch merely made an easy scapegoat. On the difficulties between the two women, see Adade Mitchell Wheeler, "Conflict in the Illinois Woman Suffrage Movement of 1913." *Journal of the Illinois State Historical Society* 76 (Summer 1983): 95–114.

TABLE 4.4. *Vote on Presidential and Municipal Suffrage by Progressive Vote in District, Illinois Senate 1913*

	% 1912 District Vote for Progressive Candidate(s)*		
	Mean	Standard Deviation	Number of Senators
Voted Against	11.9	11.4	15
Voted For	18.9	12.1	29
Did Not Vote	10.1	12.4	7
All Senators	15.6	12.3	51

* Percent vote for Progressive State Senator if Senate election held in district in 1912, percent vote for Progressive State Representatives if no Senate election in that district in 1912.
Sources: *Journal of the Illinois House of Representatives, 1913; Blue Book of the State of Illinois, 1913.*

but also the issue importance to ensure that supportive senators actually cast their votes.

Using logistic regression to differentiate supporters from non-supporters (both those who voted no and abstainers), it is also possible to test whether Progressive voter sentiment in senators' districts uniquely prodded them to both turnout out for and cast votes in favor of the suffrage bill, or whether Progressive sentiment was simply more prevalent in districts where pressure for woman suffrage already existed. This is accomplished by building a model of senators' support of the suffrage measure that includes indicators of other possible pro-suffrage influences. First, the model includes an indicator of whether or not the senator was a Republican, because that party had shown a greater openness to suffrage changes. It also includes an indicator of whether whoever held the seat for the senator's district in 1911 voted in favor of suffrage then – before Progressives could be given credit for any political pressure thereon. Finally, the model includes a measure of the relative presence of farming interests in the district, the number of farms per 100 population, because farmers' organizations had taken an early lead in pro-suffrage politics. The model produces results, presented in Table 4.5, that support the argument that Progressive influence was both unique and important. A statistically significant positive coefficient on the district's Progressive vote shares – even when controlling for the influence of party, district characteristics, and the district senator's support of the 1911 woman suffrage measure – indicates a unique pressure to cast their votes for women's voting rights on senators facing districts that had expressed their support of Progressive policies in the 1912 elections by turning larger percentages of their votes over to the new party.

Even after the Senate handed over a majority vote, suffrage activists expected the House would be a greater challenge for their legislation, as it had been for

TABLE 4.5. *Predicting Support for Presidential and Municipal Suffrage, Illinois Senate 1913 Logistic Regression Results*

	Coefficients (standard errors)
Republican	1.07
	(0.77)
% District Progressive 1912	6.25**
	(3.08)
Support Woman Suffrage 1911	1.44*
	(0.75)
Farming Interests	15.68*
	(8.79)
Constant	−3.04
	(1.06)
N	49
Log likelihood	−24.44
LR	18.53

* $p < .10$, ** $p < .05$, two-tailed t-test
Sources: U.S. Census, 1910; *Journal of the Illinois House of Representatives,* 1913; *Blue Book of the State of Illinois,* 1913.

decades. Not since the 1891 school voting rights provision was passed had the House come to a floor vote on women's voting rights; opponents had been allowed to bury measures in committee or to table consideration and allow the legislation to expire at the close of the Assembly's session. But although attempts to repeat such treatment were made in 1913, those tactics failed in the face of increased partisan pressure to pull the measure to a vote. The backing of the Progressives gave Republicans and reformist Democrats a keener interest in woman suffrage, and both groups pushed their members to help deliver the bill to the floor. Most important, even some who could not be convinced to support the legislation on the vote of final passage were entreated not to prevent others from doing so by stalling the process, beginning in committee. Consider the treatment in committee, where the suffrage bill first faced two Progressives, eleven Republicans, and twelve Democrats. In committee meeting, fourteen members endorsed a favorable report: both Progressives, eight Republicans, and four Democrats. All four supporting Democrats were reformists who had refused to vote for the machine-sponsored compromise on House Speaker. Two of the committee members – one Republican and one Democrat – supported the favorable report although they would ultimately cast their floor votes against the bill. The four absent members – three Democrats and one Republican, all from Chicago – were also opponents of the bill, but allowed the committee to endorse the legislation by not attending the meeting at which it was considered.[56]

Having survived committee, the presidential and municipal suffrage bill deliberately worked its way through readings on the floor. Two weeks after the committee reported back, the Democrat-dominated Rules Committee granted the speaker discretionary power over the decision on bringing the bill up for second reading, a power he exercised the same day. On second reading, the suffrage measure faced two challenges from the floor. First, a Chicago Democrat offered an amendment that would strike the enacting clause. That motion was laid on the table by a vote of ninety-two to thirty-five. Next, another Democrat forwarded an amendment that would require a citizen-initiated referendum on the issue before women's voting rights would take effect. This amendment was tabled by a vote of ninety-one to thirty-eight. Only eight Republicans voted to sustain the floor amendments; five of these representatives were from machine-dominated Chicago. Nearly all the Democrats supporting the floor amendments were also linked to machine politics; fifteen of the twenty-six were members of Democratic Party boss Roger Sullivan's faction, and four others were tied into Chicago politics. All of the Democrats who had refused to compromise on a machine-endorsed candidate for Speaker, in contrast, supported the motions to table the hostile amendments.

Pushed through second reading, the suffrage bill encountered further procedural challenges when its sponsor attempted to bring it up on third reading one week later. After the House refused unanimous consent to bring up the bill, Representative Dillon moved to push consideration back to the last day of the legislative session. A Republican representative countered with a substitute motion to have the roll called for the purposes of taking up Senate bills on third reading, a maneuver that would allow for the immediate consideration of the suffrage bill. In turn, a Chicago Democrat motioned for an amendment that would put the House into immediate consideration of House bills, thereby scuttling the voting rights measure, which had come from the Senate. With slightly more resistance than that mounted to the motion to table the amendments on second reading, both procedural maneuvers to put off consideration of the suffrage bill were abated, and by a vote of eighty-eight in favor, forty-five opposed, the House moved on to third reading. Finally, the House delivered legislative success for women's voting rights in presidential and municipal elections; by a vote of eighty-three to fifty-eight, the bill passed.

Success on the procedural votes and final passage was built on a base of Republican and progressive Democratic support, added to the staunch pro-suffrage positions taken by Progressives and the House's three Socialists. But both major parties had induced members who would ultimately vote against the

---

[56] Records of House Committee on Elections consideration of Senate Bill 63. (Illinois State Archives bills files, 1913, 48th General Assembly.)

suffrage measure to help push the bill through to its final consideration. Looking, for example, to Democratic support for the motion to table the amendment that would have stricken the bill's enacting clause, eleven Democrats who
would later vote against the bill helped table the hostile amendment. Thirteen
suffrage-opposing Democrats supported the motion to table the amendment
requiring a referendum before women's voting rights could take effect. And,
of course, four Democratic opponents had earlier let woman suffrage come
out of committee by voting for or abstaining from the vote on the committee's proposed favorable report. In fact, regardless of their position on the
final vote, nearly every Democrat not associated with the Sullivan machine
or Chicago politics helped push the suffrage measure through to the final roll
call.[57] Republicans kept far fewer members from voting against woman suffrage at all – just fourteen Republicans voted against final passage – but also
pulled several opponents along on the procedural votes.[58]

On final passage, the presidential and municipal woman suffrage bill garnered support from legislators competing for the "progressive" title.[59] Progressives, Republicans, and members from the progressive wing of the Democratic
Party, along with the three House Socialists constituted the winning coalition. Among Democrats and Republicans, in fact, identification with either
the Republican Party or the progressive wing of the Democratic Party was
the only discernible difference between supporters and opponents of the bill.
Logistic regression analysis of the final roll call, presented in Table 4.6, shows
that although both of these affiliations were significant predictors of support,
the nature of the legislators' constituencies had little bearing. The Progressive
Party's endorsement, and their subsequent electoral success had made woman
suffrage a party issue for both Democrats and Republicans in the Illinois legislature. Support of women's voting rights was an important part of both major
party organizations' attempts to claim the progressive label and reclaim electoral support.

As a Progressive issue, woman suffrage gained the salience it needed for
non-machine partisans to push it through the legislative process – particularly
in the House – despite machine members' resistance. Having lost so many
seats to the Progressive success, Republicans needed to diffuse the Progressive
agenda to regain their dominance in Illinois politics. Yet, the Republican Party

---

[57] On the general partisan politics of the session, including identification of machine and progressive Democrats, see Morton, *Justice and Humanity*, 67–82. Only four non-machine Democrats
from outside Chicago voted against the motions to table the enacting clause amendment,
although fifteen of this group would later vote against the suffrage bill on final passage. Six of
this group voted against the tabling of the referendum amendment and the motion to take up
Senate bills on third reading. Nine voted against taking up the suffrage bill in particular.

[58] Six of the fourteen Republican suffrage opponents voted in favor of bringing up the Senate bills
on third reading, four to bring up the suffrage bill in particular, and three to table both the
hostile amendments.

[59] Progressive Democrats identified in Morton, *Justice and Humanity*, 67–82.

TABLE 4.6. *Predicting Support for Woman Suffrage among*
Democrats and Republicans, Illinois House of Representatives 1913
Logistic Regression Results

	Coefficients (standard errors)		
	Democrats & Republicans	Democrats	Republicans
Republican	2.63**	–	–
	(1.12)		
Progressive Democrat	1.96*	2.62**	–
	(1.16)	(1.23)	
Machine Democrat	−0.78	−0.44	–
	(1.51)	(1.49)	
Chicago Representative	−0.77	0.19	−0.79
	(.94)	(1.37)	(1.38)
% District Vote Progressive	1.02	1.87	1.49
	(2.05)	(3.04)	(2.78)
Per Capita Labor	−4.81	−2.88	−9.55
	(7.60)	(10.19)	(12.48)
Constant	−1.41	−2.45	1.69
	(1.25)	(1.48)	(.89)
N	110	66	46
Log likelihood	−76.23	−43.26	−24.60
LR			

* $p < .10$, **$p < .05$, two-tailed t-test
Sources: U.S. Census, 1910; *Journal of the Illinois House of Representatives, 1913*; *Blue Book of the State of Illinois, 1913*; Morton, Richard Allen *Justice and Humanity: Edward F. Dunne, Illinois Progressive* (Carbondale and Edwardsville: Southern Illinois University Press, 1997).

was unwilling to pass the direct democracy measures central to the Progressive Party's demands. Women's voting rights became one of the set of auxiliary Progressive policies to benefit from this situation, gaining the Republican Party organization's support. Democrats also saw opportunity in the Progressive insurgence; the break within the Republican base might be exploited to build Democratic prominence in the state. Indeed, many of the Democrats elected in 1913, including the governor, were proclaimed "progressives." This partisan jockeying for the "progressive" label, along with commitment from Progressives, themselves, pulled the suffrage measure through both houses of the Illinois legislature. It pressured Republicans and Democrats to push the measure to a floor vote, despite (or perhaps because of) resistance from the machine element of the Democratic Party, and would also leverage the governor's signature. Third party success had once again brought victory for women's voting rights in Illinois.

Conclusion

As the Illinois Progressive Representative George Fitch had observed, legislators had endless choices for dealing with suffrage legislation beyond voting it up or down on final passage. Convincing legislators to work to ensure the measure reached the floor was therefore at least as important as securing their nominal favor for the policy. What third parties could offer woman suffrage was an especially clear signal that political consequences were involved for failing to bring the issue through. When a suffrage plank was part of the platform on which a successful third party ran, surviving major party politicians needed to worry about the electoral consequences of ignoring the third party agenda. These electoral concerns not only pressured individual legislators from districts where third party sentiment was strong, but also gave incentives to party organizations that faced consequence or opportunity in the third party ascendancy; looking to regain or capitalize on seats lost, major parties looked to diffuse the third party success through cooptation of its issues. Moreover, when third party legislators held the balance of power in a legislature, which happened in Illinois both in 1891 and 1913, they had the unique ability to use their place as pivotal voters on party-line issues to leverage concessions on their agenda from the major parties. If suffragist advocates could sustain their partnerships with these third parties – partnerships which grew out of common issue concerns and women's role in the parties' organizational base – the benefit of third party politics was uncommonly strong pressure for lawmakers to deliver women's voting rights.

Winning presidential and municipal suffrage was a significant political gain for Illinois women, delivered through their negotiation of coalitions that secured them the unmatched leverage of the Progressive Party. Unfortunately, it would be their last suffrage victory until passage of the U.S. Constitutional amendment. The cross-class coalition that had played such an important part in the appeal of woman suffrage endorsement to the Progressive party fell apart shortly after the passage of the 1913 suffrage bill. IESA leaders made choices that put their desire for full suffrage rights above the WTUL's commitment to working women's goals. Most public of these choices was a decision by the IESA leadership to accept the offer of infamously anti-labor newspaper publisher William Randolph Hearst to publish a suffragist version of his Chicago paper on their behalf, promising the IESA all the net proceeds thereof. It was an offer the middle class suffragists found hard to refuse for the financial windfall it promised the IESA (it reportedly generated $15,000 for the organization); but for the WTUL, it was a stark symbol of the lack of concern the suffragists held for working women's labor rights.[60] In short, the organized suffrage movement proved that although it was, indeed, a movement of women, it was not an all-encompassing woman's movement. Just as politicians had expected,

---

[60] Buechler, *The Transformation of the Woman Suffrage Movement*, 178–182.

women were a politically diverse group, and holding them together based only on their sex proved impossible. With strong evidence that women offered no hope of a new party voting bloc, the loss of labor as a political ally for the suffrage cause, and quick return to Republican dominance of state politics following the 1914 elections, political interest in the suffrage cause dissolved.

Indeed, the case of Illinois was particularly illustrative of the dynamics of suffrage politics delivered through variation in several factors that define the likelihood of suffrage extension under the programmatic enfranchisement model. Coalitions that at one point in a state's history gave electoral meaning to the issue of woman suffrage could be undone – either through missteps such as those that undid the connection between labor and suffrage in the wake of the 1913 victory, or through more benign neglect, as seemed the case of the farmer-suffrage connection in the wake of the 1891 victory. Without active coalitional politics, suffrage lost the issue definition that gave legislators electoral incentive to deliver support – quite obvious in the disappearance of a connection between farming presence in legislators' districts and their vote decisions on suffrage in the 1890s. As the programmatic enfranchisement model specifies, however, the effectiveness of coalitional politics is also shaped by broader forces in electoral politics that change the degree of lawmakers' vulnerability to coalitional constituent demands for new voting rights. This was also evident in Illinois. In a general sense, it seemed not much happened on the suffrage front during times when Republicans held secure control over state politics. More crisply, it was the moments of partisan upheaval caused by sudden third party electoral fortunes that gave rise to the most active – and successful – politics of woman suffrage.

5

Coalitional Impossibilities

Race, Class, and Failure

> The question of Woman Suffrage is a big one, for it deals with human liberty.
> But when it is proposed to accomplish it by Federal Authority it is, so far as
> the South is concerned, instantly submerged in the unanswerable question of the
> relationship between the races.
>
> – Harry P. Gamble, Democrat, former Louisiana state senator, 1918[1]

> Some of our Southern friends insist that there is a grave danger in giving Negro
> women the right to vote and for that reason they oppose the Federal Amendment,
> while willing for women to vote under state laws. I cannot believe there is such
> a menace from this source as warrants the whole Nation in refusing to adopt the
> suffrage amendment to the Federal Constitution. In my judgment, the situation
> can be handled as has been done with Negro men for the past twenty-five years.
>
> – U.S. Senator Joseph Ransdell, Democrat-Louisiana, 1918[2]

Stories of race and women's voting rights often begin and end with the question of the Fifteenth Amendment to the U.S. Constitution. The adoption of
the Constitutional protection of black voting rights divided the earliest suffrage organizers between those who supported the Amendment as progress on
voting rights and those who rejected it as an unpalatable compromise. Later,
debate over the desirability of a federal woman suffrage amendment would
be caught up in questions of the South's ability to maintain its obfuscation
of the Fifteenth Amendment. With many of the early nationally prominent
suffrage leaders arising from the abolitionist movement in the North, the reac-
tion of the suffragists to Amendment XV was remarkable, and understandably

[1] From "Federal Suffrage a Racial Question in the South" Address by Harry P. Gamble, Delivered
before the New Orleans Press Club, March 11, 1918.
[2] "Remarks of United States Senator Joseph E. Ransdell on the Suffrage Amendment to the
Constitution" June 24, 1918.

divisive. It forged a cleavage in the early, Northern movement, finally splitting women who had worked together for decades into two separate suffrage organizations in 1869: the National Woman Suffrage Association (NWSA), which denounced the adoption of black men's voting rights before (white) women's, and the American Woman Suffrage Association (AWSA), which welcomed any extension of voting rights. Although the predominantly Northern members of these organizations were able to reconcile in the 1890s, forming the National American Woman Suffrage Association (NAWSA), as the reunited "national" organization began to interest Southern women, Amendment XV again entered discussions of women's voting rights. Concerns about renewed federal interest in voting rights regulation and enforcement in a racially "redeemed" South surfaced and were channeled into aversion to woman suffrage in the form of another amendment to the U.S. Constitution. Women organizers and male politicians alike would warn of the floodgate opening that a federal amendment might bring, and appealed to states' rights arguments for the rejection of such a project.[3] Ultimately, most of the Deep South states would refuse to ratify Amendment XIX; of the former Confederate States, only Arkansas, Tennessee, and Texas approved.[4]

Although both the accounts of early Northern tension and later Southern resistance caused by the issue of race center on the Fifteenth Amendment, racial politics significantly affected the push for woman suffrage outside of the commingling of the questions of federal action on voting rights for black Americans and for women. Race and gender politics intersected at the state level as well, as a number of scholars of the Southern woman suffrage movement have argued. Both Marjorie Spruill Wheeler and Elna Green, for example, have documented how concerns for white supremacy increased the interest of some Southern white women in the suffragist cause, especially through state action, helping to fuel Southern activism after the Civil War. Enfranchisement of white women was interpreted first as a means to temper the influence of the votes of black men, then, following Southern Redemption, as further assurance against the possible resurgence of black political power. Yet, Wheeler, Green and others have observed that concern for white supremacy was also commonly offered as a justification of the anti-woman suffrage position – by Southern white women and male politicians. Woman suffrage, Southerners were reminded, would enfranchise white *and* black women. Intimating that the racial violence

---

3 On this typical characterization of the relationship between issues of race and women's voting rights: Kraditor, Aileen S., *The Ideas of the Woman Suffrage Movement, 1890–1920* (New York: W. W. Norton & Company, 1981), 163–218. Suffragists' own commentaries can be found throughout NAWSA's six-volume *History of Woman Suffrage* and in Carrie Chapman Catt and Nettie Rogers Shuler, *Woman Suffrage and Politics: The Inner Story of the Suffrage Movement* (New York, C. Scribner's Sons, 1926).

4 All the states that rejected or refused to consider Amendment XIX in the 1920s were former slave states: Alabama, Delaware, Florida, Georgia, Louisiana, Maryland, Mississippi, North Carolina, South Carolina, and Virginia.

often used in tandem with legal provisions such as the literacy test to keep black men from the polls might not be as easily meted out to women, anti-woman suffrage rhetoric warned of the slippery slope toward political equality of the races.[5] With racism marshaled on both sides of the issue, then, it has been difficult for scholars to make the case for whether and how racial politics could explain the significant resistance to state woman suffrage provisions in the South.

The consequences for the woman suffrage issue in state politics arising from racial politics is the subject of this chapter. Class politics will also enter, as race and class were (and are) intertwined, and both, I argue, served to narrow the range of political possibilities for suffragists. Race infiltrated the woman suffrage issue not only through the intersection of political discussions of blacks' voting rights and [white] women's voting rights, but also, and more importantly, by shaping the political landscape suffragists encountered when race was a particularly salient issue in party politics. Whether driven primarily by racial antagonism, or by economic or partisan goals that were facilitated by racial antagonism, racial politics created barriers to woman suffrage in ways that stretched well beyond resistance to a federal woman suffrage measure by Southern politicians. Racial politics – which could involve not only whites and blacks, but Hispanics, Asians, and Native Americans, too – fostered the creation of a number of political institutions that constrained possibilities for suffrage success. Notably, electoral laws that excluded significant portions of the male citizenry, stifled the possibility of the emergence of a third party, and often narrowed the political playing field to a single viable party served to narrow coalitional opportunities for suffragists, and constitutional procedures that made suffrage qualification changes more difficult increased the necessary size of a winning coalition. Racial attitudes – of suffragists and politicians – were not unimportant; those attitudes both dampened suffragists' inclinations to reach out to the groups that joined successful suffrage coalitions in other states, and influenced the political viability of those coalitions if and when they

---

[5] Wheeler, Marjorie Spruill, *New Women of the New South: The Leaders of the Woman Suffrage Movement in the Southern States* (New York: Oxford University Press, 1993), esp. 100–32. Green, Elna C., *Southern Strategies: Southern Women and the Woman Suffrage Question*(Chapel Hill: The University of North Carolina Press, 1997). Note these two authors disagree on the extent of the use of racist arguments by Southern suffragists. Scott, Anne Firor, *The Southern Lady: From Pedestal to Politics, 1830–1930* (Chicago: University of Chicago Press, 1970). Thomas, Mary Martha, *The New Woman in Alabama: Social Reforms and Suffrage, 1890–1920* (Tuscaloosa: University of Alabama Press, 1992). Gilmore, Glenda Elizabeth, *Gender and Jim Crow: Women and the Politics of White Supremacy in North Carolina, 1896–1920* (Chapel Hill: The University of North Carolina Press, 1996), esp. 203–24. Kraditor, Aileen S. "Tactical Problems of the Woman-Suffrage Movement in the South" in *History of Women in the United States: Historical Articles on Women's Lives and Activities*, vl. 19, ed. Nancy F. Cott (Munich: KG Saur, 1992), 272–90.

did form. If coalitional politics really were the key to voting rights for women, as I have argued in the previous chapters, political institutions and identity politics that constrained coalitional possibilities would deal a significant blow to the chances for women's voting rights.

Turning to the states of Louisiana and New Mexico, this chapter demonstrates that the question of woman suffrage faced both institutional and coalitional barriers built by racial politics outside the conflicts over either the meaning and importance of the Fifteenth and Nineteenth Amendments to the U.S. Constitution or the utility of enfranchising white women at the state level for the maintenance of white supremacy. Louisiana's racial question was one of black and white, but that did not imply steadfast resistance to women's voting rights from lawmakers who feared being turned out of office by blacks, as the white supremacy rhetoric might have implied. Instead, the one-party political system built on the back of white supremacy created a range of political obstacles for the extension of voting rights, even to white women only. In New Mexico, racial politics were not about black and white, but rather Spanish American and Anglo.[6] This case reveals that politics to *protect* racial minority rights also had important implications for the woman suffrage question. These politics also built institutional barriers that made woman suffragists' goal more difficult to obtain. And laws protecting minority rights did not necessarily diminish the difficulty for successful coalition-building that stemmed from racial attitudes.

Louisiana – Racism, Democracy, and Personal Politics

As in other Deep South states, consideration of and organization for woman suffrage in Louisiana did not begin until after the Civil War, and activity on the issue was slow to develop over the ensuing decades. Yet the constitution rewriting of Reconstruction and Redemption offered opportunities that were not ignored. Even before any suffrage organization existed in the state, several women petitioned the Louisiana Constitutional Convention in 1879 for the inclusion of women's voting rights, asking if full suffrage was deemed infeasible, at least school suffrage be granted on account of women's interest in the raising of children. The convention, in producing Louisiana's first Redemption constitution, included a small concession to the women in the form of a clause that permitted women to hold "any office of control or management under

---

[6] The term "Spanish American" is derived from practice in the nineteenth and early twentieth centuries; those who had been citizens of Mexico and their descendants were typically referred to as such, or simply as "Spanish" – and sometimes also as "natives." Although contemporary dialogues might classify this distinction as ethnic rather than racial, both Anglo Americans and Spanish Americans at that time referred to themselves as separate races. Because race is a social construction, characterizing the tension between these two groups as racial, rather than ethnic, seems most appropriate.

the school laws of the state."[7] Before the next Constitutional Convention, held in 1898, Louisiana would have its first woman suffrage organizations. Two women's clubs, the Portia Club and the Era Club, formed by white society women in New Orleans, took up the issue of woman suffrage in the 1890s, and in 1896 joined to form the first "state" woman suffrage association. There is no evidence that this Louisiana State Suffrage Association (LSSA) actually had members from outside New Orleans, and it was gone by 1900; in that year, NAWSA officially recognized the Era Club as its state affiliate in Louisiana. Before it passed out of existence, however, Louisiana's first state suffrage organization faced a new Constitutional Convention in 1898 at which the first voting rights for women in the state would be granted.[8]

Called for a more thorough Redemption of the state following an 1896 election cycle marked by violence, fraud allegations, and the strongest showing against the Democrats since the 1879 Constitution was adopted, the 1898 convention made all other constitutional provisions secondary to the business of forming new electoral qualifications. On their second day in session, the convention delegates approved a resolution that required "[t]hat no ordinance or proposition intended to become a part of the Constitution, nor any resolution, motion or order referring to or concerning any provision in the Constitution, shall be considered by this Convention until the report of the Committee on Suffrage and Elections shall have been made to and finally acted upon by this Convention."[9] To establish Democratic dominance in the state, the 134 Democratic delegates would adopt a set of voting qualifications that included the payment of poll taxes for two years and demonstration of "literacy" through the ability to properly fill out a voter registration form. The literacy requirement could be waived, however, through either a "grandfather clause" or property qualification; men who themselves qualified to vote in

---

[7] Lindig, Carmen, *The Path from the Parlor: Louisiana Women 1879–1920* (Lafayette, Louisiana: University of Southwestern Louisiana), 37–41. HWS, vol. IV, 678. The clause was apparently not used until the mid-1880s.

[8] It is worth noting that, although populist parties were key parts of successful woman suffrage coalitions in other states (such as the Farmers' Alliance that helped Illinois women win their first voting rights), no connection between woman suffrage and the populism that emerged in Louisiana appears to have been made. Organized suffrage activism by women had not yet emerged, and the women who were just beginning to organize were of a social class whose direct interests were opposed to a small-farmers' rights movement: the society women of the Portia and Era Clubs were typically from plantation wealth, even if not living on a plantation. See Lindig, *The Path from the Parlor*, 36–68, 110–30.

[9] *Official Journal of the Proceedings of the Constitutional Convention of the State of Louisiana, 1898* (New Orleans: H. J. Hearsey), 74. In the election of 1896, the Republican-Populist Fusion candidate for governor, John N. Pharr, had taken 43% of the state vote, leaving Democrat Murphy J. Foster just 57%. Democrats had been polling well more than 60% since the 1879 Constitution. On the mob violence and fraud allegations leading up to the 1898 Constitutional Convention, see Shields, Thomas Walton, "The Political and Social Background of the Suffrage Changes of 1898 in Louisiana," (M.A. Thesis, Louisiana State University, 1930).

Louisiana prior to January 1, 1867 or whose fathers or grandfathers did were exempt from the literacy test, as were men who could demonstrate that they owned at least $300 worth of assessed property.[10]

The voter qualifications, and the intended consolidation of Democratic power, clearly turned on appeals to white supremacy, although there was dissention over the inclusion (or exclusion) of foreign-born voters. In his opening remarks, the president of the convention, E. B. Kruttschnitt of New Orleans, articulated the delegates' purpose as a charge from "the people of the State to eliminate from the electorate the mass of corrupt and illiterate voters who have during the last quarter of a century degraded our politics.... With a unanimity unparalleled in the history of American politics they have entrusted to the Democratic party of this State the solution of the purification of the electorate."[11] It would soon become clear that the vulnerability to corruption at the polls caused by a lack of education or property was only a concern insofar as that vulnerability was to Republican influence. Not only did the grandfather clause allow for the inclusion of illiterate white voters, but it also contained a provision that "grandfathered" in all foreign-born residents, so long as they had been naturalized before 1898. The newspapers implied, although delegates attempted to deny, that this provision was inserted especially for the protection of the sizable Italian immigrant community in New Orleans, a constituency generally understood to be part of the Democratic machine in that city.[12] Blacks, however, were repeatedly linked to the influence of the Republican Party, and

---

[10] *Constitution of the State of Louisiana*, 1898, Art. 197, Sec. 1–5. The registration form required filling in the blanks of this statement: "I am a citizen of the State of Louisiana. My name is ___. I was born in the State (or country) of ___, Parish (or county) of ___, on the day of ___, in the year ___. I am now ___ years, ___months and ___days of age. I have resided in this State since ___, in this parish ___, and in Precinct No. ___, of Ward No. ___, of this parish, since ___, and I am not disfranchised by any provision of the state." Also disfranchised were "[t]hose who have been convicted of any crime punishable by imprisonment in the penitentiary, and not afterwards pardoned with the express restoration of the franchise; those who are inmates in any charitable institution, except the Soldiers' Home; those actually confined in any public prison; all indicted persons, and all persons notoriously insane or idiotic, whether interdicted or not" (Art. 202). Two of the convention delegates were not Democrats: a Populist from Winn Parish and a Republican from Iberville Parish.

[11] *Official Journal of the Proceedings of the Constitutional Convention of the State of Louisiana, 1898*, 9. The president's opening remarks have been edited to delete a spelling error clearly made by the recording clerk.

[12] The allegations and denial of the strategic protection of Italian immigrant voters were read into the convention's record on March 18 (page 122). For a discussion of the Italian and other immigrants in the New Orleans machine, see Reynolds, George M. *Machine Politics in New Orleans, 1897–1926* (New York: Columbia University Press, 1936), 11–15. For more on the partisan politics of disfranchisement, see J. Morgan Kouser, *The Shaping of Southern Politics: Suffrage Restriction and the Establishment of the One-Party South, 1880–1910* (New Haven: Yale University Press, 1974). Pages 152–65 deal with the 1879 and 1898 Louisiana Constitutional Conventions. Also see Richard M. Valelly, *The Two Reconstructions: The Struggle for Black Enfranchisement* (Chicago: University of Chicago Press, 2004).

ultimately the target of disfranchisement. At the end of the convention, the chairman of the Committee on the Judiciary, Thomas J. Semmes – one of Louisiana's representatives in the Confederate Senate – offered a speech on the accomplishments of the delegates, stressing and defending their accomplishments as both partisans and believers in white supremacy:

This is the work of a Democratic Convention. This is the work of the Democratic party of the State, represented by its selected agents appointed to do that work. If we have done anything wrong, anything which will dissolve the dissolution or disintegration or defeat of the Democratic party, then we ought to be condemned. It has been stated in some quarters that we have been actuated to a certain extent by party spirit. Grant it. What of it? What is the State? It is the Democratic party. [Applause from delegates noted.] . . . We met here to establish the supremacy of the white race, and the white race constitutes the Democratic party of this State. There is, therefore, in my judgment, no separation whatever between the interests of the State and those of the Democratic party.[13]

In a convention so focused on designing electoral qualifications for the benefit of a single party, what became of appeals for woman suffrage? Without a widespread and well-organized movement, and with only a single petition signed by forty-one women, woman suffrage won consideration in the 1898 Convention. Its consideration, it seems, was tied to ideas about the connection between taxation and suffrage rights, and to the contributions white women might make to Louisiana politics. The first resolution on the issue of woman suffrage, introduced by a district attorney from the northern parish of Natchitoches who had no apparent link to the organized suffragists, called for women property owners, otherwise duly qualified, to have the right to vote at special elections regarding taxation.[14] The LSSA's petition to the convention was later introduced by A. W. Faulkner, a long-serving state representative. In it, the women made a strategic enfranchisement appeal, asking that they be granted suffrage on the same terms as men while stressing the contributions educated,

---

[13] *Official Journal of the Proceedings of the Constitutional Convention of the State of Louisiana, 1898*, 374–75. Semmes went on to defend Section 5 of Art. 197, the "grandfather" clause that included naturalized foreign-born residents, claiming its sole purpose was to protect white supremacy, to allow illiterate white populations, "that ancient Acadian population" that voted with the Democrats "to wrest from the hands of the Republican Party, composed almost exclusively of negroes the power which, backed by Federal bayonets, they had exercised for many years," to retain their voting rights. Clearly, however, these were not the people to which the naturalized foreign-born exemption applied. Semmes was working hard to sell Democracy and white supremacy as synonyms, even in the face of necessary practical deviations from that creed.

[14] *Official Journal of the Proceedings of the Constitutional Convention of the State of Louisiana, 1898*, 43. The next year, Breazeale would go on to the U.S. Congress, where he served three terms. His Congressional biography is available at http://bioguide.congress.gov. Natchitoches was a cotton-growing parish with a majority black population (60%) according to the 1890 U.S. Census.

white women could make to the state's electorate. Leaders of LSSA and its constituent Portia and Era clubs, along with Carrie Chapman Catt from NAWSA, were also allowed a hearing by the convention, after which Faulkner promptly offered a resolution of thanks to the women "as an evidence of appreciation of their presence and intelligent and interesting addresses to the convention." Faulkner's resolution also called for the Committee on Suffrage and Elections "to take cognizance of the same."[15] The resolution was promptly adopted. Women's voting rights never entered the floor discussions of the suffrage clauses, and were not mentioned in any of the leadership's speeches, but the taxpaying woman suffrage clause proposed earlier became part of the 1898 Constitution.

It is difficult to establish exactly why and how the convention acted to adopt the limited woman suffrage clause – not only is there no record of consideration of the taxpayer woman suffrage clause in the convention proceedings, but the women offered very little account of their own experiences. What evidence there is suggests the woman suffrage cause was likely forwarded by a small set of friendly political entrepreneurs. In their entry in the NAWSA-compiled *History of Woman Suffrage*, Louisiana suffragists state only that, "Dr. Henry Dickson Bruns, a member of the Suffrage Committee, bent every effort to secure Full Suffrage for women as the only means to effect the reform in political conditions so much desired."[16] Bruns was also sent a letter of thanks by Louisiana suffragist Kate Gordon for his support of woman suffrage in the convention.[17] It is apparent that Bruns, a physician and Anti-Lottery Democrat from New Orleans, did not quite toe the party line on the state's suffrage qualifications, as he refused to sign the final 1898 Constitution on the objection that the "grandfather" clause was unconstitutional.[18] His support of woman suffrage seemed born of a genuine personal political conviction in favor of government reform; he served in no other government office after the convention, but continued in support of reform activities and eventually appeared at a NAWSA conference.[19]

[15] *Official Journal of the Proceedings of the Constitutional Convention of the State of Louisiana, 1898*, 48–49, 64. Caldwell was a cotton growing parish; blacks constituted 53% of the population in 1890 according to the U.S. Census.

[16] HWS, vol. IV, 681.

[17] Letter from Kate Gordon to Henry Dickson Bruns April 9, 1898 (Bruns Family Papers, 1839–1917 [MS-BRUNS], Louisiana Division, New Orleans Public Library).

[18] Biographical information from summary overview of Henry Dickson Bruns Papers (Bruns Family Papers, 1839–1917 [MS-BRUNS], Louisiana Division, New Orleans Public Library). Anti-Lottery Democrats were a faction within the Democratic Party with the central concern of ending the state's lottery franchise. A franchise had been granted to a private corporation by the state, which paid $40,000 annually back to the state for the privilege, but was estimated to pull in profits many times that amount. The profits were allegedly used, in part, to influence government officers. Shields, Thomas Walton, "The Political and Social Background of the Suffrage Changes of 1898 in Louisiana," 39–42.

[19] Bruns addressed the 1903 NAWSA conference held in Louisiana. His remarks encouraged suffragists to take account of the electoral incentives of legislators, and not to "rely upon wise

Whether the adoption of tax suffrage was an attempt to redress the concerns of committed reformers like Bruns, or a concession to Bruns' pressure alone, the absence of woman suffrage from the extended deliberations of the other suffrage clauses suggests that Democrats saw little strategic advantage for the party in (white) women's votes.

Although it granted only limited suffrage, the 1898 Constitution offered Louisiana suffrage advocates a new opportunity to establish the effect of woman suffrage at the polls. The Era Club formed a committee, led by the woman who would run the club in the coming decades, Kate Gordon, to organize a campaign to register and turn out women property holders in New Orleans to vote on a coming municipal tax issue. Their stated intent was to establish that women were a reforming force for politics, which they hoped to demonstrate by helping to pass a sewerage and drainage tax that had been proposed to redress the public health concerns presented by the city's lack of sufficient infrastructure for water and sewer services. Work on the voting drive began with the task of identifying women taxpayers from city records, who were then sought out first for their signatures on a petition to put the tax increase on the ballot, and again either to go to the polls or to make use of the special constitutional provision for women's votes to be cast by proxy. Era Club members reported casting several hundred votes by proxy for women who would not visit the polling places themselves. The tax carried and the Era Club women were quick to claim credit for aiding its passage. They also took sides in the legal battle that followed over the method of selection of the newly formed Sewerage and Water Board, coming out in favor of an appointive board, rather than the elective board desired by the city and state administrations.[20] In their efforts to show their electoral strength, they were antagonizing the "machine" or "Regular" Democratic Party politicians, who had just consolidated power through the 1898 Convention. This was, unfortunately, the beginning of a tense relationship between suffrage activists and the Democratic Party – particularly the New Orleans machine. Antagonism of the machine would prove a difficult barrier to overcome, particularly given the political environment created by the 1898 Constitution.

The political conditions that resulted from the 1898 Constitution, in fact, were much as the framers had hoped. As illustrated in Table 5.1, Louisiana politics were effectively reduced to a single-party, whites-only system as citizen participation in elections was severely constricted – by legal barriers, racial violence, selective law enforcement, and intra-party coordination by elites. The

and eloquent appeals to Legislatures and conventions. It is in the campaigns for the election of the legislative bodies that you should marshal your forces and use to the full the all-sufficient influence with which your antagonists credit you." See HWS, vol. V, 66–67.

[20] For the Era Club position, see HWS, vol. IV, 684. For the positions of the administrations, see the resultant Louisiana Supreme Court case *State ex rel. Saunders v. Kohnke et al.* (No. 14,598 Supreme Court of Louisiana 109 La. 838; 33 So. 793; 1903 La. LEXIS 444 January 19, 1903). The administration position lost the court case, and the members it added to the board through a bill passed by the 1902 state legislature were removed from office.

TABLE 5.1. *Voter Turnout in Louisiana Gubernatorial Elections*[21]

Election Year	Turnout	Voting Age Male Population	% Voting Age Male Turnout	% Vote Democratic
1872	126,969	189,766	66.9	42.6
1876	160,963	203,277	79.2	52.5
1879	114,038	213,409	53.4	64.6
1884	132,282	230,297	57.4	67.1
1888	188,740	243,808	77.4	72.5
1892	178,302	265,639	67.1	68.9
1896	203,814	295,791	68.9	56.9
1900	74,421	325,943	22.8	78.3
1904	53,622	361,533	14.8	89.0
1908	67,683	397,124	17.0	87.1
1912	55,542	425,869	13.0	89.5
1916	128,892	447,769	28.8	62.5
1920	55,115	469,669	11.7	97.6

number of black voters in the state dropped from 129,760 in 1896 to 5,380 in 1900 – hardly surprising given the stated antiblack intent of the Constitutional Convention. But the political participation of whites was also affected in the face of heightened control of the process by Democratic elites. Democrats chose candidates through conventions until 1906, and then through primaries that discouraged challengers by requiring a candidate to earn a majority (not plurality) to advance to the general election. Election laws were also written to make ballot access for new parties extremely difficult, including the requirement of a ten percent return in a general election before a group running a candidate could attach its party label to its candidate on the ballot.[22] With little real choice offered, electoral participation of even qualified voters waned. The only up-tick in a trend of declining voter turnout beginning in 1900 was in 1916, the year a prominent Democrat, John M. Parker, bolted the party and ran on a Progressive ticket in the general election (only possible because of the 1912 Roosevelt presidential candidacy); the percentage of voting age males participating in the general election jumped from 13.0 in 1912 to 28.8 in 1916, only to bottom out again at 11.7 percent in the next election.

In a political system that offered so few options for those legally included, it would be difficult for woman suffragists to find electoral leverage for their cause. There were, quite simply, few challengers to the status quo. Interest groups with mass bases were not central in electoral politics that included

[21] Population numbers extrapolated from U.S. Census reports of voting age male populations of 1880, 1890, 1900, 1910, and 1920 (simple linear smoothing). Turnout is for the general election, from *Congressional Quarterly's Gubernatorial Elections, 1787–1997* (Washington, DC: Congressional Quarterly, 1998).

[22] Reynolds, *Machine Politics in New Orleans*, 78–92.

so few of "the masses." And the purposeful restraint on third party politics, which offered particularly influential suffrage partnerships in other states, rendered such opportunities for Louisiana suffragists rare. What did evolve in Louisiana politics as a result of the constrained, one-party system was an ever-stronger machine element in New Orleans politics. As New Orleans accounted for approximately one-fourth of the state's white population, and its representatives accounted for one-fifth of the membership in the Louisiana House of Representatives and nearly one-fourth of the Senate, the power of the city machine in state politics was formidable. Although a reformist challenge would surface, culminating in the Parker candidacy for governor, Louisiana suffragists would never be able to surpass the machine opposition that stood between them and their goal of women's voting rights, even when they appealed on the grounds of white supremacy and states' rights, and even as they attempted to imitate the same personal politics they witnessed among Democratic Party elites.

Southern Ladies' Organizations – Society Club Suffrage Politics

In many ways, organization for woman suffrage in Louisiana actually mirrored the exclusivity and factionalism of Louisiana state politics after 1898. The suffrage "movement" in the state was never about mass, grass-roots participation, but was instead centered on a set of elite white women who were eventually driven into separate, discordant factions. No organizations for suffrage existed outside of New Orleans until 1913, when suffrage societies emerged in Shreveport and Baton Rouge. Between 1900 and 1913, the Era Club was the only organization working for women's voting rights, and was only doing so as part of its club activities, which also included charitable fundraising and campaigning for legislation to regulate child labor, improve public services, and combat the city's somewhat infamous vice districts. Not only was the Era Club busy with pursuits other than suffrage work, it was also carrying out its activities with a very limited membership. Begun as a social club, and not a movement or political organization, the Era Club required both prepayment of fairly hefty dues and sponsorship by two existing members for a new woman to join its ranks. In 1911, the president of the club, Judith Hyams Douglas, described its membership as "New Orleans' foremost Physicians, having charge of the woman's dispensary, Dentists, Journalists, Attorneys, Philanthropists, and Presidents of the all the leading Woman organizations, together with many teachers."[23] Douglas also mentioned that the club met just twice a month and recessed from May until October, although the Executive Board and some committees met several times during the summer. It would be difficult to describe the Era Club as an active *movement* for women's voting rights.

---

[23] Era Speech, 1911 (Judith Hyams Douglas Papers, Louisiana State University Libraries Special Collections, Baton Rouge). On the Era Club's membership, activities, and policies, see also the Douglas' other Era speeches (1908, 1910) in the same collection and the Era Club Minutes, 1915–1920 (New Orleans Public Library) and HWS.

In 1913, as suffrage clubs were beginning to develop in other parts of the state, the New Orleans organization split in two. Women who had been involved with the Era Club since its founding left to form the Woman Suffrage Party of Louisiana (WSPL), apparently because of conflicts with new leaders, sisters Kate and Jean Gordon. A letter from one of WSPL's founding members, Sake Meehan, to Era's departing legislative committee chair (and former president), Grace Chamberlain, in June of 1913 discussed the reasons women like Chamberlain were abandoning the Era Club:

I think the fact that you women who worked so hard in the Era Club had to work in an atmosphere of jealousy and dominant authority and all that kind of thing reacted on the health of every one of you. I don't believe the same work done in a different atmosphere and with the help and encouragement of those associated with you, and with a feeling that you could go right ahead and do what you thought was right and no one would criticise [sic] or get offended, or anything of that sort, would have affected you badly at all. I think you have carried on the work of the Era Club for years, a few of you, under the most trying circumstances, sacrificing your nerves and health, and the Gordons have calmly appropriated to themselves the results of your labor when they were good, and blamed you when they were not all that was expected. I hope in a few months more everyone will be able to see those women exactly as they are, selfish, arrogant, and in many ways inferior to the women they speak of slightly.[24]

The Gordons had clearly personally alienated a number of the former Era Club members, but disagreements about the proper strategy for a suffrage campaign were also brewing. In the 1912 legislative session, Kate Gordon had asked New Orleans attorney Martin Manion to introduce a bill that would have given women the right to vote in primary elections. As the Democrats had already established a whites-only primary election system, this was a pointed attempt to win voting rights for white women in a way that brought no chance of coincidental enfranchisement of black women. Although the primary suffrage legislation never made it out of committee, this was a point of departure for Louisiana suffragists. Those who stayed on under the Gordons' leadership would pursue a "South-specific" strategy marked by racial antagonism, personal legislative lobbying, and resistance to a woman suffrage amendment to the U.S. Constitution. Suffragists who left the Era Club, however, were unwilling to place states' rights over women's voting rights. Although certainly not marked by any concern for the rights of black women, WSPL members advocated for a federal woman suffrage amendment, whatever the cost to the racial order might be.[25] Unfortunately, neither group's strategy would earn the support of the New Orleans machine; reformist women, committed to white supremacy or not, held little appeal for politicians whose power rested on patronage and electoral control.

---

[24] Letter from Sake Meehan to Grace Chamberlain, June 28, 1913 (Grace German Chamberlain Papers, Louisiana State Museum, Historical Center, New Orleans, Lousiana).

[25] Some of the women who felt this way but remained in the Era Club were kicked out of the club in 1918. See Era Club Minutes, June 29, 1918 (New Orleans Public Library).

With apparent confidence in their personal political leverage, Era Club leaders attempted to work directly with Democratic politicians, including the New Orleans machine headed by Mayor Martin Behrman, and made use of club members whose husbands were in the state legislature. Two of their sponsors for suffrage legislation in the Louisiana General Assembly, Frank Powell in the House and George Wesley Smith in the Senate, were, in fact, the husbands of members of the Executive Board of the club. Working outside Democratic politics, however, was flatly refused, no matter the consequence to other alliances. For instance, although the Era Club Executive Board actively discussed the political advantages of endorsing John M. Parker as a reformist Democrat candidate for the governor's office in October of 1915, a representative of the WCTU who extended an invitation to club members at a regular meeting the next month to attend an informational session with the Prohibition Party candidate was turned out by Kate Gordon. Gordon informed the WCTU woman, with no apparent sense of her duplicity, that "partisan politics could not be injected into the Era Club."[26]

While the Era Club drew a strict line between Democratic politics and other partisan politics, they seemed unconcerned about conflict in attempts to court both machine and reformist factions within the Democratic Party. As the club undertook the project of purging city voting lists of names they suspected were fictitious creations of the New Orleans machine, they sent delegates to meet with Mayor Behrman, hoping to gain his endorsement of suffrage legislation.[27] They opposed a school bond issue backed by the mayor, and then seemed incredulous when they sensed that the city machine had helped defeat the referendum that would have given women the right to hold office in the state school system. Their initial confidence in the machine's support of the amendment apparently stemmed from a donation made by a wealthy New Orleans society woman to establish a tuberculosis hospital for the city; the donation was made on the condition that the woman might be allowed to sit on the hospital board, which could only occur if the constitutional amendment passed. When the Era Club leadership took the deal for granted and chose to work against the bond measure, Jean Gordon reported to Era Club members "how the amendment to Art. 210 was again defeated, word having gone forth from the bosses to 'give it to the women in the neck' for daring to interfere with the financial plans approved by the ring."[28]

In contrast to the Era Club program, the WSPL adopted a model based on NAWSA suggestions for a statewide campaign to increase suffrage sentiment

[26] Discussion of Parker candidacy on October 7, 1915; of Prohibition candidate November 13, 1915. Era Club Minutes (New Orleans Public Library).

[27] Voting list project discussed on October 9, 1915. "Calling on" city's candidates discussed January 10, 1916. Meeting of Mayor Behrman and donor Mrs. John Dibert to "ask his advice and influence" discussed October 19, 1916.

[28] Era Club minutes November 11, 1916 (New Orleans Public Library). See also HWS, vol. VI, 222–23 for Kate Gordon's telling of the incident.

among both legislators and voters, and rejected the placement of states' rights above women's voting rights. While WSPL leaders also engaged in legislative lobbying, the organization prioritized a concerted effort to develop suffrage organization outside of New Orleans, believing such organization might influence legislators that lobbyists could not. WSPL officer Mrs. Edgar Cahn wrote to legislative committee chair Grace Chamberlain about the plans for this approach shortly after the WSPL was formed:

Did you read George Fitch's article 'The Noiseless Suffragette' in *Colliers*, week of August 9th, telling about the passing of the bill in Illinois, etc. Fitch is in the legislature, from Peoria. He is friendly to suffrage, and his article is a good one, and contains a few lessons for us. I think the 'noiseless' way is the best, myself, – it is just what you have worked on, and I believe a carefully selected committee, like yours will be, can go down to the legislature and do more by working quietly and in a personal sort of way with the assembly members than in any other way. But I think the state work ought to be carried on vigorously so as to have a sentiment at home to back up the weak members.[29]

Despite the WSPL concern for building "suffrage sentiment" throughout the state, their approach was still marked by a concentration on personal and "society" connections. WSPL officers endeavored to build organizations of club women in places other than New Orleans, often working directly through the structure of the General Federation of Women's Clubs. They wrote personal correspondence to club women across the state, attempting to interest them in the suffrage cause and appeared at some local club meetings in places like Baton Rouge and Lake Charles. Yet, several other organizational decisions distinguished the WSPL approach. Notably, in an effort to extend their possible influence, WSPL membership outreach efforts included deliberate recruitment of women from the "country" parishes to serve in the organization's leadership positions. There was also a strict prioritization of suffrage work within the WSPL that was not characteristic of the Era Club. While serving as chair, Sake Meehan had decided even to keep the WSPL out of the efforts to amend the state constitution to allow women to serve on school and charitable boards.[30]

Ultimately, although some differences in organizational and lobbying strategy were evident, both the heavy reliance on personal connections to lobby legislators and a general "reformist" ideology were consistent across Louisiana's suffrage groups, as was a lack of cooperation with any organizations other

---

[29] Letter from Cahn to Chamberlain, August 19, 1913 (Grace German Chamberlain Papers, Louisiana State Museum, Historical Center, New Orleans, Louisiana). As the Louisiana suffragists made a practice of addressing each other formally by last name (unless close friends), and because they listed themselves by their husbands' names in their publications, several women can only be identified as such, including Cahn.

[30] WSPL activities discussed in the correspondence of Grace Chamberlain with Sake Meehan and Mrs. Edgar Cahn (Grace German Chamberlain Papers, Louisiana State Museum, Historical Center, New Orleans, Louisiana).

than women's clubs. By far the most consequential distinction between the feuding suffrage factions was their stance on the federal suffrage amendment issue. The Gordons were so committed to the idea of white supremacy and its link to states' rights that they also established the Southern States Woman Suffrage Conference (SSWSC), an organization specifically aimed at uniting Southern suffragists against the proposed national amendment in the name of states' rights and preservation of white supremacy, and formed the Louisiana Suffrage Association as the state's official SSWSC organ. Rejecting the states' rights strategy, WSPL leaders worked diligently to herd Louisiana women into their own campaign and challenged the Gordons' organization's status as the state affiliate of NAWSA. Louisiana would have two, feuding state organizations until ratification of Amendment XIX closed the woman suffrage question. Yet, the treatment of legislation for women's voting rights by state lawmakers during the years that society women battled for ownership of the suffrage cause did not suggest that the internal division was the greatest barrier to success. Rather than turning directly on the issue of the connection between woman suffrage and race politics, failure of woman suffrage in Louisiana seemed marked by resistance of an urban, Democratic machine to the causes of socialite reformers. But it was racial politics that drove the state to the one-party system that empowered the machine, and racial and class politics that kept suffragists from working directly with the machine's voters for support.

Facing One-Party Politics and an Effective Machine – Legislative Gains, Electoral Losses

While a push for women's voting rights had been slow to come to the South, it had finally arrived in Louisiana in the form of politicized clubs of society women. Having no alliances built with organizations that might wield electoral leverage – certainly due in part to a declination to forge such partnerships, but also to a great extent to a limited choice set in an electorally contracted state – Louisiana suffragists relied on a strategy of directly lobbying politicians for their support. Although organization for suffrage split over personal grievances and relative commitments to states' rights, white supremacy, and woman suffrage, there was, nevertheless, no inclination to challenge the system of Democratic rule. The result, rather than steadfast resistance, as suggested by an assumption that Southern Democrats were resolutely opposed to expansion of the franchise, was a set of legislative gains followed by electoral loss. Rather than finding their opposition in the plantation parishes, where white elites stood to lose the most if the argument that woman suffrage would open the electoral floodgates held true, the insurmountable hurdle lay in New Orleans. Repeatedly, New Orleans representatives in the General Assembly attempted to block legislation for woman suffrage. When finally allowed to pass the legislature on condition of a public referendum of approval before enactment, women's voting rights were thwarted by New Orleans voters – despite approval from nearly every other parish in the state.

Introduced for the first time in 1908, the resolution to amend the state constitution to allow women to hold office in the state's school systems produced the Era Club's first legislative victory for women's rights in 1912. The club had secured sponsorships for the measure from two New Orleans lawmakers – Martin Manion in the House of Representatives and William Byrnes in the Senate. Despite these endorsements, the measure faced opposition from other New Orleans legislators. In the House, the roll call vote showed sixty-eight in favor and thirty opposed; eleven of the opponents were from New Orleans. Manion, however, won reconsideration of the measure, and pulled twenty-one more legislators, including six from New Orleans, into the yes column, while losing only eight to the opposition. It seemed Manion had brokered success despite resistance. Following the vote in the House, Byrnes pulled the measure easily through the Senate, and the Era Club faced its first referendum campaign.[31]

There is, unfortunately, very little evidence of Era Club activity to promote the amendment at the polls. In the months before the measure passed the legislature, the club had conducted a petition campaign under the direction of Grace Chamberlain. That campaign had involved sending petition forms to various organizations across the state, asking to have the forms signed by the membership and returned. Era Club leaders had deemed the petition campaign a success, and perhaps saw little else to do to stir up public sentiment. Working with three women's organizations – the Newcomb College Alumnae, the State Nurses' Association and the Federation of Women's Clubs – the Era Club remained active in publicizing their position. There is no record, however, that the suffragists made any attempt to target voters in any more systematic way, nor gained any support from an organization that might have been able to leverage the electoral support of its members. Moreover, there is no evidence to suggest that any of the legislators who voted in favor of the constitutional amendment worked to secure its passage at the polls. The result on Election Day was that not a single parish returned a majority for the amendment.[32]

Despite an unwillingness to consider primary suffrage for women in 1912, and the sound defeat of the limited measure for women's office-holding at the polls, the House of Representatives would consider an amendment for full

---

[31] *Official Journal of the House of Representatives of the State of Louisiana, 1912* (Baton Rouge: New Advocate), 74–75, 232, 256, 392, 684–86, 835–36. Gilley, B. H. "Kate Gordon and Louisiana Woman Suffrage" in Nancy Cott, ed. *History of Women in the United States*, vol. XIX (Munich: KG Saur), 254–71. There is really very little systematic to the voting patterns, consistent with the idea that this was still "personal politics." For those legislators not from New Orleans, supporters' and opponents' home parishes were equally likely to be agrarian and black-majority, and displayed effectively equal levels of share-cropping.

[32] In fact, the summary of Louisiana suffrage activity written by Gordon states there were only two public campaigns, one in 1915 and one in 1918. HWS vol. VI, 222–24. Documents and letters regarding the petition drive in the Grace German Chamberlain Papers (Louisiana State Museum, Historical Center, New Orleans, Louisiana).

woman suffrage in their next three sessions, finally passing it in 1918. The new interest in a woman suffrage amendment to the state constitution was surely not the result of consideration by a new set of actors; because Louisiana legislators faced election every four years, 107 of the 117 members in the 1912 House returned for the 1914 session.[33] Instead, the new interest seemed tied to a rising reformist sentiment in state politics. Formed in 1910 with the intent to lessen the influence of the New Orleans machine in state politics, the Louisiana Good Government League had backed their own candidate, Luther Hill, for governor in 1912. When the League's candidate won the Democratic primary, Mayor Behrman's efforts to maintain control of the city and its legislative delegation heightened. Behrman, however, found it necessary to make symbolic concessions to the reformist movement, such as selecting leading businessmen for city positions, a strategy promoted by the League in the name of "government efficiency." Although Behrman managed to retain control of the city, the League's first success was the beginning of years of strong factional politics within the Louisiana Democratic Party that would turn on anti-machine "progressive" appeals for government reform and a New Orleans organization intent on retaining its power.[34]

Thus, a resolution for a constitutional amendment for woman suffrage found its way to the floor of a Louisiana House of Representatives that was growing increasingly sensitive to the push for reform, and increasingly aware of who stood to lose or gain if that push was effective. Although Martin Manion again agreed to introduce the Era Club's sponsored legislation, and even help guide it through readings, when the measure reached a vote, the New Orleans legislator abandoned it. The final roll call produced a vote of sixty in favor and forty-one opposed – Manion and twelve other New Orleans representatives among them.[35] Far short of the two-thirds majority vote required to pass a

[33] *Official Journal of the House of Representatives of the State of Louisiana*, 1912 and 1914 (Baton Rouge: New Advocate). The turnover of ten members was due only to deaths and resignations.

[34] Reynolds, *Machine Politics in New Orleans*, offers a thorough account of the rise and effect of reformism in state politics. His evidence comes not only from newspaper accounts and government documents, but also interviews with several key players in state politics during that time. As Reynolds documents, "progressive" was probably a proper label for some of the faction, whereas others quite clearly were not really interested in anti-machine reforms, but rather specifically in the displacement of the Behrman machine.

[35] Manion's sponsorship announced before the legislative session in the publication of the Era Club, *The New Citizen* (April 1914, 10). Legislative history from *Official Journal of the House of Representatives of the State of Louisiana*, 1914, 617–18, 727–30. It is possible that Manion voted "no" strategically, intending to have the vote reconsidered if it failed. Although he motioned for reconsideration, however, he did not follow through. In addition, Manion was not the only New Orleans delegate who voted against the woman suffrage measure despite having voted in favor of the amendment to Article 210 in 1912. Representatives Friedrichs, Gahagan, Generally, Kantz, Kronenberger, and Rando did the same.

constitutional amendment, full woman suffrage had met its first defeat on the floor of the Louisiana House.

After the final roll call, several legislators found it necessary to read explanations of their vote into the record. Although most referenced their beliefs about what the will of the people was on the issue, Robert Roberts, an attorney from Webster parish in northern Louisiana, opened his remarks with a statement that made clear his support was for white women's voting rights only, and then moved on to the partisan implications of the question:

Louisiana's best product is its white womanhood. Nobody will deny that statement. Some of them want the ballot. Some of them do not. They all have the right to the ballot... woman's suffrage is going to come. It is going to come in Louisiana and in every State of the Union.... If it does not come through the Democratic party, as other reforms have come, it will come through the Progressive party.[36]

No longer simply about the personal politics that suffragists had been cultivating, the idea of white woman suffrage was beginning to take on partisan meaning in state politics. Through a connection to the ideas of the reform movement that was starting to swell, full voting rights for (white) women had earned consideration by the Louisiana House. But in those same partisan terms, opposition to woman suffrage was also consolidating. In 1914, this meant New Orleans representatives were resistant to voting for the suffrage amendment – even some who had been personally persuaded to go along with the office-holding amendment in 1912 – whereas a number of supporters couched their votes in the progressive terms of the people's right to decide through referendum. Other sources of factionalism in Louisiana politics – namely racial composition and farming interests in legislators' home parishes – had not yet become clearly enmeshed in the question of women's voting rights. This can be seen in a simple analysis of the voting patterns of representatives from outside New Orleans on the 1914 issue, using the representatives' district characteristics to predict their supportiveness of the issue. As shown in Table 5.2, neither the percentage of the district's population that was black nor the concentration of (small) farming interests, as measured by the per capita number of farms, was a statistically significant predictor of the votes of representatives from outside New Orleans. When the progressive faction bolted the Democratic Party in the next election, however, clearer divides on the suffrage issue would be evident.

Although it came a full election cycle later than it had in so many other states, the Progressive Party movement had consequences for electoral politics in Louisiana. Louisiana reformer and Good Government League vice president John M. Parker had been nominated as Theodore Roosevelt's Vice President on the Progressive ticket in 1916. When Roosevelt declined the candidacy,

---

[36] *Official Journal of the House of Representatives of the State of Louisiana*, 1914, 729–30.

TABLE 5.2. *Predicting Support for the Woman Suffrage Amendment among Representatives not from New Orleans, Louisiana House of Representatives 1914 and 1916*

	1914	1916
Member of Progressive Party	–	1.77*
		(.90)
Per Capita Farms	6.84	12.22**
	(4.60)	(5.10)
Percent Black	−1.13	2.56
	(1.49)	(1.58)
Constant	0.54	−1.84**
	(.71)	(.83)
N	82	86
Log likelihood	−51.46	−56.22

Note: Entries are coefficients from logistic regressions, standard errors in parentheses. $*$ $p < .10$, $**p < .05$, two-tailed t-test.
Sources: United States Census, 1910, 1920; *Official Journal of the House of Representatives of the State of Louisiana*, 1914 and 1916.

Parker turned his attention to state office, and ran on the Progressive ticket in Louisiana's first seriously contested general election for governor since the 1898 constitution had been adopted. Parker polled 48,085 votes in the 1916 election, just 2,496 votes less than had elected Luther Hill in the last election. The competition, however, had brought more voters into the general election, and Parker's total accounted for just more than 37 percent of the turnout. Although Parker did not take the governor's office, the consequences of his campaign spilled over into the legislature: sixteen Progressives joined the previously all-Democratic body – twelve in the House and four in the Senate. Campaigning in explicit opposition to the organization that ran New Orleans, Parker had led a charge that heightened factionalism within the Democratic Party, while also demonstrating the potential for electoral consequences for the party if the reformist demands could not be settled internally. With Progressives and reformist Democrats staking out their position in favor of woman suffrage, it would lose out to machine and "Regular" Democrat opposition in the 1916 session. But the move toward Democratic reconciliation would bring a compromise in favor of the suffrage amendment in the 1918 session, as the New Orleans machine officially and publicly entreated its delegation to allow the measure to pass and be sent along to the voters.[37]

Division on the question of woman suffrage in the 1916 House clearly pitted "reformist" country parish legislators against "Regular" Democrats and the New Orleans machine. On the final roll call of fifty-nine in favor and

[37] Reynolds, *Machine Politics in New Orleans*, 175–93.

fifty opposed, only four of the city's twenty-four representatives voted for the amendment, and just two members elected on the Progressive label voted against it. Using logistic regression to predict support for the suffrage amendment among members from outside of New Orleans (Table 5.2) shows that Progressive and country-parish representatives were far more likely to vote in favor of the measure than their less-rural counterparts. Not only did the Progressive label predict a representative would support the measure, but so, too, did the percent of his district that was engaged in farming. Indeed, the results indicate that support for woman suffrage came from those legislators who should have opposed the measure if lawmakers believed granting white women voting rights would open the electoral floodgates: those from agrarian parishes, where black populations were often larger. Rather than a threat to white supremacy, it seems Louisiana politicians saw in woman suffrage a threat to the New Orleans-based faction that many felt had come to dominate state politics. Louisiana suffragists' antagonism of the Behrman machine in New Orleans through repeated "reformist" initiatives of their own, including their electoral showings on previous tax and bond issues, may have made out-state politicians hopeful that women voters might temper the Behrman organization's influence. Several of the Progressive legislators, in fact, made a connection between woman suffrage and anti-machine sentiment in the explanations they offered on the floor for their votes in favor of the amendment. L. A. Moresi, a plantation owner, himself, offered the most direct comment on the issue, stating, in part:

Our great Democratic president has said that the matter of equal suffrage is not one for national consideration, but one to be decided by each State. It can only be decided by the entire electorate of this State, and even though I was personally opposed to equal suffrage, I feel that I should not stand in the way of the electorate passing on this measure.... My additional reason for voting in the affirmative is because this session of the General Assembly, instead of curtailing expenses, has been one of extravagance.... Our people are suffering from political evils and are growing restive at the dearth of real beneficial legislation.... We seem no longer to represent the tax payers; instead the ominous shadows of political intrigue are athwart our legislative halls and political tyranny, oppression, and greed supplants reason and self-abnegation.[38]

Although Louisiana legislators did not see the opening of electoral floodgates to the black population in the adoption of woman suffrage, at least as state law, state politicians certainly understood that white supremacy and Democratic dominance were built on one another. Compromise to maintain the

---

[38] *Official Journal of the House of Representatives of the State of Louisiana*, 1916, 293–96. Moresi was a representative of Iberia parish, which was both highly agrarian and more than 40% black. His comments were corrected for typographical errors on the part of the recording clerk or publisher. Other floor statements referenced the need for the people to decide the issue and belief in the referendum as a Democratic [party] process. Two statements against the measure claimed that not enough women expressed an interest in the right to vote.

one-party system was in the interest of both agrarian and urban elites, and by the 1918 session of the General Assembly, most of the declared Progressives had been brought back into the Democratic fold.[39] The issue of woman suffrage benefited from its own compromise in 1918, when Mayor Behrman issued a public instruction to the New Orleans delegates in the state legislature to let the constitutional amendment pass. Behrman, however, stopped far short of actually endorsing women's voting rights. In the publication of his instructions, Behrman noted his own "personal" reservations about the idea of woman suffrage. By the time of the requisite public referendum on the amendment, however, Behrman's personal reservations had been converted into an instruction to city ward leaders to deliver votes against women's voting rights. Just days before the issue went to the voters, the machine's united position against the amendment was reported to the newspapers. The coverage by the New Orleans *Times-Picayune* – which was fairly sympathetic to woman suffrage on its editorial pages – laid out the decision and its expected implications in simple terms:

> . . . the seventeen ward leaders of New Orleans, in caucus Wednesday, decided to oppose the woman suffrage amendment to the State Constitution at the election next Tuesday. All the other amendments will receive the organization's support. . . . Although there have been rumors that the leaders might divide on the suffrage question, Wednesday's action is reported to have been binding on all, an agreement having been reached to stand as a unit . . . it will be a blow to the hopes of the suffrage advocates who entertained hopes of inducing the organization to vote with them. . . . The endorsement or approval of a constitutional amendment by the organization usually carries with it a majority of from 15,000 to 18,000, and in most instances in the past has decided the issue. A heavy vote in the state, equally one-sided, is the only offset.[40]

Votes in the 1918 House were certainly consistent with an instruction from the Behrman machine. Fifteen of the city's representatives voted in favor of the amendment, twelve of whom had voted against it in 1916. There were also developments in the support offered by legislators from outside of New Orleans. Although the measure retained most of its supporters from 1916, with "Progressivism" quieted, so, too, was the distinctive pattern of support from the formerly Progressive representatives: former Progressives split half in favor and half opposed in the 1918 vote. More pronounced in the 1918 vote was the pattern of support from legislators who hailed from more predominantly black districts. Although many legislators from districts with large black populations had signed on in support in the 1916 session, the division along the lines of

---

[39] Most legislators claiming the Progressive label in 1916 had dropped it by the 1918 session, and several actually resigned, allowing Democrats to take their places.

[40] "Organization Will Oppose Suffrage" *The Times-Picayune*, October 31, 1918. The article also referenced the instruction by Behrman to the New Orleans delegates in the legislature to pass the measure, and his announcement of his personal disapproval of woman suffrage. For supportive editorial treatment by the *Times-Picayune*, see especially October 30 and November 3, 1918.

TABLE 5.3. *Predicting Support for Woman Suffrage Amendment among Representatives not from New Orleans, Louisiana House of Representatives 1918*

	Logistic Regression Coefficient (standard error)	
Former Progressive Party Member	−.77	−
	(.84)	
Per Capita Farms	9.33	1.60
	(7.74)	(9.53)
Percent Black	5.33**	8.33**
	(2.45)	(3.85)
Vote in 1916 session	−	3.81**
		(1.27)
Constant	−1.42	−3.12**
	(1.27)	(1.48)
N	72	67
Log likelihood	−36.85	−31.49

* p < .10, **p < .05, two-tailed t-test

Sources: U.S. Census, 1910, 1920; *Official Journal of the House of Representatives of the State of Louisiana*, 1918.

racial composition of legislators' home districts in 1918 was stark. Setting aside the legislators' 1916 votes, and using the same measures of representatives' Progressive identification and the prevalence of farming and black residents in their districts to predict their 1918 votes, the logistic regression results in Table 5.3 show the only systematic predictor of support for the woman suffrage amendment in 1918 was a larger black population in the home district. Dropping the Progressive term – as legislators' themselves had – but adding a control for their vote in the 1916 session demonstrates that whereas most simply repeated their votes in 1918, larger black populations pushed still more legislators to support the amendment. In fact, only one representative from a district where blacks constituted more than half the population voted against the suffrage amendment in 1918; eight had done so in 1916.[41] No longer an issue of country-parish versus machine factional politics, positions on woman suffrage were now a matter of legislators from the black-belt versus those who were not.[42]

[41] *Official Journal of the House of Representatives of the State of Louisiana*, 1918, 298–99. Percent parish population black and per capita farms from the 1920 U.S. Census reports.

[42] A number of agrarian parishes were not previously home to large plantations, thus not heavily populated by former slaves. Pearson's correlation between percent of the parish population that was black and the per capita number of farms (excluding New Orleans) is .32 (p = .002).

Race, it seems, had finally become a central deciding factor on the question of woman suffrage for Louisiana legislators. Yet, rather than forming opposition to the idea of opening the electoral system, legislators from districts where blacks could be the strongest electoral force if enfranchised were those most likely to support voting rights for women. After years of Era Club appeals for woman suffrage as a state measure, and to provide for the enfranchisement of white women only, it appears that Louisiana legislators finally had reason to follow that course. The reason, however, was provided by events outside the state. By the time the Louisiana General Assembly met in 1918, the Eighteenth Amendment to the U.S. Constitution, which would create the federal prohibition on alcohol, was making the rounds of the states and headed for ratification. Once Prohibition was in place, many sensed, the federal woman suffrage amendment would also gain ground in Congress. Even Democratic President Woodrow Wilson's public position on the issue of woman suffrage had converted from a states' rights stance to support of a federal amendment – which he stated publicly in January of 1918.[43] Debate among Louisiana politicians thus finally came to woman suffrage as a racial question only once the threat of renewed federal intervention in state electoral laws actually looked imminent. For the first time, the governor had engaged the woman suffrage question in his inaugural address to the legislature, and came down in support on the grounds of preserving the racial order so carefully cultivated by state electoral laws:

The women of the State should be given equal suffrage with the men, and a [state] Constitutional amendment should be submitted to that effect.... Equal suffrage by amendment to the Constitution of the United States will not find favor in Louisiana and the rest of the South for reasons that are obvious. Let all the states make national control of suffrage unnecessary and undebatable [sic] by granting equal suffrage through the State Constitutions, and thus retain control of the whole question of suffrage ourselves, and, with it, our sovereignty.[44]

Although the Senate followed the House in supporting the state constitutional amendment, displaying similar patterns of support from New Orleans and black-belt parish lawmakers, Louisiana would not adopt a woman suffrage

---

[43] The President justified his position change by stating he supported the amendment as "a war measure." In reading correspondence between Wilson and NAWSA leaders, Eleanor Flexner saw more of a personal conversion, with the war rhetoric as public packaging. Flexner, Eleanor and Ellen Fitzpatrick, *Century of Struggle: The Woman's Rights Movement in the United States* (Cambridge, MA: Belknap Press, 1996), 272, 377.

[44] *Official Journal of the Senate of the State of Louisiana*, 1918 (Baton Rouge: Ramires-Jones Printing Co.), 31–32. Several legislators also felt it necessary to qualify their support of woman suffrage as submitted only under the threat of a national amendment. Representative T. Sambola Jones of Baton Rouge stated simply: "I vote yea for STATE female suffrage, and stop right there. I wish it strictly limited to state lines." *Official Journal of the House of Representatives of the State of Louisiana*, 1918, 299.

amendment before Congress passed the national measure.[45] True to their pledge before the election, the New Orleans organization returned a majority vote against the amendment at the polls. The final count on the suffrage amendment in the city was 5,411 in favor and 14,492 opposed. Despite a majority in favor returned from forty-eight of the sixty-three other parishes, even the next most populous Caddo (Shreveport) and East Baton Rouge, the amendment lost: the state totaled 23,077 against and 19,573 for woman suffrage. Picking up support from the black belt had been enough to carry woman suffrage in the legislature, but the black-belt parishes combined offered far fewer possible popular votes than the city of New Orleans.[46] And inside New Orleans, Louisiana suffragist organizations were no match for Behrman's political machine. The machine promised patronage, doled out strategic personal favors, looked the other way on vice violations; suffragists sent letters and petition blanks, made speeches, and took out newspaper advertisements.[47] Perhaps more important was the fact that the suffragists had no organizational alliances to help turnout the vote on their side of the issue in New Orleans, while they faced a political machine designed expressly for delivering votes on Election Day.

After the election, suffragists accused Behrman of "turning the vote of his henchmen against the suffrage bill" and suggested he did so because he feared for his own electoral fate at the hands of women voters.[48] And it appears their allegations were well-founded, even if the fault implied was not completely accurate. Machine politicians may have stood in the way, but suffragists had done nothing that gave them reason not to do so. They had formed no alliance with any of the machine's base of working class and immigrant voters; unlike women in other states, Louisiana suffragists had not even attempted to reach

---

[45] With only 39 members, statistical analysis of the Senate is not as informative as for the 118-member House. The nine New Orleans Senators showed more resistance to the Behrman instruction and split five in favor and four opposed. Among the Senators from outside New Orleans, those who voted no average 38.8% black population in the home district, whereas supporters averaged 46.3%. Although the difference is in the same direction as in the House, with just thirty cases that difference does not reach conventional levels of statistical significance ($p = .36$).

[46] Of the thirty-four parishes with populations greater than forty percent black, twenty-nine returned majorities in favor of woman suffrage. Even if every vote cast in those parishes had been in favor of the amendment, however, the total yes vote would have grown by only 4,080.

[47] On the campaign work carried out: Era Club minutes October 5, 1918 shows the club engaged only in a letter and petition drive. Various articles from the *Times-Picayune* document the same for the WSPL as well. "Working to Promote Woman's Suffrage" October 4, 1918; "Inaugurate Active Suffrage Campaign" October 29, 1918; "Suffrage Workers Look to City Vote" October 30, 1918; "Women are Sure of Big Victory for Suffrage" November 4, 1918. A half-page advertisement was run by a group of women who did not identify with either state organization on November 3, 1918.

[48] Quotation from Era Club minutes, November 17, 1918 (New Orleans Public Library); Behrman electoral incentive accusation in letter to the editor by Jean Gordon, New Orleans *Times-Picayune*, November 7, 1918.

beyond class lines (and certainly not beyond racial lines) to see common ground with other groups interested in the issues the social clubs addressed, such as protection of child laborers, vice regulation, and improved schools. Undoubtedly Louisiana suffragists had fewer opportunities to do so, given the state's restrained political environment, but the few possibilities that existed to reach out to urban voters through the venues of women's settlement house and factory inspection work were largely passed over.[49] Moreover, the machine faction of the Democratic Party was hardly solely responsible for the loss; the entire Democratic Party had been complicit in creating a system where voter turnout was both low and manipulable. Woman suffrage had faced a general, midterm election in a state where Democratic dominance brought out less than a quarter of the voting-age male population in presidential elections. Many of the groups that would help woman suffrage pass in other states, such as Farmers' Alliance and Grange organizations, had been effectively closed out of Louisiana politics. Racial politics had narrowed the field of coalitional possibilities available to suffragists, even if they had been able to see past their own racial and class prejudices.

Beyond Black and White – Race, Coalitions, and Institutions in the West

Issues of white and black were not the only racial politics that had consequences for woman suffrage. Whiteness was defined in reference to a number of other groups, including Asian, American Indian, and "Spanish" – all most frequently encountered in the West. In thinking about "how the West was won" for woman suffrage, then, it is important to consider the role of racial politics. Just as in the South, the politics of race defined both state institutions and state electorates in ways that had consequences for women seeking voting rights. With early federal control of American Indian populations, including their removal to reservations and denial of citizenship status until the passage of the Indian Citizenship Act in 1924, questions of their voting rights were settled by most Western states through the definition of electors as U.S. citizens, and often

---

49 A majority vote in one New Orleans precinct was attributed to such a connection. The New Orleans *Times-Picayune* reported that "[t]he First Precinct of the Tenth Ward gave 75 for and 10 against. This is on the river front in the factory district, and a ward worker from that section advanced the opinion that this showing was due to the influence of Mrs. Martha D. Gould, factory inspector, who has a strong personal following there, and has done a great deal of work among the factory employees of that district." ("Suffrage Loses City by Majority of About 9000" November 6, 1918.) There is no evidence in Louisiana suffrage leaders' correspondence or the Era Club records, however, that working to make these sorts of connections was a regular activity, even though some suffragists, including Jean Gordon of the Era Club, were well-involved in factory inspection and the settlement house activities in New Orleans. See Lindig, *The Path from the Parlor*.

as taxpayers, as well.[50] Asian immigrants could also be excluded by citizenship requirements, and again federal policy helped define that exclusion through legislation that defined citizenship as impossible for many of this group, starting with the Chinese Exclusion Act in 1882.[51] "Spanish" Americans, however, were given citizenship through the treaty that brought their territories into the United States: the treaty of Guadalupe Hidalgo, which annexed the lands that would become the states of Arizona, California, New Mexico, Texas, and parts of Colorado, Nevada, and Utah.[52]

With their citizenship guaranteed through the actions of the federal government, the Spanish American population presented an important racial question to Anglo American settlers in the West. As with black Americans in the South, federal regulation of Spanish American citizenship rights meant that whites[53] were obligated either to accept equal political status or to work to create legal definitions of electors that circumvented such equality. Yet there was a difference between the racial politics of the West and South: Spanish Americans had far more agency to protect their political rights than blacks. The choices negotiated by white Westerners and Spanish Americans in this regard had implications for women seeking voting rights. Who might be included or excluded from state politics shaped both the landscape of group politics in the state – and thereby the coalitional possibilities for woman suffragists – and the formal institutional requirements for changing states' voting rights qualifications.

To understand these dynamics, New Mexico is a particularly useful case. By the time of the final push for statehood in 1910, Spanish descendent residents accounted for a significant proportion of the population in New Mexico. Estimates from the U.S. Census suggest more than forty percent of New Mexico's citizens were Spanish American.[54] The large Spanish-American population had

[50] Arizona, Idaho, Nevada, New Mexico, Utah, and Washington all had both citizenship and tax-paying requirements during early statehood. Idaho, New Mexico, and Washington specifically excluded "Indians not taxed."

[51] On the politics of Asian immigrant exclusion and the Chinese Exclusion Act in particular, see Andrew Gyory, *Closing the Gate: Race, Politics, and the Chinese Exclusion Act* (Chapel Hill: The University of North Carolina Press, 1998).

[52] The treaty actually gave former Mexicans living on these lands the right to elect either to remain Mexican citizens or to choose U.S. citizenship. If they did not express a desire to remain Mexican citizens within one year, they would be assumed to have elected U.S. citizenship. See Treaty of Guadalupe Hidalgo, February 2, 1848, Art. VIII and IX.

[53] Although the term "white" as we understand it today would actually include many who fall here into the category of "Spanish American," it seems consistent with late-nineteenth- and early-twentieth-century terminology to call the Anglo Americans in the region "white." In their own writings, Anglo and white were often interchangeable for those who lived in the region.

[54] Based on the 1900 Census, individual-level sample, identification of Spanish surnames, and excluding American Indian populations the estimate for New Mexico is 43%. Data and documentation available from: Steven Ruggles, Matthew Sobek, Trent Alexander, Catherine

a significant influence both on the writing of the state constitution and on the politics of the early state. Yet, early suffrage activism in the state was carried out through entirely Anglo women's organizations. This racial exclusivity would have discernible consequences for New Mexican women, as would a difficult constitutional amendment process that also resulted from racial politics. Granted only school suffrage the first state constitution, New Mexican women faced a nearly impossible amendment process, which required a three-fourths vote in both houses of the legislature and then a three-fourths vote of public approval in the state, including a two-thirds majority in each county. Although the amendment process was a key political victory for Spanish American politicians, ensuring the electoral rights of the racial minority group could not be amended out of the state constitution, it was a disastrous obstacle for woman suffrage. Provisions for women's voting rights in New Mexico would never surmount even the legislative hurdle.

New Mexico, Its Constitution, and the Anglo-Spanish Conflict

Race as an impeding factor to woman suffrage in New Mexico could be found among the suffragists, themselves. Organization for woman suffrage in the territory (and the early state), such as it was, was carried out exclusively by and targeted to Anglo women. The women organized themselves in fits and starts, without the help of any organizers from NAWSA, beginning in the early 1890s.[55] At the time of the 1910 state Constitutional Convention, there was no official woman suffrage organization in New Mexico. The only known contacts made to the convention by women in support of woman suffrage were from women's clubs; the state Federation of Women's Clubs sent a petition for school suffrage, and the Woman's Club of Albuquerque sent a letter indicating that their membership wished the delegates to endorse school suffrage.[56] In a 1917 report to NAWSA, New Mexico suffragists wrote, "[o]ur suffrage leagues are closely interwoven with the state Federation of Women's Clubs... our membership consists almost entirely of home makers, who have become suffragists

A. Fitch, Ronald Goeken, Patricia Kelly Hall, Miriam King, and Chad Ronnander, *Integrated Public Use Microdata Series: Version 3.0* [Machine-readable database]. Minneapolis, MN: Minnesota Population Center [producer and distributor], 2004.

[55] The only documentation that appears to exist of these organizational efforts is a letter from Mrs. M. J. Borden to Mrs. Kellum, dated March 27, 1917. Borden responds to a request by Kellum to provide an early history of the movement in New Mexico by stating that all of her documentation has been lost in her move from New Mexico to California, but that by her memory they first held a meeting in 1893 and formed a "temporary suffrage organization." To her memory, the group met twice and got a grand total of about six people to speak for suffrage (New Mexico State Records Center and Archives (NMSRCA), Santa Fe, Miscellaneous Records, Political Issues, #40B, Women's Suffrage in New Mexico, 1917–1919. Correspondence).

[56] Jensen, Joan M., "Disfranchisement is a Disgrace: Women and Politics in New Mexico, 1900–1940." *New Mexico Historical Review* 56 (1981): 5–35. The letter can be found in the Territorial Archives of New Mexico, Constitutional Convention Collection (NMSRCA).

through suffrage debates in the Women's Clubs."[57] Working for suffrage through the base of the women's club movement was an approach common in many states, as it reduced the start-up costs of organization. In New Mexico, however, it was also a de facto decision to exclude Spanish American women from the effort, as the state's women's clubs were Anglo domains.[58] There were undoubtedly political costs to this decision. The potential influence of Spanish American women lobbying their own thirty-five delegates was lost, as was the opportunity to connect to any organizations that could wield the influence of Spanish American voters. Moreover, the racially segregated appeal for woman suffrage could have incited the Spanish population's already growing uneasiness about their representation in New Mexico's government to be projected onto the debate about women's voting rights.

Failure to appeal to Spanish American politicians had consequences in the 1910 Constitutional Convention beyond the exclusion of full voting rights for women. The convention granted New Mexico's women only a tenuous right to vote in school elections; women otherwise qualified were permitted to vote for school officers only if the elections were held separately from all other elections and under the condition that male voters in the school district did not submit a petition, signed by the majority, to "suspend" this right in their district. This small victory for woman suffrage was offset, however, by an unprecedented institutional obstacle to the extension of women's electoral rights beyond the schoolhouse: the constitution required any amendment to its electoral qualifications clauses to first receive a three-fourths majority vote in both houses of the state legislature, and then the approval of three-fourths of the state's voters, including two-thirds of each county's voters. By many accounts, both the decision regarding the limited nature of women's voting rights and the difficulty of amending the state's voter qualifications turned on the positions of the Spanish American delegates to the convention. Although a minority in the convention – accounting for just 35 of the 100 delegates – Spanish Americans represented nearly half of the seventy-one member Republican Party caucus in the convention.[59] Constituting such a large bloc of the majority party gave the Spanish American delegates significant leverage on the product of the convention, resulting in the unique and effectively unamendable protection of the voting rights of a racial minority population – and a unique institutional challenge for women seeking new voting rights from the state.

---

[57] "Outline of Progress of the Women in New Mexico from October 1909 to November 1917" (NMSRCA, Miscellaneous Records, Political Issues, #40C, Women's Suffrage in New Mexico, 1917–1919, Resolutions, Outlines, Dispatches, Bills).

[58] Jensen, "Disfranchisement is a Disgrace," 7–8.

[59] Only one Spanish American delegate identified as a Democrat. Summary information about the delegates and the rules of the convention from Dorothy I. Cline, *New Mexico's 1910 Constitution: A 19th Century Product* (Santa Fe: The Lightning Tree, 1982).

Spanish American delegates' interest in preventing discrimination against Spanish American men in voting qualifications was a straightforward protection of their constituencies. Accounts that placed the decision to limit women's voting rights to school elections on the part of the Spanish American delegates, offered by several of the white delegates in their summaries of the 1910 convention, painted resistance to woman suffrage as a response to constituency interests as well. Edward Tittmann, a Democratic delegate from Sierra County, presented one such claim in an article for the *New Mexico Historical Review*:

One provision which caused much debate and considerable compromise was the one that gave women the right to vote in school elections. The Spanish speaking delegates, faithfully representing the then prevailing ideas of their people, were opposed to the theory that it was a good thing to let women vote. If you will read the first Section of Article VII on Elective Franchise, and use your imagination, you will see the kind of compromise that had to be made by the opposing parties in order to get the idea of votes for women in school elections into the Constitution.[60]

Tittmann's claim was that Spanish Americans in the New Mexico territory were steadfastly opposed, for largely cultural reasons, to the extension of any voting rights to women, and that the limited and tenuous nature of woman suffrage in the state constitution was the result. Substantiating that claim is difficult. Because of the votes of the Republican majority in the convention, verbatim minutes of the proceedings were not provided, and a rule requiring thirty members to call for a roll call vote was instituted. Thus, neither floor discussion nor roll call votes on the suffrage provisions were recorded. According to newspaper accounts, the decision to grant women the right to vote at school elections was voted on at least twice by a rising or voice vote, with a final vote total of fifty-one in favor and thirty-three opposed. From these accounts, it is possible to establish the positions of fifteen of the delegates: ten Republicans and five Democrats – three of the Republicans have Spanish surnames. The positions of these members on school suffrage are displayed in Table 5.4. With at least one delegate from each party, and at least one Anglo and one Spanish American on both sides of the issue, it is clear that support for school suffrage for women crossed both partisan and racial lines. Although there are too few Spanish-American delegates in this list to make any definitive claims about a racial divide on the issue, given the total of fifty-one in favor, at least two Spanish-American delegates other than Luna must have lined up in support of suffrage extension. Thus, there is evidence that Spanish American delegates

---

[60] Tittmann, Edward D. "New Mexico Constitutional Convention: Recollections" *New Mexico Historical Review* 28 (1952): 176–86. Quote from p. 182. Heflin, Reuben W. "New Mexico Constitutional Convention" *New Mexico Historical Review* 21 (1946): 60–68. Heflin was also a Democratic delegate.

TABLE 5.4. *Position of Delegates on School Suffrage,*
New Mexico Constitutional Convention, 1910

Name	Political Party	Position on School Suffrage
Bursom	Republican	Yes
Canning	Republican	Yes
Childers	Democrat	Yes
Dougherty	Democrat	Yes
Fall	Republican	Yes
Field	Republican	Yes
Heflin	Democrat	Yes
Lawson	Democrat	Yes
Lindsey	Republican	Yes
Luna	*Republican*	*Yes*
Spiess	Republican	Yes
Stover	Republican	Yes
Miera	*Republican*	*No*
Saxon	Democrat	No
Sena	*Republican*	*No*

Spanish surnames in bold italics.

could be persuaded to support women's voting rights, but their relative absence from the press accounts leaves their level of support in question.[61]

Votes on the issue of woman suffrage before and after the Constitutional Convention evince a similar pattern of Spanish American and white representatives' support. In the Territorial Assemblies of 1874 and 1895, roll call votes on the motion to indefinitely postpone – that is, effectively kill – a bill that would have granted women full suffrage rights were recorded. Evident in these votes is a pattern similar to that exhibited in the fifteen available delegate positions on school suffrage at the Constitutional Convention. Opposition to woman suffrage was common among Spanish American politicians, with nearly ninety percent of the Spanish American legislators voting to kill the woman suffrage bills in 1874 and 1895. Yet, it is also evident both that the issue did not divide delegates along strict racial lines, and that Anglo politicians were not over-whelmingly supportive of the issue. Indeed, fully half of the Anglo legislators voted to kill the woman suffrage bill in 1895. Division on the question after

[61] Luna is Solomon Luna, of Valencia County, widely regarded as the preeminent Spanish American delegate at the convention and a leader in the New Mexico Republican Party. Sources for positions on woman suffrage: "Women at School Elections," *Santa Fe New Mexican*, November 9, 1910 and Heflin, Reuben W. 1946. "New Mexico Constitutional Convention," *New Mexico Historical Review* 21: 60–68. Dougherty clearly stated his support for woman suffrage was limited to school suffrage only.

the Constitutional Convention exhibited a similar pattern. Although votes on suffrage legislation did not fall along strict racial lines, the opposition was consistently predominantly Spanish American. A breakdown of support in the House and Senate on a woman suffrage measures considered in 1917 and 1919 shows that even in the last session before the national suffrage amendment was adopted, Spanish American legislators provided the majority of the opposition to women's voting rights.

Yet there are reasons to believe that Spanish American politicians' resistance to woman suffrage measures was political, not cultural, as some white politicians had claimed. Even before New Mexican women had full voting rights, Spanish American women were moving into politics – with the aid of Spanish American men. Adelina Otero-Warren, niece of Republican leader Solomon Luna, was appointed superintendent of Santa Fe schools by Democratic Governor Ezequiel Cabeza de Baca in 1917; she was re-elected to the same office on the Republican ticket in 1918. After full woman suffrage was granted by the national amendment, Spanish American women quickly moved into government positions beyond the school system. Soledad Chávez Chacón won the office of secretary of state on the Democratic ticket in 1922, and in 1924 was "acting governor" for more than a month while the governor was out of the state. Otero-Warren was also a candidate for high elective office in 1922, when the state Republican Party chose her as their candidate for the U.S. House of Representatives.[62] Spanish American women were not absent from politics – they were, however, absent from the organizations pushing for a woman suffrage amendment to the state constitution. Several women leaders of the Spanish American community, including Otero-Warren, were eventually tapped for the suffrage cause, but only by the Congressional Union (CU), the national organization working specifically for an amendment to the U.S. Constitution. Spanish American women were not part of the delegations of suffragists that met with state legislators during session. Just how the Anglo exclusivity to suffrage organizing was interpreted by lawmakers, of course, is difficult to ascertain. But with just a few Spanish American women in the CU, and none in the NAWSA-affiliated suffrage societies that grew out of the General Federation of Women's Clubs, Spanish American politicians might have feared that women's voting might be almost exclusively Anglo, and thus a possible threat to their continued representation in state politics.[63]

---

[62] Salas, Elizabeth "Soledad Chávez Chacón, Adelina Otero-Warren, and Concha Ortiz y Pino Three Hispana Politicians in New Mexico Politics, 1920–1940" in Melanie Gustafson, Kristie Miller, and Elisabeth I. Perry, eds. *We Have Come to Stay: American Women and Political Parties 1880–1960* (Albuquerque: University of New Mexico Press, 1999), 161–74.

[63] Joan Jensen, "Disfranchisement is a Disgrace," 14–15, established biographies of 107 women active in the New Mexican suffrage campaigns. Only seven were Spanish American; six of whom were involved through the CU and one whose affiliation was unclear. Newspaper reports observed the tension between the CU strategy for woman suffrage through a national amendment and the NAWSA-sponsored strategy for a state amendment. "Suffragists Organizing"

While the racial politics of suffrage activism in New Mexico may have provided reasons for Spanish American politicians to worry about the electoral consequences of women's voting rights, the racial politics of the constitutional definition of New Mexico's suffrage qualifications presented suffragists with their greatest challenge: the constitutional clause that made amendment of electoral qualifications provisions nearly impossible. Inclusion of this clause was, according to all available accounts, a Republican initiative meant to preserve the rights of Spanish American men, who formed a significant portion of both their electoral base and their convention delegation.[64] One of the clauses protected by the requirement for practically unattainable majorities in both the legislature and the public provided that:

The right of any citizen of the State to vote, hold office, or sit upon juries, shall never be restricted, abridged or impaired on account of religion, race, language or color, or inability to speak, read or write the English or Spanish languages.[65]

The other clause covered by the difficult amendment procedure set out the general qualifications of voters – the first of which was being a male citizen – and established the exception that allowed women to vote at school elections.[66]

Republican delegates to the convention claimed no connection between the decisions to allow for limited women's voting rights and to create the amendment difficulty for the suffrage clauses, including W. E. Lindsey, who became governor of the early state.[67] Regardless of intent, however, the result of the difficult amendment procedures was the effective freezing of New Mexican women's voting rights at school suffrage only status. Although a suffrage bill was introduced at every legislative session following statehood, none ever surmounted even the legislative hurdle of a three-fourths vote in each house, despite state party platforms that endorsed woman suffrage and several governors' willingness to make strong public endorsements of woman suffrage. Moreover, the difficulty of the amendment process deterred support for attempts to achieve woman suffrage through state politics even from suffrage

---

The Christian Science Monitor, March 6, 1917 observed "[e]qual suffrage advocates in New Mexico continue to be divided as to submission of an amendment by the present legislature, one organization favoring submission and the other contending that the cause of suffrage would be best served by making the fight for support of the national amendment." Reports of meetings between suffragists and Republican Party leaders and suffragists indicate all present were white. See "It was a Sorry Day When the Suffrage Bill Lost" *Albuquerque Morning Journal*, March 11, 1917.

[64] Larson, Robert W. *New Mexico's Quest for Statehood, 1846–1912* (Albuquerque: The University of New Mexico Press, 1968), 272–86.

[65] Article VII Sect. 3.

[66] Article VII Sect. 1.

[67] Lindsey's claims are cited often in his wife's correspondence (NMSRCA, Santa Fe, Miscellaneous Records, Political Issues, #40B, Women's Suffrage in New Mexico, 1917–1919. Correspondence).

organizations. New Mexico was the last state to establish a NAWSA affiliated association, as the national organization did not even attempt work in
New Mexico until 1916, and even then sent only one representative to assess
the possibility of facilitating efforts to lobby for the *national* amendment. The
perception that the state constitutional provisions were unamendable left New
Mexican women on their own while neighboring states received organizational
and financial assistance from NAWSA – despite pleas from suffrage leaders in
the state.

First support from a national suffrage organization in New Mexico actually
came from the CU, which sent organizers to the state in 1915 to recruit New
Mexican women to the push for the national amendment. Deanne Lindsey,
ardent suffrage advocate and wife of W. E. Lindsey, reported to Anna Howard
Shaw of NAWSA in December of that year, as she entreated the national
leader to send assistance to the state, that "the Congressional Union people
are coming so often and making ground upon the theory that the only way
New Mexico can win suffrage is by the National Government."[68] Lindsey's
request for NAWSA assistance met resistance from that organization, however.
In April of 1916, she wrote again for aid, this time specifically addressing the
reluctance of the NAWSA leadership to invest in the state:

It seems to me that the National should have an organization in the state. It is folly
to say that we cannot do anything as a state. The Attorney General says that the
[amendment] clause referred to does not necessarily bar the women from voting, as it
was to insure the Spanish Americans their rights especially. Mr. Lindsey was a member
of the constitutional convention. I was with him in Santa Fe and knew of it at the time. I
therefore leave it to the judgment of your Committee as to what you had best do under
the circumstances. If you do not come, the state is turned over to the Congressional
Union and many will join and feel that the National neglected us. We would have the
state if an organizer came. Therefore I await your judgment and will do all that I can in
case you decide that it is best to come.[69]

That is, not only was the amendment process, itself, a daunting obstacle to
woman suffrage in New Mexico, but it also prevented the New Mexican
women from receiving precious assistance from NAWSA in their efforts, as
the national organization was reluctant to expend such resources in obvious
vain. When a NAWSA organizer finally arrived in New Mexico in May of
1916, it was only a ten-day trip, which included the business of recruiting New
Mexican suffragists for the planned NAWSA demonstrations at the Democratic
and Republican national conventions that summer. Although a New Mexico

[68] Letter from Deanne Lindsey to NAWSA president Anna Howard Shaw, December 7, 1915
(NMSRCA, Santa Fe, Miscellaneous Records, Political Issues, #40B, Women's Suffrage in New
Mexico, 1917–1919. Correspondence). Deanne Lindsey chaired the legislative committee of
the New Mexico Federation of Women's Clubs and the suffrage committee of the New Mexico
WCTU.
[69] Letter from Deanne Lindsey to NAWSA corresponding secretary Hanna Patterson, April 4,
1916 (NMSRCA, Santa Fe, Miscellaneous Records, Political Issues, #40B, Women's Suffrage
in New Mexico, 1917–1919. Correspondence).

affiliate of NAWSA was established through this visit, there is no evidence that the national organization ever offered significant organizational or financial assistance to the state. And when the CU came to New Mexico to organize, it was expressly for purpose of lobbying the state's members of Congress to pass the national suffrage amendment.[70]

Despite New Mexican suffragists' organizational challenges, partisan interest in woman suffrage in the state peaked after the national party organizations adopted suffrage planks in 1916, and New Mexico's state party organizations did the same in their own conventions. The state party endorsements came as the Republican Party struggled to pull together its old "Santa Fe Ring" machine and new progressive factions, and Democrats jockeyed to pick off Republicans who supported more progressive policies. As the Republican Party began to lose ground to pushes for progressive Republican and Democratic fusion tickets, woman suffrage became an active agenda item. The party organization went so far as to organize Republican Women's Clubs to campaign for both the party's candidates and women's voting rights under the leadership of a prominent California suffrage activist engaged for the project by the Republican Party leadership, Dr. Jessie Russell.[71] Suffragists reaped another benefit from the Republicans' attempts to keep the party together: progressive Republican W. E. Lindsey received the party nomination for lieutenant governor.[72] Lindsey not only won the election for that office, but took over as New Mexico's chief executive less than two months into his term when Democratic governor Ezequiel C. de Baca died in office. With the husband of the state's most visible suffragist, Lindsey, now in the governor's office and endorsement of the cause from the party organizations, political conditions seemed fairly promising for a woman suffrage measure in 1917, even in the face of previous losses and the general sentiment that the state's suffrage qualifications were unamendable.

---

[70] HWS, vol. VI, 435–36; "Sentiment Here is Sounded by Suffrage Leader" *The Evening Herald*, May 19, 1916. According to HWS, although New Mexican suffragists requested the return of the organizer who came in May of 1916, Lola Walker, that request was denied. Another organizer, Gertrude Watkins, was sent in January of 1917 to do some organizational work. There is no other mention of NAWSA presence in the state in HWS, newspaper coverage, or New Mexican suffragists' correspondence, however, until a visit from Carrie Chapman Catt as part of the NAWSA president's "ratification tour" after the national amendment passed Congress in 1919.

[71] "Women Organize Republican Clubs," undated newspaper clipping in Thomas Catron papers (Center for Southwest Research, University of New Mexico); "Women's Work and Women's Clubs," *Los Angeles Times*, September 10, 1916; "New Mexico Women Working for Vote," *Las Vegas Optic*, September 18, 1916; "Women Go After the Right to Vote," *Las Vegas Optic*, October 13, 1916.

[72] Various correspondence in the political papers of New Mexico's Republican U.S. Senator Thomas Catron document the progressive-machine (or "ring") conflict in the Republican Party, and the Democratic attempts to benefit from it electorally. On the Lindsey candidacy, one letter, dated September 17, 1916 and addressed to "Hening" reads, in part, "I had Charlie Speiss nominate Lindsey for Lieut. Governor, believing it would force him back into the party and that it would bring all of the progressives back with him" (Center for Southwest Research, University of New Mexico).

TABLE 5.5. *Votes on Woman Suffrage Amendment by Party and Race, New Mexico House of Representatives 1917*

		Voted No	Voted Yes
Democrat	Anglo	3	10
	Spanish American	4	1
Republican	Anglo	2	5
	Spanish American	17	5

New Mexican suffragists reported that, although they had not intended to wage a state campaign in 1917, lawmakers introduced a suffrage amendment into the state legislature, and a lobbying campaign was undertaken. Governor Lindsey not only publicly supported the cause, but he also facilitated meetings between suffragists and party leaders.[73] Assistance from the governor and promises from the parties, however, did not deliver a suffrage victory – nor even a simple majority in favor of the measure in either house of the legislature. Lindsey could not manage to bring the majority of his fractionalized Republican Party legislators along on the final vote, encountering, as previously highlighted, a tendency for greater resistance from Spanish American lawmakers, who accounted for twenty-two of the twenty-nine Republicans in the House, and six of fourteen Republicans in the Senate. Representatives' votes, in fact, seemed far more related to their race than their partisan affiliation. As Table 5.5 shows for the House vote, the racial divide on the suffrage question was evident among both Republicans and Democrats; Spanish Americans simply constituted a larger bloc of the Republican vote.[74]

Although the 1917 measure had not even approached the necessary three-fourths legislative majority, one final attempt at woman suffrage was made in New Mexico in the next legislative session. Facing a still-divided Republican Party, and without suffrage supporter Lindsey in the chief executive position, it is not clear why suffragists should have been hopeful for success in 1919. When the House voted on the proposed suffrage amendment, the measure fared marginally better than it had in 1917, but with only twenty-six of fifty representatives in favor, the vote was still far short of the two-thirds mark. Although Democrats were nearly unanimous in their support of woman suffrage in the 1919 session, a significant portion of the Republican House members, including most Spanish American legislators, were still opposed.

[73] "New Mexico Women Declare for Suffrage," *Christian Science Monitor*, February 23, 1917; "It Was a Sorry Day When the Suffrage Bill Lost, but a Glad Day Too Because It Lost by So Little; to Keep Trying," *Albuquerque Morning Journal*, March 11, 1917.

[74] Multivariate analysis of the House vote, including measures of legislators' race and party and the presence of labor interests and residents of Mexican origin in legislators' districts showed only legislators' race significantly predicted their votes, with Spanish American legislators, of course, less likely to vote yes ($b = -2.76$, s.e. $= .93$, $p = .003$).

Republican resistance did not go unaddressed by the party. Days after the House defeat, as the legislature neared the end of the session, the new Republican governor, O. A. Larrazolo, issued a statement chastising legislators – Republicans, in particular – for failing to deliver on a set of campaign promises, including the enfranchisement New Mexican women. Larrazolo's message exhibited frustration with Republicans who refused to back the party platform, and warned of electoral consequences for the party if its members in the legislature could not cohere on the highly visible policy decisions of woman suffrage and prohibition of alcohol:

I take it for granted that no [R]epublican member of the present legislature who opposes the enactment of these laws will have the hardihood to again solicit the support of the voters of the state at the polls for any office ... such conduct can bring but one result, and well-merited at that, namely the defeat of the party at the polls in the next election.[75]

The next day, the Senate passed the suffrage amendment. New Mexican suffragists had their first legislative victory, but the session expired without reconsideration of the amendment in the House. New Mexican women would have to wait for ratification of the federal amendment – which was ratified by New Mexico's state legislature – for full access to the ballot box.[76] A struggle between Progressive and machine Republicans may have brought New Mexico's first serious consideration of women's voting rights, but those same factional politics could not carry the policy all the way over the state's high majority vote hurdles. The constitutional amendment clause adopted to protect the role of New Mexico's Spanish American population in the state's politics had, indeed, ensured that no change to the state's suffrage qualifications could be made without their approval.

Just as in the South, racial politics in the West created both institutional arrangements that made success for suffrage legislation difficult and barriers to effective coalition-building for women's voting rights. Constitutional provisions for difficult amendment procedures blocked the Anglo majority of the state from overturning Spanish American rights, but also discouraged attempts to change state law to extend voting rights to any other group, including women. Not only did New Mexican women face the difficulties of attaining support from supermajorities in the legislature and the public, but they did so with very little assistance from national organizations. Even when New Mexico's suffragists pleaded for resources from NAWSA in the form of trained

75 Speech of Governor O. A. Larrazolo, *Proceedings of the Fourth State Legislature, State of New Mexico, House Journal* (Santa Fe: State Record Print, 1919), 440–41. Same speech printed in "Lawmakers Scored for their Failure to Pass Suff Law," *Santa Fe New Mexican*, March 13, 1919.
76 Vote on ratification was seventeen yes, five no in the Senate (the same five that voted against the 1919 measure) and thirty-six yes, ten no in the House. All but two no votes were from Republicans. HWS, vol. VI, 437.

organizers and campaign funding, the national organization's leaders resisted on account of the state constitution's "unamendability." When investment finally came from the national suffrage organizations, both NAWSA and the CU, it was in the form of organizational assistance to pursue the national suffrage amendment.

Conclusion – The Place of Race in the Struggle for Woman Suffrage

Although many discussions of race and the push for woman suffrage in the United States center on the tension between the questions of black voting rights and women's voting at the federal level, much of the mechanism of racial politics is lost by that focus. Looking to racial politics revolving around black and white in Louisiana and Spanish American and white in New Mexico has revealed that the resistance to woman suffrage in states facing "racial questions" was not about fears of opening electoral floodgates, as the discourse surrounding the national woman suffrage amendment suggested. It is true that inside state politics, race built barriers to woman suffrage by inciting state lawmakers to design electoral institutions that constrained electoral politics. But resistance to woman suffrage did not come from those lawmakers whose electoral interests would be directly threatened by empowering racial minorities. Instead, it came from several sets of political actors that benefited from the constrained environment, including, at times, the racial minorities, themselves.

Feeding into the resistance of some politicians in these environments was the circumscribed character of suffrage coalitions. Race and class identities led to suffrage organizations that were the domains of elite white women, who made little to no effort to build coalitions with other women, let alone groups that could have electoral leverage on lawmakers. Neither Louisiana nor New Mexico suffragists had partnerships with the organizations that were key suffrage allies in other states, such as labor unions or farmers' associations. In other states, those partnerships were built through women who reached across social class; middle class suffragists in Illinois worked with working class women of the WTUL, urban, middle-class suffragists in Michigan partnered with farming women of the Grange. Where women could not reach out past their racial and class identities, they paid the price of lost political leverage for the suffrage cause. Suffrage coalitions, however, were not only constrained by suffragists' identities, but also by the more limited range of opportunities for partnerships that race politics created. This dynamic was most pronounced in Louisiana, where Democratic power consolidation was accomplished by cutting much of the population out of the political process – both through legal qualifications and through electoral and ballot access laws that constrained choice. Thus some potential partners for suffragists, such as an effective farmers' movement, never emerged and others, such as the Progressives, were quickly suppressed by one-party politics.

6

The National Story

> The passage of the amendment is the result of fifty years or more of concerted, never-ceasing effort. . . . The victory at Washington is, therefore, no sudden development, no unexpected event. On the contrary, it is a long-overdue climax.
> – Carrie Chapman, National American Woman Suffrage Association, 1919[1]

In 1919, the Susan B. Anthony Amendment, barring states from making distinctions in voter qualifications on the basis of sex, was passed by the U.S. Congress. Ratification came the next year, when Tennessee became the state that put the amendment over the three-fourths threshold. The overarching goal of the organized American woman suffrage movement was achieved. As NAWSA president Carrie Chapman Catt pointed out to the press, that achievement was long in coming, the result of a protracted campaign carried out by activists across the country. Moreover, it was the result not only of the decisions that politicians made in the Capitol in 1919 and in statehouses through the following months, but of decisions made by politicians across the country, across more than fifty years' time. This chapter is meant to tell the national story of woman suffrage in exactly this way – as one that unfolded in important ways over both geography and time.

Tracing the specifics of the politics of suffrage extension in Colorado, Michigan, Illinois, Louisiana, and New Mexico, previous chapters have detailed the process of state decisions on women's voting rights. These accounts demonstrated how women gained electoral inclusion through programmatic enfranchisement; women were granted voting rights when state lawmakers had reasons to believe such action would win approval from important groups of existing voters. Political parties and interest groups played central roles in this

[1] From Catt, Carrie Chapman, "Why Suffrage Fight Took 50 Years," *The New York Times*, June 15, 1919.

process. With women's expanding functions in interest group organizations, including farmers' associations and labor unions, woman suffrage found its way onto the agendas of groups that wielded significant electoral pressure. Partisans, with incentives based in the political enterprise of developing and maintaining winning coalitions, were more willing to expand the electorate when well-organized constituents demanded the change. Politicians' vulnerability to those constituent demands was even greater when elections were more competitive. A particularly helpful form of party competition came from interest groups that became third party challengers. Suffragists were able to gain endorsements from a number of minor political parties, and when candidates from those third parties subsequently carried significant vote shares, major party interest in addressing women's voting rights was peaked. Even more instrumental were third party endorsers who were actually elected to the legislature, where their legislative bargaining directly produced gains for the woman suffrage cause.

The case studies have also revealed a set of factors that reduced women's chances for gaining voting rights. Racial and class politics, in particular, built a set of barriers to effective lobbying for woman suffrage – both by hindering the construction of pro-suffrage coalitions and by increasing the institutional hurdles for enfranchisement. Where (and when) race and class identities were particularly salient, suffrage organizations begun by middle and upper class women had difficulty forging the sorts of partnerships that were key to programmatic enfranchisement. In some instances, the relatively homogeneous sets of women who constituted suffrage organizations made appeals for strategic enfranchisement; attempts were made to convince lawmakers to grant voting rights to only white, or educated, or propertied women. Such appeals were generally unsuccessful. The incentives for strategic enfranchisement, the granting of voting rights by a party simply to reap the votes of the newly enfranchised group, were often simply lacking, and the definition of an appropriate group of women too legally difficult. In the Northern state of Michigan, a failed attempt at strategic enfranchisement by some Republican lawmakers through an English literacy requirement suggested legislators were dubious of the effective implementation of the policy to ensure it enabled only the desired native, educated, white women to vote. In Louisiana, Democrats could be sure that most white women would vote for the party's candidates – but only because the party's dominance of state politics was nearly perfect, and thus new voters unnecessary. The story of Louisiana thus also revealed some of the institutional difficulties induced by the politics of race. Where whites struggled to keep racial minorities out, electoral rules were defined to limit choice, and thus heighten elite control. Such systems provided diminished opportunity for electoral leverage to deliver women's voting rights. In New Mexico, the concerns of a racial minority about their continued inclusion in state politics also led to sticky electoral institutions; difficult rules for changing electoral qualifications helped keep Spanish American men politically empowered, but also kept New Mexican women out of the electoral arena.

Given the insights gained from the case studies, this chapter returns to the national story of women's voting rights, to the question of whether the coalitional, partisan politics story that emerged from the detailed accounts actually typified the process of women's enfranchisement. This entails both a comparison of all forty-eight (relevant) states to explain action and inaction on the issue of women's voting rights, and an analysis of the consideration of woman suffrage by the national political parties and the U.S. Congress. By first comparing the states that did adopt woman suffrage, in the years in which they did so, I offer a general description of the political conditions that encourage expansion of the electorate. To test whether the political context identified does, indeed, push states to act on the issue of suffrage extension, I then employ an analysis that compares the conditions of these states, in these times, to both the previous conditions of these states and the conditions of non-adopting states. Then, by mapping developments in national partisan politics to developments in consideration of the issue of suffrage at the federal level, I show how the programmatic enfranchisement account also helps to explain the politics surrounding the Anthony Amendment.

State-Level Enfranchisement: Parties and Constraints on Coalitions

The case studies in previous chapters provide evidence to suggest that state-level provision of voting rights for women resulted from politicians' need to meet constituent demands for electoral expansion. Woman suffrage, that is, was provided through programmatic enfranchisement. Suffragists' success in joining political forces and creating durable and credible coalitions was key to programmatic suffrage extension. Third parties, in particular, offered a uniquely credible claim about the electoral costs to be paid by major party actors who failed to respond to demands for suffrage rights, and, at the times when third party candidates were actually elected, added legislative bargaining tactics to the call for voting rights extension. But the case studies have also revealed that the political makeup of a state could reduce the possibility of enfranchisement of any sort. Particularly, where racial and class interests caused politicians to create institutional barriers to the expansion of the electorate – such electoral rules that limited the scope of electoral politics and thus blocked the formation of effective coalitions between woman suffrage activists and interest groups able to exert electoral leverage – women paid a high price.

There are two questions to answer to assess the validity of the argument that the extension of voting rights to women was driven by partisan interests in the demands of pro-suffrage coalitions. First, within states that did adopt woman suffrage, were the conditions consistent with a programmatic story of enfranchisement? Were states that adopted woman suffrage characterized by competitive partisan environments? Were strong electoral support for third parties and third party members in the legislature common at the time at which adoption occurred? Second, were these states, at these times, different from states that never acted on the woman suffrage issue? Were states with racial and class interests that constrained possibilities for rights and reform based coalitions less likely to expand their electorates? Did the strong presence of typical suffrage allies, such as a formidable farming interest, increase states' likelihood of extending voting rights to women? I provide the answers to these questions through a number of analyses that compare the characteristics of states that enfranchised women, highlighting what was common in their political circumstances at those moments, and missing from the politics of states that failed to act on woman suffrage.

Turning first to the partisan conditions of states at the time measures granting women state-level voting rights were adopted, Tables 6.1 and 6.2 display a number of indicators of party competition and third party strength. The suffrage measures considered here, which include provisions for the right to vote in all elections (Table 6.1), only in presidential elections, or in primary elections (Table 6.2), are measures that made women into constituents of consequence to state party organizations, and thus are of central interest.[2] Perhaps most striking is the evidence consistent with the argument that strong leverage for women's enfranchisement came from third parties sympathetic to the woman suffrage cause when those parties garnered their own electoral leverage. The fourth column in each table reports the level of electoral support for "reform" parties in the gubernatorial election immediately preceding the adoption of woman suffrage, and the entries in the table are sorted in descending order of this vote.[3] Nine of the fifteen full woman suffrage adopters and six of fifteen presidential or primary suffrage adopters acted after an election in which the reform party garnered more than 5 percent of the gubernatorial vote. Further evidence of common involvement of third parties in the adoption of woman

---

[2] Data for these tables are from *Congressional Quarterly's Gubernatorial Elections 1787–1997*; state constitutions; *Partisan Division of American State Governments, 1834–1985* ICPSR Study No. 16; and The National American Woman Suffrage Association, *Victory: How Women Won It* (New York: The H. W. Wilson Company, 1940). Banaszak, Lee Ann, *Why Movements Succeed or Fail: Opportunity, Culture, and the Struggle for Woman Suffrage* (Princeton: Princeton University Press, 1996) and McCammon, Holly J., Karen Campbell, Ellen Granberg, and Christine Mowery "How Movements Win: Gendered Opportunity Structures and U.S. Women's Suffrage Movements, 1866 to 1919," *American Sociological Review* 66 (2001): 49–70, make a similar distinction between these types of enfranchisement measures and those that gave women voting rights only in school or municipal elections. Like both, I include primary suffrage only for Southern states, where one-party dominance made primary suffrage so consequential.

[3] Reform parties are those concerned with a program of policies meant to promote "good government" and/or increase representation of less affluent interests in American politics. These parties, which all fit woman suffrage into their political programs at some point between the start of the woman suffrage movement and 1920, were: Progressives, Prohibitionists, Populists, Socialists, Labor, and Greenbacks.

TABLE 6.1. *Partisan Conditions as States Adopted Full Woman Suffrage*

State and Year	Party of Governor	Governor Margin of Victory	% Vote Reform Party	% Seats Third Party	% Seats Largest Party (Party Name)	Constitutional Amendment Vote
New York 1917	Republican (Progressive)	10.1	52.6†	0% Upper 1% Lower	71% Upper, 64% Lower (Republican)	majority of each house, 2 successive legislatures
Colorado 1893	Populist	4.9	46.7	33% Upper 44% Lower	44% Upper, 50% Lower (Republican)	2/3 of each house
Idaho 1896	Republican	12.5	29.0	25% Upper 25% Lower	61% Upper, 72% Lower (Republican)	2/3 of each house
Montana 1914	Democrat	3.0	23.6	6% Upper 20% Lower	41% Upper, 58% Lower (Democrat)	majority of each house
Oklahoma 1918	Democrat	1.9	20.8	2% Upper 0% Lower	77% Upper, 71% Lower (Democrat)	majority of each house
California 1911	Republican	5.8	12.4		80% Upper, 86% Lower (Republican)	2/3 of each house
Nevada 1914	Republican	7.9	6.8	13% Upper 8% Lower	55% Upper, 51% Lower (Republican)	majority of each house, 2 successive legislatures
Oregon 1912*	Democrat	5.2	6.8		90% Upper, 97% Lower (Republican)	majority of each house, 2 successive legislatures

(*continued*)

TABLE 6.1 (continued)

State and Year	Party of Governor	Governor Margin of Victory	% Vote Reform Party	% Seats Third Party	% Seats Largest Party (Party Name)	Constitutional Amendment Vote
Arizona 1912*	Democrat	9.1	5.8		95% Upper, 89% Lower (Democrat)	majority of each house
Kansas 1912	Republican	5.0	0.0	0% Upper 1% Lower	87% Upper, 57% Lower (Republican)	3/5 of each house
Utah 1896	Republican	5.6	0.0		61% Upper, 69% Lower (Republican)	2/3 of each house
Wyoming 1890‡	Republican	10.8	0.0		81% Upper, 82% Lower (Republican)	2/3 of each house
Michigan 1918	Republican	15.2	0.0		71% Upper, 88% Lower (Republican)	2/3 of each house
South Dakota 1918	Republican	17.3	0.0		78% Upper, 69% Lower (Republican)	majority of each house, 2 successive legislatures
Washington 1910	Republican	29.6	0.0		93% Upper, 94% Lower (Republican)	2/3 of each house

* Adopted through initiative petition and referendum
† Fusion ticket of Republicans and Progressives
‡ Included in first state constitution

TABLE 6.2. *Partisan Conditions as States Adopted Presidential and Primary Woman Suffrage*

State and Year	Party of Governor	Governor Margin of Victory	% Vote Reform Party	% Seats Third Party	% Seats Largest Party (Party Name)	Constitutional Amendment Vote
Nebraska 1917	Democrat (People's Ind.)	2.3	49.3*		70% Upper, 60% Lower (Democrat)	3/5 of each house
Minnesota 1919	Democrat	14.8	30.3	30% Upper 29% Lower	70% Upper, 71% Lower (Republican)	majority of each house
Illinois 1913	Democrat	10.7	26.1	4% Upper 27% Lower	49% Upper, 49% Lower (Republican, Democrat)	2/3 of each house
Wisconsin 1919	Republican	13.0	17.4	12% Upper 17% Lower	82% Upper, 78% Lower (Republican)	majority of each house, 2 successive legislatures
Arkansas 1917	Democrat	44.5	5.5		100% Upper, 97% Lower (Democrat)	majority of each house
Texas 1918	Democrat	67.2	5.2		100% Upper, 97% Lower (Democrat)	2/3 of each house
Missouri 1919	Democrat	0.3	0.0		67% Upper, 53% Lower (Democrat, Republican)	majority of each house

(continued)

TABLE 6.2 (*continued*)

State and Year	Party of Governor	Governor Margin of Victory	% Vote Reform Party	% Seats Third Party	% Seats Largest Party (Party Name)	Constitutional Amendment Vote
Ohio 1919	Democrat	1.2	0.0		64% Upper, 62% Lower (Republican)	3/5 of each house
Indiana 1917	Republican	1.8	0.0		50% Upper, 64% Lower (Republican)	majority of each house, 2 successive legislatures
Iowa 1919	Republican	3.7	0.0		90% Upper, 86% Lower (Republican)	majority of each house, 2 successive legislatures
Maine 1919	Republican	4.6	0.0		94% Upper, 73% Lower (Republican)	2/3 of each house
Kentucky 1920	Republican	8.5	0.0		53% Upper, 68% Lower (Democrat)	3/5 of each house
Rhode Island 1917	Republican	15.1	0.0		66% Upper, 64% Lower (Republican)	majority of each house, 2 successive legislatures
Tennessee 1919	Democrat	24.8	0.0		N/A	majority of each house, 2/3 in next session
North Dakota 1917	Republican	60.8	0.0		88% Upper, 86% Lower (Republican)	majority of each house, 2 successive legislatures

* Technically, both candidates were fusionist: Democrat/People's Independent and Republican/Progressive

suffrage is in the frequency of their presence in the legislatures that passed provisions for women's voting rights; ten of these adopting states (across the two tables) had at least one third party legislator present when woman suffrage passed.

Competitive elections, the tables highlight, were also frequent antecedents to the adoption of women's voting rights. As a measure of statewide partisan competition, the third column of the tables report the governor's margin of victory in the previous election, and the entries of states with no third party votes are sorted in ascending order of this margin. The tables show that among those states with no significant third party presence, seven adopted their suffrage measures following a particularly close gubernatorial election – one in which the winner beat the first runner-up by less than six percentage points. Thus, at the time of woman suffrage adoption in most states, politicians were facing increased electoral vulnerability – either through major party competition for control of government or through an electoral threat from third party ascendance – to whatever constituent demand for women's voting rights there might have been.

There is another observation to be made in these tables relevant to the political conditions under which woman suffrage was adopted across the states: woman suffrage was adopted under both Democratic and Republican control. This fact would have provided further evidence to attentive politicians at the national level that "women" as a category would not be likely to define a single partisan constituency, and thus made poor candidates for strategic enfranchisement.

Although they provide a useful description of the partisan environment at the time of woman suffrage adoption, Tables 6.1 and 6.2 offer only snapshots of those moments, and thus cannot speak to whether or not these actions were undertaken at times of particularly amenable conditions in the course of state politics. I perform statistical analyses to test the argument that indeed they were undertaken at such moments. First, however, recall that the histories of the case studies suggested that victories, indeed, occurred at moments when partisans were more electorally vulnerable. Figures 6.1 and 6.2, which locate suffrage adoption in the partisan trends of gubernatorial elections across the case study states of Michigan and Illinois, speak to these observations and to these data's ability to capture them. The graphs track party competition, as captured by the governor's margin of victory and share of the two-party vote, and reform party strength, as measured by the percentage of the gubernatorial vote, from 1870 through 1920 and indicate the time of adoption of each woman suffrage measure in the state's timeline.[4]

The figures indeed corroborate the case study observations that woman suffrage measures were adopted at points of electoral vulnerability in the party politics of each state, where newly emerging reform parties were taking noticeable

[4] Electoral data for figures drawn from *Congressional Quarterly's Gubernatorial Elections 1787–1997*.

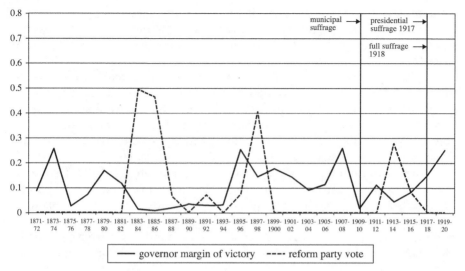

FIGURE 6.1. Margin of Victory for Governor, Third Party Vote, and Time of Suffrage Adoption in Michigan.

shares of the gubernatorial vote and/or where partisan battles were particularly close. In Michigan (Figure 6.1), the broadly supported municipal suffrage compromise came at a moment of sharp major party competition, and the statewide suffrage measures in the wake of the electoral upheaval created by Progressives in 1912. Of course, in the Michigan case, although full suffrage measures had actually first passed the legislature at the moment of Progressive ascendancy, repeated (though close) referenda failures meant legislative victory was not converted to policy until 1917. In Illinois (Figure 6.2), full woman suffrage was, in fact, adopted immediately following a decisive electoral showing by the Progressive Party. Figure 6.2 captures this, locating presidential and municipal suffrage adoption at a peak in reform party support. School suffrage came with more limited electoral success for the Farmers' Alliance, but the figure nonetheless captures that the measure also came at a point at which the major parties were particularly competitive. It is also worth noting that some of the periods of suffrage movement frustration map well onto less competitive periods. For example, Figure 6.2 shows that the period in which the movement particularly struggled to assert itself in legislative politics despite a budding partnership with labor groups, the late 1890s through about 1910, was the time at which partisan competition, by these measures, was less strong.

Of course, the case studies also demonstrated that more than partisan dynamics were important – the story was one of coalitional politics that pushed politicians' to respond. The presence of a strong farmers' association for suffragists to partner with was key in Michigan. And in Illinois, especially, it was evident that organized labor could be invested in the cause and important to

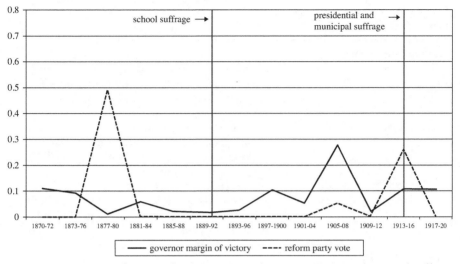

FIGURE 6.2. Margin of Victory for Governor, Reform Party Vote, and Time of Suffrage Adoption in Illinois.

leveraging success. Moreover, race and class interests shaped political institutions that made *effective* coalition-building difficult in Louisiana and New Mexico. Thus, explaining the action – or inaction – of states on the issue of women's voting rights should entail taking account of all these factors, and comparing both adopters and non-adopters across time. This is accomplished by modeling the adoption of woman suffrage within an event history framework.

Modeling the "Hazard" of Woman Suffrage
I have argued that coalitional and party politics were responsible for state action on the issue of women's voting rights. Party competition, the success of reformist third parties, the entrenchment of racial and class interests in state politics, the availability of coalitional partners – all of these factors shaped the chances of woman suffrage gaining both sufficient support and the issue salience it needed to push through the political process. The argument, then, implies a dynamic process: a state's likelihood of extending voting rights to women changed as its political and social environment changed. An event history, or "hazard model," approach can account for these dynamics by building a model of the likelihood ("hazard") of woman suffrage adoption using yearly data. Essentially, the estimation is of the likelihood of voting rights being extended in each state, in each year, as a function of the partisan environment, racial composition, class structure, suffrage organization, and availability of coalitional partners specific to that place and time.

Ideally, the model would include measures of all the factors that contributed to the coalitional politics of programmatic enfranchisement across all forty-eight states for every year from the start of the woman suffrage movement

TABLE 6.3. *Variables for Event History Analysis Descriptions, Observed Ranges 1892–1920*

Party Environment	
Party Competition	Governor's margin of victory in the last election, subtracted from 1, so that higher values indicate a more competitive partisan environment
	Observed range 0.0 to 1.0
Reform Party Vote	Percent of the gubernatorial vote that went to a candidate running on a reform party label: Progressive, Prohibition, Populist, Socialist, Labor, and Greenback
	Observed range 0.0 to .77
Third Party Legislators	Percent of the lower legislative chamber members identified with a party other than "Republican" or "Democrat"
	Observed range 0.0 to 1.0
Suffrage Organization	
State Members	State membership in NAWSA, per 1,000 state population
	Observed range 0.0 to 12.49
NAWSA Budget	Annual NAWSA budget, per 1,000 U.S. population
	Observed range .05 to 1.21
Race	Percent state population non-white*
	Observed range .002 to .60
Class	Percent state population living in urban areas*
	Observed range .02 to .92
Coalitional Partner Possibilities	
Farms	Number of farms per capita in state*
	Observed range from .01 to .48
Labor	Number of manufacturing workers per 1,000 state population, logged*
	Observed range 1.78 to 5.49
	OR
	Per capita investment in manufacturing, logged*
	Observed range 2.52 to 6.32

* Linear smoothing applied between Census years

until the adoption of Amendment XIX to the U.S. Constitution in 1920, which banned state voter qualifications based on sex. This presents some measurement challenges. Not all of these data are available across that entire time span; getting data all the way back to 1848 proves quite difficult. Additionally, although measuring the level of third party presence and party competition is relatively straightforward, gauging the availability of coalitional partners consistently across states and time is not. All the measures employed in the analysis are described briefly in Table 6.3; here I take up the rationale and the consequences of each measurement strategy.

Assessing the partisan environment through gubernatorial election returns has thus far proven quite informative, and thus the same measures for the competitiveness of state party politics and the electoral success of reform parties will be retained. As the Illinois case revealed a particularly strong influence of third parties when their members were inside the legislature, bargaining for woman suffrage, a measure of third party presence in the state house will also be helpful. Using the data on party compositions of state legislatures collected by Walter Dean Burnham allows for the addition of the percentage of the lower house members that identified with a party label other than "Republican" or "Democrat" from 1874. Thus, the first trade-off: the time series cannot run all the way back to 1848.

Measuring the level of suffragist organization also shortens the time horizon. State memberships in the National American Woman Suffrage Association (NAWSA) are available only from 1893 through 1920.[5] There is also some conceptual distance between the level of organized state suffrage activity and the measure. In some states, NAWSA membership will be an underestimate of suffrage activity, either because women were affiliated with another national organization such as the Congressional Union, as were New Mexico suffragists, or not affiliated with any national organization at all, as was the case with one of Louisiana's two feuding state suffrage groups. Still, NAWSA was the largest national organization, and cast the widest membership net. It is also the only for which such state-level numbers are available. Ideally a measure should also be included to gauge the resources of these suffrage organizations; the case of Illinois, for instance, showed that political resources made suffragists attractive partners for third parties such as the Progressives. Although a consistent metric is not available across states and years, the annual budget for NAWSA is available for the years 1892 through 1920. Yet, because of the federated nature of NAWSA, and its standard practice of funneling money and paid organizers to state suffrage campaigns, to a great extent the national organization was able to smooth the supply of suffrage work across states.[6] This measure, then, is a fair approximation the concept of resources available to the states, although it varies only over time, and not across states.

Entrenchment of racial interests rose within a state as the (free) non-white population increased. That is, although Illinois and Michigan certainly had black residents, because blacks represented a relatively small proportion of the state population, whites were not consistently preoccupied with maintaining their separation and supremacy.[7] In Louisiana, in contrast, both political identities and institutions were built on concerns about race. In New Mexico, race was also central, although the non-white population of concern was Spanish

---

[5] The NAWSA data were provided by Lee Ann Banaszak and used in her book *Why Movements Succeed or Fail: Opportunity, Culture, and the Struggle for Woman.*

[6] HWS discusses regular assistance for state campaigns.

[7] Note this does not imply an absence of important racial politics; it only implies a relative degree of dominance of state politics by racial politics.

American. Capturing the entrenchment of racial interests in state politics and the barriers to extending voting rights to women that were consequently built are thus captured by a measure of the percentage of the states' populations that were non-white. This measure, derived from U.S. Census data, includes blacks, Asians, American Indians, and Spanish Americans in the category "non-white."[8] In states with large non-white populations, class politics were tied to race politics. In other states, rising industrialization and urbanization supported the growth of both the middle class, from whose ranks suffragists and other "reformist" interest groups rose, and the working class. Therefore, a measure of the urbanization – the percent of the population living in urban areas – will also help to control for the effect of class structure on the defining of the electorate.

Representing the availability and strength of potential suffrage coalition partners proves the most difficult for this analysis. Third party organizations were one of the most effective partners suffragists found, and measures have already been introduced to account for their presence in state politics. Other effective partners for suffragists found in farmers' associations, such as the Grange in Michigan, and labor organizations, as in the case of the WTUL in Illinois, are not so easily translated into a consistent measure across years and states. Given the centrality of farmers and laborers in the case study accounts, however, an approximation, at least, is essential. Again, the U.S. Census provides a useful set of measures. Counts of the number of farms per capita approximate the availability of members of farmers' associations, and their relative importance in the state population. Census counts of manufacturing workers and capital investment in manufacturing serve as a gauge of the presence of labor interests in the states. The complication with the labor measures,

---

[8] Leaving the population percentages constant for the ten years between Censuses would not appropriately capture changes in population demographics. It was obviously necessary to account for the huge change in the free population made by the mass emancipation of slaves during the Civil War. It was also important to capture trends of migration within the country and immigration into the country as somewhat gradual processes, rather than huge changes in population characteristics every ten years. Thus, the 1860 slave populations were added to the free black populations in 1865 and a general linear smoothing was applied to make each year between censuses a step in the direction of the next census observation. It would have been ideal to also capture the other immigrant populations that had difficulty establishing their "whiteness." The measurement difficulty is that these varied over both states and time; the Irish and Italian populations might have struggled in some locations until the early twentieth century, in other places they may have been politically incorporated and racially assimilated in the late nineteenth century. Moreover, the U.S. Census, itself, gives us a good indication of contemporary ideas of "race" – only blacks, American Indians, and Asians were counted separately from whites in this time period. Spanish American populations were estimated from the Spanish surname counts available from the individual-level Census data samples provided by IPUMS. (Steven Ruggles, Matthew Sobek, Trent Alexander, Catherine A. Fitch, Ronald Goeken, Patricia Kelly Hall, Miriam King, and Chad Ronnander. Integrated Public Use Microdata Series: Version 3.0 [Machine-readable database]. Minneapolis, MN: Minnesota Population Center [producer and distributor], 2004.)

of course, is the inability to distinguish the influence of unions rather than corporate interests. I return to that complication in the discussion of the analysis results.

With all of these measures in hand, it is now possible to build a model of the hazard of woman suffrage adoption.[9] The likelihood of woman suffrage adoption occurring in a given state and year is modeled as a function of the set of explanatory factors, and each state has an observation every year from 1893, or the first year of its statehood, if later, until: (1) the state adopts state-level woman suffrage, or (2) Amendment XIX to the U.S. Constitution is ratified.[10] Before turning to the results of the full model, however, it is useful to have a sense of the bivariate relationship between each explanatory factor and the likelihood of suffrage adoption. For such an analysis, similar to the investigation of cross tabulations in cross sectional data analysis, bivariate event history model results are presented in Table 6.4. Each entry in the coefficient column of the table is the coefficient obtained when that variable is the only variable in a Cox proportional hazards model of the likelihood ("hazard") of woman suffrage adoption using data on all states between 1892 and 1920.[11] A negative coefficient indicates that a higher value on that factor decreased the likelihood that woman suffrage would be adopted in a given state and year, a positive coefficient indicates an increase in the likelihood would result from a higher value.

Of particular note in Table 6.4 are the positive coefficients produced on the measures of the partisan environment: reform party strength at the polls and in the legislature were related to a greater likelihood of woman suffrage adoption, as were closer vote margins. The results also indicate that suffrage extension was more likely to occur where activism was greater, as indicated by the positive and statistically significant coefficient on the measure of state membership

[9] Formally stated it is: $h(t, X, \beta) = h_0(t)e^{x\beta}$ where,

$$X\beta = \beta_1 Party\ Competition + \beta_2 Third\ Party\ Vote + \beta_3 Third\ Party\ Legislators$$
$$+ \beta_4 Suffrage\ Members + \beta_5 NAWSA\ Budget + \beta_6 Race + \beta_7 Urban + \beta_8 Farms$$
$$+ \beta_9 Labor$$

Note the model includes a term integrating time, t – essentially, the year of the observation. The mode also implies a functional form for the likelihood or hazard, as denoted by $h_0(t)$.

[10] Note that this causes Wyoming to drop from the sample. I explored expanding the time series by dropping the suffrage activism measure, with little impact on the substantive results.

[11] Use of Cox's partial likelihood approach allows estimation of the relationships between the explanatory variables and the hazard of suffrage adoption without imposing any distributional assumptions on that hazard, thus making the results a good approximation of cross-tabular information. For an overview of the Cox model see David W. Hosmer Jr. and Stanley Lemeshow, *Applied Survival Analysis: Regression Modeling of Time to Event Data* (New York: John Wiley & Sons, Inc., 1999). Because the Cox model is estimated through partial likelihood, it is unable to handle covariates that do not vary across units (here, states). As a result, I am unable to produce a Cox estimate for the bivariate relationship between the likelihood of woman suffrage adoption and the NAWSA budget, which does not vary by state.

TABLE 6.4. *Bivariate Relationships with Likelihood of Woman Suffrage Adoption Cox Proportional Hazards Models*

	Coefficient	Standard Error
Party Environment		
Party Competition	1.34	0.86
Reform Party Vote	4.15***	1.43
Third Party Legislators	5.07***	1.95
Suffrage Organization		
State Members	0.38**	0.16
Race	−5.54***	1.98
Class	0.14	0.92
Coalitional Partner Possibilities		
Farms	−0.18	4.41
Labor – workers	−0.53**	0.25
Labor – capital	−0.44*	0.26
Regional Differences		
South	−0.88	0.64
West	1.63***	0.50

*** $p < .01$, **$p < .05$, *$p < .10$

For all entries, number of suffrage adoptions = 29. Standard errors are adjusted for clustering of observations by state. Exact partial likelihood estimation.

in NAWSA. Turning to the constraints on woman suffrage coalitions, the negative relationship between the presence of non-white populations and adoption of woman suffrage is quite pronounced. In states where politics needed to deal with the rights and interests of non-whites – whether by protecting or eliminating their electoral inclusion – expanding the electorate was decidedly less likely. The estimated relationships between class structure, as approximated by urbanization, and the potential for coalitions with farmers' associations, as captured by the relative number of farms, are far less stable. A strong labor presence – in both capital and workers – was common to a less likely environment for woman suffrage. Labor unions might have made strong suffrage allies, but that relationship does not seem straightforward. Also included in Table 6.4 are estimations of simple regional differences from a model that included both variables indicating region. This simple model picked up the general geographic pattern to women's voting rights adoption, with Southern states least likely to act on the issue, and Western states most likely to do so.[12]

---

[12] The excluded comparison group being Northern states. For a map of the regional pattern, see Chapter 1. South includes the former slave states: Alabama, Arkansas, Delaware, Florida, Georgia, Kentucky, Louisiana, Maryland, Mississippi, Missouri, North Carolina, South Carolina, Tennessee, Texas, Virginia. West: Arizona, California, Colorado, Idaho, Iowa, Kansas, Minnesota, Montana, Nebraska, Nevada, New Mexico, North Dakota, Oklahoma, Oregon, South Dakota, Utah, Wyoming, Washington. North: Connecticut, Illinois, Indiana, Maine,

Of course, although the bivariate relationships in Table 6.4 help describe the conditions under which voting rights were expanded by the states, the real empirical leverage lies in embedding all of the possible explanations for action or inaction on the issue of suffrage rights into a single model. We want to see the relative importance of all these factors in determining a state's propensity to extend voting rights to women, while also ruling out spurious relationships. The results of the analysis of the full model, therefore, are presented in Table 6.5; hazard ratio comparisons are displayed in Table 6.6.[13] Several versions of the model were estimated; high correlations between the measures of potential coalitional partners – farms, labor workers, and manufacturing capital – make embedding all in the same model precarious. The results largely sustain the relationships discovered in the bivariate models, and are consistent with the argument that partisan state politics drove the process of women's enfranchisement. Importantly, the positive and statistically significant coefficients for reform party vote shares and third party representation in state legislatures support the argument about the role of this unique sort of partisan leverage on the issue of woman suffrage. In times and places in which reform party support in the electorate was stronger, and where seats were held by third party politicians, the likelihood of adopting a woman suffrage measure increased, even when controlling for the influence of suffrage activism and other interests.[14] And when these two partisan incentives reinforced each other, as they did in a number of states, the partisan push for suffrage rights was decidedly intense.

Massachusetts, Michigan, New Hampshire, New Jersey, New York, Ohio, Pennsylvania, Rhode Island, Vermont, Wisconsin, West Virginia.

[13] To include both measures of suffrage activism, one of which varies only by year and not by state, and also to recover statistical efficiency, I use a parametric event history approach, adding a distributional assumption that allows an estimation of whether the likelihood of suffrage adoption increased over time in some way for which the explanatory variables do not account. As stated earlier, because the Cox model is estimated through partial likelihood, it is unable to handle covariates that do not vary across units (here, states). The parametric approach relies on the same proportional hazards assumption made by the Cox model, but also imposes a distributional assumption on the baseline hazard. In this case, I impose a Weibull distribution. There are trade-offs in making the assumption. There are gains in efficiency, essentially because the model uses all the information about the timing of events, rather than just their order, as in the partial likelihood approach of the Cox model. Yet, it also simply imposes a shape on the baseline hazard that increases monotonically over time (although to what degree is estimated); changes in the likelihood of suffrage adoption are driven by changes in the explanatory variables, and the overall likelihood increases with time. Non-parametric (Kaplan Meier) graphs of the survivor function lend support to the assumption, however. The results presented generally hold under other parametric assumptions. Also, allowing some states to be more susceptible to change through the addition of a frailty term (shared by region) does not change the substantive results, and the frailty term is statistically insignificant under most specifications.

[14] Adding a variable for the vote percentages for *other* third party movements did not change these results and the coefficient on that variable was statistically insignificant: $b = -2.60$, s.e. $= 1.97$ in Model 1.

TABLE 6.5. *Event History Model Results Log Relative Hazard Form Coefficients and Robust Standard Errors*

	Model 1	Model 2	Model 3
Party Environment			
Party Competition	1.10	1.89*	1.20
	(1.04)	(1.02)	(0.84)
Reform Party Vote	1.94**	3.21***	1.92**
	(0.94)	(0.89)	(0.83)
Third Party Legislators	3.71***	3.02**	3.32***
	(1.20)	(1.31)	(1.33)
Suffrage Organization			
State Members	0.30***	0.22***	0.24***
	(0.05)	(0.03)	(0.04)
NAWSA Budget	3.41***	3.43***	3.30***
	(0.83)	(0.85)	(0.83)
Race	−5.05***	−3.50*	−3.65**
	(1.69)	(1.96)	(1.85)
Class	0.37	3.12	1.32
	(1.15)	(2.16)	(1.75)
Coalitional Partner Possibilities			
Farms	11.87***		
	(3.71)		
Labor – workers			−0.69**
			(0.33)
Labor – capital		−1.36**	
		(0.53)	
Constant	−9.23	−4.85	−6.28
	(3.09)	(3.62)	(3.50)
Shape parameter, ρ	1.41	1.67	1.49
	(0.98)	(1.00)	(1.05)
Log Pseudo-likelihood	−8.72	−4.68	−7.94
Wald χ^2	110.65***	147.56***	130.14***
Time at risk	1072	1073	1065
Number of Failures	29	29	29

*** p < .01, **p < .05, *p < .10
Standard errors are adjusted for clustering of observations by state.

The hazard ratios, which indicate the effect of a standard deviation change in each explanatory factor on the odds of suffrage adoption occurring, suggest such a surge in reform party voting could boost the chances of suffrage adoption by a third, whereas a similar magnitude increase of third party members in the legislature increased the chances by more than 50 percent. Constraints on state politics presented by racial interests also had a significant effect on the likelihood of suffrage adoption. Salient racial interests made woman suffrage less politically viable; the chance of enfranchising women in states with

TABLE 6.6. *Hazard Ratios for Standard Deviation Changes in Variables*

	Hazard Ratio	95% Confidence Interval	
Party Competition	1.35	0.78	2.32
Reform Party Vote	1.33	1.02	1.75
Third Party Legislators	1.53	1.17	2.00
State Members	1.22	1.15	1.31
NAWSA Budget	3.02	1.78	5.13
Race	0.43	0.25	0.75
Class	1.08	0.67	1.75
Farms	1.62	1.20	2.17
Workers	0.57	0.33	0.96
Capital	0.32	0.13	0.76

All hazard ratios except Workers and Capital derived from Model 1 estimates.

sizable non-white populations was less than half of the chance for those without significant numbers of non-white residents.

The results regarding the role of activism merit close attention. Although activism increased the likelihood of woman suffrage adoption, as evidenced by the positive coefficients on both activism measures, the results seem inconsistent with an account that would define the main role of activism in producing the desired policy change as one of developing insurgency. Indeed, the relative sizes of the coefficients and their relative impact on the hazard of state adoption of woman suffrage indicate that what mattered most was not the "demand" for woman suffrage within a state as evidenced by the number of women joining the cause, but the organization's overall development as an attractive coalition partner to other interests. The large positive coefficient on the measure of NAWSA's budget and its decidedly large effect on the hazard of woman suffrage adoption indicate that woman suffrage became more likely as the organization's coffers offered increasing financial incentives to possible political allies to lend their support. In contrast, having women organized to signal a level of demand from the group in the state had comparatively little effect on the likeliness that the state would acquiesce to such demand; in fact, such demand had the smallest impact of all the significant factors included in the model. The importance of having political resources to offer, including money to offer campaign contributions, stresses the primary role of suffrage activism as one of maneuvering to create and maintain credible and durable coalitions.

There is an additional concern about interpreting the increasing size of NAWSA coffers as *the* explanation for successful state adoption of woman suffrage: it does not help us determine *which* states were vulnerable to NAWSA activities. That NAWSA's organizational resources peaked at the time of increased success for women's voting rights is accurate. Figure 6.3, which indicates the number of state woman suffrage adoptions in each year, and

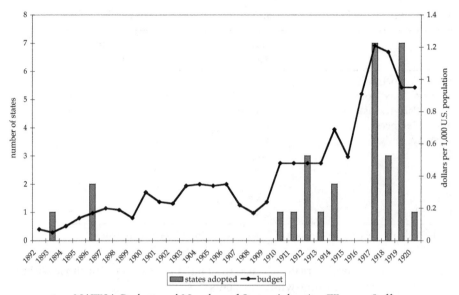

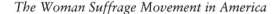

FIGURE 6.3. NAWSA Budget and Number of States Adopting Woman Suffrage.

overlays the yearly NAWSA budget totals, shows increased state-level success as NAWSA resources grew. Yet NAWSA resources cannot be the whole story – or even the most informative – about when and how suffragists achieved their goals. There were clearly suffrage victories long before NAWSA had a sizable resource base. More important, there were clearly holdouts even after NAWSA had amassed a hefty treasury. State politics shaped both the realization of suffrage success before activism peaked, and the chances that suffragist resources could actually be leveraged. And there is certainly evidence that NAWSA made choices about where to expend their resources based in large part on their assessments of whether state political conditions made a suffrage victory likely there. In the case studies presented in earlier chapters, for example, Colorado and New Mexico suffragists found themselves pleading with NAWSA for support, arguing against the national organization's assessments of their chances. In contrast, in the politically promising conditions of the 1918 Michigan referendum campaign, NAWSA responded readily to requests for assistance with infusions of cash and organizational assistance.

There are several other subtle points about the interplay of supply- and demand-side factors in determining the outcome of states' policies on women's voting rights, some of which are partially analytical technicalities. Although my line of argument has been that activism and political opportunities in the partisan environment interacted to facilitate the adoption of woman suffrage in the states, the models presented in Table 6.5 did not interact the measures gauging activism and the partisan environment. There are reasons for this, mostly technical in nature. First, and most technical, the rare events nature of the data – only twenty-nine events from which to draw information about the conditions under which suffrage adoption occurred – makes the estimation of such an interactive model analytically infeasible. Yet, there are several ways in which the interactions between these supply and demand factors are already built into the model. The measures of third party influence, for instance, already capture some of that interaction; the measures are of the relative presence in electoral and legislative politics of third parties that actually endorsed woman suffrage. As demonstrated in the case of Illinois in Chapter 4, such endorsement depended on both the needs of the third party and the resources offered by suffragists. And the endorsement criterion is necessary for third party presence to facilitate the adoption of woman suffrage; when a measure of the electoral success of other third parties is added, it does not produce a statistically significant effect on the likelihood of state action.[15]

The interaction of supply and demand is also caught up in the rise of successful suffrage organizing, especially given that the measure of suffragists' financial resources is for the national organization, which undoubtedly benefited from increased fundraising capabilities as its cause looked more hopeful. In fact, modeling the determinants of state success after truncating the time series by cutting off all observations after 1915, when NAWSA fundraising began to reach its peak levels, produces a set of estimates, displayed in Table 6.7, that suggests partisan factors were even more important in earlier successes. The estimated effect of party competition, notably, is more than four times the size it was in the full time series, whereas the coefficients on the measures of reform party presence in state politics are also slightly larger. Ultimately, however, the strongest evidence that the arrangement of the partisan environment encountered by suffragists *conditioned* the effectiveness of their organizational resources lies in the analysis of lawmakers' decisions in previous chapters, rather than in the results of this event history analysis – although clearly this analysis sustains the claim that both must be taken into account to explain the action or inaction of states on women's voting rights.

To illustrate the relative roles of the level of activism signaling "demand" and the structure of the political environment activists encountered more clearly, it is particularly useful to turn to several state examples. Illinois, as detailed in Chapter 4, adopted woman suffrage in 1913, with strong support from Progressives. Using the results of the hazard model of suffrage adoption, it is possible to estimate Illinois's chances of resisting the push for woman suffrage, given its political and social conditions in 1912 and 1913. In 1912, just one year before the state would grant women's voting rights, the model suggests that Illinois was quite resistant to the suffrage cause; the estimated probability that

---

[15] $b = -2.60$, s.e. $= 1.97$, $p = .19$.

TABLE 6.7. *Event History Model Results Years Prior to 1915*

	Coefficient (robust s.e.)
Party Environment	
Party Competition	4.58**
	(2.22)
Reform Party Vote	2.45*
	(1.42)
Third Party Legislators	3.80***
	(1.38)
Suffrage Organization	
State Members	0.28***
	(.08)
NAWSA Budget	3.38**
	(1.62)
Race	−3.23
	(3.84)
Class	0.10
	(2.25)
Coalitional Partner Possibilities	
Farms	5.92
	(8.00)
Constant	−10.19
	(3.22)
Shape parameter, ρ	.96
	(.71)
Log Pseudo-likelihood	−19.15
Wald χ^2	69.30***
Time at risk	900
Number of Failures	11

*** $p < .01$, ** $p < .05$, * $p < .10$
Standard errors are adjusted for clustering of observations by state.

Illinois could continue to hold out on the issue was .82.[16] Just one year later, however, much had changed in Illinois politics, and the probability that the state could continue to deny women's voting rights dropped to .52, suggesting suffragists had an even chance in 1913. Nearly all of the reduction in the state's predicted chances of continuing to deny woman suffrage came from the success of the Progressives; retaining all of the characteristics of Illinois from 1912 except adding the 1913 level of reform party voting and the percent of state legislators from third parties (Progressives and Socialists in this case) moves the estimated probability that Illinois could continue to withhold women's voting rights from .82 to .55. Consistent with the evidence in Chapter 4, party politics

[16] All predicted probabilities refer to the value of the survival function of Model 1 in Table 6.5 given the values of the explanatory variables as described in the text.

explained the *timing* of woman suffrage adoption in Illinois – why Illinois was able to gain a suffrage victory in 1913, not earlier or later.

What about the question of states that continued to holdout in the face of ever-increasing suffrage resources and activity? Chapter 5 demonstrates that Louisiana was one of those cases. Although suffragists were hopeful when the state legislature passed a suffrage amendment in 1918, machine politics easily defeated the measure at the polls. The hazard model captures Louisiana's drastic change in political receptivity to woman suffrage in the last few years before the national amendment passed; only some of the state's declining resistance to women's voting rights was attributable to the increasing resource base of suffragists. Using 1912 again as a reference point – in part to illustrate how different Louisiana's chances were from Illinois's at that time – the hazard model estimates a probability of Louisiana's continued refusal to grant women's voting rights of .98. Woman suffrage simply had no chance for success in Louisiana in 1912, a statement that squares with the evidence from the state. In 1912, Louisiana politicians were still trying to decide if women ought to be allowed to hold office in the state school system, and simply refused to consider voting rights. For 1918, the year the state constitutional amendment passed the legislature, the model estimates a probability of continued denial of women's voting rights of just .30. Some of that change was because of the growth of suffragist resources; keeping Louisiana's 1912 conditions, but imposing the NAWSA budget and the number of Louisiana NAWSA members from 1918 yields an estimated probability of .72. But also involved in the decreased resistance to woman suffrage predicted by the hazard model for 1918 was a suddenly competitive partisan environment driven by Progressive surge at the polls. In neighboring Mississippi, where Democratic politicians still held consolidated control, resistance to suffrage held steady as well. Even at the height of NAWSA's organizational strength, Mississippi conditions predicted no change, with a probability of .73. Mississippi never adopted woman suffrage at the state level – and even refused to ratify the national amendment until 1984.

Capturing the effect of the availability of potential suffrage allies and the political opportunities afforded by a more differentiated class structure was more difficult for the hazard model. Urbanization may have offered resources or political opportunities that helped build political strength for the suffrage cause, but although the coefficients on this measure of class structure are positive, they are less stable and fail to reach statistical significance at conventional levels. And although the case studies demonstrated that both farmers' associations and labor unions could lend strong political leverage to the suffrage cause, high (negative) correlations between the available measures for each made including both simultaneously in the hazard model infeasible.[17]

---

[17] Adding both measures to the same model more than doubles the coefficient on Farms and renders the Labor measures statistically insignificant, a common result in the face of highly collinear measures.

Estimated in separate hazard models, the effect of a strong presence of farmers was positive and that of a large labor base was negative. Where agrarian
economies thrived, the chances for women's voting rights also grew; the hazard
ratio in Table 6.6 indicates a significant farming interest drove the chances of
woman suffrage up by more than 60 percent. With a massive suffrage lobbying effort mounted by the Grange, the Michigan case in Chapter 3 shows just
how much influence a strong farmer-suffrage alliance could have on legislator
decisions and returns for suffrage at the polls. Conversely, where a manufacturing economy drove the state, the chances for suffrage dropped by at least 50
percent. In Chapter 4, the Illinois case illustrates how helpful a coalition with
organized labor could be, but also how difficult such a relationship was for
predominantly middle class suffragists to maintain. The availability of labor
partners did not mean a coalition could be forged. Furthermore, a labor base
did not necessarily imply strong union organization; the measure could as easily be capturing corporate influence, which had no interest in the commonly
reformist sentiments of suffrage activists.

The Politics of National Woman Suffrage

Although state politics may be key to understanding the provision of voting
rights to American women, it is nonetheless true that woman suffrage was an
issue that played in the national venues of political party conventions and the
U.S. Capitol. Suffragists, of course, both sought and eventually won an amendment to the U.S. Constitution barring sex discrimination in voting rights. In
their pursuit of what would come to be known as the Anthony amendment,
the need to somehow incentivize partisan politicians' interests in forwarding a
constitutional amendment was a recognized and thorny problem for national
suffrage movement leaders – one that seemed particularly crystallized in the
wake of the adoption of the Fifteenth Amendment. Susan B. Anthony, for
example, in her testimony on woman suffrage before a congressional committee in 1884, spoke at length about women's political disadvantage in seeking
the vote because of their political heterogeneity, which she contrasted with the
advantage of black men based on politicians' expectations of partisan cohe-
siveness:

Of course the negro was not asked to go begging the white man from school district
to school district to get his ballot [as women are]. If it was known that we could be
driven to the ballot-box like a flock of sheep, and all vote for one party [like black men],
there would be a bid made for us; but that is not done, because we cannot promise
you any such thing; because we stand before you and honestly tell you that the women
of this nation are educated equally with the men, and that they, too, have political
opinions. . . . We all have opinions, we all have parties. Some of us like one party and
one candidate and some another. Therefore we cannot promise you that women will
vote as a unit when they are enfranchised.

Anthony even went so far as to clarify that she deemed the expectation that women would vote for a party simply because it pushed for woman suffrage a foolish one:

Suppose the Democrats shall put a woman-suffrage plank in their platform in their Presidential convention, and nominate an open and avowed friend of woman suffrage to stand upon that platform; we cannot pledge you that all the women of this nation will work for the success of that party, nor can I pledge you that they will all vote for the Republican party if it should be the one to take the lead in their enfranchisement. Our women will not toe a mark anywhere; they will think and act for themselves, and when they are enfranchised, they will divide upon all political questions.[18]

As Anthony's remarks suggest, the national story of woman suffrage involved the protracted difficulty of overcoming barriers to political success built by gender. Suffragists not only needed to find a way to navigate past ideas about women's capacity for politics and the propriety of a change in gender roles, but they needed to do so without violating their feminist convictions in women's equality – to do so without suggesting that women would be somehow less varied in their political convictions than men or more easily controlled by partisan gestures. To move the politics of woman suffrage past arguments about gender roles, past politicians' ability to dismiss the issue on account of their own attitudes about women's place, suffrage organizers would eventually realize a need for a partisan meaning for their issue. Knowing that the promise of a women's voting bloc was a disingenuous and untenable pledge, it took both time and experience to uncover an alternative path into partisan politics.

Activism Frustrated – Woman Suffrage outside Partisan Politics
The frustration Susan B. Anthony voiced in the 1884 suffrage hearing with the standing of women's voting rights in partisan politics derived from little attention to the issue at the national level despite constant petitioning of the party conventions and members of Congress by suffrage leaders. At the national level, the first partisan success for the woman suffrage issue was a small one: a plank in favor of the enfranchisement of women in the 1872 party platform of the Prohibition Party. At their convention in Columbus, Ohio that year, the minor party's delegates chose to state simply, "[t]hat suffrage should be granted to all persons, without regard to sex."[19] Although no major political party touched

---

[18] Anthony's remarks are reprinted in the *Congressional Record-Senate*, January 25, 1887, 996. Other suffragists testifying during the hearing, including Helen Gouger and May Wright Sewall, also stressed the multi-partisan leanings of the leaders of the movement and/or women generally.

[19] McKee, Thomas Hudson, *The National Conventions and Party Platforms of All Political Parties* (Baltimore: The Friedenwald Company, 1901), 158. The Prohibition candidate for President that year garnered 5,608 votes nationwide, which was less than a tenth of a percent of all votes cast. Johnson cites an 1869 Prohibition platform adopted in Chicago, Illinois that also called for woman suffrage. Johnson, Donald Bruce, *National Party Platforms, Volume I, 1840–1956* Revised Edition (Urbana: University of Illinois Press, 1978), 45–46. But 1872 was the first national nominating convention to include the woman suffrage platform.

on woman suffrage that year, the Republican national convention delivered the first major party plank on the status of women, which recognized the party's "obligations to the loyal women of America" and conceded that "the honest demand of any class of citizens for additional rights should be treated with respectful consideration."[20] In these first years after the Civil War, then, it seemed that perhaps the Republicans might be persuaded that their extension of the franchise to black males bound them to be stewards of woman suffrage as well. Indeed, four years later, the Republican platform congratulated Republican state legislatures for adopting policies that extended the property rights of women and allowed women to fill offices in school administrations and charitable organizations. Republicans still stopped far short, however, of calling for women's enfranchisement or political empowerment, and simply reasserted that demands by women for rights ought to be "treated with respectful consideration."[21] And that would be the last that either major party would have to say about women's rights in its national platform for two decades.

Despite the lack of engagement from the major political parties, woman suffrage was not a dormant issue through the latter part of the nineteenth century. Third parties continued to address the idea of woman suffrage, with several adopting planks in favor of the issue at their national conventions. Perhaps unsurprisingly, given the integration of women activists into the temperance movement, the Prohibition Party in particular stood as a steady supporter over the decades. The party repeated its direct endorsement of woman suffrage in 1876 and 1880, and stated its position in 1884 with even more clarity, announcing that its membership would "hold to and will vote for woman suffrage." That sort of stalwart support from Prohibitionists would endure into the twentieth century.[22] Beginning in the 1880s, mentions of support also came from parties associated with labor interests, including the Greenbacks, the Union Labor Party, and the Socialist Labor Party, although the positions taken were less forceful. The Greenback Party's 1884 plank, for example, called for a national referendum on the issue, whereas the 1888 plank of the Union Labor Party asserted that woman suffrage was "properly within the province of state legislation."[23] Thus, although it appeared that perhaps politically organized labor interests sensed some political imperative to support woman suffrage, their initial stands signaled less than full commitment to the cause. Moreover, with none of these third parties exacting any noticeable influence in national

---

[20] Johnson, *National Party Platforms*, 47.

[21] McKee, *The National Conventions*, 172.

[22] And over this time, the party held steady (and low) in the presidential race: 9,522 (.1%) in 1876 and 10,305 (.1%) in 1880.

[23] Language of the planks found in McKee, *The National Conventions*. The Greenback plank read: "For the purpose of testing the sense of the people upon the subject, we are in favor of submitting to the people an amendment to the Constitution in favor of suffrage, regardless of sex, and also on the subject of liquor traffic" (McKee, 217).

elections, their support did little to bring woman suffrage to the mainstream of partisan politics.

Although the major national parties as yet showed little interest in woman suffrage, and although suffragists' third party supporters had yet to make much headway in national elections, the issue did receive some attention in national politics in the decades after the Civil War. As with early consideration in many states, however, the politics of woman suffrage at this point were personal rather than partisan. A delegation of woman suffragists was regularly sent to and received by committees in the U.S. Congress, with the committees often granting the suffragists an official hearing. Indeed, the Senate established a select committee on the rights of women, which became a regular venue for suffragists' petitions and testimony. Hearings generally entailed speeches by suffragists and platitudes from members of Congress. The resolution adopted in the Senate committee at the conclusion of the 1882 suffrage hearing there was a characteristic response: "That the committee are under obligation to the representatives of the women of the United States for their attendance this morning and for the able and instructive addresses which have been made, and that the committee assure them that they will give to the important subject of woman suffrage that careful and impartial consideration which its grave importance demands." With only the woman suffragists petitioning and lobbying on behalf of voting rights for women, party politicians seemed bound only to treat the individual activists with the personal respect due them on account of their class and gender, rather than to engage their political cause.[24]

Still, the Senate granted woman suffrage its first consideration on the floor of the U.S. Congress during its 1887 session, bringing the issue up for debate and a roll call vote. Newspaper accounts generally associated the push for a vote on the suffrage amendment in this session with an individual senator, Henry William Blair, a Republican from New Hampshire. Indeed, the *New York Times* went so far as to lament on the suffragists' behalf that the measure was not forwarded by a different senator, not because any different outcome was to be expected, but because his pageantry would have been more entertaining. "If they had entrusted their cause to Senator Hoar," the paper declared, "they might not have got more votes, but they would have got a good deal more enjoyment from the campaign... when partisanship is not involved, he is of fine and pungent flavor."[25] As the *Times* suggested, debate on

---

[24] The 1882 hearing and resolution are reported in *The New York Times*, January 21, 1882. The suffragists' comments during the Senate hearings of 1880 and 1884 are reprinted in the *Congressional Record-Senate*, 1887, 992–1002.

[25] Quoted passage from *The New York Times*, January 26, 1887. George Hoar was a prominent Republican senator from Massachusetts (grandson of Founder Roger Sherman). Blair became so much the personality attached to the woman suffrage cause in the Senate in this time period that an extended essay published in the *Times* on the daily business of the Senate, a full paragraph was devoted to Blair and his "admirers" in the ladies' gallery. See "Senators on the Floor." *The New York Times*, September 28, 1890.

the floor generally reflected the personal, rather than partisan, considerations brought to bear on the issue of voting rights for women. The opposing senators mainly invoked appeals to norms or "natural laws" of gender that segregated men's and women's spheres as their main impetus for resistance to the suffrage amendment. In summation of his long speech on the amendment, for example, Joseph Brown of Georgia pronounced that the woman suffrage "movement is an attempt to reverse the very laws of our being, and to drag woman into an arena for which she is not suited, and to devolve upon her onerous duties which the Creator never intended that she should perform."[26] Supporters generally argued against this sort of resistance with claims about women's capacity and appeals to Republican principles, pointing to examples of women as rulers in other countries and even as voters in Washington Territory. And the result was a resounding defeat of the amendment by a vote of only sixteen in favor and thirty-four opposed. In fact, more senators – twenty-six of them – were absent for the vote than voted in support of it.

Although the Senate's contemplation of the woman suffrage amendment hardly seemed partisan, it is true that there were no Democrats among the sixteen supporters. Indeed, Southerners – all of whom were Democrats – were the Senate's most vocal opponents. And traces of reasoning for a Southern resistance were scattered in their commentary. Most notably, Brown's speech touched upon the possibility that "the ignorant and less refined portions of the female population" might be most likely to vote. Brown expounded upon a Southern interest in this fact, imploring his fellow senators to "comprehend the fact if universal suffrage should be established that we will, especially in the Southern States, add a very large number to the voting population whose ignorance utterly disqualifies them from discharging the trust." The reference was, of course, to the large population of black women in the South, and to the difficulty that Southern Democrats might face in doubling the number of people whose votes would need to be suppressed or controlled to maintain Democratic control in the South. Yet, although this sort of partisan consideration may have driven Southern, and thereby Democratic, opposition, it seems Republicans were unconvinced. More Republicans voted against the bill or failed to show up for the vote than voted for it, an outcome that hardly

---

[26] Brown's remarks from the *Congressional Record-Senate*, 1887, 983. For as much as Blair was recognized as the amendment's protagonist, Brown, a Democrat, was its known adversary. If anyone should have played a partisan card, it should have been Brown, a well-known partisan opportunist. He was Democratic governor of Georgia before and during secession, became a Republican politician during Reconstruction, and switched back to the Democratic fold as Redemption took hold. He was also known to use public goods for his own private gain, having been involved in convict leasing and in forwarding railroad interests (he was at one point head of the Western Atlantic Railroad Co.). See "Joseph Emerson Brown," *Biographical Directory of the United States Congress*; and "Georgia's New Senator," *The New York Times*, November 26, 1880.

TABLE 6.8. *State Characteristics by Senators' Votes on Woman Suffrage in U.S. Senate, 1887*

	Yes	No		Did not Vote	
		All	Republicans	All	Republicans
Partisan Competition Scale	.94	.85	.89	.85	.84*
Farms Per Capita	.07	.08	.07	.08	.07
Labor – Manufacturing $ per 1,000	4.3	3.7*	4.1	3.8	4.3
Percent Population Urban	38	25*	35	31	40
Percent Population Black	1	22*	5	13	1.5
Percent Population Racial Minorities	2	22*	7	15*	2
Percent Population Foreign Born	25	11*	24	17	26
Percent Population Female	47	49	47	48	48
Number of Senators	16	34	11	26	14

* Statistically different from "yes" voters, p < .05, two-tailed t-test

suggests Republicans believed the argument that woman suffrage would challenge Democratic dominance in the South.

With a roll call vote on the suffrage amendment, it is possible to compare systematically the possible incentives of supporters and opponents. Table 6.8 provides a description of supporters and opponents of the measure by reporting the state characteristics of the average senator who cast a vote in favor of the amendment, the average senator who voted against the amendment, and the average senator who failed to appear for the Senate's consideration and vote on the measure.[27] The table also further breaks down opponents and nonvoters to display separately the description of the average Republican in each of those categories, so that possible differences in political incentives between supporters (all Republican) and opponents within their own party might be discerned. Comparison of the first two columns reflects the Southern unison on opposition to woman suffrage. The description of the difference between the average supporter and opponent reflects the differences between Northern and Southern states: an opponent was significantly more likely to come from a state that was less urban, had less manufacturing and fewer immigrants, and had more racial minorities than a supporter. Yet Southern opposition alone did not imply defeat for the amendment. With just sixteen of the Senate's forty-one Republicans supporting the measure, the lack of Republican support was nearly as troubling for suffragists as the Southern Democratic resistance. Looking to

[27] The measures used here are almost entirely the same as those used in the statistical analysis of state action in the previous section. Additional measures of population characteristics come from the U.S. Census.

the third column of Table 6.8, however, fails to suggest a racial, partisan – or any other political – imperative that might differentiate Republican supporters and opponents. Indeed, the only discernible difference among Republicans was that those who felt the need to attend the Senate session and actually cast their votes were from more partisan competitive states than those who failed to attend. That partisan competition was related to being present to vote, rather than which side the senator chose, would seem to suggest only that electoral competition placed higher demands on Senators to participate in the body's decisions.

Although the last decade of the nineteenth century brought woman suffrage victories in a number of states, including the full enfranchisement of women in Wyoming, Colorado, Idaho, and Utah, the issue languished in national politics. Suffrage activists continued their petitioning of Congress, but the Anthony amendment was not reported out of committee in either chamber. The inclusion of woman suffrage in the Populist agenda, however, seemed to exert some pressure on the politicization of women's rights. Republicans explicitly addressed the idea that women's activism might have partisan consequence through a plank in their party platform in 1892. Still, the Republican stance was more vague commentary on the political role of women, and promised no specific rights – suffrage or otherwise:

The Republican party is mindful of the rights and interests of women, and believes that they should be accorded equal opportunities, equal pay for equal work, and protection to the home. We favor the admission of women to wider spheres of usefulness and welcome their co-operation in rescuing the country from Democratic and Populist mismanagement and misrule.[28]

By the early part of the twentieth century, it seemed suffragists were becoming more cognizant of the need for partisan – rather than personal or principled – support for their cause. The national leadership of the NAWSA had always committed itself to nonpartisanship, in part to avoid engendering partisan resistance to their cause or alienating suffragists with differing partisan sympathies. Yet, nonpartisanship on the part of the organized movement was also important because, as Anthony's commentary in the 1884 committee hearing suggested, arguments for equal rights for women were deeply tied to arguments about women's equality with men – including their equal capacity to think about politics and choose a partisan side.[29] These tensions – between the need for partisan efforts on their behalf and their commitments to a feminist logic for suffrage; between the leverage on political outcomes that a partisan approach could offer and the risk of narrowing support for the issue by attaching partisan meaning – challenged the movement's leadership. What emerged was the logic

---

[28] Johnson, *National Party Platforms*, 109.

[29] See Marilley, Suzanne M., *Woman Suffrage and the Origins of Liberal Feminism in the United States, 1820–1920* (Cambridge, Massachusetts: Harvard University Press, 1996).

of petitioning at the state level for limited enfranchisement of women by simple acts of the legislature. Given that the U.S. Constitution reserved the power to define the qualifications of electors for President to state legislatures, and that most state constitutions left it within state legislators' prerogative to set the definitions of qualified voters for many state and municipal offices, it seemed possible that suffrage rights for women might be won with a narrower base of support. This state-level strategy was forwarded by NAWSA's Henry Blackwell in the latter part of the first decade of the twentieth century, although it seems even Blackwell was still struggling with how, exactly, it would work. "The more I consider it, the more I feel convinced," wrote Blackwell in 1909 to the president of the Illinois chapter of the NAWSA, "that each state society would be wise if it would petition *exclusively*, and *at each session of its state legislature* for the *National* (i.e., presidential) suffrage by simple act of legislation." That the approach would bring change sooner because an act was institutionally easier to pass than a constitutional amendment was straightforward logic. That having a political party decide woman suffrage was in its interest meant that the party did the work of convincing members of the legislature to support the issue was also an easy to understand feature of the strategy. Yet *how* to get partisan interest was still a missing piece. At this point, Blackwell made use of a logic he surely must have questioned, asserting that "sooner or later, one of the two great National parties, having control of a legislature, in order to secure the women's votes, will hold a caucus . . . and make it *a party issue*."[30] Not only had NAWSA leaders already realized the political dubiousness of the promise of votes from women in return for their enfranchisement, but this logic gave suffrage activists no agency other than attempting to demonstrate political unity among women. And that strategy was never pursued by NAWSA.

Having realized the importance of partisan interest in extending voting rights, what NAWSA activists had yet to comprehend fully was how activism might engender that interest outside of the strategic enfranchisement framework. That is, without promising women would deliver a new vote margin for a specific party, how could partisan interest be conveyed or cultivated? The missing piece of Blackwell's strategy was an understanding of how the preferences of existing voters could pressure the parties into seeing a political imperative for supporting women's enfranchisement. Suffragists, in other words, needed a programmatic enfranchisement strategy. There was already evidence of this fact in the politics of women's enfranchisement at the state level. As detailed in Chapter 2, for example, Colorado's suffrage politics suggested a successful programmatic enfranchisement path. And as political circumstance

---

[30] Letter from Henry Blackwell to Catharine Waugh McCulloch, March 3, 1909. Papers of Catherine Waugh McCulloch, Schlesinger Library of the Radcliffe Institute for Advanced Study. Emphasis in original. Blackwell is also given credit for forwarding the strategy in the HWS, vol. 5, 369.

would have it, an opportunity not unlike the one in Colorado presented itself at the national level within just a few years' time. In 1912, the national partisan landscape was changed by the bolting of Theodore Roosevelt from the regular Republican Party to run on the ticket of a new Progressive "Bull Moose" label. Herein, woman suffrage found its first truly partisan meaning in national politics, and its first serious consideration by national lawmakers.

From Personal to Political – The Programmatic Path to the Nineteenth Amendment

By 1911, NAWSA activists had come to the full realization that they needed some way to exert electorally-based influence on lawmakers' positions on the suffrage issue. Among the strategies to emerge in explicit response to this understanding was a new organizational plan, called the "plan for political district organization." The plan, as laid out in official correspondence from the NAWSA leadership to its affiliated state organizations, entailed "the enrollment, without dues, of the adult population in favor of woman suffrage, in every political district in the state." The idea of the organization, which would become known as the Woman's Party, was for suffragists to organize themselves in a structure that mimicked the political parties, with district committees and even precinct captains. This structure was intended to be used to both drum up and demonstrate the existence of district-based demand for woman suffrage; to both prepare such that if a "referendum occurs the election district or precinct will be carried for woman suffrage," and "to put behind every legislator a woman suffrage constituency."[31]

Although the idea of the Woman's Party was for direct influence on major party lawmakers, its institution was a timely, if unknown, preparation for a different partisan opportunity. In the summer of 1912, the Republican Party, because of growing internal fissures over its policy platform and leadership choices, fractured. The dynamic former President Roosevelt led an exodus from the regular Republican fold, and the national Progressive "Bull Moose" party was formed. With just months before the next national elections, the Progressives found themselves in need of an instant party structure. The leadership turned to existing organizations as the basis for that structure, and the well-organized suffrage movement was a prime potential partner. Not only did suffragists have skills and resources useful to the new party, but extension of the franchise also fit well with the reform agenda that the Progressives were advocating. In a platform that already featured several other policies that would increase citizens' involvement in governance, including the rights of initiative, referendum, and direct election of U.S. senators, voting rights for women was a credible addition. And so suffragists found themselves, for the first time,

---

[31] Quoted passages from memo on "Plan for Political District Organization in the States," attached to letter from NAWSA to board members, January 23, 1911. Catharine Waugh McCulloch Papers.

with the interest of a political party that was expected to garner more than single-digit percentages at the presidential polls.

To be sure, the support for woman suffrage was not an immediate part of the Progressive agenda. Roosevelt had been noncommittal during his previous time in the White House, and – as a Progressive candidate – first took the position that women had not yet demonstrated sufficient interest in being enfranchised. Candidate Roosevelt, however, made a very public conversion to full support of woman suffrage in June. The rhetoric Roosevelt offered on the suffrage issue suggested that Progressives in fact believed endorsement of woman suffrage would not only garner them the support of the movement, but also appeal to the labor interests that they were attempting to attract to the Progressive ticket. Given that organized labor had already demonstrated their own interest in the extension of woman suffrage, including explicit demands from the American Federation of Labor (AFL) for partisan endorsement of woman suffrage, the connections Roosevelt drew were unsurprising. In one speech, Roosevelt claimed he "grew to believe in woman suffrage not because of associating with women whose chief interest was in woman suffrage, but because of finding out that the women from whom I received the most aid in endeavoring to grapple with the social and industrial problems of the day were themselves believers in woman suffrage." Indeed, his comments on woman suffrage in his speech at the Progressive Party convention were about the need of workingwomen for the power of the ballot. "Workingwomen have the same need for protection that workingmen have," was Roosevelt's first comment on his suffrage stance at the convention, and the rest of his remarks on woman suffrage carried on the workingwoman theme.[32] The convention then went on to adopt a plank pronouncing the party's full support for equal voting rights for women:

The Progressive Party, believing that no people can justly claim to be a true democracy which denies political rights on account of sex, pledges itself to the task of securing equal suffrage to men and women alike.[33]

By late summer, it seemed the Progressive endorsement had brought some results for both the new party and for the suffrage cause. Women workers,

[32] Roosevelt had been friendly to the idea of woman suffrage but unwilling to make any call for government action while in office. See, for example, coverage of his response to suffragist lobbying in *The New York Times*, October 18, 1908. Leading up to the 1912 exodus from the Republican Party, Roosevelt declared that he believed that there should be a referendum of women on the issue of woman suffrage. See "Roosevelt is for Woman Suffrage," *The New York Times*, February 3, 1912. Public announcement of Roosevelt's suffrage conversion came on June 12, 1912. See "Roosevelt a Suffragist," *The New York Times*, June 13, 1912 and "Suffrage Secret is Told," *The New York Times*, June 17, 1912. Quote from Roosevelt public speech appears in "How Women Won Roosevelt to Them," *The New York Times*, August 31, 1912. The AFL made an explicit demand for a woman suffrage plank in the Republican national platform in 1908. See "What Labor Demands," *The New York Times*, June 18, 1908. Roosevelt's entire convention speech was reprinted in *The New York Times*, August 7, 1912.

[33] Johnson, *National Party Platforms*, 176.

many from the suffrage movement, were employed in the essential day-to-day business of the party. Women fundraised and provided administrative and clerical services. They assisted in district canvassing for the new party. And some well-known women activists with strong ties to the suffrage movement were deployed by the party for higher-profile public appearances. Most notable was the Progressives' use of Chicago's Hull House founder and NAWSA vice president Jane Addams as a draw for crowds across the country, including a whirlwind tour of the Pacific states.[34] Woman suffrage, in exchange, was receiving more attention in the realm of partisan politics. In August, *The New York Times* reported that there were expectations that Taft or at least some regular Republican candidates for state offices might "take up woman suffrage as a counter move to Col. Roosevelt's campaign in that direction." Yet, the *Times* also noted that although the Republican candidate for governor in Ohio seemed to be pursuing that strategy, Taft's campaign claimed he would not follow. At this point the *Times* and the Taft campaign seemed to fail to understand fully the coalitional reasons for support of woman suffrage, as the reasoning for the lack of support from the Taft campaign followed a strategic, rather than programmatic, enfranchisement logic:

The opinion here is that in years past States have remained Republican or Democratic regardless of woman suffrage and that the granting of this suffrage in particular states did not change the political complexion in these States one whit. As the men had voted before, so the women voted afterward. It is thought that will be the case in November. In suffrage states the vote, it is anticipated, will be multiplied by two, but the ratio between Taftites, Bull Moosers, and Democrats will not be shifted by the addition of the women's vote.[35]

Although it appeared that the regular parties doubted that woman suffrage would bring them the votes of women, both Republicans and Democrats made symbolic gestures to "women" – perhaps just in case some might be swayed. Most visibly, each party appointed a few women to posts within the party organization and eventually created women's bureaus or departments. As the campaign progressed, however, competition between the parties to claim the mantle of "reform" through women's involvement or women's issues grew. In an extensive piece on the involvement of women in the party organizations, *The New York Times* highlighted this pattern:

As a matter of fact, very little is being said about votes for women by any of the women connected with the three parties. Laws to better the lot of women and children is what is being urged, and each organization is doing everything possible to prove that this

---

[34] Documentation of the involvement of women, particularly suffragists, in the work of the Progressive Party is collected in the Papers of Catherine Waugh McCulloch. See also "Women Get Seats in All Party Councils," *The New York Times*, August 14, 1912, which reports the comparative extent of involvement of women in the Progressive Party organization and also comments on how the women workers in all the parties were suffragists.

[35] "Taft to Avoid Suffrage," *The New York Times*, August 12, 1912.

result will brought about more rapidly by the election of Gov. Wilson, Mr. Taft, or Col. Roosevelt, as the case may be.[36]

Within the Taft campaign, the women's department pushed the idea that the Republican Party was tied to the interests of the clubwomen who had worked for reforms in the interest of women and children. Their attempt was to claim that the Republican Party was the home of those truly interested in reform principles, rather than their own voting rights. "Republican women," wrote the secretary of the department in a letter to *The New York Times*, "are working now, as they have worked in campaigns since 1888, for principles.... They know the Republican Party has stood always for the welfare of women, as well as for the votes of women... their work in this campaign is not for man or woman, not to attract suffragists or anti-suffragists... but to make known to all that that best interests of all lie in continuing Republican policies." Taft, however, never would become a supporter of a national woman suffrage amendment.[37] The refrain within the Democratic women's bureau was quite similar – women's role in pushing for government reform and policies that benefited workers was touted. "Women should add their influence to those who are struggling to bring politics into the open, to make politics the business of the whole people," remarked the chair of the Democratic women's department to the *Times*. She also pointed to Wilson's record on laws to protect "women wage earners," proclaiming that "[w]hat he has done on behalf of women, children, the home, health, &c., fills a large pamphlet." Rhetoric from the Progressive women's bureau was similar, but more explicitly bore the theme that woman suffrage was part of accomplishing a reform agenda. Of the connection between suffrage and Progressive sentiment, the Progressive chair remarked that "[i]t is no longer women for the vote alone, it is women standing for the right and protection of working women, the preservation of children, help to the stranger aliens, insistence on health standards, and, above all, freedom of thought and action."[38]

In November, the Progressives took 27.4% of the popular vote for president, and eighty-eight electoral votes. The Progressive success in splitting the Republican base – Taft won only eight electoral votes – allowed the Democrat, Woodrow Wilson, to take the office of President with only 41.8% of the popular vote. It also put Democrats in solid control of both houses of Congress. Thus, although the Progressive Party failed to take the White House, and won only a handful of congressional seats, their electoral influence provided leverage for Progressive causes on those in office. Without concessions to its Progressive

[36] "Women as a Factor in the Political Campaign," *The New York Times*, September 1, 1912.

[37] Letter to the editor of *The New York Times* by Mary Wood, Secretary, Department of Women's Work, Republican National Committee, September 7, 1912 (published September 9, 1912). Taft's wife, in fact, would become associated with an anti-suffrage organization.

[38] Quotes of Republican and Progressive women's department chairs from "Women as a Factor in the Political Campaign," *The New York Times*, September 1, 1912.

faction, the Republican Party stood on losing ground. And without some appeal at least to those Independents who had been swept into the Progressive push, Democrats stood no chance of garnering a safe electoral majority. With woman suffrage a conspicuous feature of the Progressive platform, it seemed that the incentives for programmatic enfranchisement of women were in place. In fact, if politicians generally believed the evidence that women's enfranchisement was unlikely to tie women to any particular political party, woman suffrage would have seemed one of the policies on the Progressive platform that would be least threatening to politicians' power – certainly less so than the devolution to the people of the power to choose Senators and to legislate through the initiative and referendum.

To be sure, the place of woman suffrage in the electoral politics of 1912 did not win the issue instant consideration in the new Congress. Still, it would appear on the floor of the Senate before the next election cycle, and face a roll call vote there in March of 1914. True to the partisan infusion the issue received in 1912, consideration of the suffrage amendment on the floor was markedly different than its previous contemplations. This time, although commentary on gender roles was not entirely absent, rather than long speeches on women's place and lighthearted ponderings about senators' personal interest in the issue, the discourse surrounding the enfranchisement of woman was primarily of partisan interests in suffrage rights, and of the federal government's role in defining electoral qualifications. Indeed, a number of senators felt it necessary to explain their positions on the Anthony amendment as constrained by states' rights principles. One Texas senator explained that, "I believe women should be accorded the right to vote. [But] I am not yet convinced that this question of suffrage is a proper subject for Federal jurisdiction." Another senator from Maryland explained he would vote against the amendment on "the ground that I believe it is a matter for regulation by the States." In due course, woman suffrage was interwoven with positions on the desirability of the Fifteenth Amendment, so much so that there was an attempt to add language to the Anthony amendment that some believed might undo the federal protections of blacks' voting rights.[39]

Although the Anthony amendment ultimately failed to pass, this time it garnered the support of more than one-third of the Senate. Again, the roll call votes enable some systematic investigation of the possible incentives behind senators' positions, the results of which are displayed in Table 6.9. This time, the support crossed party lines; fourteen Democrats, twenty Republicans, as well as the Senate's sole Progressive cast their votes in favor of woman suffrage. With floor debate entwining the perils of the Fifteenth Amendment and any federal action on woman suffrage, however, it is unsurprising that Southern senators remained almost unanimously opposed, with just three willing

---

[39] Consideration of the Anthony amendment appears in the *Congressional Record-Senate*, 1914, 5088–108. Quoted passages on page 5091.

TABLE 6.9. *State Characteristics by Senators' Votes on Woman Suffrage in U.S. Senate, 1914*

	Yes		No		Not Voting	
	Suffrage States	Non-suffrage States	All	Non-South	All	Non-South
Percent Vote Progressive	30	25	21	26	26	29
Partisan Competition Scale	.85	.80	.66	.89	.79	.85
NAWSA Membership per 1000	.1	1.5	1.3	2.1	.5	.6
Farms Per Capita	.06	.08	.09	.07	.08	.07
Labor – Manufacturing $ per 1,000	3.9	3.8	4.1	4.3	4.1	4.2
Percent Population Urban	44	38	36	46	42	46
Percent Population Black	1	5	19	2	8	2
Percent Population Racial Minorities	5	6	21	5	11	6
Percent Population Foreign Born	17	16	10	18	14	16
Percent Population Female	46	47	49	48	48	48
Number of Senators	16	19	34	16	26	20

Entries are means within each category.

to vote in favor of the new federal amendment. The only other unmistakable pattern in the votes was the support from senators representing states in which women were already enfranchised. Of the twenty senators representing states in which women were able to vote in statewide elections, sixteen voted for the Anthony amendment; only one voted against the federal suffrage provision. Although it might be tempting to attribute this pattern to the notion that these senators felt they might be voted out of office by "women" if they failed to cast their votes in favor of the Anthony amendment, it is just as consistent with the interpretation that these senators felt accountable to all of their constituents who had expressed an interest in women's voting rights – male and female. Indeed, given that most states at this point had incorporated woman suffrage through a constitutional amendment process that included a public referendum registering majority support for woman suffrage among male voters, and that the balance of power between the two major parties had not been drastically changed in the aftermath, the latter interpretation seems far more likely.

Despite the loss for the Anthony amendment in the 1914 Senate session, the push onto the partisan politics agenda for the issue of woman suffrage provided by the Progressives in the 1912 elections cemented its place there. In their next national conventions in 1916, the Democratic and Republican national parties finally addressed the issue of woman suffrage formally, although each did fall short of endorsing the Anthony amendment and took a decidedly states' rights stance on the issue:

The Democratic Party – We recommend the extension of the franchise to the women of this country, State by State, on the same terms as to the men.

The Republican Party – The Republican party, reaffirming its faith in government of the people, by the people, for the people, as a measure of justice to one-half the adult people of this country, favors the extension of the suffrage to women, but recognizes the right of each State to settle this question for itself.[40]

Despite the pressure the major parties faced to respond to the issue of woman suffrage, the final push toward the amendment still took further effort on the part of suffrage activists and their supporters. The Anthony amendment would face three more votes in the Senate and three more in the House before it finally found its way into the ratification process. Given the apparent leverage of state-level suffrage measures on senators' votes in 1914, the tactic of pressing more states for adoption of woman suffrage provisions for the sake of increasing pressure for the federal amendment was aggressively pursued by NAWSA. NAWSA President Catt introduced the so-called "Winning Plan" at an "emergency convention" of the organization in 1916. Billed as the venue for debate and discussion of the proper strategy for NAWSA to pursue in the interest of "the uniformity [of activism] that is essential to the final success now within our reach," the convention opened with debate among those activists who preferred to use movement resources strictly toward lobbying for congressional action, those – mostly Southern – activists who preferred suffrage to come without adoption of the federal amendment, and those activists who endorsed the plan of tandem action. Catt's plan, however, seemed a forgone conclusion, and was adopted and implemented in short order.[41] Over the ensuing two and half years, seventeen states adopted policies that enlarged the voting rights of women at the state level, many through legislative enactment of provisions qualifying women as voters for presidential electors. As the previous section and chapters show, coalitional, partisan politics were key to those victories.

In the Senate's final consideration of the Anthony amendment in 1919, the fruits of suffragists' long and complicated campaign were evident. When

---

[40] Johnson, *National Party Platforms*, 199, 207.
[41] Catt, Carrie Chapman. "Crisis in Suffrage Movement, Says Mrs. Catt," *The New York Times*, September 3, 1916.

the Senate passed the measure by a vote of fifty-six in favor and twenty-five opposed (with fifteen Senators not voting), forty-one of the amendment's supporters were from states with woman suffrage provisions. Moreover, just five Senators hailing from states where women were permitted to vote in at least some statewide elections cast their votes against the federal provision. And congruent with the coalitional, cross-partisan nature of the protracted suffrage campaign, the vote was bipartisan: nearly half of the chamber's Democrats and more than 70 percent of its Republicans supported the amendment on the final floor vote. To be sure, the victory was not a complete one. Most notably, although challenged, notions of maintaining proper gender roles and questions about women's capacity for politics were still entertained as legitimate points of contention on the Senate floor. Yet, woman suffrage was engaged far more in terms of its political meaning.

In this final consideration, resistance to the Anthony amendment was still heavily southern, and explicitly tied in floor debate to concerns over any way in which further federal control of voting laws might undo the repression of blacks' voting rights in the South. "This [legislation] opens up anew the negro question in all the Southern States," declared one senator from Florida, "and I warn my colleagues from the South who are supporting this measure that they are 'playing with fire,' which is likely to produce another 'reconstruction' conflagration in our Southland." There are reasons to believe, however, that the concerns were not only about avenues for federal intervention, but also about the viability of extending Southern repression tactics to black women. That same Florida senator, for example, went on to quote a passage from *The Crisis*, the publication of the National Association for the Advancement of Colored People (NAACP) that pointed to such a possibility. "It is going to be more difficult to disfranchise colored women in the South than it was to disfranchise colored men. Even Southern 'gentlemen,' as used as they are to the mistreatment of colored women, can not in the blaze of present publicity physically beat them away from the polls." Although the Senator was using the passage in an attempt to indict suffragists, notably Jane Addams who held officer positions in both the NAACP and NAWSA, on the charge of meddling in Southern racial politics in the interest of forwarding the Republican Party, its content presented a salient concern for Southern politicians. The "negro problem" was one of overcoming legal obstacles to keeping blacks in a politically and economically subordinate position; without control over the legal apparatus that enfranchised women, the Southern states would, in fact, be dealing with a greater "problem."[42] Nonetheless, the behavior of Southern senators from states that had already adopted woman suffrage (Texas, Arkansas, and Tennessee) was consistent with the notion that other political considerations pressured them away from casting

[42] *Congressional Record-Senate*, 1919, 90.

TABLE 6.10. *Predictors of Voting in Favor of Woman Suffrage in U.S. Senate,*
1919

	All Senators	Non-Southern Senators
Percent Vote Progressive	7.1	11.3*
	(6.0)	(5.5)
Partisan Competition Scale	−1.4	9.0*
	(2.7)	(4.2)
Republican Senator	1.1	0.7
	(1.2)	(1.5)
State Has Woman Suffrage	1.3	0.5
	(0.8)	(1.3)
NAWSA Membership per 1,000	0.2	−0.8
	(0.6)	(0.8)
Farms Per Capita	−18.9	19.7
	(12.1)	(41.9)
Labor – Manufacturing Dollars per 1,000	−1.9	−0.2
	(1.2)	(0.9)
Percent Population Urban	−0.1	−0.3
	(3.5)	(3.8)
Percent Population Racial Minorities	−3.2	27.0
	(5.0)	(31.4)
Number of Senators	79	56

Entries are coefficients and standard errors from a logistic regression. Standard errors are corrected for clustering by state.

their votes based on the "negro problem" logic: none voted against the federal amendment.

That the sources of support and opposition to woman suffrage on this final vote were firmly rooted in political considerations is made clearer in a systematic analysis of the roll call votes, the results of which are presented Table 6.10. The statistical analysis performed is a multivariate model of support for woman suffrage, wherein state characteristics representing incentives for programmatic enfranchisement are used to predict the likelihood that a Senator cast his vote in favor of the Anthony amendment. Most of the included explanatory factors are the same predictors used in the models of state activity on woman suffrage in the previous section: competitiveness of elections in the state, level of NAWSA membership, number of farms, manufacturing capital, urbanicity, and the presence of racial minorities are all included. One important difference for the model of senators' votes is that in consideration of the federal amendment the relevant third party pressure is taken to be the state electorate's receptiveness to the Progressive push in national politics, and thus the included measure of third party influence is the percent of the state's vote that went to the Progressive presidential ticket in 1912. Another important difference is that whether or not the state has already adopted suffrage may act on senators' willingness to extend suffrage rights to women at the federal level, and so an indicator variable for whether or not the state already had some form of voting rights for women in statewide elections is included.

The model is estimated first for all Senators and then again using only the votes from non-Southern senators. Given the unique preoccupation among Southern senators with the implication of federal intervention in voting rights, and their unique ability to make a resonant states rights' argument premised on the tenuous maintenance of racial order, Southern senators perhaps stood uniquely able to resist the coalitional pressures for political support for the Anthony amendment.[43] Indeed, the contrast between the two models suggests that non-Southern senators were uniquely affected by partisan incentives. All else equal, among senators from non-Southern states, greater two-party competition and greater influence of the Progressives at the polls in the 1912 elections indicated a greater likelihood that they would cast their votes in favor of the Anthony amendment. This is evident in the positive, statistically significant coefficients on the Progressive vote and partisan competition variables in the results of the model when estimated using just non-Southern senators, displayed in the second column of Table 6.10. When Southerners are included, those relationships are masked. That is, the first column of the table, displaying the results when all senators who cast their votes on the Anthony amendment, shows no significant relationships between any of the possible incentives and the likelihood of voting in favor of the amendment.

As important as it is to notice that Progressive sentiment and party competition in senators' home states were significantly linked to their propensities to vote in favor of the Anthony amendment, it is also noteworthy that the indicator of whether their state had woman suffrage was not a significant predictor of senators' final votes. This result speaks to the importance of understanding the state politics that drove adoption of suffrage in the first place. It suggests that the most important piece of information for senators was not that women were enfranchised in their home states, but that important influences in their preexisting male electorates had already conveyed their political interest in having women's voting rights enacted. In other words, what mattered most in the Senate's decision to pass the Anthony amendment at this moment was not simply that more Senators were accountable to women voters, but that they

---

[43] The model was also estimated as a fully interactive one, using all senators and interacting each predictor with a "dummy" variable indicating the senator was from a Southern state. The results for the baseline coefficients, which would indicate the effects among non-southern senators, were substantively and statistically similar to those generated when the model was run on non-Southern senators only. These results are robust to alternative specifications. In contrast, with few yes voters among Southerners, the results for the interactive terms (or for a South-only model) are more fragile to alternative specifications, but are suggestive that the adopters in the South were from places where the Progressives had greater influence.

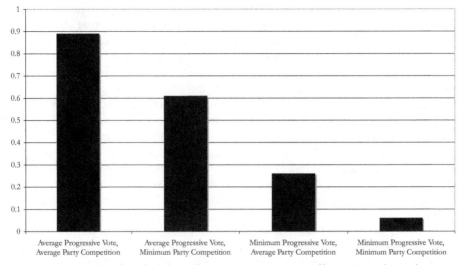

FIGURE 6.4. Predicted Probability of Supporting Woman Suffrage Amendment by State Partisan Incentives, U.S. Senate 1919.

felt themselves beholden to the political pressures that had put woman suffrage into effect in their states.[44]

To illustrate the connection between partisan incentives and non-Southern senators' likelihood of voting for the Anthony amendment on its final passage, Figure 6.4 compares the predicted probabilities that a Senator with specific partisan profiles in his state would vote in favor of the amendment. The probability displayed in the first column of the figure is calculated from the results of the model for non-Southern senators presented in Table 6.10 based on a Republican Senator from a non-suffrage state with otherwise average state characteristics. Such a Senator, the model predicts, would have nearly a 90 percent chance of voting in favor of the amendment. That the "average" senator, even from a non-suffrage state, was very likely to support the amendment is certainly consistent with the outcome that more than 70 percent of non-Southern senators did, indeed, cast their votes in favor. What the subsequent columns highlight, however, was just how much a senator's likelihood of supporting the measure dropped off when the politics in his home state reflected

[44] In fact, if an additional variable is added to the model to indicate whether or not woman suffrage was adopted in the state before the Progressive push, the coefficient on indicator on simply having suffrage goes decidedly to zero (b = .09, s.e. = 1.3, p = .94), whereas the indicator for the early adopters is positive, although still not significant by conventional standards (b = 2.6, s.e. = 2.2, p = .25). Other coefficients and standard error are not significantly changed in this alternative specification. This pattern is consistent with the argument that the relevant information that pushed the Senate from rejecting the amendment in 1914 to accepting it in 1919 was the change in their information about the importance of woman suffrage in ongoing partisan politics.

little sentiment in favor of the Progressive agenda and/or little competition for voters among the major political parties. Moving the senator's state-level partisan competition measure to the minimum among the non-Southern states, as column two shows, would move his likelihood of supporting the Anthony amendment down to near 60 percent. The third column shows the impact of Progressive sentiment in the state to be even greater. Replacing the average Progressive vote share with the minimum would move the Senator's likelihood of voting in favor of the amendment down to less than 30 percent. And if an otherwise average senator faced a home state where the third party movement received its least support and the major parties were least competitive, the fourth column in the figure illustrates that he would be almost certain to vote against the amendment.

Conclusion

This chapter began with the argument of NAWSA president Carrie Chapman Catt that the final victory for woman suffrage, the amendment to the U.S. Constitution, needed to be understood as the product of the years of activism that came before it. Embedded in that history was the cumulation of suffrage politics fought and decided across the states over the decades before the national amendment was won. This chapter has demonstrated both how those state-level decisions mattered in the politics of the national amendment and how those state decisions must be understood as products of politicians who felt pressured for the change by their existing constituents.

Whatever feats of organization suffrage activists accomplished, enfranchisement ultimately lay in the decisions of lawmakers – party politicians. Those politicians were unconvinced in the partisan utility of enfranchising women for the promise of their votes. Both politicians' own ideas about gender, including their assumptions that women would follow the leadership of their own husbands, fathers, and brothers, and the evidence fed back to them from early-adopting woman suffrage states suggested women would vote both Democratic and Republican – and, as men did, maybe occasionally for some third choice.[45] The incentive to deliver woman suffrage, then, needed to be cultivated in some other way, through some other political avenue. Ultimately, this chapter demonstrates, because the extension of voting rights to women was driven by politicians' responsiveness to the demands of already-enfranchised constituents, the strength of organizing women in support of their own voting rights did not lay in developing insurgency or "demand." Instead, what mattered most was the development of organizational resources that made woman suffrage

---

[45] For an academic treatment of women's voting patterns immediately following enfranchisement demonstrating the partisan similarity of women's and men's voting, see Joel H. Goldstein, *The Effects of the Adoption of Woman Suffrage: Sex Differences in Voting Behavior – Illinois, 1914–21* (New York: Praeger, 1984).

organizations attractive coalition partners for other groups – including third party organizations – who could in turn leverage power within partisan politics to affect policy change. Yet, where no such partnerships for suffrage could be built, women's voting rights remained a political impossibility.

The limitations suffrage activists faced as they pursued state-level enfranchisement were certainly fundamentally shaped by gender – and yet also, we have seen, in often-interconnected ways, by race. Importantly, the working notions of gender and "women's" interests constructed by white, middle-class suffragists affected the viability of coalitions built in favor of and opposed to extending voting rights to women. Moreover, it also shaped the political institutions proponents of woman suffrage faced; states facing salient political conflicts along the lines of racial identities had a strong tendency to build the infrastructure of politics in ways that resisted group-based challenges to the status quo. The result was that states with large non-white populations often presented nearly impossible political challenges for suffragists – no matter how large suffrage organization memberships and budgets grew. And when enough state-level sentiment in favor of woman suffrage had been registered such that the issue of a federal constitutional amendment finally achieved real consideration, the concern of maintaining racial order in the face of gender-based voter protections provided ammunition for stalwart Southern resistance.

Although it is true that the story of woman suffrage must be told with reference to its entire political history to uncover the sources of the movement's failures and successes, this chapter has also shown that the success of the Progressives in the 1912 election cycle was a particularly important political turning point for the fate of federal protection of women's voting rights. The Progressives' endorsement of the issue and integration of the organized suffrage movement, coupled with their critical role in deciding the outcome of the presidential election and partisan composition of Congress forced both major parties to respond to woman suffrage on the national level for the first time. Republicans, needing to herd bolters back into the party, and Democrats, unable to count on winning another election with far less than half of the popular vote, were uniquely pressured in these circumstances. The issue of woman suffrage was poised for a programmatic response only in the wake of the Progressive experience. When the final vote on the Anthony amendment was taken, the support was bipartisan and regional – drawing support from legislators in direct relation to the Progressive vote in 1912. And yet this response only came once suffragists had converted that Progressive leverage into a string of new suffrage states between 1915 and 1919.

7

From the Outside In

On the outside of politics women fought one of the strongest, bravest battles recorded in history, but to these men inside politics, some Republicans, some Democrats, and some members of minority parties, the women of the United States owe their enfranchisement.

– Carrie Chapman Catt and Nettie Rogers Shuler,
National American Woman Suffrage Association[1]

Women's Voting Rights – Coalitional Success in Party Politics

By the time the Nineteenth Amendment to the U.S. Constitution was ratified in 1920, woman suffrage in some form was already a reality in nearly every state. Thirty states had changed their laws to do away with sex qualifications to vote in elections of national consequence, either by striking the word male from the suffrage clauses of their state constitutions, or by amending state law to remove the sex qualification for presidential electors or primary voters. Statements that "women won the right to vote in 1920" – fairly common in histories of American politics – therefore, seem wildly inaccurate. Not only had some American women voted long before the election of 1920, but some American women would be waiting for decades more for their voting rights. The Nineteenth Amendment barred states from denying voting rights on account of sex; just like the Fifteenth Amendment, it made no guarantees against a myriad of other discriminating qualifications states might choose to impose. Women who could not pay a poll tax, pass a literacy test, or a "moral character" evaluation; American women who lost their citizenship by marrying a non-citizen man and women from immigrant groups barred from naturalization; and many American Indian women, via citizenship denials and other avenues, were all

---

[1] From *Woman Suffrage and Politics: The Inner Story of the Suffrage Movement* (New York, C. Scribner's Sons, 1926), 493.

still easily and legally excluded by state voter qualifications after the Nineteenth Amendment took effect. The Amendment was the crowning glory of organized suffragist activism, but both before and after its passage, state politics shaped women's inclusion in the American electorate.

The preceding chapters have engaged the question of state decisions on voting rights for women before the Nineteenth Amendment. I have argued that extending voting rights is a process of partisan politics, and hence that positive outcomes for the woman suffrage movement were driven by partisan considerations. Although in Chapter 1 I detailed two sets of partisan incentives that enable suffrage extension – what I term *strategic* and *programmatic enfranchisement* – success for suffragists (as previous chapters show) came in the form of programmatic enfranchisement. That is, changes in state laws came when suffragists could build coalitions with groups able to leverage for their cause from *inside* party politics; woman suffrage was delivered by politicians as part of a program of policies meant to appease their existing constituents. Suffragists surely attempted to gain voting rights on account of their promise of a voting bloc for a single political party – through strategic enfranchisement – but such attempts were marked by failure. In most instances, politicians saw far too much variation in the category "women" to believe that their party would benefit from a "women's vote." "It would only double the vote without changing the result" was an argument suffragists heard often enough against their cause to feature it in a 1917 publication refuting common anti-woman suffrage arguments.[2] Those places in which the women who would be enfranchised were quite likely to be loyal to a single party were states where one party had already established secure dominance, most notably in the Redeemed Democratic South, but also in Northeastern Republican strongholds. Where one party dominated, "women" were not needed as a new voting bloc, even if they could offer it through the imposition of the same means used to establish partisan homogeneity of the male electorate.

Forging partnerships with groups that could wield electoral and partisan influence for their cause, therefore, was key for suffragists.[3] Although suffragist propaganda and lobbying tactics might have changed preferences of both lawmakers and ordinary citizens, without electoral and/or partisan costs and benefits attached, legislators had little reason to work actively for the cause. Suffragists could change preferences; effective partnerships added salience. Large interest groups, such as farmers associations or labor unions, added electoral

[2] *"The Blue Book": Woman Suffrage, History, Arguments and Results*, edited by Frances M. Björkman and Annie G. Porritt (New York, National Woman Suffrage Publishing Co., Inc., 1917), 183.

[3] That pressure from inside party politics was key was certainly realized by the NAWSA leaders who strategized on how finally to win the Congressional vote on the national amendment. Carrie Chapman Catt's famous "winning plan" was to win enough state battles so that suffragists might more readily claim electoral pressure for their cause from enfranchised women. Park, Maud Wood, "The Winning Plan" in *Victory: How Women Won It*, National American Woman Suffrage Association, ed. (New York: The H. W. Wilson Company, 1940), 123–39.

consequence to the issue. Particularly persuasive partners were found in third parties. Not only did significant vote shares for third parties bring increased major party responsiveness to woman suffrage when it was part of the third parties' agendas, but third party members in state legislatures added the pressure of partisan legislative bargaining to the cause.

Yet developing and maintaining such coalitions was not a simple task for suffragists, nor was it always a strategy they pursued vigorously. Clashes over prioritization of goals ruined more than one suffrage partnership, even with other women's groups. In Illinois, for example, suffragists had gained labor union support through an alliance with the Women's Trade Union League. That partnership decayed, however, as middle-class suffragists' actions made it clear that women's workplace rights were deemed subordinate to voting rights. The connection between woman suffrage and third party politics grew both from the involvement of suffrage-interested women in the social movements at the base of a number of third parties, and from the recognition by third party politicians that well-organized, politically trained suffragists offered a resource base that such new parties desperately needed to take on their major party opponents. Of course, woman suffrage was not the central political goal of any of these parties, and in the trade-offs of party politics, the relationship did not always produce new voting rights.

Although this account has centered on the politics of women's voting rights before the Nineteenth Amendment, there are insights that apply more broadly in American politics. First, the frameworks of programmatic and strategic enfranchisement give us a new way to look at why the American electorate has expanded at particular historical moments – and perhaps also why it has sometimes contracted. Taking up the case of black voting rights, I turn to those questions in the next section – although American history obviously supplies many more cases to explore. There is also an important observation about the role of third parties in the development of American politics in this account of women's voting rights. Although many appeared only briefly, and many only at the level of state politics, one legacy of a number of third parties during the nineteenth and early twentieth centuries was a significant redefinition of the American electorate. I discuss what possibilities this insight may open for future representation of minority interests. Finally, I offer some thoughts about how the story of woman suffrage adds to existing work that pushes for scholars to broaden and deepen their conceptualizations of "women's rights" and "women's interests" in matters of politics.

History Repeating Itself? Electoral Exclusion and Inclusion of Black Americans

In Chapter 1, I argue that the enfranchisement of blacks in the United States through the passage of the Fifteenth Amendment was accomplished through strategic enfranchisement. Republicans, barely clinging to their national majority position, worked to grant blacks voting rights, anticipating that the party could profit from its claim as the liberator of the country's slave population by reaping the votes of these new citizens. Blacks were seen as a promising voting bloc, one the Republicans sorely needed, especially to have any electoral hope in the readmitted Confederate states. Yet, gaining voting rights via strategic enfranchisement did not necessarily win blacks' full incorporation into party politics. As argued by Paul Frymer, the certainty of Republicans about support from blacks after the Civil War made them a "captured constituency," a group whose political demands did not weigh heavy in party policy-making because party leaders believed they had nowhere else to go. The ultimate consequence was that when the new voting bloc was no longer necessary to produce the national domination Republicans hoped for, it was promptly abandoned. Having solidified their national control by 1896, Republicans allowed the South to be fully Redeemed.[4]

Redemption in the South meant, of course, that most black Americans were once again disfranchised; less than 10 percent of black Americans lived outside the former slave states at the turn of the twentieth century.[5] Their re-enfranchisement would take further federal intervention, which would not come for decades. In the second round of the politics of black voting rights, however, it is less clear that the simple strategic enfranchisement model applies. Democratic administrations delivered the most significant victories for black voting rights since the Fifteenth Amendment in the form of the Twenty-Fourth Amendment, which outlawed the poll tax upon its ratification in 1963, and the 1965 Voting Rights Act, which suspended the literacy test in a number of Southern states and set up a system of federal examination of voting rights and registration practices in areas with conspicuously low voter turnout or registration.[6] Did Democrats act merely on the strategy of capturing the votes of black Americans? As the party that had worked for decades to exclude blacks, it is much less clear that Democrats were sure to reap the votes of the newly enfranchised. Pursuing the black vote entirely for its own sake was a far riskier proposition for Democrats in 1965 than it had been for Republicans 100 years earlier.

The partisan politics of the twentieth century re-enfranchisement of blacks, in fact, seem quite inconsistent with the strategic enfranchisement story. In

---

4 Frymer, Paul, *Uneasy Alliances: Race and Party Competition in America* (Princeton, NJ: Princeton University Press, 1999), 49–86. Walton, Hanes Jr., *Black Republicans: The Politics of the Black and Tans* (Metuchen, NJ: The Scarecrow Press, Inc., 1975). Kousser, J. Morgan, *The Shaping of Southern Politics: Suffrage Restriction and the Establishment of the One-Party South, 1880–1910* (New Haven, CT: Yale University Press, 1974).

5 According to the 1900 U.S. Census, 90.9% of black Americans resided in the former slave states; the former Confederate states alone accounted for 82.7%.

6 The literacy test was specifically banned in Alabama, Georgia, Louisiana, Mississippi, South Carolina, and Virginia. Areas that fell under federal examination were those with registration or turnout in the 1964 presidential election that was less than 50 percent of the voting age population.

the 1960 presidential election, both Kennedy and Nixon carried civil rights promises in their campaigns. As John F. Kennedy entered office, he did so with a Congress controlled by Democrats, but also without an overwhelming victory at the polls and in the face of a challenge from within his own party. Harry Byrd, the powerful Virginia Senator, had taken electoral votes from Alabama, Mississippi, and Oklahoma. The intraparty struggle meant that Kennedy and his supporters within the party needed to be responsive to their base constituency, but also reach out to new supporters. Enfranchising blacks could be part of that strategy, but with Southern blacks constituting only a third or less of the Deep South state populations, winning their votes would not override the opposition mounting from Southern whites. Lyndon Johnson, whose 1964 victory over Barry Goldwater was far more decisive, lost all the states in the heart of the Deep South – Alabama, Georgia, Louisiana, Mississippi, and South Carolina – and by significant margins.[7] Johnson's campaign promise to deliver on the civil rights agenda Kennedy had begun had not harmed the national popularity of the Democratic ticket, which took 61.1 percent of the popular vote, but it had crystallized the consequences for the party in the South. Thus, although the black rights strategy seemed a risky formula for electoral success based simply on the votes of those who would be re-enfranchised in the South, it might have held some promise as part of a larger new Democratic agenda that could win without the Solid South.

Not only was the advantage for Democrats acting to gain solely the black vote unclear, so, too, was their ownership of the black rights issue. Indeed, Republicans had not been totally inactive on the issue of black rights, even if they had been less than effective. Civil rights measures had been passed under Republican watch in 1957 and 1960 – the first civil rights legislation to be enacted since Reconstruction. Moreover, although Democrats were at the helm when the Twenty-Fourth Amendment and the 1965 Voting Rights Act passed, both were carried by a bipartisan vote. The new-found interest of both parties in legislation to protect the rights of blacks points in the direction of a programmatic enfranchisement story, rather than a strategic one.

To say that the voting rights victories of the Civil Rights Movement were the result of programmatic enfranchisement, of course, begs the question of who the "inside" partners of disfranchised blacks were. As the literature on the Civil Rights Movement, like that on the woman suffrage movement, is concentrated on understanding the building and maintenance of activism by the disfranchised group, an answer to that question is still difficult.[8] Yet as scholars

---

[7] In these former Democratic strongholds, Johnson's shares of the popular were: Alabama 30.5%, Georgia 45.9%, Louisiana 43.2%, Mississippi 12.9%, South Carolina 41.1%. He also lost Goldwater's home state of Arizona, capturing only 49.5% of its popular vote.

[8] And those who look at the decisions of party elites on the issue of race in the 1960s do not dig into the question of whether and how coalitions might have mattered. Carmines and Stimson look only to mass attitudes, not group politics. Carmines, Edward G. and James A. Stimson, *Issue Evolution: Race and the Transformation of American Politics* (Princeton: Princeton University

in that same literature continue to confront evidence of significant black insurgency long before national politicians noticed or reacted to the "Civil Rights Movement," uncovering the partnerships disfranchised blacks forged and the role of those alliances in leveraging the nation's political attention may be key to understanding why black insurgents were successful at particular historical moments, and not at others.[9] Undoubtedly, some of the leverage came from other blacks – blacks now living and voting in Northern urban centers, whose support was becoming increasingly important to politicians who sought to rule these cities. By 1960, more than 40 percent of black Americans lived outside the South; Illinois's population was more than 10 percent black, and New York, New Jersey, and Pennsylvania were all approaching that benchmark.[10] Moving North, however, did not sever family and community ties to the South, nor did Northern blacks escape racial discrimination. Their situation fostered a group interest in further protection of all blacks' voting (and civil) rights.[11]

Labor unions also might have stood to gain from an empowered black population in the South, where blacks desperate for employment were used to break unionizing and strike attempts. Although such circumstances bred racial antagonism, there was also recognition from some union leaders of the promise

Press, 1989). Frymer credits pressure from black activists and international allies with pushing the Kennedy Administration's response; action on voting rights was alleged to be simply a smaller concession than full civil rights, a compromise to quell the activism, satisfy allies, and yet not alienate too many whites. There is no role for other domestic pressure. Frymer, *Uneasy Alliances*, 96–98. McAdam notes only that "external support" of the movement peaked in the mid-1960s, which he captures in dollars given. Although his claim is that external support was greater when outsiders perceived "opportunity posed by an indigenous protest campaign," and mentions support from "groups drawn from the ranks of labor, northern students, organized religion, and such traditional liberal organizations as the American Civil Liberties Union and Taconic Foundation," he does not unpack the details of how those connections were made and what party politicians made of them. McAdam, Doug, *Political Process and the Development of Black Insurgency, 1930–1970* (Chicago: The University of Chicago Press, 1982).

9 A growing number of scholars have pushed for an understanding of the black protest movement that pushes further back in history that *the Brown v. Board of Education* decision in 1954. Fairclough, Adam, *Race and Democracy: The Civil Rights Struggle in Louisiana, 1915–1972* (Athens: The University of Georgia Press, 1995); McAdam, *Political Process and the Development of Black Insurgency*. The question here is why the nation responded at the moment it did, in the way it did, when both black insurgency in demand of political rights and Southern whites' attempts to quell those demands (e.g., lynching) date to before the 1960s?

10 U.S. Census 1960. Percentages were: Illinois 10.2%, New York 8.4%, New Jersey 8.5%, Pennsylvania 7.5%. The Northern migration left smaller numbers in some former slave states: Kentucky 7.1%, Missouri 9.0%. South Carolina was the state with the largest proportion of black residents at 34.8%.

11 On the Northern migration, new life in cities, involvement in politics, and continued discrimination, see St. Clair Drake and Horace R. Cayton, *Black Metropolis: A Study of Negro Life in a Northern City* (Chicago: The University of Chicago Press, 1993). On the development of black racial group interest in modern-era partisan politics, see Michael Dawson, *Behind the Mule: Race and Class in African-American Politics* (Princeton, NJ: Princeton University Press, 1995).

of a class, rather than race, based politics. George L. P. Weaver, an officer of the Congress of Industrial Organizations (CIO), wrote of that organization's racial policy in 1944 that

The CIO is committed to the philosophy that a long-range national program is needed for combating racialism in the United States. This program must dig down to the basic causes, one of the most important being economic. It stems from the fear of job insecurity and competition.... As the gap is narrowed and the black and white worker, on an equal plane, struggle together to eliminate their collective standards, many of these fears are swept away during the struggle.[12]

Weaver went on to list a set of specific goals of the CIO, which would improve the living and working conditions of both white and black workers. The first on the list was equal access to union membership and protection. Other objectives included equal pay, benefits, and education. The final item was "equal voting rights in electing public officials."[13]

There were other partnerships that might have increased the likelihood of the programmatic enfranchisement of Southern blacks in the 1960s. College students, particularly politically active in this decade, were also drawn to the black rights cause. The National Council of Churches lobbied for political action on black rights, and clergy within the Catholic Church were also often-vocal supporters of the Civil Rights Movement.[14] Unpacking the leverage that all these groups might have had on party politicians' decisions on the issue of black voting rights will take digging into political decisions outside the Oval Office. Yet the payoff might be a better understanding of how the rights of blacks were suddenly a salient concern in American politics in the 1960s, despite black protest activity that dated back to the days of Redemption.

Third Parties, American Political Development, and the Representation of Minority Interests

Third party politics have been given considerable credit for, at points in American history, changing the way the state governs. The Progressives ushered in direct democracy practices, from initiative and referendum provisions, to the

---

[12] Weaver, George L. P., "The Role of Organized Labor in Education for Racial Understanding," *The Journal of Negro Education*, 13 (Summer 1944): 414–20. Quoted passage on pp. 414–15. Weaver (who was African American) went on to serve in the Kennedy Administration as Assistant Secretary of Labor for International Affairs.

[13] Weaver, "The Role of Organized Labor", 417–18. The CIO was arguably the most racially progressive of the major union organizations and not only included a significant number of black members, but also actively pursued issues on blacks rights, including through its Southern organizing effort known as "Operation Dixie." See Foner, Philip, *Organized Labor and the Black Worker* (New York: Praeger, 1974).

[14] On the National Council of Churches: Findlay, James F., "Religion and Politics in the Sixties: The Churches and the Civil Rights Act of 1964," *The Journal of American History* 77 (June 1990): 66–92. On the Catholic Church, see Fairclough, *Race and Democracy*.

direct election of U.S. Senators, which dramatically changed the playing field of party politics. With their emphasis on government efficiency, Progressives are also credited with encouraging an increased reliance on government "expertise" and growing regulatory powers.[15] Populists, driven by the concerns of small farmers and urban laborers, promoted an agenda that influenced policy on banking, tariffs, and education.[16] More generally, third parties have also been credited with rearranging the electoral coalitions at the bases of the major parties.[17] Looking carefully into the politics of woman suffrage has shown that third parties were also often key in redefining the American electorate.

There was a unique place for disfranchised women in party politics when third parties emerged; the active contribution of women to fledgling party organizations was regularly rewarded with the active pursuit of women's voting rights. And victories were not uncommon. Although not ideologically inconsistent with these parties' main objectives, increasing the electorate in this way was not at the top of the list of grievances that drove politicians and voters out of the major party fold. Yet their role in the political process that doubled the size of the American electorate was unmistakably significant. Even just three members elected to a state legislature, as we saw with the Farmers' Alliance in the case of Illinois, could wield enough pressure on major party politicians to yield some concession on the issue of state voter qualifications. As we continue to open the question of the lasting effects on American politics from small and fleeting electoral successes of third parties, we need to look not only to their central causes, but to the auxiliary issues they addressed in pursuit of both organizational and electoral viability.

The story of third party politics in the American context, and the sometimes "unintended" consequences thereof, in fact, has major implications for how we think about the normative desirability of the electoral laws that drive the American party system, driving at basic questions of representation. More than one scholar has seen a "tyranny of the majority" in the two-party system in the United States, arguing that the winner-take-all design of American elections often leaves minorities without effective representation.[18] Although a proportional representation system is often suggested as the remedy, such a radical change to the to the nation's federated network of electoral laws would be a

---

[15] For a concise overview, see David R. Mayhew, *Placing Parties in American Politics: Organization, Electoral Settings, and Government Activity in the Twentieth Century* (Princeton: Princeton University Press, 1986), 308–18. On the expansion of regulatory power, see Stephen Skowronek, *Building a New American State: The Expansion of National Administrative Capacities, 1877–1920* (Cambridge: Cambridge University Press, 1982).

[16] Sanders, Elizabeth, *Roots of Reform: Farmers, Workers, and the American State, 1877–1917* (Chicago: The University of Chicago Press, 1999).

[17] Rosentone, Steven J., Roy L. Behr, and Edward H. Lazarus, *Third Parties in America* (Princeton, NJ: Princeton University Press, 1984).

[18] For example, Frymer, *Uneasy Alliances*. Guinier, Lani, *The Tyranny of the Majority: Fundamental Fairness in Representative Democracy* (New York: The Free Press, 1994).

daunting political task. Far short of such a system overhaul, smaller changes that could increase the frequency and vitality of third party challengers, such as easier ballot access for third party candidates, hold promise of increasing responsiveness to minority interests – even if those minorities are unable to mount such a challenge on their own, and perhaps even if they have no votes to offer. As we saw in the case of woman suffrage, third parties in a two-party dominant system, facing all of the organizational challenges that implies, have reasons to reach out to citizens that the major parties do not. Often needing infrastructure and organizational capacity as much as votes, third parties reached out to and incorporated the interests of disfranchised women. Those same incentives could bring greater representation of the interests of other groups who lack electoral strength, and even electoral rights, but who can offer a set of skills or existing networks to facilitate the organizational efforts of third parties.[19] Moreover, of course, these third parties need not win elections to exert influence on the policymaking decisions of major party politicians; simply cutting into major party vote shares provides incentive for concessions to third party demands. And taking just a few seats in the government can empower third party politicians with even more leverage in the policy process. In other words, electoral rules need not change so drastically as to facilitate the rise of a multiple party system to increase minority influence in American politics; changes that might facilitate simply a temporary exit option through minor parties inside the dominant two-party structure could increase the representation of minority interests.

Rethinking the Categories of Women's Politics and Women's Rights

More than one scholar has tried to understand the place of women's interests in American politics. Typically noted are a set of initial "women's policy" gains following the Nineteenth Amendment and then a period of dormancy for a "women's agenda" until the 1960s and 1970s reinvigoration of the women's movement.[20] The political history of woman suffrage hardly makes the

[19] This, of course, does not totally alleviate a fundamental problem of representative politics: that it takes resources to have influence, that it takes some resource base to gain other resources, and that some people have more access to opportunities for resource accumulation than others. It does, however, provide more opportunity for influence in electoral politics for those who have a more limited set of resources, including those without voting rights, and those with group-based resources (such as the networks of indigenous institutions within racial and ethnic minority communities), but short on individual resources. On the consequences and origins of resource differences: Verba, Sidney, Kay Lehman Scholzman, and Henry E. Brady, *Voice and Equality: Civic Voluntarism in American Politics* (Cambridge, MA: Harvard University Press, 1995); Burns, Nancy, Kay Lehman Scholzman, and Sidney Verba, *The Private Roots of Public Action: Gender, Equality, and Political Participation* (Cambridge, MA: Harvard University Press, 2001).

[20] For an explicit engagement of the question of the two periods, see Harvey, Anna, *Votes Without Leverage: Women in American Electoral Politics, 1920–1970* (Cambridge: Cambridge

outcome of women's near immediate incorporation into partisan politics on the basis of their class, race, ethnicity, religion, and other demographic characteristics, rather than their sex, surprising. Women were not enfranchised with any anticipation that they would ever offer a "women's bloc" for any particular party.[21] Politicians were fully aware that the women organized as suffragists were not the only women that would enter party politics, and presupposed that women not identified with the movement would continue to have a different political agenda after their enfranchisement. Moreover, even organized suffragists displayed a range of partisan leanings, and woman suffrage was enacted under both Republican and Democratic watches in the states. Suffragists were pursuing changes in voting rights qualifications that excluded them based on their sex, but appeals for rights based on their political promise as a sex, we have seen, rang hollow in partisan circles.

Seeing that the admission of women into the electorate came as the result of suffragists aligning with other interest groups ought to open other women's rights questions as issues not of women versus men, but of particular women, their interests, and the coalitions they build around those interests. That is, even when policies are construed as having disproportionate or more direct influence on women because of their sex, women's positions on and level of engagement in those policies are shaped by a range of heterogeneous political interests. Pushing further on the question of women's rights and women's policies will also mean asking whether we have appropriately defined what a "women's issue" is. Is it feminist? Is it any policy that touches on gender roles? Any policy that interests more women than men? Or perhaps any issue that exhibits a difference between the way men and women of similar social backgrounds understand or support it? Much about the history of women's voting rights suggests that it was an issue of race and class interests – not just for women,

---

University Press, 1998). On early policy success, see Skocpol, Theda, *Protecting Soldiers and Mothers: The Political Origins of Social Policy in the United States* (Cambridge, MA: The Belknap Press of Harvard University Press, 1992). On the 1960s and 1970s, see, for example, Ann N. Costain and W. Douglas Costain, "Strategy and Tactics of the Women's Movement in the United States: The Role of Political Parties" and Jo Freeman, "Whom You Know versus Whom You Represent: Feminist Influence in the Democratic and Republican Parties" both in *The Women's Movements of the United States and Western Europe: Consciousness, Political Opportunity, and Public Policy*, Mary Fainsod Katzenstein and Carol McClurg Mueller, eds. (Philadelphia: Temple University Press, 1987). On women's issues in contemporary party politics, see Sanbonmatsu, Kira, *Democrats/Republicans and the Politics of Women's Place* (Ann Arbor: University of Michigan Press, 2002) and Wolbrecht, Christina, *The Politics of Women's Rights: Parties, Positions, and Change* (Princeton: Princeton University Press, 2000). Sanbonmatsu also promotes un-bundling women's issues to see the different politics underlying the outcomes.

21 For more discussion on the "women's bloc" as historical myth, see Jo Freeman, *A Room at a Time: How Women Entered Party Politics* (Lanham, MD: Rowan & Littlefield Publishers, Inc., 2000).

but for men, as well. Yet gender surely shaped the understanding of the issue across men and women who were located inside the same racial groups and of similar class status.

Reconceptualizing the idea of "women's issues" could also redefine our understanding of where we see "women's influence" in politics. Scholars have already begun this project by bringing to light the ways in which women's incorporation into the electorate and party organizations changed the practices of American partisan politics.[22] But shifting attention from policy gains to the practice of politics does not engage the question of whether the dearth of "women's policy" gains observed between the adoption of the Nineteenth Amendment and the 1960s is real, or an artifact of an incomplete definition. Those who observe a dormancy in the political salience and success of "women's policy" issues tend to define those issues as ones that disproportionately affect women because of their sex and/or societal gender roles, such as mothering. Yet, the era of agitation for woman suffrage provides examples, certainly, of policy changes that were facilitated by women activists – organized *as women* – that were not targeted specifically at remedying sex differences. Prohibition was aided by the work of the *Women's* Christian Temperance Union. General labor rights and reforms, not just special accommodations for women workers, were furthered by the *Women's* Trade Union League. Characterizing the period between the end of the suffrage movement and the beginning of the feminist movement of the mid-twentieth century as a period of dormancy may rely too heavily on the definition of women's issues ascribed to, and sometimes actively defended by, middle-class, white women activists.

Conclusion

This has been an account of how electoral rights are gained by groups in a system based on electoral politics. Short of revolution, the story must necessarily be political. Existing political institutions must be maneuvered, and existing political coalitions engaged. Thus, getting rights through politics takes not only the changing of preferences, but the attainment of political saliency for the interests of those who have no pressure of their own to exert from the inside of political institutions and ruling coalitions. Although excluded groups often pursue insurgency or lobbying strategies meant to influence the preferences of elites and the public, party politics are not solely responses to public opinion or the appeasement of preferences. As political scientist and party politician Charles Merriam wrote in 1923, "of great significance in the composition of

---

[22] See, especially, Kristi Anderson, *After Suffrage: Women in Partisan and Electoral Politics before the New Deal* (Chicago: The University of Chicago Press, 1996); and Paula Baker "The Domestication of Politics: Women and American Political Society, 1780–1920" *American Historical Review* 89 (June 1984): 620–47.

any political party are the numerous types of social groupings."[23] Group-based politics help to signal the salience of preferences, to broker the priority of issues in party agendas. Only under rare political circumstances does the excluded group's promise of electoral support lead a party to seek their enfranchisement for the sake of their votes alone. More often, gaining access to electoral politics requires partnering with groups already inside party politics, who can cultivate the issue salience needed to deliver new voting rights.

---

[23] Merriam, Charles, *The American Party System: An Introduction to the Study of Political Parties in the United States* (New York: The Macmillan Company, 1923), 3.

Appendix: Additional Notes on Measures and Analyses

Measures and Analyses in the Case Studies

Decisions about the measures to use and the statistical tools and models to employ in the quantitative analyses of the case studies were not straightforward to make. There were competing factors at play, namely the need to make the best and most appropriate use of the data available in a particular state at a particular moment on the one hand and the importance of enabling ways of thinking about the cumulation of the evidence across time and geography on the other. Given, however, that the cross-state analyses presented in Chapter 6 were intended to do some of the cumulating work, in the case studies I proceeded with the foremost goal of making the individual best-use decisions. This included making individual decisions based on the general rule of presenting in the text the least complicated analysis necessary. These decisions imply that rather similar hypotheses may be evaluated with different modeling or statistical approaches. Sometimes, for example, there were enough legislators voting – and, importantly, voting in different ways – to make multivariate analysis sensible and feasible, and sometimes there were not. Similarly, in some places and times two measures might present issues of collinearity if employed in tandem in multivariate analysis, whereas in other places they did not. A notable example of the latter issue would include varying degrees of overlap between available measures of the presence of farming interests and labor interests in districts. I have endeavored, however, to provide footnotes that explain the choices I made, and that often offer the results of alternative specifications of the analysis.

A Note on Measuring Interest Group Influence

Across all the case studies, when I seek to assess the effects of pro-suffrage coalitions on legislative decisions, I map the relative presence in each district of the constituent group that the partner represents onto vote decisions of legislators. There are two common sets of interest organizations that tended to be involved: farmers' groups and labor organizations. I outline here my general method of measuring their potential influence in legislative districts.

When the suffrage partner is a farmers' organization, such as the Grange, I use the per capita number of farms in the district. This number is calculated from the county-level reports of number of farms and population in the most recent U.S. Census (e.g., the 1900 Census for a 1901 vote). Sometimes this measure is scaled to number of farms per 100 population in the district, for ease of presentation; the relative information, of course, remains the same. As most state legislative districts map onto county lines (even though they often span multiple counties), the county numbers do fairly well in capturing district numbers. There is an unavoidable measurement error when a county is split across multiple districts, but this is most often the case for urban districts, which likely do, in fact, have a fairly uniform distribution of (a small number of) farms across the districts.

When the partner is a labor organization, the best available measure is the per capita number of workers employed in manufacturing in the district. This number is calculated in a fashion similar to the farming measure, using county-level Census records of the number of workers and population. Unfortunately, the Census reports do not report these counts in 1910. Thus at times too far removed from the 1900 and 1920 Census counts, I rely on a measure of per capita investment in manufacturing. This measure is typically logged before analysis, as it is quite skewed in its raw form. As discussed in Chapter 6, the two measures are highly correlated where they appear in the Census together, albeit not perfectly so. There is once again an unavoidable measurement error when a county is split across multiple districts. That is most often the case for urban districts, which is a bit more troublesome for the labor measure, as sections of the city surely have different distributions of labor constituencies. This may, in fact, mute the analyses' ability to pick up connections between labor constituencies and votes on suffrage. Conclusions of "no relationship" are thus made with particular care and caveat.

Although I argue that the presence of the interest group's constituency base is, in fact, key information for legislators about the likely electoral consequences of their responsiveness to the interest group's demand for new voting rights, this consequence is of course contingent upon the degree to which legislators perceive the interest group as being able to exercise its potential influence. In general, I rely on the historical record in each case to provide this information by delineating the times at which the relevant suffrage partners held sway in state politics. It would also be helpful on this score to have systematic measures of the organizational capacity of the groups, but such data are generally unavailable. The historical record did uniquely provide a simple measure of such capacity for the Grange in Michigan in 1910 – an indication of whether each legislative

TABLE A.I. *Mean Farms per 100 Population by Grange Organizational Strength, Michigan House Districts, 1910*

	Strong Grange Organization	Grange Organization Not Strong
Mean	9.72	7.78
Std. Error	1.29	0.55
N	15	85

Note: Mean difference is not statistically significant at conventional levels.
p = .17, two-tailed t-test, unequal variances assumed.

district had a local Grange with at least 1,000 members, derived from membership information reported in Trump, Fred, *The Grange in Michigan: An Agricultural History of Michigan over the Past 90 Years* (Grand Rapids: The Dean-Hicks Co., 1963). It is thus possible to make some observation about whether the organizational presence of the Grange mapped onto the type of district with larger potential leverage. Table A.1 reports the mean number of farms per 100 population in 1910 across two categories of Michigan's state house districts: those with a strong organizational presence of the Grange and those without. The reported means are at least suggestive that organizational capacity and the relative presence of the constituent base of the group were connected. Even though the means indicate a greater presence of farms in districts where the Grange was organizationally strong, the difference of nearly 2 farms per 100 population fails to reach traditional levels of statistical significance.

One might suggest embedding a measure of urbanicity into analyses using the farm and labor measures, hoping that it would net out "other" urban-rural patterns and leave more clearly the farmer and/or labor element meant to be captured. Unfortunately this typically introduces serious issues of collinearity. Although I do employ this strategy when it is feasible – at least in alternative specifications reported on in footnotes – I am, once again, most reliant on leveraging other contextual information from the historical record about the *timing* of *expected* connections between legislative decisions and the interest group measures (i.e., qualitative information about when the groups are pushing for suffrage and when they are not) to assess the notion that the inferences from these analyses are valid.

Event History Analysis: Adding Controls for Constitutional Amendment Procedures

In Chapter 1, I argued that the institutional rules governing the process of suffrage extension could also shape the likelihood of state action on the issue. In Chapter 5, I argued that racial interests built institutional barriers that

TABLE A.2. *Partisan Incentives under Initiative Provisions,*
Cox Model – Log Relative Hazard Form Coefficients

	Initiative Provision	No Initiative Provision
Reform Party Vote	3.54	3.41**
	(4.87)	(1.63)
Party Competition	−3.28	1.14
	(3.43)	(.92)
State Suffrage Membership	4.53*	.40**
	(2.70)	(.17)
N	55	1025†
Number of Failures	7	22

*** $p < .01$, ** $p < .05$, * $p < .10$. Standard errors are adjusted for clustering of observations by state.
† This number for the Reform Party model. Party Competition N = 1,035; State Members N = 1,033.

made suffragist success more difficult. That line of argument suggested that the institutions are endogenous to politicians' preferences for greater electoral participation, making embedding institutions, rather than the interests that shaped them, into the statistical model presented in Chapter 6 perhaps an inappropriate approach. Further complicating statistical analysis of the question of constitutional amendment procedures, in particular, as the political institution with perhaps the most direct effect on suffrage extension, is the relative lack of state variation in procedures during the specific time period in question. With some variance on provisions for initiative rights in the time period, however, I make some attempt here to explore the significance of this particular innovation in constitutional amendment procedures.

Initiative Rights: Changing the Impact of Party Competition

The major role of initiative rights was to bypass or manipulate the partisan procedures of state legislatures. Yet, under rules that allowed citizens to initiate constitutional amendments to change suffrage qualifications, reform parties continued to be important to the suffrage cause. Alliances with reform parties added networks for mobilizing public preferences in favor of woman suffrage, which could result in either a successful initiative, as in the case of Arizona, or a passage of woman suffrage by the state legislature in preemption of an initiative, as in the case of Arkansas. Having more suffrage activists on the ground in the state also became more important, as their role became one of convincing masses of voters rather than handfuls of legislators.

Because so few states provided for initiative rights in this time period – Arizona, Arkansas, Michigan, Nebraska, Ohio, Oklahoma, and Oregon – it is difficult to illustrate their effect with statistical confidence. But splitting the sample by whether or not initiative rights were in effect and then running simple bivariate Cox models with just the variables for partisan incentives and state suffrage demand allows some comparison. These results, presented in Table A.2, suggest that suffrage adoption was more likely to occurr in initiative rights states when reform parties were doing well electorally, major party competition was not especially close, and state activism was high. In states without initiative provisions, the viability of reform parties was just as important, but suffrage rights tended to be granted at times when the major parties were more competitive. And while suffrage activism also affected the likelihood of suffrage adoption in these states, its effect was markedly diminished. In sum, initiative rights may have granted suffragists more direct influence on the passage of woman suffrage.

Index